AMERICAN LITERATURE

KENNIKAT PRESS SCHOLARLY REPRINTS

Dr. Ralph Adams Brown, Senior Editor

Series on

LITERARY AMERICA IN THE NINETEENTH CENTURY

Under the General Editorial Supervision of

Dr. Walter Harding

University Professor, State University of New York

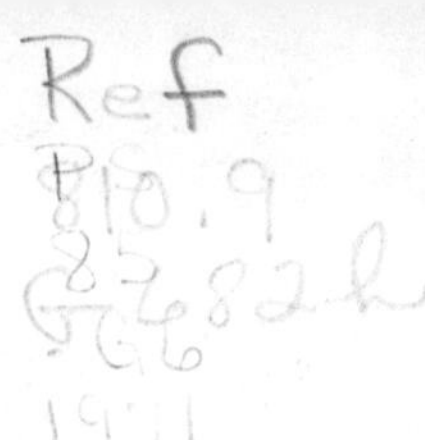

Hand-Book

of

American Literature

Historical, Biographical

and Critical

By
Joseph Gostwick

KENNIKAT PRESS
Port Washington, N. Y./London

HAND-BOOK OF AMERICAN LITERATURE

First published in 1856
Reissued in 1971 by Kennikat Press
Library of Congress Catalog Card No: 78-121942
ISBN 0-8046-1304-4

Manufactured by Taylor Publishing Company Dallas, Texas

PREFACE.

A SERIES of Hand-books intended to give a concise account of modern literature, must be incomplete without some brief review of books published in the United States. Many of the lighter productions of American writers have been lately reprinted, and rather widely circulated, in England; but we have no fair, general view of a literature, comparatively fertile when we consider its short time of cultivation, and already including such names as Edwards, Franklin, Hamilton, Irving, Bryant, Channing, Sparks, Bancroft, Prescott, and Ticknor. In the present manual, an attempt has been made to describe faithfully the various features of American Literature. In justice to many able writers, whose works could not be adequately noticed in a review designed for the use of the general reader, it must be observed, that the American Library is comparatively rich in its special departments, including works on the several sciences, and on law, politics, and divinity.

Among the writings found serviceable in the preparation of this manual, we must name a series of notices of American authors inserted in a reprint of the *History of English Literature* (*Chambers's Educational Course*); also, the biographical and critical notices accompanying Mr Griswold's selections from poets and prose-writers. In several instances, critical opinions have been borrowed—of course, with acknowledgment—from the *North American Review*.

CONTENTS.

INTRODUCTION.

THE present volume belongs to a series of Hand-books of Literature, and contains a brief review of American contributions to history, biography, poetry, prose-fiction, and other departments, during the period 1640–1854. American literature belongs almost entirely to our own times. Several works possessing, at least, an historical interest were produced during the colonial period, and about the time of the Revolution—and these, with the early records and biographies of the States of New England, have seemed worthy of notice in our review; but the writings of the eighteenth century were mostly theological and political, and few books of the class commonly included in reviews of general literature were produced before the year 1820.

The North American Review (commenced in 1815) complained, during its early years, that it could scarcely find American books to be noticed. After the lapse of about twenty-five years, the same Review found a difficulty in keeping pace with the productiveness of the press. During this time, the departments of history and biography had been enriched by the writings of Prescott, Sparks, Bancroft, Wheaton, and other authors; Irving, Cooper, Ware, Kennedy, and many other writers, had appeared in the field of prose-fiction; poetry had been represented by Bryant, Sprague, Halleck, and Longfellow; in mathematics, Dr Bowditch had produced his commentary on the *Mécanique Céleste;* the works of Audubon, Silliman, Bigelow, Morton, and other special authors, had extended the literature of science; Webster, Duponceau, and Pickering, had published the results of their studies in philology; theology and Biblical criticism had been cultivated by Channing, Norton, Stuart, Robinson, and others too numerous to be mentioned here; while a very large proportion of educational works had made America, in this department, almost independent of the old country.

America, however, has few professional authors, excepting editors of newspapers. The best writers have wisely avoided dependence on booksellers, and have been engaged in commercial pursuits. Their poems, essays, and reviews, have been written as recreations, after the cares of banking and bookkeeping. 'Authorship,' says a reviewer,[1] 'is the least lucrative profession in the United States. Every prudent man avoids it as he does a pestilence. A writer who attempts to live on the manufactures of his imagination, is continually coquetting with starvation.' That this should be the case to a greater extent in America than in England, is mainly owing to the want of international copyright law between the two countries. It is an unavoidable difficulty that American authors must write under the shade of the greatest names in English literature; but in the present system, they must also be discouraged by a competition altogether unfair. The stripling, if we may so speak, has to carry weight in his contest with a giant. In plainer words, the American author, or his publisher, must demand dollars as the price of a new book, while the best English works on the same topic may be offered at the cost of a few cents, because they have been seized and reprinted, without any payment made either to the writer or the original publisher. The injury thus inflicted on British authors, and other proprietors of copyrights, is indeed serious, yet can hardly be compared with its moral consequences on the other side of the Atlantic. It is a melancholy fact, that so many thousands of persons are found, after repeated remonstrance, willing to derive profit, instruction, and entertainment from the labour, enterprise, and commercial risk of neighbours to whom they will yield no remuneration. It is sad that a law as old as the world itself should be evaded or laughed at, simply because an expanse of water lies between the debtor and his creditor, and the latter, unhappily, has no power to enforce his claims. These remarks fairly represent the views of at least a majority of the best writers in the United States. With reference to the fatal labours of Sir Walter Scott—whose works have afforded delight to many thousands of American readers—a reviewer has well expressed the sentiments of many of his more generous countrymen. The passage may be quoted, as a proof that the strongest and most earnest arguments have been urged in the States, as on this side of the water, in opposition to the system commonly styled piracy.

'We have no notion of human nature—of just and generous human nature, at least, which we hold the American to be—if the

[1] E. P. Whipple, one of the writers in *The North American Review*.

reader, who, bending over the instructive or affecting page, holds friendly and useful communion with its author's mind, finds his pleasure enhanced by the reflection of its being obtained in fraud and defiance of the author's right. Not many of our countrymen would bring a good relish to the stalled ox served up *gratis* from their helpless neighbour's herd: we do not know them, if they prefer that the intellectual food they so relish should be seasoned with the thought of making no return to the producer. We insist that it is a mere unfounded and offensive libel to say, that of the hundreds of thousands, the millions, who on this side of the water have found so much of the charm of their lives in the writings of Scott, there is any number deserving to be counted who have satisfaction in the remembrance of having contributed nothing to keep that great heart from breaking. Had American laws been but as honest as American feelings—had very much less than what was there due from us been rendered—one of the most melancholy chapters in literary history would not have been written. One of the sublimest spirits that the inspiration of the Almighty ever endowed would have conquered in the tremendous, and, as it was doomed to be, fatal endeavour to render to others the dues which this proud and pretending people, profuse of every other tribute to his genius but justice, so cruelly withheld from him. The wizard harp of the North might still—who knows?—have been charming mankind with its else inexhaustible enchantments.[1] As it was, the creator of those worlds of delight struggled with desperate and agonised bravery, and died. We Americans helped ourselves to the fruit of his mighty toils, and extolled it largely, and, being mindful to have it at the cheapest, we let him have his struggle to himself, and we let him die.' [2]

With regard to the effects of the piratical system on the integrity of literature, numerous details might be mentioned to prove that the 'glory,' which Lord Camden declared to be the sole proper reward of science, is quite as insecure as the more substantial boon. We might notice—if any doubt existed respecting such facts—examples of mutilated editions, false reprints, books abridged and revised by the simple process of tearing out many leaves, and various other bibliographical curiosities, including 'a complete edition of Lord Bacon's works' without the *De Augmentis* and *Novum Organum*. 'If the thing is suffered to go on,' says the Review already quoted, 'different books under the same name will presently be in the hands of English and American scholars. References will be no guides in reading. The best fruits of the mind of each country will be ludicrously travestied in the other's view. The identity of the great monuments of genius and study will be confounded and lost.'

[1] This was written in 1842. [2] *North American Review*, No. 55.

On the moral effects of the system, several grave statements by American writers might be quoted. We give the following passage, because it cannot be fairly regarded as the complaint of an unsuccessful author. The writer has been chiefly engaged in reviewing and editing the works of his countrymen, and has been comparatively well rewarded for his labour. Speaking of the refusal of Congress to protect the copyrights of foreigners, he observes that 'it effectually deprives us of most of the really great works with which the presses of Europe are teeming, while it gives us nearly all they produce that is frivolous and vicious. It costs a great deal of money, as well as labour, to prepare the market for large works; there must be much advertising, a large distribution of copies, elaborate abstracts in reviews and journals, and many other means to create a demand; and the expenses of these means must be added to those of the mechanical manufacture. Yet now, as has been shewn by numerous instances, as soon as a house with enterprise and capital has issued a readable impression of a work, and secured for it such a circulation as promises a fair remuneration, some base fellow is sure to bring out, on dingy brown paper and small type, a deluge of cheap copies, with which he reaps all the advantages of the first publisher's efforts, and leaves him with his stock unsold, and his investment unreturned. It is true, that notwithstanding these dangers, a few of the more indispensable histories and other fruits of true cultivation are reprinted here; but they are generally issued in the most compact and cheap style, sometimes much abridged, and nearly always without those charts and plates which add so much to the value of many foreign editions. A recognition of the foreign author's right of property would at once remedy this part of the evil entirely.'[1]

[1] 'On the other hand, there is extraordinary activity in the republication of the light and licentious literature of the time. It is sickening to lean over the counters of the shops where cheap books are sold, and survey the trash with which the criminal folly of the government is deluging the country. Every new issue deepens the wide-spread depravity, and extends the demand for its successor. As but little capital is required for the business, and the returns are quick, these leprous spots are constantly springing up in the cities; and to gratify the prurient tastes which they create, the literary sewers of Paris and London are dragged for the filthiest stuff which floats or sinks in their turbid waters. The demoralisation increases, and the novels of Paul de Kock, disgusting as they are in the original (in which a racy style and sparkling wit render them attractive, despite their moral deformity), are made worse by the addition of gross obscenity by the translator; and from those of Eugene Sue the reflective portions, which serve to neutralise the effects of the narrative, are left out. All private morals, all domestic peace, fly before this withering curse, which the Congress persists in sustaining, by its refusal to recognise the rights of the foreign author. For, if the respectable publishers could be protected in their business, they would furnish good editions of good books, that would give a healthy tone to the common sentiment, and drive this profligate literature into oblivion; if the foreign author were protected in his rights, he would be but a competitor of the native author, and would have an inducement to support those liberal principles of society which are here established, thus

These statements may be received as substitutes for several theories intended to explain the defects of American literature, especially its want of a distinct national tone.

It is fair to observe, in connection with this notice of their difficulties, that writers on the other side of the water enjoy certain facilities in the acquirement of reputations. Their field of enterprise is not crowded like that of literature in the old country. Of many names included in the following review, it may be truly said, that they owe their prominence partly to their early appearance. In the beginning of the next century, literary distinction will not be so easily gained as it has been during the last thirty-five years. Every reader knows that in England we have a legion of authors who either have written or could write such verses as would have been famous a hundred years ago. The poetry contributed by Americans during recent years has been received in the old country with a degree of favour hardly granted to home productions of the same class. Our reviews have been carried over the water, and have seemed to gain importance by the voyage. The young American author who has been noticed in the English journals, suddenly finds himself famous, while he hardly knows on which side of the Atlantic his reputation had its origin. In short, the fame of several minor poets has been spread by echoes, rather than by the power of any original voice. There are certain localities where the shout of a child sounds like the voice of a congregation.

While we trust that the present work may be regarded as a fair general survey of American Literature, it is necessary to observe, that it does not pretend to define strictly the proportionate merits of many living writers, or to anticipate the verdicts of future time on the works of the present age. It is obviously a difficult task to notice, with a view to just proportions, the writings of many contemporaries, and it will be easy to criticise 'the distribution of materials and the relative degrees of attention' paid to several names included in our pages; while it is more than probable that some few names worthy of notice have been omitted. Such defects, in details implying questions of opinion and taste, can have little importance, when compared with the general fairness of a review. It should be remembered that a survey of recent literature must be written without the aid derived from opinions matured by time. The true and permanent fame of good books

strengthening them here, and diffusing them in his own country; and if the American were thus admitted to a competition in his own market with the European, our best intellects would be busy with the instruction of the people, which is now in so large a degree surrendered to the supporters of aristocracies.'—*Griswold.*

arises, in the first place, from the fact that they are read and esteemed by men of superior intelligence. These readers have the power of extending their own opinions, which are infinitely more durable than the tastes and fashions of the multitude. It is not by the votes of majorities that the rulers of literature maintain their sway. In every period, the readers who fairly appreciate the best writers are comparatively few; but their thoughts remain steadfast from one age to another, and ever extend their influence, until the decision once pronounced by two or three voices becomes the recognised judgment of the world. Verdicts which now appear as the results of individual judgment, have, in truth, required centuries for their consideration. As an example, the relative degrees of merit in the dramatists of the sixteenth century, have been fully estimated, for the first time, in the present age. The contrast between Shakspeare and his contemporaries may now seem obvious to every reader, but was probably never seen by the admirers of Marston and Webster. These remarks may suffice to shew the difficulty—to say nothing of the presumption—of any attempt to arrange strictly in the order of merit the names of many living writers.

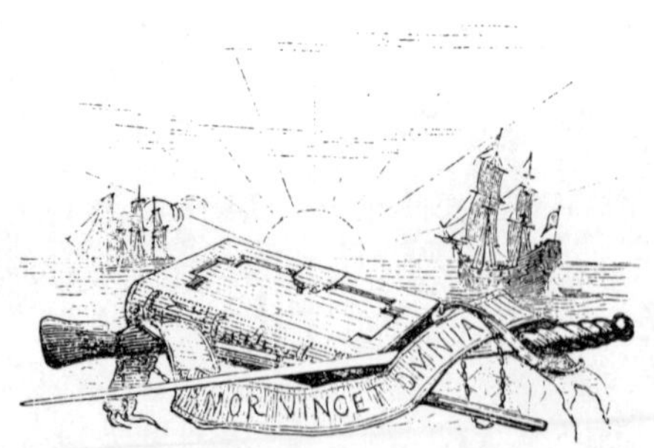

AMERICAN LITERATURE.

FIRST PERIOD.

1620-1800.

HISTORY AND BIOGRAPHY.—1631-1728.

A GLANCE at the early history of the colonial times will be sufficient to shew, that we must not expect to find here any writings to be classed with elegant literature. The Pilgrims who arrived at Plymouth in 1620, and their followers who settled the states of New England, had generally a respect for learning in its relation to theology; but of imaginative works, or any other form of literature written for amusement, they knew little or nothing. The cares of planting, building, and defending their property—'the wilderness-work' of the new colonies, as an old writer quaintly says—gave full employment to the majority; while the few superior men—such as Cotton and Hooker—who enjoyed leisure, devoted it to the study of theology and church-discipline. Even the religious teachers in these times had their share of worldly cares. Roger Williams, who proclaimed, in the year 1631, the doctrine of entire liberty of conscience, and afterwards founded the colony of Rhode Island, wrote several small books and pamphlets; but his life was not passed in quiet studies. 'My time,' he says, 'was not spent altogether in spiritual labours; but day and night, at home and abroad, on the land and water, at the hoe, at the oar—for bread.'

During the early colonial period, including the latter part of the seventeenth century, the literature most worthy of notice consisted of journals, records, biographies, and various materials of history which have been serviceable to Bancroft, Hildreth, and other recent writers. The works of Winthrop, Hubbard, Cotton, Eliot, and other chroniclers and divines of the earliest time, might be left unnoticed, if we regarded an elegant style as the standard of worth in books; but to pass over such works as Winthrop's *Journal*, the writings of Roger Williams, or the *Magnalia* of Cotton Mather—books reflecting the life and progress of a people—would imply a narrow and arbitrary definition of literature. We would rather regard it as the record of life, work, and thought, than as the plaything of idle minds; and, consequently, would prefer the diary of the laborious settler to the light tale or essay of more elegant authors who have little or nothing to say. The pamphlets of Williams, the founder of the colony of Rhode Island, have, with regard to style, no claims upon our attention; yet their uncouth diction gave expression to some of the most important ideas connected with the welfare of mankind.

It would be tedious and useless to enumerate the titles and dates of the scattered materials of history found among early documents; and to give specimens of the crude diction used by many of the old colonists who wrote diaries of public and private transactions, would serve no good purpose. To indicate the fact, that America possesses a rich store of annals of her early times, it may suffice to mention, besides the *Journal of Governor Winthrop*, a few other works; such as Winslow's *Good News from New England*, and Mourt's *Relation*, both giving 'a detailed and most interesting narrative of the affairs of Plymouth Colony, for the first three years after the landing of the Fathers. These and various documents relating to the discovery and colonisation of the New World, it is well known, were collected at the time they were printed, by the indefatigable Samuel Purchas, and published by him in an abridged form, in that invaluable store-house of historical knowledge which he entitles his *Pilgrimes*. The number of these tracts and pamphlets, however, was so great, that even that immense repository could contain but a small part of them.'[1] Bishop Kennett's catalogue, entitled *Bibliothecæ Americanæ Primordia* (1713), occupies a quarto volume of 275 pages. For numerous tracts and papers interesting to the special student of American history, we may refer to the publications of the Massachusetts Historical Society, and to the valuable collection edited by Peter Force.

[1] Colonel Aspinwall's collection of books and manuscripts relating to America contains 771 distinct works, including many curious early documents—such as Gosnold's *Brief and True Relation of the Discoverie of the North Part of Virginia*—that is, New England—1602; and John Clarke's—physician of Rhode Island—*Ill News from New England*. These statements are taken from an article in the *North American Review*, No. 92.

John Winthrop (1587–1649) embarked for America in the year 1630, as the leader of those colonists who settled in Massachusetts. As governor of this colony, he displayed a noble and benevolent character, devoting fortune and health to the public service. Mather, in his *Magnalia*, says in his quaint manner: 'Our New England shall tell and boast of her Winthrop, a law-giver as patient as Lycurgus, but not admitting any of his criminal disorders; as devout as Numa, but not liable to any of his heathenish madnesses; a governor in whom the excellences of Christianity made a most approving addition unto the virtues, wherein, even without *those*, he would have made a parallel for the great men of Greece or of Rome which the pen of a Plutarch has eternised.' Governor Winthrop wrote a diary of events and transactions in the colony down to the year 1644: it remained long in manuscript, but was published about twenty years ago, and again in a new edition by Mr Savage. It is justly regarded as a curious and valuable record of the oldest times in Massachusetts, and has supplied materials for the use of Bancroft and other historians.

The plan of Winthrop's diary was adopted by William Hubbard (1621–1704), who wrote a *History of New England*, which long remained in manuscript. It must be regretted that Bancroft, who has so diligently studied these and so many other curious old documents, has not given extracts from them in the form of notes to his history: he gives merely concise references to books and manuscripts which very few readers can possess. There is here and there an unstudied graphic force in the notes of the old chroniclers, which even the accomplished historian can hardly rival.

The attempts made in versification during early times, hardly deserve any detailed notice. However rude the rhymes, they would be interesting if they had recorded events of real life, or had portrayed the manners of the colonists; but theology was dominant in verse as well as prose; or, if other topics were chosen, they were mostly of a common-place description. We find an exception in Tompson's verses; and a few lines, said to have been copied from the recitation of an old inhabitant who died in 1767, describe the bill of fare enjoyed by the early colonists, who had—

'Pumpkin at morning, and pumpkin at noon.'

'The place where we live is a wilderness wood,
Where grass is much wanted that's fruitful and good;
Our mountains and hills and valleys below
Are commonly covered with frost and with snow;

And when the north-west wind with violence blows,
Then every man pulls his cap over his nose;
But if any 's so hardy, and will it withstand,
He forfeits a finger, a foot, or a hand.

Our clothes we brought with us are apt to be torn;
They need to be clouted soon after they 're worn;
But clouting our garments this hinders us nothing—
Clouts double are warmer than single whole clothing.'

In 1623 or 1624—about three years after the arrival of the Pilgrims—William Morell, an episcopal clergyman, wrote, in Latin hexameter verse, a description of New England. It was published in England, with a translation by the author, and has been reprinted in the collections of the Massachusetts Historical Society.

The next production in verse was an English version of the *Psalms of David*, done by several of the most eminent divines, including John Eliot—usually styled 'the Apostle of the Indians'—Thomas Welde of Roxbury, and Richard Mather of Dorchester. This version—the first *book* printed in the United States—was published at Cambridge in 1640. It was dry, literal, and unmusical in the extreme, reducing the songs of Sion to such doggrel as the following:—

'The rivers on of Babilon
There when wee did sit downe,
Yea even then we mourned when
Wee remembered Sion.'

The translators, with perfect self-complacency, commended their own style, and argued 'that God's altar needs not our polishings; for wee have respected rather a plain translation, than to smooth our verses with the sweetness of any paraphrase, and so have attended to conscience rather than elegance, fidelity rather than poetry, in translating the Hebrew words into English language, and David's poetry into English meetre.' But an improved version was soon found desirable, and was prepared by the Rev. Henry Dunster, and Mr Richard Lyon. This version, styled the *Bay Psalm Book*, passed through seventy editions, and was extensively circulated in Scotland.[1]

The best verse-writer in New England, during the lifetime of the Pilgrims, was ANNE BRADSTREET, wife of the governor of the Massachusetts colony. She was born in England (1612),

[1] In England, it passed through eighteen editions, of which the last was issued in 1754.

and came with her husband to America in 1630. Her verses, considering their dates, are by no means contemptible. In her time, the French versifier Du Bartas was the favourite poet in New England. Puns and conceits of a laborious and uncouth fashion were admired as gems of thought. The learned divine, John Norton, in his funeral eulogy on Anne Bradstreet, thought it decorous to pun upon her name by saying—

> 'Her breast was a brave pallace, a *broad street*
> Where all heroic, ample thoughts did meet.'

In those days, the death of any noted divine called forth several elegies. When John Cotton, the first minister of Boston, died (1652), a versifier wrote a eulogy which might have suggested Franklin's epitaph upon himself. The eulogist regards Cotton as a book, and says—

> 'O what a monument of glorious worth,
> When in *a new edition* he comes forth,
> Without *erratas* may we think he'll be,
> In *leaves* and *covers* of eternity!'

BENJAMIN TOMPSON, who was master of the public school in Boston from 1667 to 1670, is styled the 'first native American poet.' His poem, entitled *New England's Crisis* (written in 1670–75), contains lamentations over the decay of the colony through luxurious habits, at a time when 'the women of Boston were found working to build a fort against the Indians!' Among other signs of degeneracy, Tompson deplores the curtailing of the grace before dinner, and the introduction of silk dresses, chocolate, tobacco, and French wines; while he extols the old times when—

> 'Men fared hardly, yet without complaint,
> On vilest cates; the dainty Indian maize
> Was eat with clamp-shells out of wooden trays
> Under thatched hutts, without the cry of rent;
> And the best sauce to every dish—content.'

ROGER WOLCOT—born at Windsor, Connecticut, in 1679—wrote a long poem on the Charter obtained for his native colony in 1662, and gave a versified account of the warfare with the Pequod Indians. He set a good example in celebrating American scenes and events; but his descriptions are very dull and prosaic: if he touches a poetic topic, he spoils it by some dry details; as, in describing mountains, he takes care to tell us—

> 'Twenty-four miles surveyors do account
> Between the eastern and the western mount'—

And then goes on to say—

> 'Hither the eagles fly and—lay their eggs.'

Michael Wigglesworth—born in 1631—was a verse-writer on religious topics. His principal work, *The Day of Doom*, was very popular in its time, passed through six editions in America, and was republished in London. In the style of Sternhold and Hopkins, the most solemn matters are here described in rhymes so miserable, that passages intended to be serious read as caricatures. The end of the world is announced by such signs as—

> 'They rush from beds with giddy heads,
> And to their windows run.'

ROGER WILLIAMS AND HIS TIMES.

If we regard literature as a record of the progress of culture among a people, we cannot pass over those early writings, however antiquated in their style, which have given expression to new ideas. The founder of Rhode Island would deserve to be remembered, if he had written nothing more than the article on religious liberty inserted in the charter of his colony. He wrote on theology, besides an account of his own controversy against intolerance, and prepared a key to the Indian languages. These writings, with other contemporary documents, are valuable as they illustrate the life and character of a man who, in his views of society and government, was far in advance of his times. To criticise his works, or give specimens of his quaint and rugged style, would be useless: our purpose is to give the spirit of his life and writings.

He was born in 1599, or about that time, and it is supposed that Wales was his native land. During youth, it is said that he enjoyed the patronage of Sir Edward Coke, with whose daughter he for some time held a correspondence. Before leaving England, he was admitted to orders in the established church; but it does not appear that he was appointed as curate of any parish. We are also left in ignorance of the time when his mind first embraced the great principle of perfect liberty of conscience with regard to religious creeds; but it is certain that he had not only adopted, but had fully developed this doctrine when he sailed for Massachusetts in 1630.[1] The remainder of his biography shall be

[1] 'The settlements then forming the colony of Massachusetts Bay, had been made two or three years previously. The civil code established by the colonists was founded on the institutes of Moses.' . . . . The state was secondary to the church. . . . It was ordered that 'no man should be admitted to the freedom of the body politic, but such as are members of some of the churches.'—*North American Review*, No. 120.—Gammell's *Life of Roger Williams.*

chiefly narrated by his most faithful interpreter, Bancroft, author of the *History of the United States.*

The historian's eulogistic style is appropriately employed in describing the character of Roger Williams, the founder of Rhode Island and the apostle of liberty. Enthusiasm, in this instance, has been tempered by research; the facts fully justify the conclusions, and the whole sketch might be quoted as one of the best specimens of its kind:—

'In February of the first year of the colony, but a few months after the arrival of Winthrop, and before either Cotton or Hooker had embarked for New England, there arrived at Nantasket, after a stormy passage of sixty-six days, "a young minister, godly and zealous, having precious" gifts. It was Roger Williams. He was then but a little more than thirty years of age; but his mind had already matured a doctrine which secures him an immortality of fame, as its application has given religious peace to the American world. He was a Puritan, and a fugitive from English persecution; but his wrongs had not clouded his accurate understanding; in the capacious recesses of his mind, he had revolved the nature of intolerance, and he, and he alone, had arrived at the great principle which is its sole effectual remedy. He announced his discovery under the simple proposition of the sanctity of conscience. The civil magistrate should restrain crime, but never control opinion; should punish guilt, but never violate the freedom of the soul. The doctrine contained within itself an entire reformation of theological jurisprudence: it would blot from the statute-book the felony of non-conformity; would quench the fires that persecution had so long kept burning; would repeal every law compelling attendance on public worship; would abolish tithes and all forced contributions to the maintenance of religion; would give an equal protection to every form of religious faith; and never suffer the authority of the civil government to be enlisted against the mosque of the Mussulman or the altar of the fire-worshipper, against the Jewish synagogue or the Roman cathedral. It is wonderful with what distinctness Roger Williams deduced these inferences from his great principle, the consistency with which, like Pascal and Edwards, those bold and profound reasoners on other subjects, he accepted every fair inference from his doctrines, and the circumspection with which he repelled every unjust imputation. In the unwavering assertion of his views, he never changed his position; the sanctity of conscience was the great tenet, which, with all its consequences, he defended, as he first trod the shores of New England; and in his extreme old age, it was the last pulsation of his heart. But it placed the young emigrant in direct opposition to the whole system on which Massachusetts was founded; and gentle and forgiving as was his temper, prompt as he was to concede everything which honesty permitted, he always asserted his belief with temperate firmness and unyielding benevolence.

'It was objected to him, that his principles subverted all good government. "The commander of the vessel of state," replied Williams, "may maintain order on board the ship, and see that it pursues its course steadily, even though the dissenters of the crew are not compelled to attend the public prayers of their companions."

'But the controversy finally turned on the question of the rights and duty of magistrates to guard the minds of the people against corruption, and to punish what would seem to them error and heresy. Magistrates, Williams protested, are but the agents of the people, or its trustees, on whom no spiritual power in matters of worship can ever be conferred; since conscience belongs to the individual, and is not the property of the body politic; and with admirable dialectics clothing the great truth in its boldest and most general forms, he asserted that "the civil magistrate may not intermeddle even to stop a church from apostasy and heresy."'

Meanwhile, Williams was elected as their minister by the people of Salem. The assembly of divines now declared every one worthy of banishment who would assert 'that the civil magistrate might not interfere to stop a church from apostasy and heresy;' and, moreover, they decreed that, as a punishment, a grant of public land should be withheld from the people of Salem.

'The breach was therefore widened. To the ministers, Williams frankly but temperately explained his doctrines; and he was armed at all points for their defence. As his townsmen had lost their lands in consequence of their attachment to him, it would have been cowardice on his part to have abandoned them; and the instinct of liberty led him again to the suggestion of a proper remedy. In conjunction with the church, he wrote "letters of admonition unto all the churches whereof any of the magistrates were members, that they might admonish the magistrates of their injustice." The church-members alone were freemen. Williams, in moderate language, appealed to the people, and invited them to instruct their representatives to do justice to the citizens of Salem.

'This last act seemed flagrant treason; and at the next general court, Salem was disfranchised till an ample apology for the letter should be made. The town acquiesced in its wrongs, and submitted; not an individual remained willing to justify the letter of remonstrance; the church of Williams would not avow his great principle of the sanctity of conscience; even his wife, under a delusive idea of duty, was for a season influenced to disturb the tranquillity of his home by her reproaches. Williams was left alone—absolutely alone. Anticipating the censures of the colonial churches, he declared himself no longer subjected to their spiritual jurisdiction. "My own voluntary withdrawing from all these churches, resolved to continue in persecuting the witnesses of the Lord, presenting light unto them, I confess it was mine own voluntary act; yea, I hope the act of the Lord Jesus, sounding forth in me the blast which shall in his own holy season cast down the strength and confidence of those inventions of men." When summoned to appear before the general court, he avowed his convictions in the presence of the representatives of the state, "maintained the rocky strength of his grounds," and declared himself "ready to be bound and banished, and even to die in New England," rather than renounce the opinions which had dawned upon his mind in the clearness of light. At a time when Germany was the battle-field for all Europe in the implacable wars of religion; when even Holland was bleeding with the anger of vengeful factions; when France was still to go through the fearful struggle with bigotry; when England was gasping under the despotism of intolerance; almost half a century before William Penn became an American proprietary; and two years before Descartes founded modern philosophy on the method of free reflection—Roger Williams asserted the great doctrine of intellectual liberty. It became his glory to found a state upon that principle, and to stamp himself upon its rising institutions, in characters so deep that the impress has remained to the present day, and can never be erased without the total destruction of the work. . . . . He was the first person in modern Christendom to assert in its plenitude the doctrine of the liberty of conscience—the equality of opinions before the law; and in its defence he was the harbinger of Milton—the precursor and the superior of Jeremy Taylor.'[1]

A sentence of exile was pronounced against Williams, and it was subsequently determined that he should be sent back to the old country. A warrant was sent to him, ordering him to come to Boston and embark; and when he had refused to obey, officers entered his house to enforce the order; but Williams had meanwhile escaped into the wilderness. Through the deep snow and the bitter cold, he wandered from his home, and submitted himself to the privations of savage life; 'for fourteen weeks, he was sorely tost in a bitter season, not knowing what bread or bed did mean,' and sometimes hiding at night in some hollow tree. Happily, he could speak the dialect of the Indians, and they had not forgotten his kindness. He found shelter in the cabin of a chief; and, to use his own words, 'the ravens fed him in the wilderness.' The sympathy of friends had followed him, and even his foes could not hate him: their worst charge against him implied only that his mind, being more expansive than their own, must be 'unsettled.' The excellent Governor Winthrop privately wrote to Williams, advising him to steer his course to

[1] These statements are fully supported by the writings of Roger Williams; including his *Hireling Ministry*, and the rare tract entitled *Mr Cotton's Letter, lately Printed, Examined and Answered*. By Roger Williams, of Providence, in New England. London. Imprinted in the yeere 1644. Small 4to, pp. 47. It is preceded by an address of two pages to the impartial reader.

Narraganset Bay, where he would be free from English claims and patents; accordingly, the brave man embarked in a frail Indian canoe, and, accompanied by five friends who had joined him, paddled over to the opposite shore, and landed on a nook of Rhode Island. In gratitude, he named the landing-place 'Providence,' and here he began to plant and build.

The sequel corresponded with the beginning. Williams, the homeless exile, found friends among the Indians who surrounded his infant colony: through *their* kindness, he obtained a large tract of land. He was now in a position to make himself a wealthy proprietor; but he 'reserved to himself not one foot of land, not one tittle of political power more than he granted to servants and strangers.' 'He gave away his lands and other estate to them that he thought were most in want, until he gave away all.'

He established a simple form of democracy, providing that the will of the majority should rule, but 'only in civil things,' and that God should be the sole ruler of conscience. Quakers, and followers of Anne Hutchinson and Samuel Gorton—indeed, men of all shades of religious opinion—were admitted into the new colony, which its founder declared to be 'a shelter for persons distressed for conscience.'[1]

But the noblest feature in the character of Williams remains to be told. He forgave his enemies; he did good to those who had severely treated him. For himself, he had no fear of the Indians: they knew him and loved him. Soon after the settlement of Providence, its founder discovered that the Pequod tribe had made with other Indians an alliance for the massacre of settlers in New England. Williams embarked again in his canoe, and 'cut through a stormy wind and great seas, every minute in hazard of life,' in order to dissuade two chiefs from joining the alliance; and while he stayed in the cabins of these chiefs, he was surrounded by the Pequod warriors, and 'nightly looked for their bloody knives at his own throat.' This noble interposition was the main cause of the defeat of the Pequod conspiracy. It displayed the Christian heroism of Williams, and gave to his enemies one more opportunity of exposing their own character. Their conduct, in the sequel, proved that religious bigotry can hardly be compatible with generosity. When Governor Winthrop suggested that Williams might be rewarded and recalled from exile, the majority of the ministers of Massachusetts resolved that he should still abide in disgrace at Providence.

[1] 'No person within the said colony shall be molested, punished, disquieted, or called in question for any differences of opinion in matters of religion, who does not actually disturb the civil peace.'—*Charter of Rhode Island*, 1644.

No practical Christianity, however heroic, could hide his heterodoxy.

His services were more justly appreciated by the Red Men, especially by the two chieftains of the Narragansets, in whose cabins he had been sheltered. In one of his letters, he writes:—'God was pleased to give me a painful, patient spirit, to lodge with them [the Indians] in their filthy, smoky holes, even while I lived at Plymouth, to gain their tongue.' In a later part of his life, he journeyed, once in a month, into the Narraganset territory to preach to the natives; and it is said that, not long before his death, when he heard that King Philip was marching to attack Providence, he seized his staff, and alone went out to meet the hostile force, whom he turned aside by kind words. In his civil dealings with the Indians, he gave an example which, if it had been generally followed, might have prevented the fate of many tribes. He declared that the aborigines had a right to their native soil; and in purchasing their land, he 'spared no cost towards them in tokens and presents.' When the aged chief Canonicus was about to die, he sent for 'his friend Williams,' and desired to be buried in a piece of cloth given by the good missionary.

Such was the character of the founder of the colony of Rhode Island, the foremost man in asserting the principles which now form the basis of liberty in America. Religious toleration now appears to be a maxim of common sense; but it is the result of centuries of miserable experience. The attribute of the great teacher is to look far beyond his own times, and to anticipate the results which, by a slow process, experience must bring to light. Before the year 1630, or more than half a century before Locke wrote his treatise on toleration, Roger Williams, in New England, asserted the principle of entire religious liberty, carried it into practice, and suffered for it. So far was the reformer in advance of his age, that about the time of his death, and when twenty-five years of experience in Rhode Island had confirmed his doctrine, the Puritans of Massachusetts were enacting laws for the imprisonment, whipping, and barbarous mutilation of heterodox religionists!

After reading the life of Williams, we find a striking contrast in turning to the name of another prominent character of the old times—Cotton Mather, whose voluminous writings reflect the characteristics of his period.

COTTON MATHER AND HIS TIMES.

1663-1728.

Cotton Mather may be classed with biographical writers; for his principal work, the *Magnalia*, contains memoirs of several worthies of the old Puritan times. From the death of this quaint author, in 1728, to the time when Benjamin Franklin concluded his autobiography (1757), we find hardly any other biographies deserving notice. In this period, men were too much engaged in active life to find time for writing. The contrast suggested by the names of Mather and Franklin shews how great had been the progress of intelligence and freedom in the course of half a century; or from the time when Mather accused witches and goblins of raising high winds and blowing down meeting-houses, to the day when Franklin drew the lightning from the clouds. In one point of view, Mather and Franklin resembled each other; for each, in his writings, drew a faithful portrait of his own character, and also gave notices of the characteristics of his own times. Mather, in his diary, like Franklin in his autobiography, wrote his own life and character so faithfully, that the reader may understand the writer more fully perhaps than he understood himself. His numerous works range over a great diversity of topics, and go beyond the bounds of this visible world into regions where we do not care to follow. With a reference to Mather's strange tales of *diablerie*, Flint, in his sketch of American literature,[1] has said of the old Puritan writers: 'Their first excursions into the world of imagination were not of a nature to tempt them to go much further.'

Cotton Mather, regarded as a scholar and a writer, was the representative man of New England in the latter part of the seventeenth and early part of the eighteenth century. This assertion must not be too strictly understood, as implying either that this one quaint writer epitomised all the characteristics of his times, or that his contemporaries may all be judged by his standard. He had his peculiarities, and, while foremost as a scholar and Puritan divine, in some of his opinions he halted behind the age.

He was the son of Increase Mather, president of Harvard College, and was born in Boston February 12, 1663. His mother was the daughter of John Cotton, an eminent minister of Boston. His first ancestor, Richard Mather, settled in New England in

[1] Published in the London *Athenæum*.

1635, and was pastor of the church in Dorchester. Cotton Mather was 'born to greatness.' It was expected, as a matter of course, that he must be a great scholar and prominent character. When he took his degree at college, the president, in his oration, exclaimed: 'Cotton Mather! What a name!—I should have said, what names! . . . . I trust that in him Cotton and Mather will be united and flourish again.' After his graduation, Mather studied theology, and was ordained, in 1684, as a colleague with his father in the pastorship of the North Church in Boston. In 1690, he received the diploma of Doctor of Divinity from the university of Glasgow; and in 1713, was made a Fellow of the Royal Society. His biographers have stated that he wrote in seven languages; but this must be understood with allowance for the freedom of style in which such assertions have often been made. A scholar who knows what the labour is of writing or speaking well even one language beside the vernacular, must doubt the philological powers ascribed to Mather. It is, however, true that he published 380 distinct works, of which many were single sermons or mere pamphlets. His chief writings include the *Christian Philosopher*, the *Wonders of the Invisible World*, the *Remarkables of Divine Providence among the People of New England* (one of the most characteristic), and especially the *Magnalia Christi Americana*, or Ecclesiastical History of New England, written in a very odd, quaint style, with bad punctuation, and an absurd profusion of words in italics. It contains biographies of several worthies of the old times in New England.

Superstition, and an inordinate vanity, which might almost be styled a species of self-worship, were combined in Mather's character. The superstition he shared with other minds of that age; but vanity, or self-esteem, was his peculiar trait, and made him unhappily prominent in one of the darkest passages of American history. The habit of trusting his own impressions or opinions, rather than the evidence of facts, led to lamentable errors; and so far as these errors were connected with his vanity and selfishness, they seriously affect his moral character.

Following the example of his father, Cotton Mather kept a diary, in which he recorded even his inmost thoughts and feelings, and fully displayed his eccentricities. The mixture of religious meditations with the most insignificant traits of everyday life, makes this diary, which is still extant, a very singular record. As examples of his mode of finding 'edification' in common incidents—he tells us that, while his wife was employed in brewing, he was reminded of the spiritual wants of 'thirsty souls;' while she was baking, he meditated on 'the bread of life;' and on washing-day he ejaculated, 'wash us thoroughly from sin.' Snuffing a candle, winding up his watch, hearing a clock strike, knocking at a door, mending his fire, and other incidents of equal importance, were made occasions of appropriate devout exercises. For a lady carving at his table, he prayed that 'a rich portion of spiritual comforts' might be 'carved.' Seeing a lady 'well stricken in years,' he prayed that she might be adorned with comely virtues. (For obvious reasons, we cannot employ exactly his own words.) For a very beautiful woman, he implored that she might be most concerned for other ornaments than such as are perishable. In short, he had ejaculations prepared for all persons and circumstances, and craved, 'for a tall man,' high attainments; for a lame man, the power 'to walk uprightly;' for a negro, 'the washing of the spirit;' and for a very little man, 'great blessings.'

His self-esteem may be sufficiently illustrated by one example taken from his diary; for though this refers immediately to the appointment of his father—Increase Mather—the father and son were inseparable colleagues during many years, and each shared the other's honour. The father, president of Harvard College, wished to be sent as a deputation to England, and the son hoped to succeed to the president's chair; but it so happened that the Court of the University found merit in other men besides the two Mathers, and refused to honour the elder in this matter. Of this, the son wrote in his diary as follows:—'I am going to relate one of the most astonishing things that ever befell in all the time of my pilgrimage.' This portent proves to be nothing more than the fact, that Cotton Mather had received a strong impression—an *afflatus*, he calls it—to the effect that his father would 'be carried into England.' He concludes a passage in his strange diary by ejaculating: 'What! shall my father yet appear before Cæsar! Has an angel from heaven told me so! And must I believe what has been told to me! Well, then, it shall be so! It shall be so!'

However, the court ruled that it should *not* be so, and Cotton Mather again opened his diary, and wrote: 'What shall I make of this wonderful matter?—Wait! wait!' He waited in vain; the court finally decided that Increase Mather should remain in Boston; and both father and son were left in their astonishment. The fact that their own ambition could not, in this instance, be gratified, appeared inconceivable.

Cotton Mather's writings are full of uncouth puns: in his taste for these strange ornaments of style, he was not singular: other Puritan writers loved to torture words and play fantastic tricks with language. In writing of a worthy man, unfortunately named Partridge, who suffered some persecutions, Mather chooses to describe him as 'hunted;' as having 'neither beak nor claws' for defence; as escaping 'by flight' over the sea, and finding 'covert' in Plymouth. Even at the grave, the grim punster will not leave his game, but proposes for an epitaph the word *avolavit*—'our partridge has flown away!' Mather describes his own habit of crowding his pages with many quotations, as 'salting my sentences now and then with short, instructive, and unforced intermixtures of something or other I have read of.' He seems unable to express his own thoughts without the assistance of other 'judicious writers.'

These notices of a quaint author and self-complacent character might be regarded as unworthy of record, if they were not connected with something more important in the sequel. But Mather's self-esteem made him prominent in the annals of New England: that trait of his character which appeared merely ludicrous in minor affairs, became exceedingly mischievous in the end. This quaint author and learned divine was virtually one of the chief rulers of New England. Like other men of that time—including such divines as Richard Baxter—he believed in miraculous signs, omens, haunted places, witchcraft, and other delusions; in fact, demonology formed a very great portion of his religious belief. So far, he fairly represented the lingering popular faith of those times, when 'Indian bows were seen in the sky, and scalps in the moon;' when 'northern lights became an object of terror,' and 'phantom-horsemen careered among the clouds,' or were heard galloping invisibly through the air:[1] but as Mr Upham[2] and other writers have shewn, a mischievous vanity and obstinate self-esteem made Mather's superstition more formidable than it could have been without such allies.

Four years before the outbreak of the popular delusion (or conspiracy?) in Salem, Mather 'had studied the nature of witchcraft,' and had especially examined a case occurring in the house of a neighbour. In this instance, the girl supposed to be 'troubled by witches' uttered at least one true prediction; for, speaking of Mather's book on the subject, she told him that he would 'quickly come to disgrace by that history.' The sequel made this prediction rather remarkable.

Having formed his theory, he determined to make all facts bend to it, and popular ignorance aided his efforts. In the course of his experiments in the first supposed case of 'possession,' he came to the conclusion that demons 'are well skilled in languages, and understand Latin and Greek, and even Hebrew;' but he found them imperfect 'in one of the Indian dialects!' He was assured that over himself the powers of air had no power; they 'could not enter his study.' 'Sadducees' and the Quakers

[1] Hildreth's *History of the United States*, vol. i. p. 483.
[2] Upham's *History of the Delusion in Salem*, 1692.

opposed the delusion, and Mather's reputation became involved in the controversy on witchcraft. In his book on the subject, he treated his opponents as ignorant, uncivil, and impudent persons. This book, printed in 1689, was circulated in New England, and soon reached the mother-country, where it was republished by Richard Baxter.

When the minds of the people had been sufficiently excited, and were prepared to receive new wonders, Mather found a ready assistant in Samuel Parris, minister of Salem. In February 1692, Tituba, an Indian female-servant in the household of Parris, was accused of having bewitched two of his children. She was not put to death, because her confession was so valuable as a refutation of the 'Sadducee' doctrine. The children supposed to be afflicted gained great notoriety, and new cases were soon discovered. It was one of the most curious features in the affair, that the confessions of certain parties, and the evidence given by others, so exactly accorded with the statements of Mather's book on witchcraft, that they almost appeared as quotations. This admitted two modes of explanation, but of course Mather received it as a confirmation of his own doctrine. Examinations and commitments for witchcraft became more and more numerous. In the popular panic thus excited, several poor creatures, hoping to escape the punishment of death, made absurd confessions of having practised certain witcheries. Of one aged woman, who was hanged as a witch, Cotton Mather states, that 'she gave a look towards the great and spacious meeting-house of Salem, and immediately a demon, invisibly entering the house, tore down a part of it.' To believe all that Mather had said and written of demonology, was the only way of safety: to doubt the reality of witchcraft, was to court suspicion and inquiry; and the party brought to a trial had scarcely a chance to escape conviction. When confessions, or accounts given by witnesses, were full of self-contradictions, it only suggested the notion that demons had deprived the speakers of memory! If the accused trembled, his guilt was manifest; if he stood firmly, the demon supported him. 'At the trial of George Burroughs [a minister], the bewitched persons pretended to be dumb. "Who hinders these witnesses," said Stoughton, "from giving their testimonies?"—"I suppose the devil," answered Burroughs. "How comes the devil," retorted the chief judge, "so loath to have any testimony borne against *you?*" and the question was effective.'[1] Cotton Mather decided that the evidence was 'enough,' and the jury brought in a verdict of guilty.

[1] Bancroft's *History of the United States*, vol. ii. chap. 19.

To pass over many horrible details of other judicial murders, the case of this unhappy man Burroughs was sufficient to leave a permanent blot on the names of Parris and Cotton Mather. Burroughs had preached in Salem, where, as some of the people wished him to settle, he became the rival of Parris; but his greatest offence was, that he was a sceptic in witchcraft, and had ventured to say that such a crime was impossible. When brought to the scaffold, he firmly maintained his innocence, and so moved the assembled people, that they were ready to hinder the execution; but Cotton Mather addressed them, argued that a demon 'might be disguised as an angel of light,' and the hanging was allowed to take place.

Already, in September 1692, 'twenty persons had been put to death for witchcraft, and fifty-five had been tortured or terrified into penitent confessions.'[1] A reaction followed. Many doubted the doctrine which had been supported by such terrible means; but Mather remained firm, and published his *Wonders of the Invisible World*, which received the approval of the president of Harvard College. In October, the people of Andover, with their minister, protested against the delusion and conspiracy. This, and other circumstances, encouraged many persons to speak as they thought, and dispelled the panic. Accusations of witchcraft were treated with scorn, and Mather's books lost their authority. Did Mather himself doubt? He endeavoured, as a last resource, to get up a case of witchcraft in his own parish; but the imposition was fully exposed by one Robert Calef, whom he describes as 'a malignant, calumnious, and reproachful man.'

The result of the whole is very remarkable. As Bancroft says, 'Cotton Mather never repented;' but he 'had temptations to atheism, and to the abandonment of all religion as a mere delusion,' as he confesses in his diary. He died, February 13, 1728, leaving a reputation which has been seriously injured by the researches of historians and biographers.[2] A few American writers[3] on the life and times of Mather, misguided by a desire to speak well of one of the early divines of New England, have endeavoured to mitigate the censure pronounced against him; but careful investigations of facts have fully supported the charges brought forward by Bancroft and Upham. In literature, Mather might be left in the obscure place assigned to uncouth and conceited pedants; but he will always hold a prominent place in the records of bigotry and superstition. His character remains

[1] Bancroft.

[2] See, besides the works quoted in this notice of Mather, Peabody's *Life of C. Mather*, in Sparks's American Biography, vol. vi.; Robbins's *History of the Old North Church in Boston*.

[3] See Enoch Pond's *Life of Increase Mather*.

as 'an example how far selfishness, under the form of vanity and ambition, can blind the higher faculties, stupify the judgment, and dupe consciousness itself.'[1]

THEOLOGY.

1640-1800.

It has been already observed, that during the early part of the colonial period, and before political questions assumed the ascendancy, the talents of learned men were chiefly devoted to the service of theology and the discussion of ecclesiastical questions. When the early hardships of colonisation had been overcome, and a considerable proportion of the population of the States had some share of ease and leisure, it might have been expected that elegant literature would be cultivated, and in some degree this was the fact; but the comparatively few readers who asked for works of general or light literature, could be readily supplied with imports from England, including the essays and poetry of our so-called Augustan age, and the books of preceding times. Meanwhile, the quarrel with the mother-country was beginning, and men who, in quiet times, might have written verses, were called to write political tracts. In the early part of the eighteenth century, controversial or practical divinity, and, in the latter part, political discussion, almost exclusively occupied the attention of writers who, otherwise, might have contributed to the stores of general literature. In both periods, the literature of America reflected the progress of the people. The old books of divinity, which now seem so dry and verbose, were once readable, because their doctrine was linked with the strongest affections of the Puritans of New England; and in the present day, such names as Cotton, Eliot, Hooker, Chauncey, Norton, and Edwards, are still venerated in Massachusetts.

JOHN COTTON (1584–1652), the first minister of Boston, and one of the most learned men of his times, wrote extensively on divinity and ecclesiastical government. Like Cotton Mather, and many other divines of New England, this celebrated Boston minister sometimes wrote verses; but for poetry he had no vocation. Among his verses, we find an elegy on his contemporary and friend, THOMAS HOOKER (1586–1647), first minister of Hartford, and author of *A Survey of Church Discipline.*

[1] Bancroft.

JOHN ELIOT (1604–1690), the Apostle of the Indians, devoted his life to the instruction of the aborigines. He wrote several treatises in English—among them, one on the Christian Commonwealth; but his more remarkable efforts were made in the acquisition of a knowledge of the Indian dialects. After preparing an Indian grammar, he made a translation of the New Testament into the dialect spoken by the natives in Massachusetts. This work of great labour—printed at Cambridge, N.E., 1661—was followed by the publication of the whole Bible in the same Indian dialect. Such labours deserved a greater success. The language into which Eliot translated the Scriptures is now dead, in the strongest sense of the word; for the tribes who understood and spoke it, have long since vanished from the face of the earth. Some few copies of the Indian Bible remain as monuments of Eliot's zeal and benevolence. He lived, during a great part of his life, among the Indians; taught them to spin and to cultivate the soil; and such was his faith in their intellectual powers, that he prepared for their use a system of logic. One Indian became a bachelor of arts at Cambridge; but after taking his degree, he exchanged his gown for a blanket, and went back to the forest.

Eliot's Bible was followed by NEWMAN'S *Concordance of the Scriptures*, which maintained its value until it was superseded by the work of Cruden. Newman's book was compiled in a log-cabin, and by the light of a pine-knot torch.

JOHN DAVENPORT (1597–1670), founder of the colony of Newhaven; CHARLES CHAUNCEY (1589–1672), second president of Harvard University; and JOHN NORTON (1606–1663), must be named as eminent theological writers of this early time, when missionary rather than literary labour chiefly occupied the attention of divines. Many curious tracts, illustrating the state of religious opinions, and the progress of missions among the Indians, may be found in the collections of the Massachusetts Historical Society.

In the times of the two Mathers, father and son, theology in America assumed a more controversial character, as is seen in the writings of DICKINSON, STODDARD, and WILLARD. The chief points of dispute were the doctrines of Calvin and the ordinances of the church, especially the two forms known as 'open' and 'close communion.' On this question, the controversy was decided by the writings of JONATHAN EDWARDS (1703–1758), one of the most distinguished divines and metaphysical writers in the eighteenth century. He was a native of East Windsor, Connecticut, and was mainly self-educated. His fervid piety was united with an extraordinary power of logical thinking. The universal benevolence of his heart was restricted by the stern doctrines in which his reason had been trained. He maintained the assertion, that 'true religion in a great measure consists in holy affections, in a love of divine things for the beauty and sweetness of their moral excellency;' and that true virtue consists in benevolence having for its objects all intelligent beings; but he qualified these assertions by denying that such religion and virtue could co-exist with certain theological doctrines which he regarded as erroneous. In his celebrated treatise on *The Freedom of the Will*, he displayed his powers as a subtle and conscientious reasoner. As the *Edinburgh Review* has said: 'There is not a trick, a subterfuge, a verbal sophism in the whole book.' The opinions of Dr Chalmers, Robert Hall, Dugald Stewart, and Sir James Macintosh, might be quoted in favour of the claims of Jonathan Edwards as a metaphysical writer, and as 'one of the greatest men who have owned the authority of Calvin.' Besides his *Essay on the Freedom of the Will*, Edwards wrote a *Dissertation on the Nature of True Virtue*, and another on *God's Chief End in the Creation*, besides a controversial work on *Original Sin*, and a more practical *Treatise on Religious Affections*, which has been highly esteemed by religious readers. It must be added that his style is generally rather prolix; like another deep thinker—Bishop Butler—he seems to have taken little care to reduce his thoughts to a concise form of expression. He left at his decease some thousand and upwards of miscellaneous papers.

Another JONATHAN EDWARDS (1745–1801), the son of the preceding author, was president of Union College, and wrote in a style superior to that of the first Edwards, while in his doctrines, and also in his choice of topics, he resembled his father. Among the principal works of the younger Edwards are included *A Dissertation on Liberty and Necessity*, and a controversial treatise, *The Salvation of All Men strictly Examined and Refuted*—the latter written as a reply to the less exclusive doctrine maintained by Dr CHARLES CHAUNCEY (1705–1787). The last-named theologian, who differed from the orthodox American divines of the eighteenth century, wrote, besides his work on the *Episcopate*, a treatise on *The Benevolence of the Deity*, five *Dissertations on the Fall and its Consequences*, and a work entitled *The Salvation of All Men*, which excited controversy.

JOSEPH BELLAMY (1719–1790), who adhered to the Calvinistic doctrine of Edwards, was the writer of several religious works, including an essay, *True Religion Delineated*, which gained a considerable reputation both at home and abroad. A wider view of the scheme of Calvin was defended by SAMUEL HOPKINS (1721–1803), whose chief work, *A System of Doctrines contained in Divine Revelation*, was published in 1793.

JOHN WITHERSPOON (1722–1794) was a native of Scotland, and emigrated in 1769 to America, where he was appointed president of Princeton College. His work, entitled *Ecclesiastical Characteristics*, is described as displaying 'no small share of refined humour and delicate satire;' and his other theological works have been commended for their good sense, simple style, and condensation of thoughts.

Among the other theological writers whose works, though more or less excellent in their special class, do not demand extended notices in an account of general literature, we must name JAMES BLAIR (died 1743), president of William and Mary College in Virginia, who wrote a series of *Discourses on Matthew V.–VII.;* also, NATHANIEL APPLETON, AARON BURR (president of Princeton College), SAMUEL DAVIES (president of New Jersey College), SAMUEL FINLEY, SAMUEL JOHNSON, ANDREW ELIOT, and SAMUEL COOPER.

The name of TIMOTHY DWIGHT demands a more distinct notice; for his writings in prose and verse contributed to the improvement of American literature, though his poems have no remarkable merit besides their smooth versification. On the maternal side, Dwight was the grandson of the great Jonathan Edwards, and was born in Northampton, Massachusetts, in 1752. His most important work, entitled *Theology Explained and Defended*, consists of nearly 200 sermons, preached during his presidency at Yale College. The views of the writer are moderately Calvinistic, and his style is fluent, and by no means concise. This work enjoyed a very extensive popularity in England as well as in America. Many preachers and theological students, endowed with no great originality of thought, have been indebted to Dwight's *Theology*. Besides this principal work, the author wrote a valuable and interesting account of his *Travels in New England and New York*, which gives a view of American society and manners in the beginning of the present century. President Dwight died at Newhaven in 1817.

In Religious Biography, numerous scattered memoirs may be found besides those of Roger Williams and Cotton Mather, which have been collectively noticed; but few biographical writings of general interest were produced in the colonial period.

Among all the memoirs and other writings of the Friends (otherwise called Quakers) in America, one of the most noticeable books, though it has no literary pretensions, is the *Journal* of JOHN WOOLMAN—the book of which Charles Lamb said: 'Get the writings of John Woolman by heart.'

Woolman was born in the year 1720, at Northampton, in Burlington County, West Jersey. He was educated according to the principles of George Fox, and at a very early period began to 'bear his testimony,' in a meek and inoffensive manner, against the evils of slavery. In the course of a journey in Virginia (1746), he writes in his diary: 'Two things were remarkable to me in this journey—first, in regard to my entertainment; when I ate, drank, and lodged, free-cost, with people who lived in ease on the hard labour of their slaves, I felt uneasy. . . . . Where the masters bore a good share of the burden, and lived frugally, so that their servants were well provided for, and their labour moderate, I felt more easy; but where they lived in a costly way, and laid heavy burdens on their slaves, my exercise was often great, and I frequently had conversation with them in private concerning it. Secondly, this trade of importing slaves from their native country being much encouraged amongst them [the Virginians], and the white people and their children living much without labour, was frequently the subject of my serious thoughts. I saw, in these southern provinces, so many vices and corruptions increased by this trade and this way of life, that it appeared to me as *a dark gloominess hanging over the land;* and though now many willingly run into it, yet in future the consequence will be grievous to posterity. I express it as it hath appeared to me, not once, nor twice, but as a matter fixed on my mind.' After all that has been written on the subject of slavery, we find nothing better than the sober and charitable *Considerations on the Keeping of Negroes*, written by John Woolman, and first printed in the year 1762.

The religious principles held by this benevolent man, have been censured as tending to that 'introversion of thought and feeling,' or self-contemplation, which is certainly unwholesome; but in his case, as in others, a meditative, and, as it is commonly called, a mystical piety, was accompanied by a constant and active care for the welfare of mankind. Kindness marked every step of his course. We may smile at some of his peculiarities; but it is with a feeling quite compatible with respect for both the understanding and the heart of the man whose greatest eccentricity was in wearing 'a hat of undyed fur.' This led to a ludicrous mistake. 'The thoughts of wearing hats and garments dyed with a dye hurtful to them,' had excited some doubts in his mind: he concluded that it was a custom not founded 'in pure wisdom,' and determined to wear out the garments heretofore made; but, as soon as he wanted a new covering for his head, to buy 'a hat the natural colour of the fur.' Unluckily, at the time when he adopted this change, white hats became fashionable, and were symbols of dandyism; so John Woolman, bearing thus his simple testimony against 'dyed hats,' appeared in the height of fashion, and seemed to have been carried away by the vanities of the world. Even among the Friends, many were scandalised by his singularity; but he was able to defend himself. The fact was, that Woolman, in the middle of the eighteenth century, was a sanitary reformer, and in some respects far in advance of the doctrines held by advocates of cleanliness at the present time. He even went so far as to recommend the general use of light-coloured clothes, because 'they would not hide dirt.' In his *Journal of a Tour in England*, he says:

'Having of late travelled in wet weather through narrow streets in towns and villages, where dirtiness underfoot, and the scent arising from that filth which more or less infects the air of all thickly-settled towns, were disagreeable; and being but weakly, I have felt distress both in body and mind with that which is impure. In these journeys, I have been where much cloth hath been dyed, and have at sundry times walked over ground where much of their dye-stuffs has drained away. This hath produced a longing in my mind that people might come into cleanness of spirit, cleanness of person, and cleanness about their houses and garments. Some of the great carry delicacy to a great height themselves, and yet real cleanliness is not generally promoted. . . . . Hiding that which is not clean, by colouring our garments, seems contrary to the sweetness of sincerity. Through some sorts of dyes, cloth is rendered less useful; and if the value of dye-stuffs, the expense of dyeing, and the damage done to cloth, were all added together, and that cost applied to keeping all sweet and clean, how much more would real cleanliness prevail.'

Most probably, John Woolman fell a victim to the unsanitary state of his lodgings, against which he had 'borne his testimony;' for he died of small-pox, at York, October 5, 1772.

The journal of this benevolent man deserves notice, because it illustrates the principles of a class of religionists who exercised a considerable influence on the early progress of intellectual freedom in America. They passed through a period of suffering from persecution; for the Puritans, who ruled in the several colonies, by no means professed toleration of religious differences. But ultimately the disciples of George Fox established themselves in the New World, and under the guidance of William Penn, opened there an asylum for all who were oppressed in every nation. Emigrants from England, Wales, Scotland, Ireland, and Germany, hastened to their new home; and Philadelphia—a mere cluster of three or four cottages in 1683—in the course of two years, contained 600 houses, a school-room, and a printing-office. A new state was founded in the midst of the wild Indians, but without warfare and bloodshed, such as attended the settling of New England, Maryland, and other colonies. Penn, trusting in the power of love, treated the aborigines as brethren; and his confidence was well repaid, for no Indian ever pointed an arrow or raised a tomahawk against a Quaker.

BENJAMIN FRANKLIN.

1706—1790.

It seems hardly probable that Cotton Mather and BENJAMIN FRANKLIN could have lived in one century; but, in fact, Mather was preaching and writing in Boston, while Franklin was there working on his brother's newspaper—the *New England Courant*. The old Puritan divine sometimes saw the active boy—Benjamin was then about sixteen years old—carrying about the bad, 'free-thinking paper;' and painful recollections arose of the good strict times when such a libel would have been put down by the assembled ministers. It is probable that some of the libels which grieved the old man were written by Franklin; for he was then described 'as a youth that had a turn for libelling and satire;' and during his brother's imprisonment, he took charge of the paper, and, as he says, 'made bold to give our rulers some rubs in it.'

Benjamin Franklin, born at Boston, January 17, 1706, advanced from a humble origin, and through the details of a mechanical business, to a position of great distinction in his native country. He spent a few of his early years in London, but settled as a printer in Philadelphia, where, by means of his natural ingenuity, his industry, and prudence, he quickly rose in the world. In 1732, he first published his celebrated popular calendar, commonly known as *Poor Richard's Almanac*, which he continued during about twenty-five years. As it was designed to spread useful information among the poor, all the spaces left between the remarkable days in the calendar were filled with homely proverbs, condensing the practical wisdom, the life-lore of many ages and nations. In the almanac for the year 1757, all these proverbs were collectively given as the advice of a wise old man, and in this form they obtained a very wide circulation, were copied in all the American newspapers, reprinted in sheets to be pasted on the walls of houses throughout Great Britain, and translated and widely distributed by the clergy and gentry in France.

Having secured a competency, Franklin retired from business, and hoped to find leisure for philosophical studies; but numerous public cares were imposed upon him by his fellow-citizens. He, however, found time to make those experiments in electricity which have made his name as illustrious in the records of science as in the history of his country. In his autobiography, he mentions his experiments in a merely cursory style, and seems at all times to have been indifferent with regard to the honour of discovery. As early as the year 1749, he had suggested the theory that lightning was identical with electricity, and conceived the bold idea of testing the theory by raising an iron rod to a considerable elevation, so as to conduct the electric fluid from a passing cloud. At the same time, or soon afterwards, he concluded that such a rod might be used as a conductor to protect ships and houses from the effects of lightning. The experiment was delayed, because there was no spire in Philadelphia to which the rod might be fixed; and years passed away before Franklin thought of a common plaything—a school-boy's kite—as a substitute for the proposed iron rod. In the summer of 1752, he made his kite, using a silk handkerchief stretched over two sticks, and fixing an iron point on the upright stick. A cord of silk was tied at the lower end of the hempen-string, and to this a key was fastened. With this simple apparatus, he proceeded to ask the great question of which he had already guessed the answer. To avoid vulgar ridicule, he went out on the common, while a thunder-storm was gathering, and told his intention only to his son, who accompanied him. The kite was raised: a dark cloud passed over it. Franklin gazed for some moments in anxious suspense until he observed that the loose fibres of the string were moved. He applied his knuckle to the key, and the emitted spark immediately confirmed his theory. That power in nature which had appeared a mystery beyond the reach of man's intelligence, was now identified with a power having properties already partly understood.

This grand success cast into the shade Franklin's services in other branches of science. His generosity in caring little for his own fame, and imparting freely to others a knowledge of his discoveries, was remarkable. A patent for making a stove which Franklin had invented was taken out by a London ironmonger, who only made some slight changes in its form; but the inventor, observing that this was not the only instance of the kind, refused to claim any benefit for himself. The same liberality characterised his sanitarian scheme for cleansing the streets of Philadelphia, and made him condescend to write of fireplaces and smoky chimneys. His papers on these topics are remarkably clear, concise, and practical. Other scientific papers treat of a theory of winds and water-spouts—in which he seems to have indicated some more recent theories—of improvements in navigation—the causes of the Gulf-stream in the Atlantic—the production of cold by evaporation—the causes of earthquakes—the structure of musical-instruments—and several other topics.

The latter part of Franklin's life—from 1757 to 1790—was devoted to the welfare of his country, and forms a prominent part of American history. In 1757 he went to England, and, as the agent for Pennsylvania, employed every effort to secure the liberties of the colonists, and to prevent the outbreak of war. After a second visit to the mother-country, he again crossed the Atlantic, and in his eightieth year returned to Philadelphia, landing on the spot where, sixty-three years before, he had arrived, as a runaway apprentice, with a single dollar in his pocket. The few remaining years of his life were quiet and happy. He retained his mental faculties unimpaired, fulfilled his duties as president of the state, and found leisure to pursue his favourite study of natural history. His last public act was to sign a petition praying the House of Representatives to oppose the traffic in slaves. He died April 17, 1790.

The writings of Franklin include his *Autobiography*, *Miscellaneous Essays*, the *Way to Wealth*, several historical and political tracts, scientific papers, and his official and private correspondence. The *Historical Review*, a work of considerable influence in the beginning of the Revolution, was generally ascribed to Franklin, and is included in the last edition of his works; but in a private letter to David Hume, the supposed author states that the greater part of the volume was written by another hand. The political letters of Franklin are marked by a clear and easy style, and give expression to manly and earnest feelings; while his private correspondence is full of cheerfulness and playful humour, and shews that he was capable of warm affections. The familiar essays supply models of a style of homely exposition and exhortation addressed to the masses of the people.

Franklin's character, though it may be found defective when tried by higher standards than his own, was in itself consistent and harmonious. He has been described as a utilitarian, or as a mere practical man striving to rise in the world; but it should be remembered that he was not contented to bend the world to his own uses and advantage: he endeavoured to leave it better than he found it. If he paid great attention to small gains, and laboured, in the first place, to improve his own circumstances, it was because he regarded such means as necessary to attain higher objects. For want of the practical wisdom of Franklin, many men of higher aspirations have wasted their powers and have lived in vain. No impartial reader can fail to admire the traits of self-control, disinterestedness, and quietude of temper in Franklin's autobiography.

Of his other writings, the most characteristic is the collection of maxims of prudence and economy published under the title of *Poor Richard*, or *The Way to Wealth*. Such a scheme of morality must, of course, be judged with reference to its object, which is not to form perfect characters, nor to prepare men for a higher life than the present, but to make them here more prudent, industrious, and prosperous. The man who would cultivate with success the higher faculties of his nature, must first provide for his common wants, and he will find in Franklin's maxims the beginning though not the end of wisdom.

THE WAY TO WEALTH.

'Courteous reader, I have heard that nothing gives an author so great pleasure as to find his works respectfully quoted by others. Judge, then, how much I must have been gratified by an incident I am going to relate to you. I stopped my horse lately where a great number of people were collected at an auction of merchants' goods. The hour of the sale not being come, they were conversing on the badness of the times; and one of the company called to a plain, clean old man, with white locks: "Pray, Father Abraham, what think you of the times? Will not these heavy taxes quite ruin the country? How shall we ever be able to pay them? What would you advise us to?" Father Abraham stood up and replied: "If you would have my advice, I will give it you in short; for 'A word to the wise is enough,' as Poor Richard says." They joined in desiring him to speak his mind, and, gathering round him, he proceeded as follows:—

"Friends," said he, "the taxes are indeed very heavy; and if those laid on by the government were the only ones we had to pay, we might more easily discharge them; but we have many others, and much more grievous to some of us. We are taxed twice as much by our idleness, three times as much by our pride, and four times as much by our folly; and from these taxes the commissioners cannot ease or deliver us by allowing an abatement. However, let us hearken to good advice, and something may be done for us—'God helps them that help themselves,' as Poor Richard says."—[The old man, after lecturing for some time on the virtues of industry and attention to one's own business, proceeds to shew the folly of careless expenditure] :—

"Here you are all got together at this sale of fineries and knick-knacks. You call them *goods;* but if you do not take care, they will prove *evils* to some of you. You expect they will be sold cheap, and perhaps they may for less than they cost; but if you have no occasion for them, they must be dear to you. Remember what Poor Richard says: 'Buy what thou hast no need of, and erelong thou shalt sell thy necessaries.' And again: 'At a great pennyworth, pause a while.' He means, that perhaps the cheapness is apparent only, and not real; or the bargain, by straitening thee in thy business, may do thee more harm than good; for in another place he says: 'Many have been ruined by buying good pennyworths.' Again: 'It is foolish to lay out money in a purchase of repentance;' and yet this folly is practised every day at auctions, for want of minding the Almanac.

"But what madness must it be to *run in debt* for these superfluities! We are offered, by the terms of this sale, six months' credit; and that perhaps has induced some of us to attend it, because we cannot spare the ready-money, and hope now to be fine without it. But ah! think what you do when you run in debt—you give to another power over your liberty. If you cannot pay at the time, you will be ashamed to see your creditor; you will be in fear when you speak to him; you will make poor, pitiful, sneaking excuses, and by degrees come to lose your veracity, and sink into base, downright lying; for 'The second vice is lying, the first is running in debt,' as Poor Richard says; and again, to the same purpose, 'Lying rides upon Debt's back;' whereas a free-born Englishman ought not to be ashamed nor afraid to see or speak to any man living. But poverty often deprives a man of all spirit and virtue. 'It is hard for an empty bag to stand upright.'

"What would you think of that prince or of that government who should issue an edict forbidding you to dress like a gentleman or gentlewoman, on pain of imprisonment or servitude? Would you not say that you were free—have a right to dress as you please—and that such an edict would be a breach of your privileges, and such a government tyrannical? And yet you are about to put yourself under such tyranny, when you run in debt for such dress! Your creditor has authority, at his pleasure, to deprive you of your liberty, by confining you in jail till you shall be able to pay him. When you have got your bargain, you may perhaps think little of payment; but, as Poor Richard says, 'Creditors have better memories than debtors: creditors are a superstitious sect, great observers of set days and times.' The day comes round before you are aware, and the demand is made before you are prepared to satisfy it; or, if you bear your debt in mind, the term, which at first seemed so long, will, as it lessens, appear extremely short. Time will seem to have added wings to his heels as well as his shoulders. 'Those have a short Lent who owe money to be paid at Easter.' At present, perhaps, you may think yourselves in thriving circumstances, and that you can bear a little extravagance without injury; but

'For age and want save while you may;
No morning sun lasts a whole day.'

Gain may be temporary and uncertain, but ever, while you live, expense is constant and certain; and 'It is easier to build two chimneys, than to keep one in fuel,' as Poor Richard says; so, 'Rather go to bed supperless, than rise in debt.'

'Get what you can, and what you get hold;
'Tis the stone that will turn all your lead into gold.'

And when you have got the philosopher's stone, sure you will no longer complain of bad times or the difficulty of paying taxes.

"This doctrine, my friends, is reason and wisdom; but, after all, do not depend too much upon your own industry and frugality and prudence, though excellent things; for they may all be blasted, without the blessing of Heaven; and therefore ask that blessing humbly, and be not uncharitable to those that at present seem to want it, but comfort and help them. Remember Job suffered, and was afterwards prosperous.

"And now, to conclude, 'Experience keeps a dear school, but fools will learn in no other,' as Poor Richard says, and scarce in that; for it is true, 'We may give advice, but we cannot give conduct.' However, remember this: 'They that will not be counselled, cannot be helped;' and, further, that 'If you will not hear Reason, she will surely rap your knuckles,' as Poor Richard says."

'Thus the old gentleman ended his harangue. The people heard it, and approved the doctrine, and immediately practised the contrary, just as if it had been a common sermon; for the auction opened, and they began to buy extravagantly. I found the good man had thoroughly studied my Almanacs, and digested all I had dropped on these topics during the course of twenty-five years. The frequent mention he made of me must have tired any one else; but my vanity was wonderfully delighted with it, though I was conscious that not a tenth part of the wisdom was my own which he ascribed to me, but rather the gleanings that I had made of the sense of all ages and nations. However, I resolved to be the better for the echo of it; and though I had at first determined to buy stuff for a new coat, I went away resolved to wear my old one a little longer. Reader, if thou wilt do the same, thy profit will be as great as mine. —I am, as ever, thine to serve thee,

RICHARD SAUNDERS.'

GENERAL LITERATURE AND POLITICS.

1700-1800.

In this place, we may notice, first, the few historical works produced in the eighteenth century. *The History of New England*, by Hubbard, already mentioned, was followed by a more extensive work on the same subject, written by THOMAS PRINCE (1687–1758), who employed a considerable part of his life in collecting materials. The greater portion of his valuable manuscripts was unfortunately lost or destroyed during the war of Independence. Of the succeeding writer, THOMAS HUTCHINSON, who wrote a *History of Massachusetts*, a competent critic writes, that 'he was blind except to facts,' and 'without a glimpse of the great truths which were the mighty causes of the revolutions he describes.'

'Next in character, if not in time,' says the same critic, 'came *The History of Connecticut*, by the accurate, painstaking, scrupulous TRUMBULL. It excels Hutchinson's work in spirit, and equals it, nay, surpasses it in research. Its author lived in the scenes which he describes; his heart was with the fathers of his commonwealth; he held with them one faith and one hope; he revered them as they appeared in the train-bands of the militia, or in the meeting-house; at their village toils, or in their rural legislature. A true Connecticut feeling tingled in all his veins and animated all his thoughts. He read all sorts of records; he picked up and tested traditions; he was wise in the theology of Hooker and Stone; he knew the hills and the valleys, the towns and the villages of his commonwealth; and, in fact, he got Connecticut by heart before he began writing its history. Europe he knew but little of; and in reference to it, he makes mistakes, or betrays ignorance; but Connecticut he knew thoroughly. He could tell the name, birthplace, and career of every minister that had preached a good sermon, and every militiaman that had done a notable thing. Not a savage was overcome, not a backslider censured by the church, but he knew it all. His history is Connecticut put into a book; and done, not by a philosopher with wise arrogance—not by a heretic, scoffing at men who followed somewhat the laws of Moses—not by a lawyer, shewing with what indifference to precedent the New-England fathers were perpetually entering upon untried experiments; but by an honest, true-hearted Connecticut man.'

In a literary point of view, a work far superior to those already noticed is found in *The History of New Hampshire*, by Dr BELKNAP, a writer distinguished for his clear style and spirit of research. 'The tone of feeling which pervades his volumes is truly American; national, yet candid. He knew how to exhibit the faults of our ancestors without impairing admiration for their virtues. In his writings, the new spirit in literature, which naturally grew out of our revolution, began to appear; and he united happily the earnestness of old times with the liberal purposes of free inquiry. It would not be easy to name any local history in any European language superior to the history of Belknap.'[1] The amiable author of the work so justly praised, wrote some miscellaneous essays, and, if we remember truly, a novel, entitled *The Foresters*, the earliest work of its kind in American literature. He died in early manhood.

A *History of Rhode Island*, by JOHN CALLENDER, and an *Account of the First Discovery and Settlement of Virginia*, by WILLIAM STITH, may be named among the earlier contributions to American local history. PAUL DUDLEY (1675–1751), chief-justice of Massachusetts, must be noticed as the first writer on natural history. The *History of the Five Indian Nations*, by CADWALLADER COLDEN (1688–1776), is described as a work of research and good judgment. The author, who studied the physical sciences, published in 1751 a work on the *Principles of Action in Matter*, and a treatise on *Fluxions*.

WILLIAM GORDON (died 1807) wrote a history of the American Revolution, which has been described as an unadorned narrative of facts. A more elaborate work on the same topic was written by DAVID RAMSAY (1749–1815), and first published in 1790. Hutchinson's *History of Massachusetts*, already briefly noticed, was continued by GEORGE R. MINOT (1758–1802); and about the same time SAMUEL WILLIAMS (1761–1817), who was esteemed as one of the best historical writers of his age, published *A History of Vermont*. A few years later, in 1797, ROBERT PROUD published *A History of Pennsylvania*, which has been characterised as a faithful narrative, and is frequently mentioned in Bancroft's references to authorities.

In miscellaneous writings—including essays and periodical papers—the eighteenth century has little to shew besides the popular works of Benjamin Franklin. His contemporary, EZRA

[1] *North American Review*, No. 99.

STILES (1727–1795), president of Yale College, excelled chiefly in sacred literature, but was a general scholar, and wrote the *Lives of the Three Judges of Charles I.* The name of DAVID RITTENHOUSE (1732–1796), a great and self-educated genius, who enriched his country by his mechanical inventions, belongs rather to science than to literature. His writings consist of a few memoirs on mathematics and astronomy, and were printed in the first four volumes of *Transactions of the Philosophical Society of Philadelphia.* We must not forget here that an American, LINDLEY MURRAY, wrote the well-known *English Grammar*, first published in 1795.

The writings in Verse during the latter part of the colonial period, may be very briefly noticed in this place. Passing over several names of versifiers[1] who wrote in the time 1690–1776, we may mention JOHN TRUMBULL (1750–1831), who wrote during the Revolution. His chief work, *M'Fingal*, is a burlesque in verse of the Hudibrastic style, directed against the enemies of American liberty, British officers, and other Tories. The hero, M'Fingal, is a Scotchman, a violent Tory, and justice of the peace, who makes a virulent speech against liberty, and consequently is 'tarred and feathered.' This is almost the whole plot of the poem, which owed its popularity to its patriotic character.

Trumbull was the friend and literary associate of TIMOTHY DWIGHT (1752–1817), president of Yale College, already noticed as a theological author. He wrote several poems in a better style than had been previously cultivated. His longest poem, the *Conquest of Canaan*, is an epic, and was completed in his twenty-third year. *The Prospect* was written in imitation of Thomson, and *The Flourishing Village* on the model of Goldsmith's *Deserted Village.* These poems must be noticed as having exercised a considerable influence on the improvement of style; although smoothness of versification is their chief merit.

Another of Trumbull's friends was JOEL BARLOW (1755–1812), author of a dull epic, *The Columbiad*, which at one time was unfortunately regarded as a fair specimen of American poetry. Few persons could now be found, either in the Old World or the New, who would have patience to read many pages of this epic, though it was well received on its first appearance in America,

[1] Mr Kettel, in his *Specimens of American Poetry*, preserves the names of Colman, Jane Turell, Adams, Ralph, Maylem, Godfrey, Evans, Osborn, Byles, Green, Livingston, Church, and Allen—all mere versifiers, who have no claims on our notice.

and was republished in London and Paris. Barlow estimated his own abilities more correctly when, leaving the ambitious flights of *The Columbiad*, he condescended to sing in three cantos the praises of *Hasty Pudding*—the title of one of his poems. Here, to say the least, he treated his subject with gusto. The unmerited reputation of the epic may be ascribed to the rank of the author, who was engaged in diplomacy, and resided for some time in Europe. After leaving college, he studied law, served as a chaplain in the army during the war of the revolution, edited a paper in Newhaven, and prepared a revised edition of *Watts's Version of the Psalms*. Forsaking literature, he became the agent of a fraudulent land-selling association, called the Ohio Company; but it does not appear that he understood the real character of the transactions in which he was employed. In 1795, he was appointed consul for the United States at Algiers, and superintended the redemption of American captives in the States of Barbary. After his return to America, he was engaged in planning a general history of the United States, when he was appointed minister-plenipotentiary to negotiate a treaty of commerce with France. In 1812, being invited to a conference with Napoleon at Wilna, he travelled towards that place in very severe weather, which brought on a violent inflammation of the lungs, of which he died.

Of all the verse-writers who lived in the era of the Revolution, Philip Freneau, a descendant of French Protestants, was the most poetical. The dates of his birth and death are not found; but it is known that he graduated at Princeton College, in New Jersey, in 1771, and for some years conducted a newspaper in Philadelphia. Two stanzas from his lines on an *Indian Burying-ground* may be quoted:—

'By midnight moons, o'er moistening dews,
In vestments for the chase arrayed,
The hunter still the deer pursues—
The hunter and the deer, a shade!

And long shall timorous fancy see
The painted chief and pointed spear,
And Reason's self shall bow the knee
To shadows and delusions here.'

In the department of Prose-fiction, we find only one considerable name—that of Charles Brockden Brown (1771–1810), the first American who chose literature as a profession. Brown was educated under the care of Robert Proud, the historian of

Pennsylvania, and when sixteen years old, commenced the study of law. But he had made little progress before he conceived a violent dislike of his profession, and protested against the whole system of law as a 'tissue of shreds and remnants of a barbarous antiquity.'

In 1793, without a vocation or any definite intentions, he went to New York, where he wrote visionary papers on politics and society, including a dialogue on the *Rights of Women*, which seemed to anticipate the doctrines advocated by Margaret Fuller and other American ladies in our own times. An unfinished novel, *Memoirs of Carwin*, of which we cannot find the date, may be described as an introduction to the romance of *Wieland, or the Transformation*, published in 1798. This is a strange gloomy tale of seemingly supernatural agencies, which are ultimately explained by the art of ventriloquism. As we have read only a few pages of *Wieland*, we must refer to the opinions of American critics. Prescott has said that the character of the hero, Carwin, is demoniacal rather than human; and Dana, writing of Brown, says: 'The energies of his soul were melancholy powers, and their path lay along the dusky dwelling-places of superstition and fear, and death and wo. They manifest themselves in the most striking manner, when he imparts to the dead-level, rectangular streets, and plainly constructed houses of a freshly brick-built city, the gloom, awe, and mystery which hitherto had hung over the damp, dark, intricate passages and dread chambers of inquisitions.'

Brown's second novel, entitled *Ormond*, is described as an incongruous production; but it is said that the character of the heroine, Constantia Dudley, is natural and beautiful. A third novel, *Arthur Mervyn*, describes with a painful fidelity scenes in Philadelphia during the pestilence of yellow fever which prevailed there in 1793. This tale was followed by *Edgar Huntley, the Memoirs of a Somnambulist*. In this story, the interest depends partly on descriptions of scenery, but the adventures of the hero in following a sleep-walker lead to some striking situations.

Besides three other novels—*Clara Howard*, *Memoirs of Stephen Calvert*, and *Jane Talbot*—Brown furnished many articles for magazines, edited the *American Register*, and wrote many political papers. During his short life, he suffered from feeble health, and enjoyed only scanty intervals of recreation. The fact that he wrote with great rapidity, is mentioned apologetically by an editor, Mr Griswold. Of his novels, it is said that 'the author and the printer were engaged at the same time upon nearly every one of them; and he sometimes had three or four under-way at once. In all of them are indications that he grew weary before they were finished. His style is not good; in a majority of his works, it lacks simplicity and directness, and has numerous verbal faults.'

In the department of Voyages and Travels, we may briefly notice the works of Bartram, Carver, and Ledyard, who wrote in the eighteenth century. JOHN BARTRAM (1701–1777), a native of Pennsylvania, travelled from Canada to Florida in pursuit of his favourite science, botany, and published in London (1751) his *Observations* on natural history, collected during his tour. This work was followed by his *Description of East Florida* (1774), which contains a pleasing account of the Seminole Indians.

JONATHAN CARVER (1732–1780), a native of Connecticut, travelled almost 7000 miles in his attempt to explore the interior of North America, and to penetrate to the Pacific Ocean, between 43° and 46° north latitude. He failed to surmount the difficulties of his undertaking, but gathered many notices of the population and natural history of the country. The account of his travels was published in London, 1778, and in Boston, 1797.

Another native of Connecticut, the enterprising traveller JOHN LEDYARD (1751–1789), sailed with Captain Cook in his second voyage, and afterwards travelled on foot more than 6000 miles east of St Petersburg. This resolute attempt to explore the north of Europe and Asia, was opposed by the Russian government. In his subsequent attempt to trace the source of the Niger, the traveller proceeded no further than Cairo, where he was seized with sickness, and died. Ledyard's journals of travel contain one passage that ought not to be forgotten. His fine eulogium on the kindness of woman, is a summary of his own experience, and therefore is more valuable than a thousand sentimental essays. It is as follows:—

'I have always remarked that women in all countries are civil and obliging, tender and humane; that they are ever inclined to be gay and cheerful, timorous and modest; and that they do not hesitate, like men, to perform a generous action. Not haughty, not arrogant, not supercilious, they are full of courtesy, and fond of society; more liable in general to err than man, but in general also more virtuous, and performing more good actions than he. To a woman, whether civilised or savage, I never addressed myself in the language of decency and friendship, without receiving a decent and friendly answer. With man, it has often been otherwise. In wandering over the barren plains of inhospitable Denmark, through honest Sweden, and frozen Lapland, rude and churlish Finland, unprincipled Russia, and the wide-spread regions of the wandering Tatar; if hungry, dry, cold, wet, or sick, the women have ever been friendly to me, and uniformly so. And to add to this virtue, so worthy the appellation of benevolence, their actions have been performed in so free and kind a manner, that if I was dry, I drank the sweetest draught, and if hungry, I ate the coarsest morsel with a double relish.'

General Literature had made some progress, while theology was losing its exclusive sway, when the circumstances of the impending war gave a new impulse and direction to authors and readers. Politics now gained a prominence almost equal to that enjoyed by theology in the early times of the colonies. Among the writers who acquired reputations by their works published during the revolutionary crisis, we must name JAMES OTIS, author of *A Vindication of the Conduct of the House of Representatives in Massachusetts;* also JOHN DICKINSON, who wrote a series of letters entitled *Fabius*, advocating the adoption of the federal constitution; RICHARD HENRY LEE, who wrote *The Farmer's Letter;* and his brother ARTHUR, who wrote the political papers bearing the signature *Junius Americanus*.

ALEXANDER HAMILTON (1757–1804) was the greatest writer, and we might perhaps say statesman, of the revolutionary time. He was born in the island of Nevis. On his father's side, he was descended from a decayed Scotch family, and his mother belonged to the Huguenots of France. At seventeen years of age, Hamilton first appeared as a political speaker at a great meeting held in the open air, when he eloquently protested against the measures of the home government. He next engaged in a controversy with the clerical Tories of the episcopal church. In 1775, he joined a company of military volunteers, and took a part in the first act of armed opposition to the ministry. His services attracted the notice of General Washington, in whose family he resided during several years. After his retirement from the army, Hamilton studied law, came to the bar in 1782, and in the same year was elected member of the congress of the confederation. In this capacity, his services were highly important, and subsequently, in the New York assembly (1786), and in the convention for the formation of a federal constitution, 1787. 'There is not,' says Guizot, 'one element of order, strength, or durability in the constitution which he [Hamilton] did not powerfully contribute to introduce into the scheme.'

Assisted by his friends Madison and Jay, Hamilton commenced the celebrated series of essays known under the name of *The*

Federalist. When the government was organised, he was appointed secretary of the treasury; and so faithful and unremitting were his services in this office, that his successors enjoyed almost a sinecure, for his labours had reduced the work to an easy routine. Yet, so scanty was the payment for these important services, that Hamilton found it advisable to leave the cabinet, and resume his profession of law, in order to provide for the wants of his family. He was again called to public duties by the disputes with France, and re-entered the army as first officer under Washington. After the death of his commander (1799), he returned to the bar.

Hamilton, like his contemporary Fisher Ames, had a dread of ultra-democracy, and the expression of his fears gave rise to injurious suspicions of his motives; but it appears that no charge can be maintained against the consistency of his public life. In the federal convention, he proposed that the offices of the president and the senators should be held 'during good behaviour;' and argued that incalculable mischief must result from the too frequent elections of a chief-magistrate, attended, as they must be, by the transfer of an immense power of patronage. Addressing another speaker, he said: 'You and I, my friend, may not live to see the day; but most assuredly it will come, when *every vital interest of the state will be merged in the all-absorbing question of "Who shall be the next president?"*' This safe prediction was very soon fulfilled. In the year 1800, at a crisis when, if a president had not been speedily chosen, the government must have perished, the competition of the two parties was so eager, that equal votes appeared for Jefferson and Burr, and the voting was repeated *thirty-five times* in the House of Representatives before the former could gain a majority of one state!

In 1804, Hamilton fell in a duel with Aaron Burr, vice-president of the United States; or, considering the circumstances of the affair, it would be more correct to say he was assassinated. Burr gave the challenge; and Hamilton, dreading the stigma of cowardice, went, without any intention of injuring his opponent, to the appointed place of meeting at Weehawken, near New York, and was slain.

The Federalist, the most prominent work of the revolutionary times, was written chiefly by Alexander Hamilton, but included papers contributed by James Madison and John Jay. This work, designed to elucidate and support the principles of the constitution of the United States, is esteemed as a 'political classic.' To quote *The Edinburgh Review*—'It exhibits an extent and precision of information, a profundity of research, and an acuteness of understanding, which would have done honour to the most illustrious statesmen of ancient or modern times.' Hamilton was also the author of *Phocion*, a series of letters in favour of clemency to loyalists; and wrote, in 1793, the papers signed *Pacificus*.

JOHN ADAMS, second president of the United States, commenced, in 1755, a diary which contains valuable contributions to the materials of American history. He also wrote *A Defence of the American Constitution*, and numerous political papers and letters, which have been collected and edited by his grandson Charles Francis Adams.

THOMAS JEFFERSON (1743–1826), third president of the United States, desired that it should be engraved on his monument that 'he was the author of the Declaration of Independence;' but the validity of his claim has been disputed. His other writings consist of the *Notes on Virginia* (1781), autobiography, correspondence, and various state-papers which were edited by Randolph. In his excursions into general literature, he betrayed shallowness and presumption; and his views of religion, morals, and politics were borrowed from the French revolutionists. He patronised and eulogised the democrat writer THOMAS PAINE (1737–1809), who emigrated to America in 1774, and here published the tract entitled *Common Sense*, which had a remarkable success, because its doctrines fell in with the popular excitement of the times.

FISHER AMES (1758–1808), a bold writer and speaker, gained a high reputation chiefly by the enthusiasm and lively style of his political papers and orations; but these were commonly deficient in sobriety and fair argument. That he was a fearless advocate, may be easily proved by his assertions of opinions by no means popular in his day. He described 'the turnpike-road of history' as 'white with the tombstones of republics,' and regarded 'the rabble of great cities as the standing army of ambition.' The following short extract—intellect in a democracy—is quoted from an *Essay on American Literature*:—

'Intellectual superiority is so far from conciliating confidence, that it is the very spirit of a democracy, as in France, to proscribe the aristocracy of talents. To be the favourite of an ignorant, multitude, a man must descend to their level; he must desire what they desire, and detest all they do not approve: he must yield to their prejudices, and substitute them for principles. Instead of enlightening their errors, he must adopt them; he must furnish the sophistry that will propagate and defend them.'

This is a fair specimen of the one-sided declamation in which Ames indulged. It is obvious that his assertions, *mutatis mutandis*, might have been as fairly applied to monarchies and aristocracies. Logic has too commonly a slender connection with political discussions.

NEWSPAPERS AND OTHER PERIODICALS.

1690-1800.[1]

The first newspaper in North America was commenced at Boston in 1690; but of this only one copy has been preserved,[2] and it seems probable that it was very soon discontinued. On the 24th of April, in 1704, *The Boston News-letter* appeared. 'In 1719, it obtained a rival at Boston, and was imitated at Philadelphia. In 1740, the number of newspapers in the English colonies on the continent had increased to eleven, of which one appeared in South Carolina, one in Virginia, three in Pennsylvania —one of them being in German—one in New York, and the remaining five in Boston. The paper at first used was of the foolscap size; and only one sheet, or even half a sheet, was issued weekly. The papers sought support rather by modestly relating the news of the day, than by engaging in conflicts; they had no political theories to enforce, no revolutions to hasten. In Boston, indeed, where the pulpit had sent Quakers and witches to the gallows, one newspaper, *The New England Courant*, the fourth American periodical, was established in 1721 by James Franklin, as an organ of independent opinion. Its temporary success was advanced by Benjamin, his brother and apprentice, a boy of fifteen, who wrote pieces for its humble columns; worked in composing the types, as well as in printing off the sheets; and carried about the papers to the customers. The little sheet satirised hypocrisy, and spoke of religious knaves as of all knaves the worst. This was described as tending "to abuse the ministers of religion in a manner which was intolerable." "I can well remember," writes Increase Mather, then more than fourscore years of age, "when the civil government would have taken an effectual course to suppress such a cursed libel." In July 1722, a resolve passed the council, appointing a censor for the press of James Franklin; but the house refused its concurrence. The ministers persevered; and in January 1723, a committee of

[1] For the details in this section, we are chiefly indebted to the writer of the article, 'Periodical Literature of the United States,' *North American Review*, No. 85.

[2] Trübner, *Bibliographical Guide to American Literature*. Bancroft mentions the *News-letter* as the first newspaper.

inquiry was raised by the legislature. Benjamin Franklin being examined, escaped with an admonition; James, the publisher, refusing to discover the author of the offence, was kept in jail for a month; his paper was censured as reflecting injuriously on the reverend ministers of the gospel; and, by vote of the house and council, he was forbidden to print it, "except it be first supervised.""[1]

After Benjamin Franklin had eloped from Boston, the *Courant* continued to be published in his name, because an order of the General Court had forbidden the publication on the part of James. In 1734, *The Weekly Post-boy* was started in Boston, and was followed in 1748 by *The Independent Advertiser*, also published in the metropolis. Out of Boston, the first newspaper was *The American Weekly Mercury*, commenced in Philadelphia, 1719; followed by *The New York Gazette* in 1728. Besides these, we find, in 1750, *The Rhode Island Gazette*, begun in Newport, 1732; *The Pennsylvania Gazette*, started in 1728; *The Maryland Gazette*, dating from 1728; *The Virginia Gazette*, from 1736; two successive *South Carolina Gazettes*, 1731 and 1734; and five other papers—three in New York, and two in Pennsylvania. Of these two, one was a German paper.

In the times of political excitement, after 1750, newspapers increased rapidly in number; and in 1790, there were about seventy in the United States. 'The press was introduced into the wilds of Kentucky in 1786, and into Tennessee in 1793. . . . . In 1795, a newspaper was established at Cincinnati, then an Indian trading-post, on the extreme border of western civilisation.'[2]

The earliest papers were commonly printed on a half-sheet of pot paper; but now and then, when a pressure of news required a supplement, a whole sheet was given. There was only one advertisement in the first number of *The News-letter*. The editor, Campbell, a Scotchman, must have acquired a very respectable position in society, for he was appointed as justice of the peace. In 1718, he announced that, after fourteen years' experience, he found it impossible to crowd 'all the public news of Europe' into a half-sheet of pot paper! His greatest trial was the competition of Franklin's *Courant*. That small spitefulness which now forms the sole animating principle of too many provincial papers, was almost coeval with the press in New England. First, *The Courant*, in its prospectus, most invidiously described *The News-letter* as 'a dull vehicle;' a form of abuse oddly like one of our modern slang phrases. The Scotch editor replied by stating, that

[1] Bancroft.
[2] Trübner's *Bibliographical Guide to American Literature.*

a new paper had appeared, edited by a 'Jack-of-all-trades,' 'good at none, and giving some very, very frothy, fulsome account of himself.' This was a free translation of Franklin's motto—*homo non unius negotii.* With such spirit was this gentlemanly argument conducted, that Campbell was stimulated to give a whole sheet every week for two months; but when the excitement had passed over, he returned to his primitive half-sheet of pot.

The *New England Journal*, after an independent life of fifteen years, was united with *The Boston Gazette*, and so continued until 1752. During its separate existence, it took a leading part in religious disputes, and among its contributors we find a waggish minister, the Rev. Mather Byles, who reminds us that the stern old times of Puritanism have passed away. He was a man of considerable learning, and corresponded with Pope, the English poet; but his inveterate punning made him the Joe Miller of Boston. He was not only humorous, but was the cause of humour in others; and the good people of Boston seem to have been especially amused by an encounter of wit between Byles and his fellow-townsman Joseph Green. The latter, who wrote rhymes, tells us that 'on one occasion, when Byles was engaged to conduct divine service on board a vessel, finding no collection of psalmody, he wrote for the edification of the crew a metrical psalm.' Green describes how Byles lamented that even David had never written 'a proper psalm to sing at sea,' and to supply the supposed defect, produced from his own poetic resources a psalm of a very dreary character, as a few lines will shew. He

'Sat down, took out his book, and said:
"Let's sing a psalm of Mather Byles."

At first, when he began to read,
Their heads the assembly downward hung;
But he with boldness did proceed,
And thus he read, and thus they sung:

"With vast amazement we survey
The wonders of the deep,
Where mackerel swim, and porpoise play,
And crabs and lobsters creep."'

Another paper, *The Weekly Rehearsal*—afterwards styled *The Boston Evening Post*—was edited by a humorous and satirical printer named Fleet. He sometimes inserted a joke in the place of an advertisement, if we may accept the following as a joke:—

'To be sold by the printer of this paper, a negro man, about thirty years old, who can do both town and country business very well, but will suit the country best, where they have not so many dram-shops as we have in Boston.'

Hawthorne, in his pleasant review of old American newspapers, says, 'no advertisements are more frequent than those of a "negro fellow, fit for almost any household work;" a "negro woman, honest, healthy, and capable;" or "a negro man very fit for a tailor,"' &c.

We can find no books of the latter part of the seventeenth and early part of the eighteenth century which give concise and lifelike sketches of the people of those times. To collect the traits of popular life, we must search through many old records, pamphlets, and old newspapers. This work has been partly done for us by the graphic writer already quoted, who gives, as the result of his porings over old newspapers, a pleasant sketch, from which we may borrow some paragraphs :—

OLD NEWS. 1719-1744.

'The first pages of most of these old papers are as soporific as a bed of poppies. Here we have an erudite clergyman, or perhaps a Cambridge professor, occupying several successive weeks with a criticism on Tate and Brady, as compared with the New England version of the Psalms. Of course, the preference is given to the native article. . . . .

In vain we endeavour to throw a sunny and joyous air over our picture of this period; nothing passes before our fancy but a crowd of sad-visaged people, moving duskily through a dull gray atmosphere. It is certain that winter rushed upon them with fiercer storms than now, blocking up the narrow forest-paths, and overwhelming the roads along the sea-coast with mountain snow-drifts, so that weeks elapsed before the newspaper could announce how many travellers had perished, or what wrecks had strewn the shore. The cold was more piercing then, and lingered further into the spring, making the chimney-corner a comfortable seat till long past May-day. By the number of such accidents on record, we might suppose that the thunder-stone, as they termed it, fell oftener and deadlier on steeples, dwellings, and unsheltered wretches. In fine, our fathers bore the brunt of more raging and pitiless elements than we. There were forebodings, also, of a more fearful tempest than those of the elements. At two or three dates, we have stories of drums, trumpets, and all sorts of martial music, passing athwart the midnight sky, accompanied with the roar of cannon and rattle of musketry; prophetic echoes of the sounds that were soon to shake the land. Besides these airy prognostics, there were rumours of French fleets on the coast, and of the march of French and Indians through the wilderness, along the borders of the settlements. The country was saddened, moreover, with grievous sickness. The small-pox raged in many of the towns, and seems, though so familiar a scourge, to have been regarded with as much affright as that which drove the throng from Wall Street and Broadway at the approach of a new pestilence. There were autumnal fevers, too, and a contagious and destructive throat distemper—diseases unwritten in medical books. The dark superstition of former days had not yet been so far dispelled as not to heighten the gloom of the present times. There is an advertisement, indeed, by a committee of the legislature, calling for information as to the circumstances of sufferers in the "late calamity of 1692,"[1] with a view to reparation for their losses and misfortunes. But the tenderness with which, after above forty years, it was thought expedient to allude to the witchcraft delusion, indicates a good deal of lingering error, as well as the advance of more enlightened opinions. The rigid hand of Puritanism might yet be felt upon the reins of government, while some of the ordinances intimate a disorderly spirit on the part of the people.'

At a later period—the time of the old French war—we find the papers full of indications of the military spirit that moved the colonies. 'In the letters of the provincial officers, it is amusing to observe how some of them endeavour to catch the careless and jovial turn of old campaigners. One gentleman tells us, that he holds a brimming glass in his hand, intending to drink the health of his correspondent, unless a cannon-ball should dash the liquor from his lips.' We read of 'bears driven from the woods by the uproar of contending armies, and prowling within a mile or two of Boston. In the advertising columns, also, we are continually reminded that the country was in a state of war. Governor Pownall makes proclamation for the enlisting of soldiers, and directs the militia colonels to attend to the discipline of their regiments, and the select men of every town to replenish their stocks of ammunition. The magazine, by the way, was generally kept in the upper loft of the village meeting-house. The provincial captains are drumming up for soldiers in every newspaper. Sir Jeffrey Amherst advertises for bateau-men, to be employed on the lakes; and gives notice to the officers of seven British regiments, dispersed on the recruiting-service, to rendezvous in Boston. Captain Hallowell, of the province ship of war *King George*, invites able-bodied seamen to serve his majesty, for fifteen pounds, old tenor,[2] per month. By the rewards offered, there would appear to have been frequent desertions from the New England forces; we applaud their wisdom, if not their valour or integrity. Cannon of all calibres, gunpowder and

[1] The delusion in Salem, of which some account has been given in the notice of Cotton Mather and his Times.
[2] A New England currency.

balls, firelocks, pistols, swords, and hangers, were common articles of merchandise. Daniel Jones, at the sign of the Hat and Helmet, offers to supply officers with scarlet broadcloth, gold lace for hats and waistcoats, cockades, and other military foppery, allowing credit until the pay-rolls shall be made up.'[1]

Magazines, and other periodicals less ephemeral than newspapers, had little success before the Revolution. *The Boston Weekly Magazine*, begun in 1743, lingered through only four numbers; and *The Christian History*, starting with the religious excitement under Whitefield, came to a close in two years—1743–45. *The American Magazine and Historical Chronicle* was issued monthly for more than three years, beginning in 1743. Passing over other attempts of short duration, we find *The General Magazine*, commenced by Franklin about the time 1741, and may notice *The Pennsylvania Magazine*, begun by Robert Aitken in 1775, which owed its celebrity mainly to contributions by the notorious Thomas Paine. His 'necessary apparatus' for writing a leading article 'included,' as Aitken says, 'a decanter of brandy.' Altogether, about a dozen periodicals of a class above newspapers were commenced before the Revolution; but as they exerted no considerable influence on life in America, they require no lengthened notice. The first successful magazine was *The Portfolio* (1801). Charles Brockden Brown, the novelist, tried a *Monthly Magazine and American Review* in 1794, but it was a failure. The times were more favourable to the excitements of politics than to the quiet pursuits of literature.

[1] Hawthorne's paper on *Old News*.

SECOND PERIOD.

1800-1855.

POETRY.

ALLSTON — PAULDING — PIERPONT — DANA — SPRAGUE — WILDE — HILLHOUSE—DRAKE—BRYANT—NEAL—PERCIVAL—HALLECK—BRAINARD—DOANE—EMERSON.

In order to include the names of a few writers who preceded Irving and Bryant, the second period in American literature may be defined as extending from 1800 to the present time; but it should be observed that nearly all the best works in poetry, prose-fiction, history, biography, and criticism—to say nothing of special writings in the several sciences—have been produced within the space of the last thirty-five years; while American readers have had free access to all the rich stores of modern English literature.

It seems idle to speculate on all that might have been done by writers in the United States, who have had to contend against circumstances very unfavourable to the development of a national literature. This remark may be especially applied to poetry and prose-fiction. Instead of complaining that poets and novelists have done little to illustrate life on the western side of the Atlantic, we might as reasonably express our surprise that so much has been done within the space of a short lifetime, and in a country where the writings of Scott, Campbell, Wordsworth, Byron, Bulwer, Dickens, Thackeray, and a host of other English authors, have been so *cheaply* circulated.

Mr Griswold, whose definition of poetry appears to be exceedingly liberal, has given, in his work on the *Poets and Poetry of America*, the names of more than one hundred and forty authors who have written verses since the Revolution. This abundance of materials makes our task of selection rather difficult, and it is very probable that we may omit to mention names as worthy of notice as some that may be included in our brief review. To explain our reasons for passing over many of the inferior names, it may be sufficient to quote the remarks of an intelligent American critic—E. P. Whipple. Speaking of the selection by Mr Griswold, he says: 'Some of the authors whom he has included in the list are unworthy of the honour of having their feebleness thrust into notice. From others of more pretensions, he has copied too unsparingly. A few of his critical notices reflect more credit upon his benevolence than his taste. He seems to have fixed the price of admission low, in order, as the show-bills say, that the public might be more generally accommodated. King James I. debased the ancient order of knighthood, by laying his sword on the shoulder of every pander or buffoon who recommended himself by the fulness of his purse, the readiness of his jests, or the pliancy of his conscience. Editors should keep this fact in mind, and extract from it the warning and admonition it is so eminently calculated to suggest.'

In obedience to this wholesome rule, we may pass over the names of several verse-writers who succeeded Philip Freneau, and wrote before the time of W. C. Bryant. ALLSTON, the painter, included versification among his general accomplishments; but his poems have no remarkable merit. PAULDING, the novelist, wrote a poem, entitled *The Backwoodsman*, of which the design was better than the execution.

JOHN PIERPONT, author of lyrical poems which gained a considerable popularity, was a native of Litchfield in Connecticut, and was born April 6, 1785. In 1816, he published his poem, entitled *The Airs of Palestine*, which passed through several editions, and is chiefly remarkable for its smooth versification in describing the effects of music. We prefer his occasional lyrical poems, of which the following stanzas afford a favourable specimen:—

THE PILGRIM FATHERS.

'The pilgrim exile—sainted name!—
The hill, whose icy brow
Rejoiced, when he came, in the morning's flame,
In the morning's flame burns now.
And the moon's cold light, as it lay that night
On the hillside and the sea,
Still lies where he laid his houseless head;
But the pilgrim—where is he?

The Pilgrim Fathers are at rest:
When summer's throned on high,
And the world's warm breast is in verdure dressed,
Go, stand on the hill where they lie.

The earliest ray of the golden day
  On that hallowed spot is cast;
And the evening sun, as he leaves the world,
  Looks kindly on that spot last.

The pilgrim *spirit* has not fled:
  It walks in noon's broad light;
And it watches the bed of the glorious dead,
  With the holy stars, by night.
It watches the bed of the brave who have bled,
  And shall guard this ice-bound shore,
Till the waves of the bay, where the *May-flower* lay,
  Shall foam and freeze no more.'

RICHARD HENRY DANA, a native of Massachusetts, is well known as a prose-writer, especially as the author of numerous essays and reviews, published in *The North American Review*, *The United States Review and Literary Gazette*, *The American Quarterly Observer*, and other periodicals. His chief poetical works include the tale of *The Bucaneer*, *The Changes of Home*, and a didactic essay in verse, entitled *Factitious Life*. The style of these and other poems by Dana is original, and often graphic. A melancholy tone usually prevails. *The Bucaneer* is a gloomy narrative of the crimes of a pirate named Matthew Lee, 'a dark, low, brawny man,' who reigned in a solitary island. The opening of the poem, describing the quiet scenery of the pirate's island, forms a pleasing contrast with the sequel:

  'The island lies nine leagues away.
  Along its solitary shore,
  Of craggy rock and sandy bay,
  No sound but ocean's roar,
Save where the bold, wild sea-bird makes her home;
Her shrill cry coming through the sparkling foam.

  But when the light winds lie at rest,
  And on the glassy, heaving sea,
  The black duck, with her glossy breast,
  Sits swinging silently;
How beautiful! no ripples break the reach,
And silvery waves go noiseless up the beach.

  And inland rests the green, warm dell;
  The brook comes tinkling down its side;
  From out the trees the Sabbath-bell
  Rings cheerful, far and wide,
Mingling its sound with bleatings of the flocks,
That feed about the vale amongst the rocks.

Nor holy bell, nor pastoral bleat
In former days within the vale;
Flapped in the bay the pirate's sheet;
Curses were on the gale;
Rich goods lay on the sand, and murdered men;
Pirate and wrecker kept their revels then.

But calm, low voices, words of grace,
Now slowly fall upon the ear;
A quiet look is in each face,
Subdued and holy fear:
Each motion's gentle; all is kindly done.—
Come, listen, how from crime the isle was won.'

The taste displayed in many parts of the narrative is questionable, and the interest is diminished rather than increased by the use of supernatural agency, which destroys the air of reality given to some of the descriptions. This opinion, derived from a perusal of the poem, differs widely from the judgment of an American reviewer, who says of *The Bucaneer:* 'The peculiar force of the poem lies, we think, in the mingling of the natural and supernatural, and the air of reality which is thrown over both. A certain mystery shrouds the scenes, the transaction, and its consequences.'[1] Among the minor poems of Dana, the lines on the 'Little Beach-bird' have a sombre beauty. In other poems, the habitual pensiveness of Dana 'deepens into gloom.' 'His compositions,' says the critic already named, 'have more hearse-like airs than carols.' When he addresses the ocean, he says:

'Before an ear did hear thee, thou didst mourn,
Prophet of sorrows! o'er a race unborn.'

Charles Sprague, like the greater number of American writers, devoted to literature only the few leisure hours allowed by mercantile pursuits. He was born in Boston (1791), where, for several years, he held the situation of cashier of the Globe Bank. A theatrical prize-prologue first introduced him to the reading public, and was followed by other poems, of which the best are the short unassuming pieces devoted to the domestic affections. The didactic poem entitled *Curiosity*, contains passages of satire; but Sprague was deficient in the qualities of mind and temper that make a keen satirist, and was more at home with 'quiet pictures of fireside joys and sorrows,' such as *The Brothers* and *The Family Meeting*. He resembles Bryant in the harmony of his diction.

[1] *North American Review*, No. 150, p. 136.

In a style of comparison which is generally injurious to the author whom it would elevate above his true position, Sprague has been called 'the American Pope;' this unhappily reminds us of Klopstock, 'the very German Milton.' Sprague has neither the laconic force of expression, nor the pointed wit and malevolence of the English satirist; but excels in his quiet little poems, telling of household love and grief, and apparently uttered spontaneously from his own heart. His poetry, which is uniformly pure and elevated in its tone, has enjoyed a considerable popularity in America. We quote one of the shorter pieces:

THE WINGED WORSHIPPERS.

Two swallows, having flown into church during divine service, were apostrophised in the following stanzas:—

'Gay, guiltless pair,
What seek ye from the fields of heaven?
Ye have no need of prayer,
Ye have no sins to be forgiven.

Why perch ye here,
Where mortals to their Maker bend?
Can your pure spirits fear
The God ye never could offend?

Ye never knew
The crimes for which we come to weep.
Penance is not for you,
Blessed wanderers of the upper deep.

To you 'tis given
To wake sweet nature's untaught lays;
Beneath the arch of heaven
To chirp away a life of praise.

Then spread each wing,
Far, far above, o'er lakes and lands,
And join the choirs that sing
In yon blue dome not reared with hands.

Or if ye stay,
To note the consecrated hour,
Teach me the airy way,
And let me try your envied power.

Above the crowd,
On upward wings could I but fly,
I'd bathe in yon bright cloud,
And seek the stars that gem the sky.

'Twere heaven indeed,
Through fields of trackless light to soar,
On nature's charms to feed,
And nature's own great God adore.'

RICHARD WILDE (1789–1847) must be mentioned as the writer of one beautiful song—*The Lament of the Captive.* His other writings in verse consisted mostly of translations from Italian poetry. In prose, he wrote a work entitled *Conjectures and Researches concerning the Love, Madness, and Imprisonment of Torquato Tasso* (1842), in which he attempted to prove that the friendship between the poet and the Princess Leonora of Este was mutual, and that the madness of Tasso was feigned.

In the narrative sketch prefixed to the following song, we read that a solitary European was left alive after a battle between his friends and a tribe of Indians, among whom he remained in captivity. In this condition, he refused to be consoled by the kindness of his captors:—

'Nor other wish or joy the lone one had,
Save on the solitary shore to roam,
Or sit and gaze for hours upon the deep,
That rolled between him and his native home;
And when he thought none marked him, he would weep,
Or sing this song of wo, which still our maidens keep.'

THE LAMENT OF THE CAPTIVE.[1]

'My life is like the summer-rose
That opens to the morning sky,
And ere the shades of evening close,
Is scattered on the ground—to die!
Yet on that rose's humble bed
The softest dews of night are shed,
As though she wept such waste to see—
But none shall drop a tear for me!

My life is like the autumn leaf
That trembles in the moon's pale ray,
Its hold is frail—its date is brief,
Restless—and soon to pass away!
Yet, when that leaf shall fall and fade,
The parent tree will mourn its shade,

[1] There has been some dispute respecting the authorship of this song. 'The statement of Captain Basil Hall, that it was written in Germany; of others, that it was by an Irish poet; and of a third party, that it was from the Greek of Alcæus, gave rise to an amusing controversy, in which, I scarcely need state, its originality and Mr Wilde's authorship of it were established.'—GRISWOLD.

The wind bewail the leafless tree,
But none shall breathe one sigh for me!

My life is like the track of feet
Left upon Tampa's desert strand;
Soon as the rising tide shall beat,
Their marks shall vanish from the sand;
Yet, as if grieving to efface
All vestige of the human race,
On that lone shore loud moans the sea,
But none shall thus lament for me!'

JAMES A. HILLHOUSE, a native of Connecticut, wrote in a superior style several dramatic poems not intended for the stage. Of these, the best, entitled *Hadad* (1825), is founded on a Scriptural subject. It has been commended by the American reviewers as 'a chaste and beautiful production, evincing skill and taste in composition, and pure and melodious in its tone.' JOSEPH DRAKE, who died in 1820, wrote a spirited lyric on the *American Flag*, and a poem entitled *The Culprit Fay*, which displayed a poetical fancy above mediocrity. Pleasing verses, but without any examples of remarkable originality, might be selected from the specimens given under the names of Ware, Sands, Goodrich, Clason, and Leggett; but these, with many other versifiers of the same class, must be left unnoticed, in order to allow space for the writers who have made some marked progress in the cultivation of imaginative literature.

For the correctness and beauty of his diction, the truthfulness of his descriptions of nature, and the noble sentiments blended with his imaginative verses, Bryant claims, perhaps, the most prominent place among the poets of America.

WILLIAM CULLEN BRYANT, the son of a respectable physician (Dr Peter Bryant), was born, November 3, 1794, at Cummington, Massachusetts. A taste for versification appeared during his boyhood, and in his fourteenth year he published several poems, which were well received. In 1810, he entered Williams College, and after remaining here two years, studied law, and was admitted to the bar at Plymouth, Massachusetts, in 1815. In 1821, he published at Cambridge a volume of occasional poems, containing some of his best pieces—*The Ages*, *Thanatopsis* (a meditation on death), *Lines to a Waterfowl*, *Green River*, *The Yellow Violet*, and the *Inscription for the Entrance to a Wood*. In 1825, Bryant resigned the profession of law, and removed to New York, where he was engaged as one of the editors of *The United States Review and Literary Gazette*, and subsequently of *The*

Evening Post, with which he has been long connected. With reference to his writings for the newspaper press, he has described himself as one—

'Forced to drudge for the dregs of men,
And scrawl strange words with the barbarous pen.'

By this labour, however, he has acquired a competent fortune, while he has sacrificed to it the time required for making progress in his favourite pursuit of elegant literature. Nothing he has written in later years is superior to the poems published in 1821. The first edition of his collected poems appeared in 1832, and was generally received by the reviewers and the public as 'the best volume of American poetry.' It was also well received in Great Britain; and a review, written by Professor Wilson in his enthusiastic style of commendation, served to increase Bryant's popularity.

Though encouraged by success at home and abroad, he has written little. Having no remarkable variety of thought or invention, he has well understood the range of his own powers of mind, and has judiciously employed his resources, thus avoiding the fault of self-repetition often found in more voluminous writers. His poems chiefly consist of meditations and descriptions, expressed in a style of chaste beauty. Few have any great narrative interest, while of dramatic power we find no trace. This defect is common to several modern poets, who differ widely in other respects. Byron was constantly repeating his own real or imaginary characteristics; and in Wordsworth—of whose poems we should suppose Bryant to be a diligent student—we find continually but one character. The pedler in *The Excursion* is but a thin disguise of garb, and the rector is none other than Wordsworth in priest's orders. Another defect in the poems of Bryant, is their want of novelty in topics. We must complain that a writer, having command of a style so correct and elegant, has directed his attention so much to general themes—topics common to all the poets of all nations—and that he has not celebrated more frequently the peculiar aspects of life and nature in the Western World—the career of the pioneer, the adventure on the prairie and in the forest. In saying this, we remember the peculiar historical circumstances which limit the range of the American poet. We admit that poetry of the highest order cannot be composed of description—that it requires human interests, such as are found in nations with long-cherished traditions. 'America has no ruined towers, covered and beautified with legends as with ivy-leaves; no old ancestral homes, haunted by memories of ancient times. Its lakes are sublime in their extent;

but there are no points of historical interest on their shores. Its mighty rivers are associated with the industry and commerce of the present day, and also with thoughts of the future; but not with the old recollections on which imagination loves to dwell.' But, making allowance for these circumstances, we still believe that Bryant might have done more for the poetic illustration of life in America. He has devoted several poems to the memory of the Red Indians—among them, *The Indian Girl's Lament*, remarkable for its quiet pathos—but these poems can scarcely be numbered with his best productions. Perhaps, enough has been said of this defect, though it is a serious one; for, admitting the abstract correctness of our remarks, the poet and newspaper editor may remind us of his work on the *New York Evening Post* as claiming the greater part of his attention, and leaving only stray leisure hours for the cultivation of poetry. America, with all her wealth, has not hitherto been able and willing to find places for the few men devoted to the refinements of literature.

An American critic has well expressed the general estimate of Bryant's poetry:[1]—'The serene beauty and thoughtful tenderness which characterise his descriptions, or rather interpretations of outward objects, are paralleled only in Wordsworth. His poems are almost perfect of their kind. The fruits of meditation, rather than of passion or imagination; and rarely startling with an unexpected image or sudden outbreak of feeling, they are admirable specimens of what may be called the philosophy of the soul. They address the finer instincts of our nature with a voice so winning and gentle—they search out with such subtle power all in the heart which is true and good—that their influence, though quiet, is resistless. They have consecrated to many minds things which before it was painful to contemplate. Who can say that his feelings and fears respecting death have not received an insensible change since reading the *Thanatopsis?* Indeed, we think that Bryant's poems are valuable not only for their intrinsic excellence, but for the vast influence their wide circulation is calculated to exercise on national feelings and manners. It is impossible to read them without being morally benefited: they purify as well as please: they develop or encourage all the elevated and thoughtful tendencies of the mind. In the jar and bustle of our American life, more favourable to quickness and acuteness of mind than to meditation, it is well that we have a poet who can bring the hues and odours of nature into the crowded mart, and, by ennobling thoughts of man and his destiny, induce the most worldly to give their eyes an occasional glance upward,

[1] *North American Review*, No. 122.

and the most selfish to feel that the love of God and man is better than the love of Mammon.'

The style of Bryant is worthy of his thoughts—it is pure, chaste, and clear. As his thoughts are free from that mysticism which has been affected by too many modern versifiers, so his language is free from everything bombastic or forced. If we wish to find fault, we must speak of qualities wanting in his poems; for in their own kind they are, as the reviewer has said, almost perfect. They do not develop human character, nor do they arouse the passions; they are the characteristic productions of a meditative mind, endowed with imagination and an equal proportion of good taste. A few verses will justify the praise bestowed on Bryant's choice of expressions :—

TO THE EVENING-WIND.

'Spirit that breathest through my lattice, thou
  That cool'st the twilight of the sultry day,
Gratefully flows thy freshness round my brow;
  Thou hast been out upon the deep at play,
Riding all day the wild blue waves till now,
  Roughening their crests, and scattering high their spray,
And swelling the white sail. I welcome thee
To the scorched land, thou wanderer of the sea.

Nor I alone—a thousand bosoms round
  Inhale thee in the fulness of delight;
And languid forms rise up, and pulses bound
  Livelier, at coming of the wind at night;
And, languishing to hear thy grateful sound,
  Lies the vast inland stretched beyond the sight.
Go forth into the gathering shade; go forth,
God's blessing breathed upon the fainting earth!

Go, rock the little wood-bird in his nest;
  Curl the still waters, bright with stars; and rouse
The wide old wood from his majestic rest,
  Summoning from the innumerable boughs
The strange, deep harmonies that haunt his breast:
  Pleasant shall be thy way where meekly bows
The shutting flower, and darkling waters pass,
And 'twixt the o'ershadowing branches and the grass.

The faint old man shall lean his silver head
  To feel thee; thou shalt kiss the child asleep,
And dry the moistened curls that overspread
  His temples, while his breathing grows more deep;
And they who stand about the sick man's bed,
  Shall joy to listen to thy distant sweep,

And softly part his curtains to allow
Thy visit, grateful to his burning brow.

Go—but the circle of eternal change,
  That is the life of nature, shall restore,
With sounds and scents from all thy mighty range,
  Thee to thy birthplace of the deep once more;
Sweet odours in the sea-air, sweet and strange,
  Shall tell the home-sick mariner of the shore;
And, listening to thy murmur, he shall deem
He hears the rustling leaf and running stream.'

The poem entitled *Thanatopsis*—a meditation on death—has been quoted in almost all selections from the works of Bryant. It is one of the best and most characteristic of his poems:—

THANATOPSIS.

'To him who in the love of Nature holds
Communion with her visible forms, she speaks
A various language; for his gayer hours
She has a voice of gladness, and a smile
And eloquence of beauty, and she glides
Into his darker musings, with a mild
And healing sympathy, that steals away
Their sharpness, ere he is aware. When thoughts
Of the last bitter hour come like a blight
Over thy spirit, and sad images
Of the stern agony, and shroud, and pall,
And breathless darkness, and the narrow house,
Make thee to shudder, and grow sick at heart;
Go forth, under the open sky, and list
To Nature's teachings, while from all around—
Earth and her waters, and the depths of air—
Comes a still voice: Yet a few days, and thee
The all-beholding sun shall see no more
In all his course; nor yet in the cold ground,
Where thy pale form was laid, with many tears,
Nor in the embrace of ocean, shall exist
Thy image. Earth, that nourished thee, shall claim
Thy growth, to be resolved to earth again,
And, lost each human trace, surrendering up
Thine individual being, shalt thou go
To mix for ever with the elements,
To be a brother to the insensible rock
And to the sluggish clod, which the rude swain
Turns with his share, and treads upon. The oak
Shall send his roots abroad, and pierce thy mould.

Yet not to thine eternal resting-place
Shalt thou retire alone—nor couldst thou wish
Couch more magnificent. Thou shalt lie down
With patriarchs of the infant world—with kings,
The powerful of the earth—the wise, the good,
Fair forms, and hoary seers of ages past,
All in one mighty sepulchre.—The hills
Rock-ribbed, and ancient as the sun—the vales
Stretching in pensive quietness between;
The venerable woods--rivers that move
In majesty, and the complaining brooks
That make the meadows green; and, poured round all,
Old Ocean's gray and melancholy waste—
Are but the solemn decorations all
Of the great tomb of man. The golden sun,
The planets, all the infinite host of heaven,
Are shining on the sad abodes of death,
Through the still lapse of ages. All that tread
The globe are but a handful to the tribes
That slumber in its bosom.—Take the wings
Of morning—and the Barcan desert pierce,
Or lose thyself in the continuous woods
Where rolls the Oregon, and hears no sound,
Save his own dashings—yet—the dead are there;
And millions in those solitudes, since first
The flight of years began, have laid them down
In their last sleep—the dead reign there alone.
So shalt thou rest—and what if thou withdraw
Unheeded by the living, and no friend
Take note of thy departure? All that breathe
Will share thy destiny. The gay will laugh
When thou art gone, the solemn brood of care
Plod on, and each one as before will chase
His favourite phantom; yet all these shall leave
Their mirth and their employments, and shall come,
And make their bed with thee. As the long train
Of ages glides away, the sons of men—
The youth in life's green spring, and he who goes
In the full strength of years, matron and maid,
And the sweet babe and the gray-headed man—
Shall one by one be gathered to thy side,
By those who in their turn shall follow them.

So live, that when thy summons comes to join
The innumerable caravan that moves
To that mysterious realm, where each shall take
His chamber in the silent halls of death,
Thou go not like the quarry-slave at night,
Scourged to his dungeon, but, sustained and soothed

By an unfaltering trust, approach thy grave,
Like one who wraps the drapery of his couch
About him, and lies down to pleasant dreams.'

JOHN NEAL, a native of Portland, Maine, afforded a striking example of that rapidity of production which may excite a temporary admiration, but can never insure a permanent success in literature. After receiving a common school education, he was apprenticed to a shopkeeper, and remained behind the counter until he was twenty-three years of age. Soon afterwards, the power, or at least the propensity, of writing, both verse and prose, was very suddenly developed. He studied law; practised for a short time at the bar; visited Great Britain (1823-27); wrote many articles for *Blackwood's Magazine*, and other periodicals; edited *The Yankee*, a weekly journal; produced his best novel, *Seventy-six*, as the work of some few odd hours; and wrote poetry, prose-fiction, history, biography, newspaper essays and criticism, sufficient to fill fifty duodecimo volumes, all in the space of twelve years! It is with an obstinate doubt of the value of such rapid writing that we read a statement like the following:—'He is gifted,' says Mr Kettel, 'with an almost magical facility of literary composition. What to others is a work of careful study and severe labour, is to him a pastime. His writings have, in most cases, been thrown off with a rapidity that almost surpasses belief.' Neal says: 'It is no merit in me to compose rapidly. I claim no praise for it. I wish I could move more slowly, less capriciously; but I cannot. Had I a dozen hands, I could keep them all employed when I am writing poetry.' To this a reviewer has appended the note: 'In that case, half-a-dozen hands at least might be advantageously employed in blotting out, of which Mr Neal seems never to have thought. Accordingly, his verses are in a great measure vague, diffuse, overloaded with metaphors, often marked with bad taste, and, in short, destitute of all artistic excellence. Whatever poetic powers he might have, they have never been cultivated. He says of his own writing in verse: "It is poetry, or it is the most outrageous nonsense; one or the other it must be." This is dogmatic and illogical; for it is obvious that it may be a mixture of both, which is indeed the case.'[1]

[1] The above sketch might be supposed to be highly coloured. We therefore append a short extract from Mr Griswold's memoir of Neal: 'He had energy and a genius for anything or everything; and he must do something or starve. After a short deliberation, he determined, as has been intimated, to be a lawyer; but the rules of court, whatever might be his knowledge, required the devotion of years to the study of the books; and how was he to live meanwhile? He would turn author! He had scarcely any education, was ignorant even of the first principles of English grammar, and had never written a line for the press except his advertisements; but, nevertheless, he determined to be a scholar and critic, and do what no other person was then able to do in this country—gain a living by literature.'

James Gates Percival, a poetical writer, of whose powers of mind we cannot entertain that high estimate which some of his countrymen have formed, was born in Kensington parish, Connecticut, 1795, and was educated in Yale College, where he excelled in the routine of studies and as a writer of verse. His early writings were censured on account of some indications of religious scepticism, which do not appear in his later works. In general literary attainments, he excelled many American authors; but his poetry is chiefly remarkable for fluency of versification and diffuseness of style. His learning qualified him to act for some time as assistant to Noah Webster in the preparation of his Dictionary. Poetry, with Dr Percival, has evidently been treated merely as a recreation after severer studies, and has been too hastily written to live. He confesses in one of his prefaces that his verses bear 'no marks of the file and burnisher.' Consequently, we find in his poems few instances of that happy selection of words which marks classical works. Words, words flow on, as in an endless stream, while we look in vain for new thoughts and well-chosen imagery. It is said—and the remark coincides with impressions derived from his writings—that the career of Dr Percival has been marked by traits of great eccentricity, and that delicate health and immoderate devotion to study have been the causes of a morbid mental excitement and despondency which made some portion of his life unhappy. As our estimate of his poetical powers falls below that given by several American critics, it is fair to quote a more favourable judgment. 'Percival,' says a writer in the *North American Review*, 'writes with a facility but rarely equalled, and when his thoughts are once committed to the page, he shrinks from the labour of revising, correcting, and condensing. . . . . His imagination, considered as a shaping faculty, is not so great as Dana's, Longfellow's, and perhaps Bryant's; but in fancy he excels them all. Indeed, the quickness with which the latter quality works, and the disposition of Percival to hurried composition, have not been favourable to the culture of high imaginative power.'

As a favourable specimen of the shorter descriptive poems by Percival, the following lines may be quoted:—

MAY.

'I feel a newer life in every gale—
  The winds that fan the flowers,
And with their welcome breathings fill the sail,
  Tell of serener hours—
Of hours that glide unfelt away
Beneath the sky of May.

The spirit of the gentle south-wind calls
From his blue throne of air;
And when his whispering voice in music falls,
Beauty is budding there;
The bright ones of the valley break
Their slumbers, and awake.

The waving verdure rolls along the plain,
And the wide forest weaves,
To welcome back its playful mates again,
A canopy of leaves.
And from the darkening shadow floats
A gush of trembling notes.

Fairer and brighter spreads the reign of May;
The tresses of the woods
With the light dallying of the west-wind play;
And the full brimming floods,
As gladly to the goal they run,
Hail the returning sun.'

FITZ-GREENE HALLECK, born at Guilford, Connecticut, in 1795, was, like Sprague and other poetical writers, engaged during the greater part of his life in mercantile pursuits, and wrote verses as a recreation. His first volume of verse, entitled *Fanny*, appeared in 1819, and gained a considerable popularity. It was followed by *Alnwick Castle* and other poems (1827), serious and sentimental, or playfully humorous. In several of his poems —as in the *Geraldine* of Rufus Dawes, and the tale of *Lady Jane*, by Willis—there is a studied oddity in the mixture of serious or even tragic with comic and familiar passages; as in uncommon, far-fetched, and uncouth rhymes, and abrupt transitions from grave to gay. This faded imitation of Byron's mocking tone in *Beppo* and *Don Juan*, is an unpleasant affectation. 'It introduces a species of scepticism which is destructive to the enjoyment of poetry. The loftiness, purity, and tenderness of feeling which Halleck can so well express when he pleases, and the delicate and graceful fancies with which he can festoon thought and emotion, should never be associated with what is mean or ridiculous, even to gratify wit or whim. There is a kind of merry malevolence in the abasement of ennobling feelings and beautiful images, which is less pardonable than open scoffing, because more injurious.'[1] As a brief example of this style of scoffing—a few serious verses on the revolutions

[1] *North American Review*, vol. 58, p. 22.

of empires are closed with such a stale pun as the following:—

‘Empires to-day are upside down;
The castle kneels before the town;
The monarch fears a printer's frown,
A brickbat's range:
Give me, in preference to a crown,
Five shillings' change.’

That Halleck, when avoiding the affected Byronic and Mephistophelean vein of humour, could write verse in a spirited style, may be proved by one quotation:—

MARCO BOZZARIS.

‘At midnight, in his guarded tent,
The Turk was dreaming of the hour
When Greece, her knee in suppliance bent,
Should tremble at his power:
In dreams, through camp and court, he bore
The trophies of a conqueror;
In dreams his song of triumph heard;
Then wore his monarch's signet-ring;
Then pressed that monarch's throne—a king:
As wild his thoughts, and gay of wing,
As Eden's garden bird.

* * *

At midnight, in the forest shades,
Bozzaris ranged his Suliote band,
True as the steel of their tried blades,
Heroes in heart and hand.
There had the Persian's thousands stood,
There had the glad earth drunk their blood
On old Platæa's day:
And now they breathed that haunted air,
The sons of sires who conquered there,
With arm to strike, and soul to dare,
As quick, as far as they.

* * *

An hour past on: the Turk awoke;
That bright dream was his last.
He woke—to hear his sentries shriek:
“To arms! they come! the Greek! the Greek!”
He woke—to die midst flame and smoke,
And shot and groan, and sabre stroke,
And death-shots falling thick and fast
As lightnings from the mountain-cloud,
And heard, with voice as trumpet loud,
Bozzaris cheer his band:

"Strike! till the last armed foe expires;
Strike! for your altars and your fires;
Strike! for the green graves of your sires,
God, and your native land!"
They fought, like brave men, long and well;
They filled the ground with Moslem slain;
They conquered—but Bozzaris fell,
Bleeding at every vein.

* * *

Bozzaris! with the storied brave
Greece nurtured in her glory's time,
Rest thee—there is no prouder grave,
Even in her own proud clime.
She wore no funeral weeds for thee,
Nor bade the dark hearse wave its plume,
Like torn branch from death's leafless tree,
In sorrow's pomp and pageantry,
The heartless luxury of the tomb:
But she remembers thee as one
Long loved, and for a season gone;
For thee her poet's lyre is wreathed,
Her marble wrought, her music breathed;
For thee she rings her birthday bells;
Of thee her babes' first lisping tells;
For thine her evening-prayer is said
At palace couch and cottage bed;
Her soldier, closing with the foe,
Gives for thy sake a deadlier blow;
His plighted maiden, when she fears
For him, the joy of her young years,
Thinks of thy fate, and checks her tears:
And she, the mother of thy boys,
Though in her eye and faded cheek
Is read the grief she will not speak,
The memory of her buried joys—
And even she who gave thee birth,
Will, by their pilgrim-circled hearth,
Talk of thy doom without a sigh;
For thou art Freedom's now, and Fame's—
One of the few, the immortal names,
That were not born to die.'

JOHN BRAINARD, an amiable man, whose writings indicated powers worthy of a better cultivation, was a native of New London, Connecticut, and died of consumption in September 1828, at the early age of thirty-two. He graduated at Yale College in 1815, and soon afterwards undertook the editorship of *The Connecticut Mirror*. Of his poems, an American editor says:

'They were always written in haste—usually at the last moment to which he could delay, and while the printer was at his elbow, dunning for copy. They were also written without expectation of fame, and with none of the stimulus derived from a feeling of responsibility to public opinion. They always appeared in the paper as communications, and seem to have been thrown off as freely, and with as little consideration of their value, as the trees resign their leaves to the autumn winds.' As the editor of a journal, Brainard was remarkable for generosity, and maintained the character of a gentleman. This, in England, we trust, would not claim any especial recognition; but in America, where the power of the periodical press has been so often abused, it was an example worthy of being noted.

This is a better tribute to the memory of Brainard, than any that could be founded on his carelessly written poems. The *Lines on Niagara* have been commended for boldness and originality, but hardly make an exception to the general failure of poets and travellers in their descriptions of the great Falls.

George Washington Doane (born 1799), a dignitary in the episcopal church, and professor of belles-lettres and oratory in Washington College, Hartford, published in 1824 a series of devotional and occasional poems, entitled *Songs by the Way.* These have no remarkable merit, but, like many volumes of American poetry, have exercised a good influence in the diffusion of wholesome and pious sentiments. A similar remark would be sufficient to characterise the poems written by William B. O. Peabody, pastor of a congregation at Springfield, Massachusetts. The names of Grenville and Frederick Mellen, Albert G. Greene, Frederick S. Hill, James G. Brooks, and Edward C. Pinkney, may be classed with those of writers of pleasing verses not marked by any striking originality.

Ralph Waldo Emerson, the well-known essayist, has published a series of poems, lyrical in their form, but generally cold and metaphysical in their spirit. Of the exceptions, the lines to a 'Humble-bee' are among the best. We quote a few lines:—

'When the south wind in May-days,
With a net of shining haze,
Silvers the horizon wall,
And with softness touching all,
Tints the human countenance
With the colour of romance,
And infusing subtle heats,
Turns the sod to violets,

Thou in sunny solitudes,
Rover of the underwoods,
The green silence dost displaçe
With thy mellow, breezy bass.
Hot midsummer's petted crone,
Sweet to me thy drowsy tone,
Tells of countless sunny hours,
Long days, and solid banks of flowers,
Of gulfs of sweetness without bound
In Indian wildernesses found.'

WILLIS—DAWES—MORRIS—HOFFMAN—BENJAMIN—SARGENT—LONGFELLOW—WHITTIER.

NATHANIEL PARKER WILLIS, the most versatile of American magazine-writers, was born in Portland in 1807. He studied at Yale College, and after his graduation, was engaged as editor of *The Legendary* and *The Token*, published by Mr Goodrich—a gentleman better known by his *alias*, Peter Parley. Mr Willis had gained a literary reputation when he first visited Europe, and after a tour in France and Italy, came to England, where he stayed two years. In a light, sketchy, and clever style, he gave his impressions of travel, under the title of *Pencillings by the Way*. In some parts of this popular book, the writer described rather freely the personal traits of certain celebrated men to whom he had been introduced. For example, he informed his readers that Professor Wilson, in the enthusiasm of his talk about poetry, poured his tea on the outside of his cup; and that the Earl of Aberdeen crossed his hands behind him, and balanced himself on his heels. The unconscious homage paid to distinctions of rank and title, and the solemnity with which the writer commends the manners of the English nobleman, and 'the beauty of the higher classes,' seem out of place in an American book. England has her own select authors in this style, and their success seems to leave no room for foreign competition. Of our hard-working country, with its striving middle and lower classes; of the main features of our society—such as will be studied by historians in the twentieth century—we find very little in the *Pencillings* of Willis, or the *Sketch-book* of Irving.

In style, the *Pencillings*—like all the other sketches and essays by Willis—are very lively and conversational. One form of playfulness is too frequently employed, and consists in a rapid transition 'from grave to gay,' or from sentiment to mockery. Thus the description of the scenery of Scott's *Lady of the Lake* is contrasted with the humour of 'a half-intoxicated steersman,' who speaks very bad grammar. At Niagara, the sketcher cannot forget that there is a story of a tailor who, when he saw the Falls, thought it a 'very good place for sponging a coat.' This kind of liveliness belongs to the easiest style of humorous writing.

In 1835, Mr Willis published *Inklings of Adventure*, a series of tales and sketches frequently frivolous in their tone, but containing some clever descriptive passages. After his return to America, he assisted in editing *The Corsair;* and during a second visit to London, published *Loiterings of Travel*, and two dramas.

In 1843, assisted by his friend G. P. Morris, he re-established *The New York Mirror*, but soon gave up this employment, and returned to London, where he produced another series of sketches, entitled *Dashes at Life with a Free Pencil.* Numerous light essays, criticisms of art, and sketches of manners, have appeared in *The Home Journal*, a weekly gazette of literature, partly edited and written by Mr Willis; and these have been, from time to time, collected and reprinted under several odd titles.

The prose-writings of Willis have been more successful than his several volumes of poetry, and, on the whole, are more characteristic and original. It is evident that his verse-writing has been a recreation rather than a study. The old proverb, that 'good things must have time to grow,' is true in literature, and the few exceptions there are confirm the rule.

Willis first attracted notice by a series of poems on sacred subjects, which was followed by *Melanie and other Poems* (1835), and by two dramas—*Tortesa the Usurer*, and *Bianca Visconti*—in 1839. In the poems, the versification is often fluent and graceful, and a love of luxurious imagery is a prominent trait. This sometimes seems out of place in the poems on sacred or scriptural subjects; for example, the lines on the *Healing of the Daughter of Jairus*, where the subject may be said to be spoiled by rich drapery and luxuries of furniture; such as 'spice-lamps,' 'alabaster urns,' 'tassels,' 'rich curtains,' and 'silken curtains.'

Melanie is an Italian story of a tragic character, and is supposed to be told during a ramble near Tivoli. This plan admits several pleasing allusions to the scenery and classic localities of Italy.

Lord Ivon and his Daughter, a dramatic sketch in blank-verse, has been commended as one of the writer's best poems; but we regard it, with all the longer poems by Willis, as inferior to several of his short occasional and lyrical productions. Among these, the lively stanzas entitled *The Annoyer*, and the poems *Thirty-five* and *Better Moments*, are good specimens. *The Lady*

Jane is one of the numerous bantering stories which have followed Byron's *Beppo* and *Don Juan*.

In the two dramas, *Tortesa the Usurer*, and *Bianca Visconti*, marks of hasty and careless construction are apparent. The plots are defective, and the characters but slightly sketched. Lively scenes are interspersed, but in the fashion of so many separate pictures, rather than as constituent parts of the whole. To detail these incongruities, would be tiresome, and a selection of unconnected passages would be unfair. We therefore pass from the dramas to quote one of the most simple and unpretending of the occasional poems.

TO A CITY PIGEON.

'Stoop to my window, thou beautiful dove!
Thy daily visits have touched my love.
I watch thy coming, and list the note
That stirs so low in thy mellow throat.
        And my joy is high
To catch the glance of thy gentle eye.

Why dost thou sit on the heated eaves,
And forsake the wood with its freshened leaves?
Why dost thou haunt the sultry street,
When the paths of the forest are cool and sweet?
        How canst thou bear
This noise of people—this sultry air?

Thou alone of the feathered race
Dost look unscared on the human face;
Thou alone, with a wing to flee,
Dost love with man in his haunts to be;
        And the "gentle dove"
Has become a name for trust and love.

A holy gift is thine, sweet bird!
Thou 'rt named with childhood's earliest word;
Thou 'rt linked with all that is fresh and wild
In the prisoned thoughts of the city child;
        And thy glossy wings
Are its brightest image of moving things.

It is no light chance. Thou art set apart,
Wisely by Him who has tamed thy heart,
To stir the love for the bright and fair,
That else were sealed in this crowded air:
        I sometimes dream
Angelic rays from thy pinions stream.

Come then, ever, when daylight leaves
The page I read, to my humble eaves,
And wash thy breast in the hollow spout,
And murmur thy low sweet music out!
I hear and see
Lessons of heaven, sweet bird, in thee!'

RUFUS DAWES, a native of Boston, and graduate of Cambridge, edited during several years *The Emerald*, a weekly paper published at Baltimore, and wrote occasional poems, which appeared in *The Literary Gazette*. In *Geraldine*, one of his longest poems, we find a mixture of tragic with comic passages and uncommon rhymes, besides other odd traits, intended to produce a humorous effect. The whole seems to be little more than a feeble imitation of Byron's burlesque style, which has, unhappily, infected so many young writers. In his short occasional poems, Dawes was more successful.

Passing over the names of Fairfield, Griffin, Prentice, and Colton, we may notice the songs written by GEORGE P. MORRIS, who was the partner of Willis in the editorship of *The Home Journal*. Making due allowance for friendship, and for the writer's lively style, we may quote the criticism of Willis on the lyrics of his colleague: it is a fair specimen of the rapid style of reviewing practised in *The Home Journal*. 'Morris,' says his friend, 'is the best known poet of the country by acclamation, not by criticism. He is just what poets would be if they sang, like birds, without criticism; and it is a peculiarity of his fame, that it seems as regardless of criticism as a bird in the air. Nothing can stop a song of his. It is very easy to say that they are easy to do. They have a momentum, somehow, that it is difficult for others to give, and that speeds them to the far goal of popularity—the best proof consisting in the fact, that he can, at any moment, get fifty dollars for a song unread, when the whole remainder of the American Parnassus could not sell one to the same buyer for a shilling.'

CHARLES FENNO HOFFMAN (born 1806), who has written in prose many tales and sketches of nature and society, published in 1843 a poem entitled *The Vigil of Faith, a Legend of the Andirondack Mountains*. 'It contains much fine description and sentiment; the narrative is remarkably well managed, and in no other poem has Indian superstition or tradition been used with more skill or success.'[1] His songs have been very popular,

[1] Griswold.

and are commended for their lyric flow and hearty sentiment. The sonnets of PARK BENJAMIN have been praised by the best American critics. Of EPES SARGENT, it is said that 'he has written of the sea with more freshness and graphic power, with more true fancy and poetic feeling, than Falconer, or many others of a higher reputation.'[1]

HENRY WADSWORTH LONGFELLOW, professor of modern languages and belles-lettres in Harvard University, was born in Portland in 1807. At the age of eighteen, he graduated with high honours at Bowdoin College, and about the same time published several occasional poems in *The United States Literary Gazette.* After a short interval devoted to the study of law, he accepted the newly founded professorship of modern languages in Bowdoin College, and to prepare himself for its duties, left America, and passed three years and a half in travelling and residing in France, Italy, Spain, Germany, Holland, and England.

His residence in Germany, and the study of the poetical literature of this country, had a lasting influence on his taste and imagination; and it has been asserted by some, that his love of the romantic and mystical old legends of Central Europe has led him away too far from the range of topics proper for an American poet. He has, however, defended his own choice of subjects, and has protested against every narrow notion of a national literature. 'All that is best,' he says, 'in the great poets of all countries, is not what is national in them, but what is universal. Their roots are in their native soil, but their branches wave in the unpatriotic air, that speaks the same language unto all men, and their leaves shine with the illimitable light that pervades all lands.' This is true; yet it may be said, that some national division of labour is advantageous in literature. Why should an American poet reproduce German legends of the middle ages?

In 1835, when Mr George Ticknor resigned the chair of modern languages and belles-lettres at Harvard University, Longfellow was invited to take it, and since then he has resided at Cambridge, in the house formerly occupied by Washington. His life has been fortunate and happy, as his duties have corresponded well with his tastes and qualifications. In 1840, he published his first collection of poems, under the title *Voices of the Night.* The success of the volume was partly due to the melody and finish of the versification, but the chief characteristic of the several short poems consisted in giving an imaginative form of expression to moral sentiments. The direct didactic purport of the poem,

[1] E. P. Whipple.

entitled *A Psalm of Life*, might be censured by art-criticism; for it may be asked, why should the poet take the chair of the moralist, or, inviting us to hear a song, lapse into a sermon? But this ethical purport, though commonplace, was partly the cause of the wide popularity of the verses, which have been very frequently quoted. The two best stanzas shew how new imagery may give life and freshness to old and common maxims :—

'Lives of great men all remind us
We can make our lives sublime,
And, departing, leave behind us
Footprints on the sands of time;

Footprints, that perhaps another,
Sailing o'er life's solemn main,
A forlorn and shipwrecked brother,
Seeing, shall take heart again.'

The *Ballads and other Poems*, published in 1841, included several translations from the German and the Swedish. *The Skeleton in Armour*, one of the best of the original ballads, happily seizes the spirit of old Scandinavian legends. It is founded on the circumstance, that a skeleton, with some pieces of old armour, had been dug up near the Round Tower at Newport, which, as Danish antiquaries have imagined, was built by the old vikings, or Scandinavian adventurers, who, it is supposed, landed in North America long before the time of Columbus. This shadowy legend suggested to the poet the following story of a viking, or northern pirate of the old times :—

THE SKELETON IN ARMOUR.

'"Speak! speak! thou fearful guest!
Who, with thy hollow breast
Still in rude armour drest,
Comest to daunt me!
Wrapt not in Eastern balms,
But with thy fleshless palms
Stretched, as if asking alms,
Why dost thou haunt me?"

Then, from those cavernous eyes,
Pale flashes seem to rise,
As when the northern skies
Gleam in December;
And, like the water's flow
Under December's snow,
Came a dull voice of wo
From the heart's chamber:

"I was a viking old!
My deeds, though manifold,
No skald in song has told,
No saga taught thee!
Take heed, that in thy verse
Thou dost the tale rehearse,
Else dread a dead man's curse!
For this I sought thee.

"Far in the Northern Land,
By the wild Baltic's strand,
I, with my childish hand,
Tamed the ger-falcon;
And, with my skates fast bound,
Skimmed the half-frozen Sound,
That the poor whimpering hound
Trembled to walk on.

"Oft to his frozen lair
Tracked I the grizzly bear,
While from my path the hare
Fled like a shadow;
Oft through the forest dark
Followed the währ-wolf's bark,
Until the soaring lark
Sang from the meadow.

"But when I older grew,
Joining a corsair's crew,
O'er the dark sea I flew
With the marauders.
Wild was the life we led;
Many the souls that sped,
Many the hearts that bled,
By our stern orders.

"Many a wassail-bout
Wore the long winter out;
Often our midnight shout
Set the cocks crowing,
As we the Berserk's tale
Measured in cups of ale,
Draining the oaken pail,
Filled to o'erflowing.

"Once, as I told in glee
Tales of the stormy sea,
Soft eyes did gaze on me,
Burning, yet tender;

And as the white stars shine
On the dark Norway pine,
On that dark heart of mine
Fell their soft splendour.

"I wooed the blue-eyed maid,
Yielding, yet half afraid,
And in the forest's shade
Our vows were plighted.
Under its loosened vest
Fluttered her little breast,
Like birds within their nest
By the hawk frighted.

"Bright in her father's hall
Shields gleamed upon the wall,
Loud sang the minstrels all,
Chanting his glory;
When of old Hildebrand
I asked his daughter's hand,
Mute did the minstrels stand
To hear my story.

"While the brown ale he quaffed,
Loud then the champion laughed,
And as the wind-gusts waft
The sea-foam brightly,
So the loud laugh of scorn,
Out of those lips unshorn,
From the deep drinking-horn
Blew the foam lightly.

"She was a prince's child,
I but a viking wild,
And though she blushed and smiled,
I was discarded!
Should not the dove so white
Follow the sea-mew's flight,
Why did they leave that night
Her nest unguarded?

"Scarce had I put to sea,
Bearing the maid with me—
Fairest of all was she
Among the Norsemen!
When on the white sea-strand,
Waving his armed hand,
Saw we old Hildebrand,
With twenty horsemen.

"Then launched they to the blast,
Bent like a reed each mast,
Yet we were gaining fast,
When the wind failed us ;
And with a sudden flaw
Came round the gusty Skaw,
So that our foe we saw
Laugh as he hailed us.

"And as to catch the gale,
Round veered the flapping sail,
Death ! was the helmsman's hail,
Death without quarter !
Mid-ships with iron keel
Struck we her ribs of steel ;
Down her black hulk did reel
Through the black water !

"As with his wings aslant,
Sails the fierce cormorant,
Seeking some rocky haunt,
With his prey laden,
So toward the open main,
Beating to sea again,
Through the wild hurricane,
Bore I the maiden.

"Three weeks we westward bore,
And when the storm was o'er,
Cloud-like we saw the shore
Stretching to leeward ;
There for my lady's bower
Built I the lofty tower,
Which, to this very hour,
Stands looking seaward.

"There lived we many years ;
Time dried the maiden's tears ;
She had forgot her fears—
She was a mother ;
Death closed her mild blue eyes—
Under that tower she lies ;
Ne'er shall the sun arise
On such another !

"Still grew my bosom then,
Still as a stagnant fen !
Hateful to me were men,
The sunlight hateful !

In the vast forest here,
Clad in my warlike gear,
Fell I upon my spear—
Oh, death was grateful!

"Thus, seamed with many scars,
Bursting these prison bars,
Up to its native stars,
My soul ascended;
There from the flowing bowl
Deep drinks the warrior's soul,
Skoal! to the Northland! *Skoal!*"
—Thus the tale ended.'

Excelsior is a purely ideal poem, and one of the best of its kind. It is absurd to regard it as an allegory intended to represent the career of a poet; for a poet should not forsake the real world and the scenes of human life. It should be read as an imaginative expression of one sentiment or impulse—that of aspiration. Several attempts to set this poem to music have only proved that it would be well if the natural relations of music with poetry were more carefully studied. Good reading supplies all the music required by this fine poem.

EXCELSIOR.

'The shades of night were falling fast,
As through an Alpine village passed
A youth, who bore, 'mid snow and ice,
A banner with the strange device—
Excelsior!

His brow was sad; his eye beneath
Flashed like a falchion from its sheath,
And like a silver clarion rung
The accents of that unknown tongue—
Excelsior!

In happy homes he saw the light
Of household fires gleam warm and bright;
Above, the spectral glaciers shone,
And from his lips escaped a groan—
Excelsior!

"Try not the Pass!" the old man said;
"Dark lowers the tempest overhead;
The roaring torrent is deep and wide!"
And loud that clarion voice replied:
"Excelsior!"

"O stay," the maiden said, "and rest
Thy weary head upon this breast!"
A tear stood in his bright blue eye,
But still he answered, with a sigh:
"Excelsior!"

"Beware the pine-tree's withered branch!
Beware the awful avalanche!"
This was the peasant's last good-night;
A voice replied, far up the height:
"Excelsior!"

At break of day, as heavenward
The pious monks of Saint Bernard
Uttered the oft-repeated prayer,
A voice cried through the startled air:
"Excelsior!"

A traveller, by the faithful hound,
Half-buried in the snow was found,
Still grasping in his hand of ice
That banner, with the strange device—
Excelsior!

There, in the twilight cold and gray,
Lifeless, but beautiful, he lay,
And from the sky, serene and far,
A voice fell, like a falling star:
"Excelsior!"

In his translation of *The Children of the Lord's Supper*, from the Swedish of Tegner, Longfellow endeavoured to overcome the difficulty of English hexameter verse (so called), and certainly succeeded as well as any other writer in the same metre; but it was unfortunate that he adopted the same form in his tale of *Evangeline*. In other respects, this is a superior poem. It has the merit of American interest in its scenery and incidents, and its pervading sentiment is beautiful.

The story is founded on an event in the colonial history of America. When Nova Scotia—formerly known by the name Acadia—was ceded to England by the French in 1713, the French inhabitants were required to take the oaths of allegiance to the British crown. They refused to take these oaths without certain conditions, to the effect that they, the people of Acadia, should not be called upon to take up arms against their former sovereign. For some time they were allowed to hold their neutral position; but when the English had extended their territory, and had captured the French fort of Beau Séjour, the Acadians, or people of Nova Scotia, were accused of having forfeited their neutrality by giving assistance to the French and their Indian allies. It appears that this accusation was founded on the fact, that 300 Acadians had been taken in arms at the siege of Beau Séjour; but the majority were a quiet agricultural people. As they had refused to take unconditional oaths of allegiance, they were regarded as dangerous neighbours; and it was determined, in a council held by General Braddock with the British admirals Boscawen and Mostwyn, that the whole population of Acadia should be expatriated and dispersed among the colonies on the sea-board. A fleet of transports was hired to convey the exiles. In the haste of removal, families and friends were separated; husbands lost their wives, parents their children. Some escaped, and sought shelter in the woods; but the country was laid waste to prevent their subsistence. The greater number were transported to Massachusetts; other companies were sent to New York, Maryland, Carolina—some as far as Georgia. The more hardy and adventurous became hunters, trappers, or *coureurs des bois* in the West. At the peace of 1763, most of the survivors returned to Nova Scotia, or settled in Canada.

At the time of this compulsory emigration, Evangeline, the heroine of the poem, lived with her father, an Acadian farmer, at Grand-Pré, and was betrothed to Gabriel, the son of Basil the smith.

'In the Acadian land, on the shores of the Basin of Minas,
Distant, secluded, still, the little village of Grand-Pré
Lay in the fruitful valley. Vast meadows stretched to the eastward,
Giving the village its name, and pasture to flocks without number.
Dikes, that the hands of the farmers had raised with labour incessant,
Shut out the turbulent tides; but at stated seasons the flood-gates
Opened, and welcomed the sea to wander at will o'er the meadows.
West and south there were fields of flax, and orchards and corn-fields
Spreading afar and unfenced o'er the plain; and away to the northward
Blomidon[1] rose, and the forests old, and aloft on the mountains
Sea-fogs pitched their tents, and mists from the mighty Atlantic
Looked on the happy valley, but ne'er from their station descended.
There, in the midst of its farms, reposed the Acadian village.
Strongly built were the houses, with frames of oak and chestnut,
Such as the peasants of Normandy built in the reign of the Henries.'

The marriage of Evangeline and Gabriel was prevented by the burning of the village Grand-Pré, and the banishment of its

[1] A cape in Nova Scotia.

inhabitants. Overcome by the calamity, the father of Evangeline died on the sea-shore, while Gabriel and his father were carried away into exile. Thus the lovers were separated, and the remainder of the poem describes the long wanderings of the maiden in search of her betrothed:—

'Far asunder, on separate coasts, the Acadians landed;
Scattered were they, like flakes of snow, when the wind from the north-east
Strikes aslant through the fogs that darken the banks of Newfoundland.
Friendless, homeless, hopeless, they wandered from city to city,
From the cold lakes of the north to sultry southern savannas.'

The places visited by Evangeline, and the incidents of her journeys, are described in the second part of the poem, often with striking elegance and beauty, though the metre chosen by Mr Longfellow has an almost inevitable tendency to verboseness. A few lines may be quoted from the account of a voyage on the Mississippi:—

'Softly the evening came. The sun from the western horizon
Like a magician extended his golden wand o'er the landscape;
Twinkling vapours arose; and sky, and water, and forest
Seemed all on fire at the touch, and melted and mingled together.
Hanging between two skies, a cloud with edges of silver,
Floated the boat, with its dripping oars, on the motionless water.
Filled was Evangeline's heart with inexpressible sweetness.
Touched by the magic spell, the sacred fountains of feeling
Glowed with the light of love, as the skies and waters around her.
Then from a neighbouring thicket, the mocking-bird, wildest of singers,
Swinging aloft on a willow-spray that hung over the water,
Shook from his little throat such floods of delirious music,
That the whole air, and the woods, and the waves, seemed silent to listen.'

Led onward by various rumours, the maiden follows every direction, however vague and shadowy, that seems to point towards her beloved Gabriel.

'Sometimes she lingered in towns, till, urged by the fever within her,
Urged by a restless longing, the hunger and thirst of the spirit,
She would commence again her endless search and endeavour;
Sometimes in church-yards strayed, and gazed on the crosses and tombstones,
Sat by some nameless grave, and thought that perhaps in its bosom
He was already at rest, and she longed to slumber beside him.

Sometimes a rumour, a hearsay, an inarticulate whisper,
Came with its airy hand to point and beckon her forward.
Sometimes she spake with those who had seen her belovèd, and known him ;
But it was long ago, in some far-off place, or forgotten.
"Gabriel Lajeunesse !" say they ; "O yes, we have seen him.
He was with Basil the blacksmith, and both have gone to the prairies ;
Coureurs des bois are they, and famous hunters and trappers."'

At last, in Louisiana, Evangeline seems to have ended her long wanderings, for she finds the home of Basil the smith, who has become a prosperous herdsman; but, alas! his son Gabriel, restless in the absence of his betrothed, had, only some few hours before her arrival, left the homestead, and in the night his boat had passed by the journeying maiden.

Far away into the Indian territory, near the Ozark Mountains, Evangeline, guided by Basil, follows the steps of her lover; but it is all in vain. Though they hear tidings of the young man, he is always 'gone further into the wilderness.' When they reach the Jesuits' mission-station, they learn that Gabriel has been there, but has departed. The maiden stays here, hoping that 'in the autumn, when the chase is over, her betrothed will return;' but there comes only a rumour—

'"Far to the north and east," it said, "in the Michigan forests,
Gabriel had his lodge, by the banks of the Saginaw river."'

In company with returning guides, going to the lakes of St Lawrence, Evangeline leaves the mission-station, and travels on to encounter another disappointment:

'When over weary ways, by long and perilous marches,
She had attained at length the depths of the Michigan forests,
Found she the hunter's lodge deserted and fallen to ruins.'

Thus year after year passes away in the fruitless search—

'Thus did the long sad years glide on, and in seasons and places
Divers and distant far was seen the wandering maiden :
Now in the tents of grace of the meek Moravian missions ;
Now in the noisy camps and the battle-fields of the army ;
Now in secluded hamlets, in towns and populous cities.
Like a phantom she came, and passed away unremembered.
Fair was she, and young, when in hope began the long journey ;
Faded was she, and old, when in disappointment it ended.
Each succeeding year stole something away from her beauty,
Leaving behind it, broader and deeper, the gloom and the shadow.
Then there appeared and spread faint streaks of gray on her forehead,
Dawn of another life, that broke o'er her earthly horizon,
As in the eastern sky the first faint streaks of the morning.'

In the city of Philadelphia, the long pilgrimage finds a close. Here Evangeline, now advanced in years, joins the order of the Sisters of Mercy, and, while pestilence prevails, she devotes herself to attendance on the afflicted poor. It is a Sabbath-morning, when, in the alms-house, Evangeline is called to wait upon an aged man, who has been brought there to die. The closing scene is touchingly described :—

'Across the meadows were wafted
Sounds of psalms that were sung by the Swedes in their church
at Wicaco.
Soft as descending wings fell the calm of the hour on her spirit;
Something within her said : "At length thy trials are ended!"
And with light in her looks, she entered the chamber of sickness.
Noiselessly moved about the assiduous, careful attendants,
Moistening the feverish lip and the aching brow, and in silence
Closing the sightless eyes of the dead and concealing their faces.

* * * *

Many a languid head, upraised as Evangeline entered,
Turned on its pillow of pain, to gaze while she passed; for her
presence
Fell on their hearts like a ray of the sun on the walls of a prison.

* * * *

Suddenly, as if arrested by fear or a feeling of wonder,
Still she stood, with her colourless lips apart, while a shudder
Ran through her frame, and, forgotten, the flowerets dropped from
her fingers,
And from her eyes and cheeks the light and bloom of the morning.
Then there escaped from her lips a cry of such terrible anguish,
That the dying heard it, and started up from their pillows.
On the pallet before her was stretched the form of an old man.
Long, and thin, and gray, were the locks that shaded his temples;
But, as he lay in the morning light, his face for a moment
Seemed to assume once more the form of its earlier manhood
(So are wont to be changed the faces of those who are dying).
Motionless, senseless, dying he lay, and his spirit, exhausted,
Seemed to be sinking down through infinite depths in the
darkness—
Darkness of slumber and death—for ever sinking and sinking.
Then through those realms of shade, in multiplied reverberations,
Heard he that cry of pain, and through the hush that succeeded
Whispered a gentle voice, in accents tender and saint-like :
"Gabriel! O my belovèd!"—and died away into silence.
Then he beheld, in a dream, once more the home of his childhood;
Green Acadian meadows, with sylvan rivers among them,
Village, and mountain, and woodlands; and walking under their
shadow,
As in the days of her youth, Evangeline rose in his vision.

Tears came into his eyes; and, as slowly he lifted his eyelids,
Vanished the vision away, but Evangeline kneeled by his bedside.
Vainly he strove to whisper her name, for the accents, unuttered,
Died on his lips, and their motion revealed what the tongue would have spoken.
Vainly he strove to rise; and Evangeline, kneeling beside him,
Kissed his dying lips, and laid his head on her bosom.
Sweet was the light of his eyes; but it suddenly sank into darkness,
As when a lamp is blown out by a gust of wind at a casement.'

Beside the poems already noticed, Longfellow has written *The Spanish Student*, a play (1842); *Poems on Slavery* (1843); and the series entitled *The Seaside and the Fireside*. In his short occasional poems, he frequently inculcates some moral truth, as in *The Ladder of St Augustine*, which may be regarded as a concise sermon in verse. Like the *Psalm of Life*, it clothes in fine imagery common proverbs as old as the hills. For example, nothing can be more trite than the doctrine of the following verses; but the poetical illustration has a noble character:—

'We have not wings—we cannot soar;
  But we have feet to scale and climb,
By slow degrees, by more and more,
  The cloudy summits of our time.

The mighty pyramids of stone
  That wedge-like cleave the desert airs,
When nearer seen, and better known,
  Are but gigantic flights of stairs.

The distant mountains that uprear
  Their frowning foreheads to the skies,
Are crossed by pathways that appear
  As we to higher levels rise.

The heights by great men reached and kept,
  Were not attained by sudden flight;
But they, while their companions slept,
  Were toiling upward in the night.'

One more example of homely doctrine in a pleasing poetical dress must be quoted, for it is a general favourite among young readers. Carlyle, Emerson, and we must add Longfellow, make truth tiresome by their frequent iteration of the doctrine, that *to work* for self-culture, and the world's general culture, is man's true destiny and happiness; but the trite sermon seems fresh when Longfellow's sturdy blacksmith is the preacher.

THE VILLAGE BLACKSMITH.

Under a spreading chestnut-tree
  The village smithy stands;
The smith, a mighty man is he,
  With large and sinewy hands;
And the muscles of his brawny arms
  Are strong as iron bands.

His hair is crisp, and black and long,
  His face is like the tan;
His brow is wet with honest sweat,
  He earns whate'er he can,
And looks the whole world in the face,
  For he owes not any man.

Week in, week out, from morn till night,
  You can hear his bellows blow;
You can hear him swing his heavy sledge,
  With measured beat, and slow,
Like a sexton ringing the village-bell,
  When the evening sun is low.

And children coming home from school
  Look in at the open door;
They love to see the flaming forge,
  And hear the bellows roar,
And catch the burning sparks that fly
  Like chaff from a thrashing-floor.

He goes on Sunday to the church,
  And sits among his boys;
He hears the parson pray and preach,
  He hears his daughter's voice
Singing in the village choir,
  And it makes his heart rejoice.

It sounds to him like her mother's voice,
  Singing in Paradise!
He needs must think of her once more,
  How in the grave she lies;
And with his hard, rough hand he wipes
  A tear out of his eyes.

Toiling—rejoicing—sorrowing,
  Onward through life he goes;
Each morning sees some task begin,
  Each evening sees it close;
Something attempted, something done,
  Has earned a night's repose.

Thanks, thanks to thee, my worthy friend,
For the lesson thou hast taught:
Thus at the flaming forge of life
Our fortunes must be wrought;
Thus on its sounding anvil shaped
Each burning deed and thought!'

The Golden Legend is a dramatic and mystical version of an old German story, versified by a minnesinger named Hartmann von der Aue, who lived, it is said, in the twelfth century. We do not admire the supernatural machinery introduced by Longfellow in his treatment of the legend. It was in itself sufficiently improbable. We read that, in old times, there lived in Swabia a wealthy young nobleman, whom we may style Prince Henry. The plague of leprosy was prevalent in central Europe, and the prince was suddenly seized by this dreadful disease, and became an outcast from society. In vain he travelled far, and sought the aid of various celebrated physicians: they could not give him a ray of hope. At last he went to a physician at Salerno, who, according to the superstition of the times, told him that he might be cured, but only on the condition that a young maiden must freely offer her life as a sacrifice. As he regarded this as impossible, he returned home to Swabia in despair, left his castle, disposed of his riches and furniture, and retired to a little farmhouse occupied by one of his vassals. Here he lived for some time, bitterly lamenting his fate, and refusing to submit patiently to the evil which had fallen upon him. His misery touched the heart of a peasant-girl, the daughter of his vassal. She learned from her parents what the doctor of Salerno had said of the only means by which Prince Henry might be cured. It rested on her mind; and, after meditations by day and night, she resolved to offer her own life. This supernatural self-devotion is contrasted with the selfishness of the prince, who at first consents to buy health at this high price; but subsequently he relents; the life of the intended victim is spared, and the disease is cured.

In his treatment of the legend, Longfellow has freely introduced Lucifer and good angels, with other *dramatis personæ* of the old mysteries.

We have still to notice the writer's extensive work on *The Poets and Poetry of Europe*—a series of translations, with introductions and biographical notices, published in 1845. The translations are partly original and partly selected from other works. In the difficult and commonly thankless task of translating poetry from the German and other modern languages, Longfellow has apparently obeyed the orders of certain critics who have insisted on verbal fidelity.

John Greenleaf Whittier, a member of the Society of Friends, is one of the most earnest and impetuous of the writers who have attacked the evil of slavery. His sincerity and warm benevolence cannot be doubted; but the same fervour that gives spirit to his lyrics, makes him too impatient of the pains of finished composition. He regards a song as a sword—to be used in battle; and if it has a sharp point, he cares nothing about its polish. A friendly reviewer says of Whittier: 'There is a rush of passion in his verse which sweeps everything along with it. His fancy and imagination can hardly keep pace with their fiery companion. His vehement sensibility will not allow the inventive faculties fully to complete what they may have commenced.' These remarks may be applied to the anti-slavery verses, and several other poems by Whittier; but he rises, sometimes, far above the declamatory style, and gives indications of a truly poetical imagination. When free from polemical excitement, he can find suitable expressions for refined and elevated sentiments. For example, there is found not only a gentle tolerant spirit, but also sound philosophy, in the following lines on the death of an amiable and accomplished woman, who, in creed, belonged to the episcopal church:—

IN MEMORY OF LUCY HOOPER.

'They've laid thee midst the household graves,
Where father, brother, sister lie;
Below thee sweep the dark blue waves,
Above thee bends the summer sky.
Thy own loved church in sadness read
Her solemn ritual o'er thy head,
And blessed and hallowed with her prayer
The turf laid lightly o'er thee there.
That church, whose rites and liturgy,
Sublime and old, were truth to thee,
Undoubted to thy bosom taken,
As symbols of a faith unshaken.
Even I, of simpler views, could feel
The beauty of thy trust and zeal;
And, owning not thy creed, could see
How deep a truth it seemed to thee,
And how thy fervent heart had thrown
O'er all, a colouring of its own,
And kindled up, intense and warm,
A life in every rite and form,
As, when on Chebar's banks of old,
The Hebrew's gorgeous vision rolled,
A spirit filled the vast machine—
A life "within the wheels" was seen.

Farewell ! A little time, and we
 Who knew thee well, and loved thee here,
One after one shall follow thee
 As pilgrims through the gate of fear,
Which opens on eternity.
Yet shall we cherish not the less
 All that is left our hearts meanwhile ;
The memory of thy loveliness
 Shall round our weary pathway smile,
Like moonlight when the sun has set—
A sweet and tender radiance yet.
Thoughts of thy clear-eyed sense of duty,
 Thy generous scorn of all things wrong—
The truth, the strength, the graceful beauty
 Which blended in thy song,
All lovely things by thee beloved,
 Shall whisper to our hearts of thee ;
These green hills, where thy childhood roved,
 Yon river winding to the sea—
The sunset light of autumn eves
 Reflecting on the deep, still floods,
Cloud, crimson sky, and trembling leaves
 Of rainbow-tinted woods—
These, in our view, shall henceforth take
A tenderer meaning for thy sake ;
And all thou lov'dst of earth and sky,
Seem sacred to thy memory.'

HOLMES—TUCKERMAN—POE—LOWELL—STREET—TAYLOR—SAXE—BOKER—STODDART—READ.

Oliver Wendell Holmes, a physician in Boston, is the writer of a series of occasional poems—didactic, satirical, lyrical, and humorous. He was born in 1809 at Cambridge, Massachusetts ; studied at Harvard University, and after taking his degree, commenced the study of law, but soon relinquished it and adopted the medical profession, in which he has gained a high position as professor of anatomy and physiology in the university of Cambridge. Holmes is the most cheerful of the American poets ; indeed, his lighter pieces in verse may be described as little more than effusions of a playful good-humour. This quality has made him popular in America, where there is some reason to complain of a want of mirth in the higher or more educated classes, if we may accept the testimony of Emerson. He says : ' We must pay for being too intellectual, as they call it. People are not as light-hearted for it. I think men never loved life less. I question if care and doubt ever wrote their names so legibly on the faces of any population. This ennui, for which we Saxons had no name—this word of France, has got a terrible significance. It shortens life, and bereaves the day of its light. Old age begins in the nursery; and before the young American is put into jacket and trousers, he says: "I want something which I never saw before." I have seen the same gloom on the brow even of those adventurers from the intellectual class, who have dived deepest, and with most success, into active life. I have seen the authentic sign of anxiety and perplexity on the greatest forehead of the state.'[1]

In the lighter poems of Holmes, humour is generally blended with good taste. His versification is easy and fluent, and rises to dignity and chastened elegance in his serious and didactic poems; which suggest that the writer—devoting his life to literature—might have achieved greater works. As a specimen of descriptive verse, we may quote the following lines on Spring:—

THE RETURN OF SPRING.

'Winter is past; the heart of Nature warms
Beneath the wrecks of unresisted storms;
Doubtful at first, suspected more than seen,
The southern slopes are fringed with tender green;
On sheltered banks, beneath the dripping eaves,
Spring's earliest nurslings spread their glowing leaves,
Bright with the hues from wider pictures won,
White, azure, golden—drift, or sky, or sun;
The snow-drop, bearing on her patient breast
The frozen trophy torn from winter's crest;
The violet, gazing on the arch of blue
Till her own iris wears its deepened hue;
The spendthrift crocus, bursting through the mould,
Naked and shivering with his cup of gold.
Swelled with new life, the darkening elm on high
Prints her thick buds against the spotted sky;
On all her boughs the stately chestnut cleaves
The gummy shroud that wraps her embryo leaves.

* * *

Then bursts the song from every leafy glade,
The yielding season's bridal serenade;
Then flash the wings returning summer calls
Through the deep arches of her forest halls;
The blue-bird breathing from his azure plumes
The fragrance borrowed where the myrtle blooms;

[1] The writer, we presume, alludes to Daniel Webster.

The thrush, poor wanderer, dropping meekly down,
Clad in his remnant of autumnal brown;
The oriole, drifting like a flake of fire
Rent by the whirlwind from a blazing spire.
The robin, jerking his spasmodic throat,
Repeats, *staccáto*, his peremptory note;
The crack-brained boblink courts his crazy mate,
Poised on a bulrush tipsy with his weight;
Nay, in his cage the lone canary sings,
Feels the soft air and spreads his idle wings.
Thus to my heart its wonted tides return,
When sullen Winter breaks his crystal urn,
And o'er the turf in wild profusion showers
Its dewy leaflets and ambrosial flowers.
In vacant rapture for a while I range
Through the wide scene of universal change,
Till, as the statue in its nerves of stone
Felt the new senses wakening one by one,
Each long-closed inlet finds its destined ray
Through the dark curtain Spring has rent away.
I crush the buds the clustering lilacs bear—
The same sweet fragrance that I loved is there—
The same fresh hues each opening disk reveals—
Soft as of old each silken petal feels;
The birch's rind its flavour still retains,
Its boughs still ringing with the self-same strains;
Above, around, rekindling nature claims
Her glorious altars wreathed in living flames;
Undimmed, unshadowed, far as morning shines,
Feeds with fresh incense her eternal shrines.
Lost in her arms, her burning life I share,
Breathe the wild freedom of her perfumed air,
From heaven's fair face the long-drawn shadows roll,
And all its sunshine floods my opening soul!'

The satire of Holmes is partly local, but many passages may be as readily understood in England as in America. He does not spare the foibles of his countrymen, but ventures to laugh at their sensitiveness to the adulation or censure of travellers and critics; while, in serious mood, he reprobates the tyranny exercised in some matters of opinion, and reproves that extreme devotion to 'progress,' which can scarcely be described without using the Americanism 'go-ahead.'

We must here pass over the names of several verse-writers—Cranch, Palmer, Pike, Gallagher, Lunt, and others—who seem to belong to the second class of American poets. In the *Spirit of Poetry*, and other writings, by Henry T. Tuckerman, we find proofs of a refined and imaginative mind; but his prose works—

Thoughts on the Poets, and *Characteristics of Literature*—are more interesting than his poems. Several specimens of poetry are given under the name of William Crosswell, a clergyman who, for some time, was associate editor of *The Episcopal Watchman*, a religious paper published at Hartford. Among these specimens we find one of the sonnets of Wordsworth, which was probably inserted by an error of the editor.[1]

To explain our omissions of many names in this part of our review, it may be well to quote a few remarks by a candid critic.[2] With reference to numerous minor poets, or writers of verses, he observes :—'Their compositions may not deserve much eulogium; they may merely remodel old images, and repeat old forms of expression; they may rather reproduce than create; but their poetry often displays smooth versification, pure sentiment, and occasionally a happy thought. . . . In the United States, there is a great number of such persons as we have indicated. . . . If their good-natured friends would only let them alone, they would never discover that they were more gifted than their neighbours. The danger is, that they will be too much elated by flattery, and at last seriously entertain the conceit that they are great poets, who reflect honour upon the literature of their country. As every man has some friend connected with a newspaper or a magazine, this danger is not so groundless as one may at first imagine.' It is hardly necessary to add, that this warning is partly applicable to England as well as to America; but in the latter country, the condition of the newspaper-press facilitates the growth of false reputations.

Several writers have described EDGAR ALLAN POE as the most original of all the American poets, and as a melancholy example of artistic genius united with moral depravity. We are willing to believe that, in the sketches of his biography, there may be found some exaggeration of the darker traits. He was born at Baltimore in January 1811. The early death of his parents—who belonged to the theatrical profession—left him, with two other children, in a destitute condition. When about six years old, he was adopted by Mr Allan, a merchant, who brought him over to England, and placed him in a school at Stoke-Newington. After staying here some four or five years, he returned with

[1] Kettel's *Specimens of American Poetry*, vol. iii. p. 357. The sonnet begins with the lines :

'Nuns fret not at their convent's narrow room;
And hermits are contented with their cells.'

[2] E. P. Whipple, art. *Poets and Poetry of America;* in No. 122 of the *North American Review*.

Mr Allan to America, and entered the university at Charlottesville, where, it is said, he shared in the dissolute habits then too prevalent among the students. One of his biographers states, that Poe was expelled from Charlottesville; while another says, that he took the first honours of the college.

However this might be, it appears that very soon after the completion of his studies, Poe quarrelled with his benefactor, Mr Allan, who refused to pay the debts his protégé's dissipated habits had contracted. After writing an abusive letter to his patron, Poe left America, and sailed for Greece, professedly going to take part with the Greeks in their war against the Turks. He never reached his destination; and of his wild rambles and adventures in Europe we know nothing more, than that he was found in some difficulty in St Petersburg, where the American consul rescued him, and enabled him to return to his native land. Here he entered the military academy at West Point, but was soon cashiered for disobedience. We are assured by one biographer, that the origin of all Poe's subsequent misfortunes was the death of his benefactress, Mrs Allan, and the second marriage of Mr Allan, which deprived the adopted son of all hope of inheriting a considerable property. Other writers say, that Poe ridiculed and insulted the second Mrs Allan, and accordingly was turned out of doors. However the case might be, the young man, without resources, was cast upon the world, and, after some further thoughts of adopting a military life, he applied himself to literature, and appeared as a competitor for two prizes offered by the editors of the *Baltimore Visitor*. He gained both prizes—the first, by his poem on the *Coliseum;* the second, by his tale of a *MS. found in a Bottle;* but, subsequently, the adjudicators decided that, having gained the first, he must forego the second prize. When he came forward to receive the sum awarded, he was thin and pale, and his costume indicated extreme destitution. A threadbare coat was closely buttoned to hide the want of a shirt, while worn-out boots failed to conceal the want of hose. His success introduced him to new friends, by whose aid he obtained the editorship of *The Southern Literary Messenger*, published in Richmond. Having now a salary of about L.100 a year, he was bold enough to marry his cousin, a poor but beautiful and amiable girl, named Virginia Clemm—the Annabel Lee of his poetry.

The cause of his failure in Richmond, as in other places, is mildly stated in a letter written by the editor of *The Home Journal*, who appears to have been well acquainted with Poe; and as this statement seems to be both probable and charitable, we give it as a counterpoise against more serious charges made against his moral character. The editor says: 'Some four or five years since, when editing a daily paper in this city, Mr Poe was employed by us for several months as critic and sub-editor. This was our first personal acquaintance with him. He resided with his wife and mother at Fordham, a few miles out of town, but was at his desk in the office from nine in the morning till the evening paper went to press. With the highest admiration for his genius, and a willingness to let it atone for more than ordinary irregularity, we were led by common report to expect a very capricious attention to his duties, and occasionally a scene of violence and difficulty. Time went on, however, and he was invariably punctual and industrious. . . . . With the prospect of taking the lead in another periodical, he at last voluntarily gave up his employment with us; and through all this considerable period, we had seen but one presentment of the man—a quiet, patient, industrious, and most gentlemanly person, commanding the utmost respect and good feeling by his unvarying deportment and ability. Residing as he did in the country, we never met Mr Poe in hours of leisure; but he frequently called on us afterwards at our place of business, and we met him often in the street —invariably the same sad-mannered, winning, and refined gentleman, such as we had always known him. It was by rumour only, up to the day of his death, that we knew of any other development of manner or character. We heard, from one who knew him well—what should be stated in all mention of his lamentable irregularities—that, with a *single glass* of wine his whole nature was reversed; the demon became uppermost, and, though none of the usual signs of intoxication were visible, his *will* was palpably insane.'

After leaving Richmond, Poe wandered to Baltimore and New York, in search of the precarious gains of periodical literature; and about the close of the year 1838, he was engaged as editor of a magazine established by Mr Burton in Philadelphia. In this post, he was at first steady in the performance of his duties; abstained from the fatal bottle; and, in a letter to a friend, described himself as 'a model of temperance.' But he offended his employer not only by a lapse into irregularities, but also by the severe and intemperate tone of his criticisms.

Having left Mr Burton's office, Poe endeavoured to start a rival magazine, and soon afterwards was appointed editor of *Graham's Magazine*, to which he contributed several ingenious papers on cryptology, or cipher-writing. During his residence in Philadelphia, his manners, when not disguised by intoxication, were quiet and gentlemanly; but his irregularities were so frequent, that he lost his engagement, and in 1844 removed to

New York, where he gained a reputation by several magazine-papers, and especially by his poem of *The Raven.* Here, as elsewhere, if we must believe the statements of the biographer, Mr Griswold, Poe ruined himself by habits which seem to prove a case of moral insanity. In a state of destitution, he lived with his wife and his mother-in-law, Maria Clemm, at Fordham, near New York. In the midst of his misery, his mother-in-law (who must have been a brave and good soul) remained faithful, devoted to the unhappy man. She wandered in the streets of New York, selling odd poems written by her son, to provide a dinner for him; and when she had no poems, she begged for him. This might tempt a charitable mind to believe that Poe could not have been the hopeless moral outcast described by his biographer: he was still beloved by this faithful woman; but on this heroic devotion we fear no argument can be well founded in favour of the man. His wife died during this dark time, and he deplored her fate in the beautiful lyric of *Annabel Lee*, which must be quoted, as, next to *The Raven*, the most striking example of that harmony of feeling with rhythmical expression for which Poe's verses are remarkable :—

ANNABEL LEE.

'It was many and many a year ago,
    In a kingdom by the sea,
That a maiden there lived, whom you may know
    By the name of Annabel Lee;
And this maiden she lived with no other thought
    Than to love and be loved by me.

I was a child and she was a child,
    In this kingdom by the sea;
But we loved with a love that was more than love—
    I and my Annabel Lee—
With a love that the winged seraphs of heaven
    Coveted her and me.

And this was the reason that, long ago,
    In this kingdom by the sea,
A wind blew out of a cloud, chilling
    My beautiful Annabel Lee;
So that her high-born kinsmen[1] came,
    And bore her away from me,
To shut her up in a sepulchre,
    In this kingdom by the sea.

[1] The angels.

The angels, not half so happy in heaven,
    Went envying her and me—
Yes!—that was the reason (as all men know,
    In this kingdom by the sea)
That the wind came out of the cloud by night,
    Chilling and killing my Annabel Lee.

But our love it was stronger by far than the love
    Of those who were older than we—
    Of many far wiser than we—
And neither the angels in heaven above,
    Nor the demons down under the sea,
Can ever dissever my soul from the soul
    Of the beautiful Annabel Lee.

For the moon never beams, without bringing me dreams
    Of the beautiful Annabel Lee;
And the stars never rise, but I feel the bright eyes
    Of the beautiful Annabel Lee.
And so, all the night-tide, I lie down by the side
Of my darling—my darling—my life and my bride,
    In the sepulchre there by the sea—
    In her tomb by the sounding sea.'

After the death of his wife, Poe's necessities were relieved by the contributions of friends, and the faithful services of his mother-in-law. If there is anything in the sad tale of his life worthy of lasting remembrance, it is the conduct of this devoted woman, of whom Mr Willis has given the following account:—

'Our first knowledge of Mr Poe's removal to this city, was by a call which we received from a lady, who introduced herself to us as the mother of his wife. She was in search of employment for him; and she excused her errand by mentioning that he was ill, that her daughter was a confirmed invalid, and that their circumstances were such as compelled her taking it upon herself. The countenance of this lady, made beautiful and saintly with an evidently complete giving up of her life to privation and sorrowful tenderness, her gentle and mournful voice urging its plea, her long-forgotten but habitually and unconsciously refined manners, and her appealing and yet appreciative mention of the claims and abilities of her son, disclosed at once the presence of one of those angels upon earth that women in adversity can be. It was a hard fate that she was watching over. Mr Poe wrote with fastidious difficulty, and in a style too much above the popular level to be well paid. He was always in pecuniary difficulty, and, with his sick wife, frequently in want of the merest necessaries of life. Winter after winter, for years, the most touching sight to us, in this whole city, has been that tireless minister to genius, thinly and insufficiently clad, going from office to office with a poem, or an article on some literary subject, to sell—sometimes simply pleading in a broken voice that he was ill, and begging for him—mentioning nothing but that "he was ill"—whatever might be the reason for his writing nothing—and never, amid all her tears and recitals of distress, suffering one syllable to escape her lips that could convey a doubt of him, or a complaint, or a lessening of pride in his genius and good intentions. Her daughter died, a year and a half since, but she did not desert him. She continued his ministering angel—living with him—caring for him—guarding him against exposure; and, when he was carried away by temptation, amid grief and the loneliness of feelings unreplied to, and awoke from his self-abandonment prostrated in destitution and suffering, *begging* for him still. If woman's devotion, born with a first love, and fed with human passion, hallow its object, as it is allowed to do, what does not a devotion like this—pure, disinterested, and holy as the watch of an invisible spirit—say for him who inspired it?'

In 1848, Poe advertised his intention of delivering a course of lectures, in order to raise funds for the establishment of a monthly magazine. The first of these lectures was upon cosmogony, and embraced a new theory of the universe. It was read by the author at the Society Library in New York, and afterwards was published under the title of *Eureka, a Prose Poem.* Of this singular production, we can say nothing more than that it was professedly based upon intuitions—or 'dreams,' as Poe says in the preface—and had no connection with the sober inductive method of research.

The next paragraph in this sad biography seems so improbable, that we write it without a full belief in its reality, though it is indorsed by Mr Griswold. It is said that, soon after the delivery of his first lecture, Poe accidentally became acquainted with one of the most beautiful and accomplished women in New England, and that arrangements were made for their marriage. A friend congratulated Poe on his prospect of happiness; but the sequel seems as strange as the fact, that a virtuous and intelligent lady should have consented to a union with a hopeless drunkard. Poe, in reply to the congratulation, said: 'Mark me! I shall not marry her;' and his mode of breaking the engagement is described as brutal in the extreme. It is said that he deliberately left New York, and, on the evening of the day before that appointed for the wedding, was seen drunken in the streets of the city where the lady resided; that in this condition he went to her house, and there exhibited such brutal conduct, that he was turned out by the police. All this is represented as having been done in a manner perfectly prepense, and without any provocation. A biographer says: 'Here was no insanity. Poe went from New York with a determination thus to induce an ending of the engagement, and he succeeded.' Of such a tale we can say only, that it appears very improbable, and that common charity suggests that some points may have been added by the writer for the sake of effect; for if true in its description of the prepense nature of the outrage, it places Edgar Allan Poe, the man, whatever we may think of the poet, beyond the bounds of our sympathies.

After this, we are told that Poe joined the temperance society in Richmond; that his conduct shewed the earnestness of his endeavour to reform his life; and that he commenced a series of lectures, which he intended to deliver in several towns. This sudden, but, alas! short reformation, effected by the simple pledge of abstinence from alcoholic stimulus, may accord with that theory of Poe's irregularities which has been given in the letter of a friend; but we cannot see how it accords with the character of deliberate baseness above described. However, he lectured in the principal towns of Virginia in 1849; and in this year renewed his acquaintance with a lady whom he had known in his youth, and engaged to marry her. He wrote to friends letters describing his new hopes, and speaking of a future residence among scenes endeared by pleasant recollections. In October of the same year, when on his way to Philadelphia and New York, he arrived at Baltimore, and while his luggage was being carried to the train, he went into a tavern to take refreshment. Here he found some old companions, who invited him to drink. He drained the fatal cup. It does not appear that he stayed long in the tavern, or with his drinking-companions. In a few hours, he was found in the street; and, in a state of insanity, was carried to the hospital. A violent fever followed; and on the evening of Sunday, October 7, 1849, Edgar Allan Poe died, at the early age of thirty-eight.

The poetry written by Poe is almost destitute of moral characteristics, either good or bad; certainly, it is free from all objectionable features. A love of beauty and melody is the most remarkable trait in his verses; and his singular and well-known poem entitled *The Raven*, is generally allowed to be one of the most remarkable examples of a harmony of sentiment with rhythmical expression to be found in any language. While the poet sits musing in his study, and endeavours to win from books 'surcease of sorrow for the lost Lenore,' a raven—the symbol of despair—enters the room, and perches upon a bust of Pallas. A colloquy follows between the poet and the bird of ill-omen with its haunting croak of 'never more.' Though the poem is so well known, it must be once more quoted, as it is, without doubt, the best specimen of Poe's lyrical power:—

THE RAVEN.

'Once upon a midnight dreary, while I pondered, weak and weary,
Over many a quaint and curious volume of forgotten lore—
While I nodded, nearly napping, suddenly there came a tapping,
As of some one gently rapping, rapping at my chamber-door;
"'Tis some visitor," I muttered, "tapping at my chamber-door—
Only this, and nothing more."

Ah! distinctly I remember it was in the bleak December,
And each separate dying ember wrought its ghost upon the floor.
Eagerly I wished the morrow; vainly I had sought to borrow
From my books surcease of sorrow—sorrow for the lost Lenore—
For the rare and radiant maiden whom the angels name Lenore—
Nameless here for evermore.

And the silken sad uncertain rustling of each purple curtain
Thrilled me—filled me with fantastic terrors never felt before;
So that now, to still the beating of my heart, I stood repeating:
"'Tis some visitor entreating entrance at my chamber-door—
Some late visitor entreating entrance at my chamber-door:
This it is, and nothing more."

Presently my soul grew stronger; hesitating then no longer,
"Sir," said I, "or madam, truly your forgiveness I implore;
But the fact is I was napping, and so gently you came rapping,
And so faintly you came tapping, tapping at my chamber-door,
That I scarce was sure I heard you"—here I opened wide the door——
Darkness there, and nothing more.

Deep into that darkness peering, long I stood there wondering, fearing,
Doubting, dreaming dreams no mortals ever dared to dream before;
But the silence was unbroken, and the stillness gave no token,
And the only word there spoken was the whispered word, "Lenore!"
This I whispered, and an echo murmured back the word, "Lenore!"—
Merely this, and nothing more.

Back into the chamber turning, all my soul within me burning,
Soon again I heard a tapping something louder than before.
"Surely," said I—"surely that is something at my window lattice;
Let me see, then, what thereat is, and this mystery explore—
Let my heart be still a moment, and this mystery explore.
'Tis the wind, and nothing more."

Open here I flung the shutter, when, with many a flirt and
flutter,
In there stepped a stately Raven of the saintly days of yore.
Not the least obeisance made he; not a minute stopped or
stayed he;
But, with mien of lord or lady, perched above my chamber-door—
Perched upon a bust of Pallas, just above my chamber-door—
Perched and sat, and nothing more.

Then this ebony bird beguiling my sad fancy into smiling,
By the grave and stern decorum of the countenance it wore,
"Though thy crest be shorn and shaven, thou," I said, "art sure
no craven,
Ghastly, grim, and ancient Raven, wandering from the nightly
shore—
Tell me what thy lordly name is on the night's Plutonian shore!"
Quoth the Raven, "Nevermore."

Much I marvelled this ungainly fowl to hear discourse so
plainly,
Though its answer little meaning—little relevancy bore;
For we cannot help agreeing that no living human being
Ever yet was blessed with seeing bird above his chamber-door—
Bird or beast upon the sculptured bust above his chamber-door,
With such name as "Nevermore."

But the Raven, sitting lonely on that placid bust, spoke only
That one word, as if his soul in that one word he did outpour.
Nothing further then he uttered; not a feather then he fluttered—
Till I scarcely more than muttered: "Other friends have flown
before—
On the morrow *he* will leave me, as my hopes have flown before."
Then the bird said: "Never more."

Startled at the stillness broken by reply so aptly spoken,
"Doubtless," said I, "what it utters is its only stock and store,
Caught from some unhappy master, whom unmerciful disaster
Followed fast and followed faster, till his songs one burden bore—
Till the dirges of his hope that melancholy burden bore,
Of 'Never—never more.'"

But the Raven still beguiling all my sad soul into smiling,
Straight I wheeled a cushioned seat in front of bird and bust and
door;
Then upon the velvet sinking, I betook myself to linking
Fancy unto fancy, thinking what this ominous bird of yore—
What this grim, ungainly, ghastly, gaunt, and ominous bird of
yore
Meant in croaking "Never more."

This I sat engaged in guessing, but no syllable expressing
To the fowl whose fiery eyes now burned into my bosom's core;
This and more I sat divining, with my head at ease reclining
On the cushion's velvet lining that the lamp-light gloated o'er,
But whose velvet violet lining with the lamp-light gloating o'er
She shall press, ah, never more!

Then, methought, the air grew denser, perfumed from an unseen censer
Swung by seraphim, whose footfalls tinkled on the tufted floor.
"Wretch!" I cried, "thy god hath lent thee—by these angels he hath sent thee
Respite—respite and nepenthe from thy memories of Lenore!
Quaff, O quaff, this kind nepenthe, and forget this lost Lenore!"
Quoth the Raven: "Never more!"

"Prophet!" said I, "thing of evil!—prophet still, if bird or devil!
Whether tempter sent, or whether tempest tossed thee here ashore,
Desolate, yet all undaunted, on this desert land enchanted—
On this home by horror haunted—tell me truly, I implore—
Is there—*is* there balm in Gilead?—tell me—tell me, I implore!"
Quoth the Raven: "Never more."

"Prophet!" said I, "thing of evil—prophet still, if bird or devil!
By that heaven that bends above us—by that God we both adore,
Tell this soul, with sorrow laden, if within the distant Aiden,
It shall clasp a sainted maiden, whom the angels name Lenore—
Clasp a rare and radiant maiden, whom the angels name Lenore?"
Quoth the Raven: "Never more."

"Be that word our sign of parting, bird or fiend!" I shrieked, upstarting—
"Get thee back into the tempest and the night's Plutonian shore!
Leave no black plume as a token of that lie thy soul hath spoken!
Leave my loneliness unbroken!—quit the bust above my door!
Take thy beak from out my heart, and take thy form from off my door!"
Quoth the Raven: "Never more."

And the Raven, never flitting, still is sitting, still is sitting,
On the pallid bust of Pallas, just above my chamber-door;
And his eyes have all the seeming of a demon's that is dreaming,
And the lamp-light o'er him streaming, throws his shadow on the floor;
And my soul from out that shadow that lies floating on the floor,
Shall be lifted—never more!'

JAMES RUSSELL LOWELL, one of the most versatile of the younger poets of America, is the son of a clergyman of Boston, and was born in 1819. After leaving Harvard College, where he graduated in 1839, he commenced the study of law, but was soon led aside by the attractions of imaginative literature.

In early life, he joined the anti-slavery movement, and his poems have always been characterised, more or less, by a didactic and philanthropic purport. This, in many instances, becomes a fault. The doctrine which might be suitably given in an essay, is out of place, as we conceive, in a poem that seems intended to be lyrical. Poetry, though united with the interests of real life and the progress of society, should maintain its own character, and ever remain distinct from dry argument and mere declamation.

In his *Fable for the Critics*, the author seems to be fully conscious of his errors, for he says of himself—

'There is Lowell, who's striving Parnassus to climb
With a whole bale of *isms* tied together with rhyme:
* * *
The top of the hill he will ne'er come nigh reaching
Till he learns the distinction 'twixt singing and preaching.'

The 'preaching' is indeed very tiresome in numerous examples; especially when both text and sermon are equally vague and mystical.

After contributing both prose and verse to periodicals, Lowell published, in 1841, a volume of poems entitled *A Year's Life*, which contained evidence that the writer had studied the diction of our old English poets, and had, perhaps unconsciously, imitated Tennyson, as may be clearly seen in the lines entitled *The Syrens* compared with the *Lotos-eaters*. It is the tone, rather than the imagery of the poem, that betrays imitation. Redundancy of words, and uncouth combinations, such as 'rapture-quivered,' are the chief faults in the volume, which contains, however, some specimens of genuine poetry, and gives proofs that the writer possesses warm feelings and power of imagination.

In 1844, another volume of poems proved that the writer had made considerable progress in energy of thought and command of language; but the didactic tendency was made too prominent, and, in his lines entitled *L'Envoi*, the author attempted to justify his use of poetry for the advocacy of various reforms in society and government. He alludes to the common-place argument of certain critics who have supposed that America must produce a great poet because Niagara is a great water-fall:—

'They tell us that our land was made for song.'

But he maintains that the true purpose of modern poetry should be, not to celebrate the grandeur and beauty of lakes, rivers, cataracts, forests, and prairies, but to assert—

> 'The freedom and divinity of man,
> The glorious claims of human brotherhood.
> * * *
> These are realities which make the shows
> Of outward Nature, be they ne'er so grand,
> Seem small and worthless and contemptible.'

It is very true that the imaginative writer should do something more than describe woods and rivers; it is also true that he should, in his own proper style, inculcate truth and good sentiments; but a great mistake is often found very near the truth. It must be a confused notion of the mission of poetry that has led Lowell to write such lines as these—

> 'He who settles Freedom's principles,
> Writes the death-warrant of all tyranny;
> Who speaks the truth, stabs falsehood to the heart,
> And his mere word makes despots tremble more
> Than ever Brutus with his dagger could.'

This reads like a versified extract from a third-rate speech in Congress. However great the evils of society may be, it still remains true, that every department of literature should have its own distinct character, and verse should not be used for work that may be better done in prose.

These remarks must be applied to the so-called reform-poetry, but by no means to all the verses of Lowell. As we have said, he is a versatile writer, and his poems include descriptive, narrative, lyrical, humorous, and satirical, as well as didactic specimens. In the descriptive poems—such as an *Indian Summer's Reverie*—there is a considerable wealth of imagery; but it is not always distinctly arranged. The finest images are often spoiled by false associations.

In the tale of *Rhœcus*, founded on Greek mythology, the poetical part is injured by its connection with a long moral application. *Prometheus*, another of the more important poems, has a noble design, but suffers under a load of prolixity. The warmest admirers of Lowell's poems must admit, that even the best want that conciseness which finished study might have attained.

Lowell has read and admired the best sonnets and other short poems of Wordsworth, and must have noticed the examples of rich thoughtfulness compressed in single lines; or of long descriptions superseded by a few golden words. How were such effects produced? Not by rapid writing; but during many long meditations in the little garden which served as the poet's study, where he finished the composition of his verses before committing them to writing. His dislike of this last process, increased by his pens, which were 'always bad,' and his penmanship 'vile at best'—as he said—was probably the cause of many happy thoughts ascribed to sudden inspiration. Of his own 'workmanship' in poetry—that was his term—he said: 'It is rarely that I can at all please myself without much more retouching than I could recommend to a young author.'

The following quotation is an example of Lowell's quiet and pathetic mood:—

ON THE DEATH OF A CHILD.

'How peacefully they rest,
Crossfolded there
Upon his little breast,
Those small, white hands, that ne'er were still before,
But ever sported with his mother's hair,
Or the plain cross that on her breast she wore!
Her heart no more will beat
To feel the touch of that soft palm,
That ever seemed a new surprise,
Sending glad thoughts up to her eyes
To bless him with their holy calm—
Sweet thoughts! they made her eyes as sweet.

How quiet are the hands
That wove those pleasant bands!
But that they do not rise and sink
With his calm breathing, I should think
That he were dropped asleep:
Alas! too deep, too deep
Is this his slumber!
Time scarce can number
The years ere he will wake agen—
O may we see his eyelids open then!
O stern word—nevermore!
* * *

He did but float a little way
Adown the stream of time,
With dreamy eyes watching the ripples' play,
Or listening to their fairy chime;
His slender sail
Ne'er felt the gale;
He did but float a little way,
And putting to the shore,
While yet 'twas early day,
Went calmly on his way,
To dwell with us no more!
* * *

Full short his journey was; no dust
  Of earth unto his sandals clave;
The weary weight that old men must,
  He bore not to the grave.
He seemed a cherub who had lost his way,
And wandered hither; so his stay
With us was short, and 'twas most meet
That he should be no delver in earth's clod,
Nor need to pause and cleanse his feet
    To stand before his God:
    O blest word—evermore!'

The *Fable for the Critics* is a clever satire, and contains several lively sketches (in some instances, caricatures) of American authors of the present day—Emerson, Neal, Willis, Bryant, Hawthorne, and others. Generally, the sketches are given in good-humour; but the full-length portrait of a pedant, well known at Cambridge, and the caricature entitled 'Miranda,' intended for an American authoress, have sufficient bitterness. In the latter example, we dissent from the writer's opinion, that such severity was justified by the want of good taste in the lady. It is said by a critic, 'that if a woman chooses to enter the arena, and join in the athletic sports of men, she should not object to being roughly handled.' This misrepresents the case by a rather coarse comparison. A women may enter the 'arena' of literature, and may there advocate some objectionable opinions; but these may be corrected without extreme severity.

The satire on 'the heavy reviewer' is fair enough. We trust that the author has a due respect for the hard and thankless toil of sincere and careful criticism; but he knows well that criticism and reviewing are not always identical.

SKETCH OF A HEAVY REVIEWER.

''Twould be endless to tell you the things that he knew,
All separate facts, undeniably true,
But with him, or each other, they 'd nothing to do:
No power of combining, arranging, discerning,
Digested the masses he learned into learning.
There was one thing in life he had practical knowledge for
(And this, you will think, he need scarce go to college for),
Not a deed would he do, nor a word would he utter,
Till he 'd weighed its relations to plain bread and butter.
When he left Alma Mater, he practised his wits
In compiling the journals' historical bits—
Of shops broken open, men falling in fits,
Great fortunes in England bequeathed to poor printers,
And cold spells, the coldest for many past winters—

Then, rising by industry, knack, and address,
Got notices up for an unbiassed press,
With a mind so well poised, it seemed equally made for
Applause or abuse, just which chanced to be paid for;
From this point his progress was rapid and sure,
To the post of a regular heavy reviewer.

And here I must say, he wrote excellent articles
On the Hebraic points, or the force of Greek particles;
They filled up the space nothing else was prepared for,
And nobody read that which nobody cared for.
If any old book reached a fiftieth edition,
He could fill forty pages with safe erudition;
He could gauge the old books by the old set of rules,
And his very old nothings pleased very old fools;
But give him a new book, fresh out of the heart,
And you put him at sea without compass or chart—
His blunders aspired to the rank of an art;
For his lore was ingraft, something foreign that grew in him,
Exhausting the sap of the native and true in him,
So that when a man came with a soul that was new in him,
Carving new forms of truth out of Nature's old granite
New and old at their birth, like Le Verrier's planet—

* * * *

Our reviewer would crawl all about it and round it,
And, reporting each circumstance just as he found it,
Without the least malice—his record would be
Profoundly æsthetic as that of a flea,
Which, supping on Wordsworth, should print, for our sakes,
Recollections of nights with the Bard of the Lakes,
Or, borne by an Arab guide, ventured to render a
General view of the ruins at Denderah.'

The versatility of Lowell has already beguiled us into a rather lengthy notice of his poems; but we have still another phase of his literary character to notice. He can descend from the style of his serious reformatory poetry to popular satire in the Yankee dialect. Of his merits in this department, we are not competent to pronounce an opinion, and must therefore quote from an American review.[1] Speaking of the *Biglow Papers*, a critic says: 'This is an unmistakably American performance. Whether the foreign reader could fully enjoy it, we know not; but whoever knows anything of New England rustic-life, will find in it food for laughter on every page. The book is also a valuable

[1] In Putnam's *Monthly*, No. 5.

repository of the dialectic peculiarities of New England, and worth resorting to, to discover its tone of thought and mode of viewing political affairs, such as the Mexican war and slavery. . . . . Lowell's Yankee humour is genuine, and does not depend for its success upon mere slang and misspelling, which is all that there is to recommend the works of some adventurers in this department. It is at times broad, almost farcical—and again delicate and penetrating, and in either case irresistible.'

We suppose this to be an impartial judgment, and, as our object is not to reduce American literature within the limits of our own taste, but to exhibit fairly its various features, we offer no apology for our notice of the *Biglow Papers*.

They consist chiefly of a series of satirical pieces in verse, written in the Yankee dialect, and commenting on political topics, especially the Mexican war and slavery. These poems, supposed to be written by a rustic Yankee named Hosea Biglow, 'a cross between Apollo and Sam Slick,' are edited, with annotations and a tedious commentary, by the Rev. Homer Wilbur—a fictitious character of the Dryasdust school. He appends a useful Yankee glossary, and gives a few rules for reading the rustic dialect of New England. We read, that 'the genuine Yankee' avoids, as far as possible, the rough sound of *r*, and seldom sounds a final *g;* omits the aspirate in *while* and *when*, prefixes *e* to the diphthong *ou*, and reduces *au* in *daughter* to *ah*. In regard to the first vowel, he sometimes gives it a close obscure sound—as *hev* for *have;* and, in other instances, uses the broad sound it has in *fâther*—as in saying *hânsome* for *handsome.* A drawl, *ad libitum*, must be added to these peculiarities. By attention to these rules, we are enabled to read, with proper effect, the effusions of the earnest Hosea Biglow. The first is a rhymed protest against the Mexican war and a dissuasion against enlisting. Next comes a letter from a raw youth, named 'Birdofredum Sawin,' who describes the miseries of the first campaign. After other political satires, not well understood out of America, we find a debate in the senate put into 'nursery rhymes.' Calhoun is the chief speaker:—

'"Gen'nle Cass, sir, you needn't be twitchin' your collar;
Your merit 's quite clear by the dut on your knees;
At the North, we don't make no distinctions o' colour;
You can all take a lick at our shoes wen you please,"
Sez John C. Calhoun, sez he;—
Sez Mister Jarnagin,
"They wunt hev to larn agin,
They all on 'em know the old toon," sez he.

"The slavery question aint no ways bewilderin'.
North an' South hev one int'rest, it's plain to a glance;
No'thern men, like us patriarchs, don't sell their childrin,
But they *du* sell themselves, ef they git a good chance,"
Sez John C. Calhoun, sez he;—
Sez Atherton here,
"This is gittin' severe;
I wish I could dive like a loon," sez he.'

The 'Pious Editor's Creed' embraces several odd articles, such as—

'I don't believe in princerple,
But, O, I *du* in interest.

* * *

I du believe the people want
A tax on teas an' coffees,
Thet nothin' aint extravygunt—
Purvidin' I'm in office;
Fer I hev loved my country sence
My eye-teeth filled their sockets,
An' Uncle Sam I reverence,
Partic'larly his pockets.

* * *

I du believe with all my soul
In the gret Press's freedom,
To pint the people to the goal
An' in the traces lead 'em;
Palsied the arm thet forges yokes
At my fat contracts squintin',
An' withered be the nose thet pokes
Inter the gov'ment printin'!

I du believe thet I should give
Wut's his'n unto Cæsar,
Fer it's by him I move an' live,
Frum him my bread an' cheese air;
I du believe thet all o' me
Doth bear his souperscription—
Will, conscience, honour, honesty,
An' things o' thet description.'

The candidate for the presidency is as unceremoniously treated as the editor. When required 'to define his position,' he makes a profession of eclecticism, vulgarly styled trimming, and otherwise described as 'sitting on the fence.' The satire here may be more freely quoted; for while the topics are American, the treatment has a general interest—

'Ez fer the war, I go agin it—
  I mean to say I kind o' du—
Thet is, I mean thet, bein' in it,
  The best way wuz to fight it thru;
Not but wut abstract war is horrid,
  I sign to thet with all my heart—
But civlyzation *doos* git forrid
  Sometimes upon a powder-cart.
* * *
Ez to the slaves, there's no confusion
  In *my* idees consarnin' them—
I think they air an Institution,
  A sort of—yes, jest so—ahem:
Do *I* own any? Of my merit
  On thet pint you yourself may jedge;
All is, I never drink no sperit,
  Nor I haint never signed no pledge.'

Two letters from the volunteer, Birdofredum Sawin, whose morals have not been improved by the campaign, conclude the series of political verses. The appended burlesque 'notices of the press,' or fictitious extracts from reviews, are as amusing as the verses, and fairly satirise the off-hand, careless style of many newspapers.

Several names of recent writers have been omitted in our review. To describe fairly the relative merits of young authors who are still at the bar of public opinion, would be a difficult and unpleasant task. We cannot make our own opinions a basis of criticism, and we should vainly seek assistance in the pages of many reviews. After all that has been written as criticism on recent poetry, there is a want of definition and clearness. The simple dictum of Edgar Poe—that every poem should be short enough to be read in 'a single sitting'—seems as valuable as many of the rules laid down by the critics. With this apology for brevity, we may introduce the names of the younger American poets—Street, Taylor, Saxe, Boker, Stoddart, and Buchanan Read—reminding the reader that we leave the respective merits of these writers among the numerous open questions of literature.

Alfred B. Street, a lawyer, lately residing at Albany, has published descriptive poems which have passed through several editions, and have been highly commended for their graphic power. With reference to the selection of epithets, one American critic compares Street with Bryant; while another says: 'In a foreign land, his poems would transport us at once to home.' In *Frontenac*, a tale of the Iroquois, the author has added a narrative interest to his descriptive passages, of which several are clearly written with picturesque effect. The frequent recurrence of favourite epithets is justly censured by a reviewer; and the criticism may be quoted here, for this iteration is too common among young poets, and sometimes prevails as an epidemic among magazine-writers. For example, the reviewer who first happily applied the epithet 'weird' to Hawthorne's tales, must be tired of it when he finds it copied in almost every review of this author. In Street's poems, says the critic, 'it is amazing how many things *slant*. Light slants, spears slant, trees slant, brinks are "tree-slanted," banks slant, squirrels slant—all nature slants. A great many more things "shimmer" than ought to do so.'

BAYARD TAYLOR, who has written in prose lively sketches of travel in the East, is the author of *Poems of the Orient*, and various lyrical pieces. Of these, and the several poetical works by SAXE, BOKER, and STODDART, a friendly critic remarks generally, that their faults are the results of excess, not of deficiency of poetical fancy.

A short notice of the poems of THOMAS BUCHANAN READ may serve to explain our remark on the uncertainty of recent reputations. In several reviews—American and English—these poems—rather slight in texture, and consisting mostly of sentiments and descriptions given in a lyrical form—have been highly praised. It has been asserted that Read, as a poet, is superior to Bryant and Longfellow, and that one of his poems—*The Closing Scene*—is 'equal to Gray's *Elegy in a Country Churchyard*.' We have not found these eulogies warranted by a perusal of the poems; though we agree with a critic who describes the author as one 'endowed with poetic sensibility and an instinctive elegance of expression.' *The Closing Scene*, so highly commended, consists chiefly of a delineation of late autumnal scenery, and has a well-sustained tone of pensiveness.

LYDIA H. SIGOURNEY—MARIA BROOKS—HANNAH F. GOULD—SARAH J. HALE —LUCRETIA AND MARGARET DAVIDSON—FRANCES S. OSGOOD, AND OTHER WRITERS.

The poetry written by Mrs Sigourney may be noticed, not only on account of its own merits, but as representative of the general characteristics of many other productions of the same class. A reference to the number of names included in the several collections of poems by American ladies, will be sufficient to prove that our only way of treating such a profusion of materials, is to select a few fair specimens.

LYDIA HUNTLEY SIGOURNEY—a native of Norwich, in Connecticut, appeared in early life as a writer of verse characterised by feminine delicacy and religious sentiment. Her first volume of poems, published in 1815, was followed in 1822 by *Traits of the Aborigines of America;* and other poems have appeared from time to time, of which the best have been collected in a recent edition. With regard to the prevalent qualities of the poems by Mrs Sigourney—their didactic purport, tender feeling, and pious tone—they may be described as fairly representing the productions of several other American ladies, who have written poems which we cannot here notice in detail. In pathos, the authoress of *The Dying Infant*, *The Emigrant Mother*, *To-morrow*, and other poems of the same character, has few rivals among her sister-poets. Her verses are evidently the unfeigned expressions of an amiable and pious character; and it is an unwelcome task to examine strictly their value as proofs of inventive genius. An American Reviewer has fairly pointed out their defects; and we may quote his remarks, because they are applicable to so many poems of the same class.[1]

Having noticed several narrative pieces, the critic says:—'Though names are used, and persons indicated, there is really nothing there but qualities. The purest types of the affections are grasped in all their firmness and delicacy; but there is no combination of them with those other human elements which, in their union, produce character. The consequence is, that we have no representations of the affections as modified by sex, age, nation, position, or character. With remarkable distinctness of conception, and decision of expression, we have presented to us the type, but it is given in its simple unity, abstracted from all individuality. We assert confidently, that in this volume there is

[1] *North American Review*, No. 143.

not displayed one trait of character but that of the author herself. The little poems of *Harold and Tosti*, and *Bernardine du Born*, fine as they are in sentiment, have nothing but the incidents on which they are founded to entitle them to their names. . . . . But this peculiarity of bringing out a quality at the expense of all character, which we have indicated as a limitation of Mrs Sigourney's genius, is probably a chief source of her influence over the hearts of her readers. She is thus enabled to stamp a deep impression of one affection, at least, on the mind; and by detaching it from the other elements of character, by making a person stand simply for an emotion, she has completely mastered one prominent source of the pathetic. As an illustration of her power in this respect, and of her excellences in many respects, we will quote the following striking poem:—

THE EMIGRANT MOTHER.

'From my own native clime, I took my way
Across the foaming deep. My husband slept
In his new grave, and poverty had stripped
Our lonely cottage. Letters o'er the wave,
From brother and from sister, bade me come
To this New World, where there is bread for all.
So, with my heavy, widowed heart I went,
My only babe and I.
Coarse, curious eyes
Looked searchingly upon me, as I sat
In the thronged steerage, with my sick, sick soul.
But at each jeering word, I bowed my head
Down o'er my helpless child, and was content,
For he was all my world.
Storms rocked the bark,
And haggard fear sprang up, with oaths and cries,
Yet wondrous courage nerved me; for to die
With that fair, loving creature in my arms,
Seemed more than life without him. If a shade
Of weariness or trouble marked my brow,
He looked upon me with his father's eyes,
And I was comforted.
But sickness came,
Close air, and scanty food. Darkly they pressed
On feeble infancy, and oft I heard,
As mournful twilight settled o'er the sea,
The frequent plunge, and the wild mother's shriek,
When her lost darling to the depths went down.
Then came the terror. To my heaving breast
I closer clasped the child, and all my strength
Went forth in one continued sigh to God.

Scarcely I slept, lest the dire pestilence
Should smite him unawares. E'en when he lay
In peaceful dreams, the smile upon his cheek,
I trembled, lest the dark-winged angel breathed
Insidious whispers, luring him away.

It came at last. That dreadful sickness came,
The fever—short and mortal. Midnight's pall
Spread o'er the waters, when his last faint breath
Moistened my cheek. Deep in my breaking heart
I shut the mother's cry.
One mighty fear
Absorbed me—lest his cherished form should feed
The dire sea-monsters, nor beneath the sods
Of the green, quiet, blessed earth, await
The resurrection.
So, I shuddering pressed
The body closer, though its deadly cold
Froze through my soul.
To those around, I said:
"Disturb him not—he sleepeth." Then I sang
And rocked him tenderly, as though he woke
In fretfulness, or felt the sting of pain.
My poor, dead baby! Terrible to me
Such falsehood seemed. But yet the appalling dread
Lest the fierce, scaly monsters of the sea
Should wind around him with their gorging jaws,
O'ermastered me.
Nights fled, and mornings dawned;
And still my chill arms clasped immovably
The shrivelling form. They told me he was dead,
And bade me give my beautiful to them,
For burial in the deep. With outstretched hands,
They stood demanding him, until the light
Fled from my swimming eyes.
But when I woke
From the long trance, that icy burden lay
No longer on my bosom. Pitying words
The captain spake: "Look at yon little boat
Lashed to our stern. There, in his coffin, rests
The body of thy son. If in three days
We reach the land, he shall be buried there
As thou desirest."
There, from breaking morn,
My eyes were fixed; and when the darkness came,
By the red binnacle's uncertain light
I watched that floating speck amid the waves,
And prayed for land.

As thus I kept my watch,
Like desolate Rizpah, mournful visions came
Of my forsaken cottage; while the spring
Of gushing crystal, where 'neath bowering trees
We drew our water, gurgled in my ear
To mock me with its memories of joy.
My throat was dry with anguish, and when voice
Failed me to pray for land, I lifted up
That silent, naked thought, which finds the Throne
Sooner than pomp of words.
With fiery face
And eager foot, the third dread morning rose
Out of the misty deep, and coldly rang
The death-knell of my hope.
As o'er the stern
I gazed with dim eye on the flashing brine,
Methought its depths were opened, and I saw
Creatures most vile, that o'er the bottom crept,
Lizards and slimy serpents, hideous forms
And shapes, for which man's language hath no name;
While to the surface rose the monster shark,
Intent to seize his prey.
Convulsive shrieks,
Long pent within my bleeding heart, burst forth;
But from the watcher at the mast there came
A shout of "*Land!*" and on the horizon's edge
Gleamed a faint streak, like the white seraph's wing.
Oh, blessed land! We neared it, and my breath
Was one continued gasp—"*Oh, blessed land!*"

A boat was launched. With flashing oar it reached
A lonely isle. Bent o'er the vessel's side,
I saw them dig a narrow grave, and lay
In the cool bosom of the quiet earth
The little body that was mine no more.
Nor wept I; for an angel said to me:
"God's will! God's will! and thy requited prayer
Remember!"
To my hand a scroll they brought,
Bearing the name of that deserted strand,
And record of the day in which they laid
My treasure there. They might have spared that toil:
A mother's unforgetful love needs not
Record or date.
The ship held on her course
To greener shores. There came an exile's pain,
Beneath a foreign sky.
Yet 'twere a sin
To mourn with bitterness the boy whose smile

Cheers me no more, since the sea had him not,
Nor the sea-monsters.
Endless praise to Him,
Who did not scorn the poor, weak woman's sigh
Of desolate wo.
No monument is thine,
O babe! that 'neath yon sterile sands dost sleep,
Save the strong sculpture in a mother's heart;
And by those traces will she know thee well
When the graves open, and before God's throne
Both small and great are gathered.'

The poetry written by MARIA BROOKS must be noticed on account of the very high commendation bestowed upon one of her works by Dr Southey. The title of this poem is *Zophïël, or the Bride of Seven.* It was published in London in 1833, and in the following year was reprinted in Boston, United States, where it failed to attract notice. The story of the love of an angel for a mortal maiden resembles that of Byron's well-known poem; but the treatment is original. We find in *Zophïël* nothing to warrant the eulogium by Southey, who described it as the most original poem of its time, and spoke of Mrs Brooks as 'the most original and impassioned of all poetesses.' Her style is sometimes terse and expressive, but frequently harsh and disfigured by inversions of the natural order of words.

HANNAH F. GOULD is the author of numerous occasional poems which have enjoyed a considerable popularity. A lively treatment of familiar topics has recommended many of her short pieces of playful verse—such as *The Pebble and the Acorn,* and *Jack Frost.* Mrs HALE, who has written several works in prose, is the author of didactic poems of good purport and more than ordinary merit. Mrs GILMAN, chiefly known by her prose-writings, has written several lyrical poems, recommended for their grace and sprightliness, and sometimes illustrating passages in the early history of America.

Our limited space compels us to pass briefly over the names of several writers—Amelia Welby, the Misses Fuller, Alice and Phœbe Carey, the sisters Mrs Warfield and Mrs Lee and Miss Sara J. Clarke—all resident in the western states. The poetry of these ladies displays refined sentiment and cultivated taste, though it may be deficient in the power requisite to command a permanent success in the crowded field of modern literature.

The fact that so many volumes of verse, such as would have made a reputation in former times, have been produced in a few recent years, is very creditable to the state of culture among the women of America; but we may question the wisdom of the attempt to give a permanent character to effusions of fancy and sentiment which, like many other lovely things, must have their day and pass away. We refer to the several collections of specimens of *The Female Poets of America*, respectively edited by Caroline May, Buchanan Read, and Rufus W. Griswold. Poets, like other writers, must yield to the circumstances of their times; and the fame of any individual must ultimately depend on the rarity of his talent or genius. As the power of writing pleasing verses becomes more and more a common accomplishment, the standard of criticism must be raised proportionately; and writers who, in other days, might have gained comparatively lasting reputations, must now be content with an occasional notice in the corner of a newspaper. However kind the disposition of the critic, he must adopt a Malthusian doctrine as the literary world becomes densely populated. These remarks must serve as an apology for our omission or brief notice of many names included in the host of poetesses enumerated by Mr Griswold.[1]

The poems by the two sisters LUCRETIA MARIA and MARGARET M. DAVIDSON have a peculiar interest, partly owing to the melancholy charm of their biographies, written by Miss Sedgwick and Washington Irving. In these two lives, we read the same story of a precocious development of mind, especially of the imaginative powers, followed by consumption and an early death. Lucretia, the elder sister, wrote, in her childhood, poems characterised by depth of feeling, with strong impulse and aspiration, and died at the age of seventeen. After her death, when Irving called at the home of the bereaved mother, he found that the same poetic genius and the same fatal tendencies of physical constitution, were rapidly developed in the younger sister Margaret. She had written poems when she was only eight years old, and, before her fourteenth year, had acquired a power in lyrical effusions resembling that displayed by her sister. Of his last interview with Margaret Davidson, her biographer writes:—'The interval that had elapsed had rapidly developed the powers of her mind, and heightened the loveliness of her person, but my apprehensions had been verified. The soul was wearing out the body. Preparations were making to take her on a tour for the benefit of her health, and her mother appeared to flatter herself that it might prove efficacious; but when I noticed the fragile delicacy of her form, the hectic bloom of her cheek, and the

[1] *The Female Poets of America.* By Rufus Wilmot Griswold. 1849.

almost unearthly lustre of her eye, I felt convinced that she was not long for this world; in truth, she already appeared more spiritual than mortal.' Margaret died in 1838, before she had reached the age of sixteen. Her biography leaves a warning against the stimulant mode of early education. Mental powers too highly cultivated in childhood, exhaust the resources of the physical system. The perfect flower is developed at the expense of a loss of vitality and hardihood in the plant; and so the wild-flower, with its scanty petals, lives and blooms by the waysides from one century to another, while the highly-cultivated variety has a delicacy as remarkable as its beauty. Scott had a good reason for his prayer, that none of his children might be endowed with poetic genius.

The *Sinless Child* and other poems, by Mrs OKES SMITH, have been described as possessing more than ordinary merit; and several pleasing specimens might be culled from the writings of Elizabeth Hall, Emma C. Embury, Mrs Ellett, Anna P. Dinnies, and Lucy Hooper. Some traits of individuality appear in the flowing versification of Mrs FRANCES S. OSGOOD, who, like other poetesses, endeavours to blend instruction with song. Here is a stanza from the poem entitled *Labour*:—

'"Labour is worship!"—the robin is singing;
"Labour is worship!"—the wild-bee is ringing;
Listen! that eloquent whisper, upspringing,
Speaks to thy soul from out nature's great heart.
From the dark cloud flows the life-giving shower;
From the rough sod blows the soft breathing flower;
From the small insect, the rich coral bower;
Only man, in the plan, shrinks from his part.'

The fact that elegant literature has been so widely cultivated by the women of America, must be regarded as a good feature in the progress of society. 'So far as their poetry has exercised any influence on practical life, it has had a tendency to refine taste and cultivate good sentiments.'

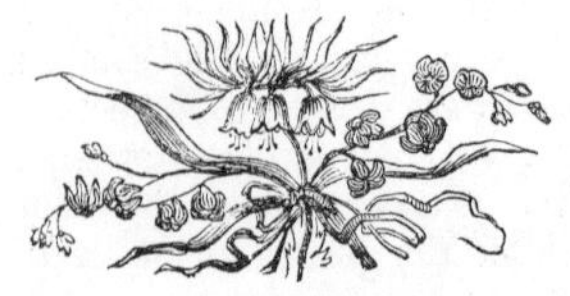

PROSE-FICTION.

ALLSTON—PAULDING—FLINT—DANA.

The wide circulation of English novels and romances—whether good or bad in moral tendency—has had an important influence on the literary taste, minor morals, and general culture of readers in the United States. The splendours of our fashionable novels have been more attractive than tales of true life in the backwoods; and too many young republicans have confessed their preference for aristocratic fictions, especially when some fraction of a dollar has sufficed as an introduction to all the solemnities described by Bulwer, Disraeli, Warren, Mrs Gore, and other novelists. While the rich and varied stores of fiction provided by the labour of British authors may be bought at a trifling outlay, the American writer of fiction comes before the public in a very disadvantageous position. He demands for his new and untried work some considerable remuneration, while his bookseller is offering the best of Scott's romances at the cost of a few cents. We have Washington Irving's own authority for the fact that, when he recommended to certain publishers the work of a young American writer, 'they even declined to publish it at the author's cost; alleging that it was not worth their while to trouble themselves about native works of doubtful success, while they could pick and choose among the successful works daily poured out by the British press, for the copyright of which they had nothing to pay.' On the moral effects of this unfair competition, an American writer offers the following remarks:[1]—

'Novels are the class of books which as yet we provide least for ourselves, and depend for most on the mother-country. They constitute a stock of reading of the utmost importance in its influence on the moral tastes and principles, and so on the political security of a nation. They are read very extensively; they are especial favourites of that period of life when the character is forming; and in the formation of character, their exciting addresses to the imagination and feelings give them an exceeding power. The hero or heroine of the fictitious tale is, to the young man or woman, for the time being, the perfection of humanity; and the condition of society, in which its gorgeous scenes are laid, presents itself as the *beau-idéal* of human life.

But the hero or heroine of the English tales we read, is an idea different from what can be realised in a republican state; and the

[1] *North American Review*, No. 116.

condition of society which, under such attractive representations, they depict, is one different from what we are to move in, and one, which for our patriotism's sake, as well as for the credit of our good judgment, we ought not to learn to love. It is unfortunate that the imaginations of our young people should be excited by it, even if the effect should be no worse than to make them look upon our far preferable institutions of republican equality and freedom, as comparatively a homely thing, and divert and abate in any degree the enthusiasm with which we ought to be trained to regard them. It is unfortunate that the merchant's daughter and the farmer's boy should get their heads too full of the Young Duke and May Dacre: there is real danger that, when such dreams are dreamed in every fifth or tenth house throughout the country, the affection with which our more venerable frame of society ought to be regarded, will be in some degree distracted and unsettled; and this would be a serious evil in a country where everything rests on the basis of opinion—where that patriotism, which is the life of our national being, looks to this only for its food. In our opinion, there is scarcely a better service of patriotism than is to be rendered by the multiplication of works in this department, in the tone of some of those in which the upright genius of Miss Sedgwick has kindled the sympathy of readers in the virtues that befit the American citizen, and awakened their veneration and love for that essential dignity and charm which every man and woman in this nation may aspire to wear. We do think, that whoever has been reading *Woodstock*, with a genuine surrender of himself to the artist's power, is in such peril of finding himself inoculated with the subtle virus of that man-worship, named *loyalty*, that he will do well presently to apply *Live and Let Live*, or some such generous febrifuge, to restore a republican sanity to his distempered blood. Works in this tone—the more abundant and more highly wrought the better—instructing the common mind of this nation to appreciate its privileges—forming it to discharge, and winning it to love, the duties of its position—will go further than any parchment Bill of Rights to perpetuate our political blessings. They must be written in America; they can be produced nowhere else. And when rulers come a little to a sense of their own duty, they will take care to provide some encouragement for the production of such works. If on every shelf in the American States, where now lies a copy of *Pelham*, we could substitute one of *Home*, or of *The Poor Rich Man and Rich Poor Man*, we hesitate not at all to say, that there would forthwith be a most substantial effect produced on the respectability of the national character, and the stability of the national institutions. Works of similar character, in much greater number—and for aught we know, of much higher order—there will be, when the grave and reverend guardians of the nation's welfare in Congress assembled, shall be disposed to attend to their duty in the premises. Readers cordially greet such works, but authors must live while they write them; and this they will have no security for doing, till legislatures shall have made that easy provision, which depends on them, for the encouragement of a literature instinct with the spirit of republican virtue.'

A clergyman, Dr Belknap, as we have remarked in our account of literature before the year 1800, made the first inroad on that prejudice against prose-fiction which had been cherished by the Puritans of New England and other colonies in early times. He was followed by Charles Brockden Brown (1771–1810), whose novels have been noticed. The increasing taste for fiction was gratified by the works, now almost forgotten, of Mrs Foster of Massachusetts, author of *The Boarding-school* and *The Coquette;* Mrs Rowson, who wrote, besides other tales, *Charlotte Temple*, a very popular novel in its day; and Royal Tyler (died in 1825), who wrote, besides some dramas, a successful romance, entitled *The Algerine Captive.*

WASHINGTON ALLSTON, the celebrated painter (1779-1843), must be numbered among the early writers of prose-fiction. He produced the tale of *Monaldi* in 1820, though it was not published until 1841. It was written for Mr Dana's periodical, *The Idle Man*, and was laid aside when that publication was discontinued. The style of the romance is good; but the interest depends rather on the metaphysical analysis of passion than on a well-developed story. It is too commonly supposed, that the great artist in music or painting must be deficient in general intellectual power and wide culture.

JAMES KIRKE PAULDING (born 1779) first appeared as an author in concert with Washington Irving, and wrote several of the papers in *Salmagundi*—a humorous and satirical miscellany, noticeable because its success had probably some influence in leading Irving away from law and commerce to a life devoted to literature. This periodical was brought to a close because the publisher, who found it very profitable, refused to give any share of his gains to the writers. Paulding, however, persevered in writing; and after giving to the public several minor pieces, produced in 1816 his *Diverting History of John Bull and Brother Jonathan*—an allegorical account of the quarrel between Great Britain and America. This was followed by *Letters from the South*, containing sketches of scenery and manners; and in the course of a few years, the industrious writer produced several other works, including a second series of *Salmagundi;* a poem entitled *The Backwoodsman; Koningsmarke*, a novel; *The Book of St Nicholas*, a series of tales said to be translated from the Dutch; and

The New Pilgrim's Progress, a humorous and satirical work. In 1831, *The Dutchman's Fireside*, commonly esteemed as the best of Paulding's novels, was published. Its scenes are laid in the district of New York, and its portraitures of the early settlers have been praised for their fidelity; but the humour of this and other tales by the same author, has not been so well appreciated in England as in America.

Westward Ho! the next novel by Paulding, has its scenery in Kentucky, and introduces several rather formidable humorists of the backwoods, especially an extravagant planter, who retreats into the forests, to escape from law and civilisation, or, as he says, 'to live independent, where there 's no law but gentlemen's law, and no niggers but black ones.' There are some pleasant traits and lively descriptions in these, as in other tales by Paulding; but the humour often descends to coarseness, and the treatment of the story is commonly rambling and without unity.

It cannot be denied that the numerous writings of this author have national characteristics and contain many graphic sketches; but their value is lessened by a want of good taste and artistic treatment. In *The Dutchman's Fireside*, the story of a night-adventure among the Indians is as lifelike as anything of the kind in Cooper's best romances. Several of the characters in *Westward Ho!* are original, and strongly though perhaps rather coarsely drawn; and *Koningsmarke* has its lively scenes of new-year's revelling and other incidents of the old settlements on the Delaware. To introduce the following extract from *Westward Ho!* it must be observed that the speaker is a settler in the backwoods, who finds civilisation pressing too close upon him when a gentleman with a *white* servant calls at his house.

KENTUCKY HOSPITALITY.

'"You must know, colonel, not long after you went away, there came a man riding along here that I calculate had just thrown off his moccasins, with another feller behind him in a laced hat, and for all the world dressed like a militia officer. Well, I hailed him in here, for you know I like to do as you would in your own house; and he came to like a good feller. But the captain, as I took him to be, hung fire, and stayed out with the horses. So I went and took hold of him like a snapping-turtle, and says I: 'Captain, one would think you had never been inside of a gentleman's house before.' But he held back like all wrath, and wouldn't take anything. So says I: 'Stranger, I'm a peaceable man anyhow, but maybe you don't know what it is to insult a feller by sneaking away from his hospitality here in Old Kentuck.' I held on to him all the while, or he'd have gone off like one of these plaguy percussion-locks that have just come into fashion. 'Captain,' says I, 'here's your health, and may you live to be a general.' 'Captain!' says the other; 'he's no captain; he's my servant.' 'What!' says I, 'one white man be a servant to another! make a nigger of himself! come, that's too bad!' and I began to feel a little savage. I asked one if he wasn't ashamed to make a slave of a feller-cretur, and the other if he wasn't ashamed to make a nigger of himself; and they got rather obstropolous. I don't know exactly how it came about, but we got into a fight, and I licked them both, but not till they got outside the door, for I wouldn't be uncivil anyhow. Well, what do you think? instead of settling the thing like a gentleman, the feller that had a white man for his nigger, instead of coming out fine . . . ., if he didn't send a constable after me! Well, I made short work of it, and licked him too, anyhow. But I can't stand it here any longer. Poor old Snowball[1] slipped her bridle the other day, and went out like a flash in the pan; so I'm my own master again, with nobody to stand in my way at all. I must look out for some place where a man can live independent; where there's no law but gentlemen's law, and no niggers but black ones. I sha'n't see you again, colonel, it's most likely, so good-by all. I expect you'll be after me soon, for I look upon it to be impossible for a man in his senses to live here much longer, to be hoppled like a horse, and not go where he pleases." And away he marched, with a heart as light as a feather, in search of a place where he might live according to his conscience.'

TIMOTHY FLINT (1780–1840), a native of Massachusetts, was educated for the Christian ministry, and for ten years laboured as a missionary in the Valley of the Mississippi. His first book, giving recollections of his mission, was published and well received in 1826, and subsequently the failure of his health made him dependent on literature. His next work was a novel, *Francis Berrian, or the Mexican Patriot;* and was followed in 1828 by *Arthur Clenning*, a very hazardous attempt to write one more Robinson Crusoe. The last of his novels, *The Shoshonee Valley* (1830), has little merit in its portraiture of character or development of a story, but its landscapes have the freshness of the writer's recollections. It is curious that Flint, who must have been well acquainted with the realities of Indian life, should choose to give a mere visionary account of it in his *Shoshonee Valley*.

His powers of description were more happily employed in his work on *The Geography and History of the Mississippi Valley* (1827)—an important contribution to American geography. It

[1] A servant who had died.

was reprinted with a condensed survey of the whole continent. During the later years of his life, Flint was engaged as editor of the *Western Monthly Magazine*, and wrote numerous magazine tales and essays, besides an historical and critical account of *American Literature*, published in the London *Athenæum*. In 1840, while passing through Natchez, on his way from Louisiana to New England, he was overtaken by the tornado which desolated that city, and for some hours remained buried under the ruins of a house. This accident seriously affected his feeble health; and after a lingering illness, he died in his native place, Reading, in his sixtieth year. His literary career, often interrupted by indisposition, was commenced when he was forty-five years old, and when failing health had disqualified him for other duties. An extract from his last novel may afford a specimen of his descriptive passages:—

COUNTRY OF THE SEWASSERNA.

'Their free domain comprised an extent of 500 leagues. The country of their compact and actual settlement is a vale, than which the earth can shew none more beautiful or more secluded—the vale of the Sewasserna. This stream, in which the poets would have placed the crystal caves of the Naiads of the ancient days, comes winding down in a clear, full, strong, and yet equable and gentle tide, from the mountains. Up its pure and ice-formed waters ascend, in their season, countless numbers of the finest salmon; and in its deep and circling eddies play trout, pike, carp, tench, and all the varieties of fish of cold mountain-rivers. The Indian, as he glides down the stream, sees the shining rocks at the bottom, covered with tresses of green waving moss, at the depth of twenty feet. This circumstance, along with its transparency, furnishes the etymology of its name, which imports the sea-green river. Streaked bass, shiners, gold-fishes, and beautiful and undescribed finny tribes, dart from their coverts along the white sand, flit from the shadow of the descending canoe, or turn their green and gold to the light, as they fan, as it were, with their purple wings, or repose in the sunbeams that find their way through the branches that overhang the banks. . . . .

The glossy gray mallard, the beautiful blue-winged teal, the green-crested widgeon, the little active dipper, the brilliant white diver; the solitary loon, raising his lugubrious and ill-omened note in unsocial seclusion; the stately swan, sailing in his pride and milky lustre slowly along the stream; the tall sand-hill crane, looking at a distance like a miniature camel; the white pelican, with his immense pouch in front; innumerable flocks of various species of geese—in short, an unknown variety of water-fowls with their brilliant, variegated, and oiled vestments, their singular languages and cries, were seen gliding among the trees, pattering their broad bills amidst the grasses and weeds on the shores. . . . .

The mountains on either side of the valley tower into a countless variety of peaks, cones, and inaccessible elevations, from 6000 to 10,000 feet high. More than half of them are covered with the accumulated snows and ices of centuries, which, glittering in mid-air, shew in the sunbeams in awful contrast with the black and rugged precipices that arrest the clouds. . . . . The rocks, cliffs, and boulders, partly of granite and partly of volcanic character, black and rugged in some places, in others porphyritic, needle, or spire shaped, shoot up into pinnacles, domes, and towers, and in other places lie heaped in huge masses, as though shook by earthquakes from the summits where they had originally defied the storms. . . . . Yet between these savage and terrific peaks, unvisited except by the screaming eagle, are seen the most secluded and sweet valleys in the world. Here and there appear circular clumps of hemlocks, mountain cedars, silver firs, and above all, the glorious Norwegian pines. . . . . The breeze that is borne down from the mountains always sighs through these evergreen thickets, playing, as it were, the deep and incessant voluntary of nature to the Divinity. . . . . In numerous little lakes and ponds, where the trout spring up and dart upon the fly and grasshopper, the verdure of the shores is charmingly repainted in contrast with the threatening and savage sublimity of the mountains, whose summits shoot down as deep in the abyss as they stand high in the air. As you turn your eyes from the landscape so faithfully pencilled on the sleeping waters, to see the substance of these shadows, the eye, dazzled with the radiance of the sunbeams playing on the perpetual snows in the regions of mid-air, reposes with solace and delight on the deep blue of the sky that is seen between, undimmed except by the occasional passing of the bald eagle or falcon-hawks, sailing slowly from the summit of one mountain to another.'

RICHARD HENRY DANA, already noticed in our account of poetical literature, is more prominent as a reviewer and essayist than as a writer of fiction. In 1821, he commenced the publication of a periodical entitled *The Idle Man*, in which he gave his stories of *Tom Thornton*, *Edward and Mary*, and *Paul Felton*. Of these, the last is the most remarkable; but it is a very gloomy description of morbid thoughts and feelings. We perhaps differ widely from several American critics in our preference of the essays and reviews to the tales and poems of Dana. An earnest, meditative vein of thought, not without a shade of melancholy, may be observed in the prose-fictions, as in the other works of this writer. Since the death of his friends Channing and Allston, he has lived in almost entire seclusion, and all his writings bear the impress of a man who dwells chiefly in the world of his own thoughts. His literary powers which, in happier circumstances, might have produced some considerable work of permanent value, have been discouraged by failing to find general appreciation; and the career of Dana is perhaps the most striking of many examples of the bad influence of the present copyright-law in America. While the most worthless and ephemeral productions of the press find all the encouragement they require, every work of time and thought must have to strive against a most unfair competition, and, indeed, can hardly be produced by any writer who has not the resources of an independent fortune. As an example of this general fact, *The Idle Man*—commenced by Dana with the assistance of Bryant the poet, Allston the painter, and other friends—gave promise of an American periodical worthy of success, and must have succeeded in a fair competition; but when a few numbers had appeared, the publisher explained that all the genius and talents of the contributors could have no chance in a contest against a host of cheap reprints of English books. Accordingly, the publication ceased; Washington Allston's tale of *Monaldi*, intended for a second volume, was laid aside for more than twenty years; and Dana, finding that America rejected his aid in building up a national literature, turned to review the books of English authors. His writings have always been highly appreciated by a select number of readers; and the following account of their characteristics appears in an American Review:—'That is the true idea of literature and art which regards them not as factitious, but as the necessary expression of the intellectual life of man. This is exhibited in the works before us, and constitutes, if we mistake not, the secret source of their attractiveness. We cannot help, if we would, seeing the writer in the writings. There is a sincerity and conscientiousness, an unaffected and honest utterance of unborrowed thoughts and feelings, which enters into our hearts, and seems to make us stronger and better. Hence their educational influence on susceptive minds cannot be slight, nor anything but good. It does us no harm when reflection is forced upon us, when we are compelled to inspect the operations of our own minds, to dwell at home. "Proneness to melancholy is not the evil of our times: we live too much abroad for that; daytime and evening, we are running at large with the common herd, or are gathered into smaller flocks and folds, called societies. No one is seen ruminating alone in the still shade of his own oak or willow." To lead us to a wise meditation will be one tendency of these works.'

Our remarks on the discouragement of thoughtful literature have been suggested by a perusal of several of the essays of

Dana. It might seem likely that these, and other writings of the same class, would be welcome to qualify the effects of a flood of shallow newspapers and cheap noxious fictions; but it would be useless to argue on this point. It has been decided, that the republic can advance without the aid of its most reflecting minds. Meanwhile, the field of literary competition, from which they are expelled, is occupied by other teachers of the people: the only diploma required is, that the author's book shall be sold for a few cents. Consequently, the lowest productions of the presses of London and Paris are spread over the counters of the cheap booksellers, and attract the masses of the people. The novels of French writers whom we need not name are very widely circulated; and it is asserted by those who ought to know the facts, that the reprints and translations are, by a wanton superfluity of mischief, made even worse than the originals—which seems scarcely possible.

WASHINGTON IRVING.

BIOGRAPHY—SALMAGUNDI—KNICKERBOCKER—SKETCH-BOOK—BRACEBRIDGE HALL—TALES OF A TRAVELLER—TALES OF THE ALHAMBRA—ABBOTSFORD AND NEWSTEAD ABBEY—CHRONICLES OF WOLFERT'S ROOST—STYLE—VARIETY—DESCRIPTIVE PASSAGES—EXTRACTS FROM THE SKETCH-BOOK.

WASHINGTON IRVING, the author of classic tales, sketches, and essays which have given delight to many thousands of readers in England and America, may be placed among the writers of prose-fiction, though his works in a great measure belong to other departments of literature. A critic, taking the higher and more comprehensive sense of the word 'poetry,' without regard to the accident of rhyme, would probably name Irving as the first of the *poets* of America. In imaginative power and variety, he finds no rival among the writers of verse in his own country; while, with regard to melody and beauty, his prose style can hardly be excelled. He is the descendant of a Scotch family, and was born in the city of New York in the year 1783. A few years afterwards, his father, who was a respectable merchant, died, leaving the care of young Washington's education to his elder brother William, who, like other members of the Irving family, had a taste for literature.

After a tour in Europe (1803-1806), Washington Irving returned to New York, and, in concert with his brother William and the two young authors Verplanck and Paulding, wrote in 1807 the humorous miscellany entitled *Salmagundi*. It consisted of light sketches of character and burlesques of manners, and was very successful; but the publisher refused to pay the writers, and consequently their association was broken up. A miscellany, published under the same title in 1819, was entirely written by Paulding.

In his next work, a *History of New York*, supposed to be written by a Dutch antiquary named Knickerbocker, Irving displayed a peculiar style of humorous writing—we might almost say he invented a new kind of humour. At first, the work was intended to be nothing more than a burlesque of a publication styled *A Picture of New York;* but as the writer proceeded, and became more conversant with the history of the early Dutch colonists of New Amsterdam, he seems to have been charmed by the somnolent humour of the old times. The quietude of rural life in the valleys lying near the Hudson and the Tappan Zee; the gravity of old fashions, and the dreamy character of old traditions —these were all blended in Irving's sketches of his favourite Dutch settlers—the creatures of his own imagination, though suggested by historical realities. This ideal treatment of Dutch characteristics is unique in literature. Irving must have found delight in his own creations, for he carried their history too far, and made a considerable book of the materials which might have been, with better effect, condensed in a few chapters.

The incidents related in Knickerbocker's history are not wholly imaginary. Wouter van Twiller, 'the Doubter,' and other Dutch governors, had their prototypes in the early annals of New Amsterdam, though it is hardly necessary to say that the real characters differed widely from their ideal portraitures.

After the publication of *Knickerbocker*, Irving entered into partnership with his brothers, who were engaged in foreign commerce, and in 1815 came to England, to carry on the business of the firm in Liverpool. Soon after his arrival in this country, he experienced a reverse of fortune. The house of Irving and Brothers was ruined by the commercial crisis which followed the peace. In literature, which hitherto he had regarded chiefly as a recreation, he now hoped to find a means of support. While American journalists—probably misled by the cheerful tone of the sketcher and essayist—imagined that he was passing a very idle and pleasant time among the 'aristocracy of the Old World,' Irving was, in fact, an obscure toiling author; having determined to write until success crowned his labour, and never to return to his friends in America until, by his literary exertions, he had placed himself 'above their pity or assistance.' He knew well the fate of Goldsmith, to say nothing of inferior writers —he understood how precarious were the rewards of literature— yet he ventured on the dangerous path, and achieved a well-deserved success. Supposing that his elegant sketches and essays would be more interesting in his native land than in England, he sent them occasionally to the United States, where they were published from time to time in a serial form. They found many admiring readers, but not the hearty welcome which greeted them when Walter Scott had pronounced them 'beautiful,' and had persuaded Murray to publish them. Meanwhile, the writer received from America certain anonymous letters, accusing him of having forgotten his native land; of being seduced by the charms of fashionable society, of living in epicurean indulgence; and assuring him, that he had lost the good-will of the public in America. The cheerful tone of his writings may perhaps explain such errors. As few readers of *The Vicar of Wakefield* would imagine the writer to be a literary drudge, compiling, translating, revising, and 'touching-up' prefaces and 'head and tail pieces for new works,' or 'modifying travels and voyages;' so few readers could think of the refined and humorous sketcher, Geoffrey Crayon, otherwise than as a very comfortable gentleman, travelling at his ease, and for his own pleasure, and often very merry at the table of some hearty old English squire, such as he had portrayed in *The Sketch-book*. The mistake was like that of a grave London reviewer, who, on the ground of certain sportive papers in *Blackwood's Magazine*, described the Ettrick Shepherd as a gourmand revelling in turtle, while, in fact, the poor poet was tending a few sheep, and struggling to pay the rent of a little farm in the Ettrick solitudes.

Happily, Irving found a friend in one as distinguished for kindness of heart as for wealth of intellect. The Crayon papers —afterwards published as *The Sketch-book*—had failed to win the favour of Murray, to whom they had been offered. Though admitting their 'tasteful qualities,' he could not regard them as altogether safe articles of trade-speculation. The refusal almost disheartened the writer, who next thought of Constable of Edinburgh as a publisher; but first determined to submit the work to the judgment of Sir Walter (then Mr) Scott. This was the turning-point in Irving's early literary career. Scott, with the generosity which was the prevailing trait in his noble character, replied very promptly, saying that it would afford him the greatest pleasure to forward the views of the striving author. These, of course, coming from such a man, were not idle words of compliment, but sure pledges of deeds of kindness, which were very speedily redeemed. A weekly periodical was at this time projected in Edinburgh, and the editorship, with a salary of L.500 a year, was offered to Mr Irving. In making the offer, Scott, with a delicacy which would seem to solicit rather than confer a favour, says: 'I have glanced over *The Sketch-book;* it is positively beautiful, and increases my desire to *crimp* you, if it be possible. Some difficulties there always are in managing such a matter, especially at the outset; but we will obviate them as much as we possibly can.' In the same letter, it was intimated that the political bias of the proposed journal might not suit the views of the American. This was indeed the case; and partly on this account, partly through distrust of his own qualifications for regular task-work, Irving gratefully declined the offer. By so doing, he lost not his hold upon Scott's kindness, which was next exerted, as he expressed it, 'to open the trenches with Constable;' in other words, to persuade this publisher to take up *The Sketch-book*. Lockhart, at the suggestion of Scott, had written for *Blackwood's Magazine* a favourable review of the Crayon sketches; and, meanwhile, Irving had determined to risk their publication on his own account.

This was a dangerous experiment, and might have proved ruinous; for the book was put into the hands of an obscure London bookseller, who failed soon after its publication. Once more, Scott appeared as a friend and helper. He arrived in London, induced Murray to undertake the publication of the book, and thus opened for Irving the path to success and fame. After fairly winning the praises of the literary world in Great Britain, Irving, in improved circumstances, returned to his native city, New York, where he was gladly welcomed by many friends. His subsequent career has been so prosperous, as to form a bright exception among the biographies of literary men. Resources derived immediately from his writings, or from the position gained by his literary talents, have made his old age, in his retirement at Sunnyside, easy and independent.

The Sketch-book was followed in 1822 by another series of papers, entitled *Bracebridge Hall*, consisting partly of sketches of old English manners, but including legends of New Amsterdam, and new portraitures of mythical Dutchmen. In 1824, the *Tales of a Traveller* appeared, containing the short novel of *Buckthorne*, intended to portray the miserable life of a poor author. Humorous exaggerations are freely employed in this story. In one example, the writer finds a fair subject for ridicule, and gives a very ludicrous caricature of a depraved taste in literature. Buckthorne, the poor author, has tried without success several styles of writing, and at last has ruined himself by publishing on his own account a sentimental poem, entitled the *Pleasures of Melancholy*. He now yields to the advice of booksellers of a certain class, who have assured him that the public no longer read for instruction, but require tales of pirates and robbers, highly spiced with burglaries, murders, and suicides. In order to prepare a proper story to add to the literature of horrors, he hires a study in a cottage not far from Chalk Farm, and here begins to muse over his plot and its characters; but the rural beauty of the neighbourhood seduces his imagination, and hinders the progress of his story. At last, he finds a proper hero, and meets 'a friend' well qualified to give assistance in suggesting scenes and incidents.

THE AUTHOR'S ADVENTURE.

'Chance at length befriended me. I had frequently, in my ramblings, loitered about Hampstead Hill, which is a kind of Parnassus of the metropolis. At such times, I occasionally took my dinner at Jack Straw's Castle. It is a country inn so named—the very spot where that notorious rebel and his followers held their council of war. It is a favourite resort of citizens when rurally inclined, as it commands fine fresh air, and a good view of the city. I sat one day in the public room of this inn, ruminating over a beef-steak and a pint of port, when my imagination kindled up with ancient and heroic images. I had long wanted a theme and a hero; both suddenly broke upon my mind. I determined to write a poem on the history of Jack Straw. I was so full of my subject, that I was fearful of being anticipated. I wondered that none of the poets of the day, in their search after ruffian heroes, had ever thought of Jack Straw. I went to work pell-mell, blotted several sheets of paper with choice floating-thoughts, and battles and descriptions, to be ready at a moment's warning. In a few days' time, I sketched out the skeleton of my poem, and nothing was wanting but to give it flesh and blood. I used to take my manuscript and stroll about Caen Wood, and read aloud; and would dine at the castle, by way of keeping up the vein of thought.

I was there one day, at rather a late hour, in the public room. There was no other company but one man, who sat enjoying his pint of port at a window, and noticing the passers-by. He was dressed in a green shooting-coat. His countenance was strongly marked: he had a hooked nose; a romantic eye, excepting that it had something of a squint; and altogether, as I thought, a poetical style of head. I was quite taken with the man—for you must know I am a little of a physiognomist—I set him down at once for either a poet or a philosopher.

As I like to make new acquaintances, considering every man a volume of human nature, I soon fell into conversation with the stranger, who, I was pleased to find, was by no means difficult of access. After I had dined, I joined him at the window, and we became so sociable, that I proposed a bottle of wine together, to which he most cheerfully assented.

I was too full of my poem to keep long quiet on the subject, and began to talk about the origin of the tavern, and the history of Jack Straw. I found my new acquaintance to be perfectly at home on the topic, and to jump exactly with my humour in every respect. I became elevated by the wine and the conversation. In the fulness of an author's feelings, I told him of my projected poem, and repeated some passages, and he was in raptures. He was evidently of a strong poetical turn.

* * * *

We were so much pleased with each other, that we sat until a late hour. I insisted on paying the bill, for both my purse and my heart were full, and I agreed that he should pay the score at our next meeting. As the coaches had all gone that run between Hampstead and London, we had to return on foot. He was so delighted with the idea of my poem, that he could talk of nothing else. He had made me repeat such passages as I could remember; and though I did it in a very mangled manner, having a wretched memory, yet he was in raptures.

* * * *

Never had I spent a more delightful evening. I did not perceive how the time flew. I could not bear to separate, but continued walking on, arm-in-arm, with him, past my lodgings, through Camden Town, and across Crackskull Common, talking the whole way about my poem.

When we were half-way across the common, he interrupted me in the midst of a quotation, by telling me that this had been a famous place for footpads, and was still occasionally infested by them; and that a man had recently been shot there in attempting to defend himself.

"The more fool he!" cried I: "a man is an idiot to risk life, or even limb, to save a paltry purse of money. It's quite a different case from that of a duel, where one's honour is concerned. For my part," added I, "I should never think of making resistance against one of those desperadoes."

"Say you so?" cried my friend in green, turning suddenly upon me, and putting a pistol to my breast: "why, then, have at you, my lad!—Come—disburse! empty! unsack!"

In a word, I found that the Muse had played me another of her tricks, and had betrayed me into the hands of a footpad. There was no time to parley; he made me turn my pockets inside out; and hearing the sound of distant footsteps, he made one fell swoop upon purse, watch, and all; gave me a thwack over my unlucky pate, that laid me sprawling on the ground, and scampered away with his booty.

I saw no more of my friend in green until a year or two afterwards, when I caught a sight of his poetical countenance among a crew of scapegraces heavily ironed, who were on the way for transportation. He recognised me at once, tipped me an impudent wink, and asked me how I came on with the history of Jack Straw's Castle.'

The pleasant humour of many sketches in the *Tales of a Traveller*, is varied by passages of pathos and narratives of romantic adventure. *Wolfert Webber*, a tale of a money-digger, takes us back to the old traditions of New York, and is one of the best of Irving's Dutch legends.

After his return to America (1832), Irving fixed his residence near the scenes peopled by his own imagination. 'He purchased the old mansion of the Van Tassels, on the Hudson, close by the margin of the Tappan Zee, and in the vicinity of "Sleepy Hollow"—as quiet and sheltered a nook as the heart of man could desire, in which to take refuge from the cares and troubles of the world.' This retreat he called 'Wolfert's Roost,' and repaired and renovated it 'with religious care, in the genuine Dutch style, with sundry relics of the glorious days of the New Netherlands.' It is pleasant to find an author thus able to indulge his own imagination and taste, and to blend his real with his ideal life. A sketch of his own dwelling and its locality is included in the papers collected under the title of *Chronicles of Wolfert's Roost*. We there read that the Roost is 'an old-fashioned stone-mansion, all made up of gable-ends, and as full of angles and corners as an old cocked-hat.' The imaginative sketch of Wolfert and the quaint historian Knickerbocker, who are supposed to have been residents in the old 'roost,' is so characteristic of the writer, that one passage must be quoted. It describes the quiet time after the Revolutionary war, when the Dutch antiquary took up his abode in the mansion, and began to explore its dreamy and haunted neighbourhood.

WOLFERT'S ROOST.

'Years and years passed over the time-honoured little mansion. The honeysuckle and the sweet-brier crept up its walls; the wren and the phœbe-bird built under the eaves; it gradually became almost hidden among trees, through which it looked forth, as with half-shut eyes, upon the Tappan Zee. The Indian spring—famous in the days of the wizard sachem—still welled up at the bottom of the green bank; and the wild brook, wild as ever, came babbling down the ravine, and threw itself into the little cove, where, of yore, the water-guard harboured their whale-boats. . . . .

Here, then, did old Diedrich Knickerbocker take up his abode for a time, and set to work with antiquarian zeal to decipher these precious documents, which, like the lost books of Livy, had baffled the research of former historians; and it is the facts drawn from these sources which give his work the preference, in point of accuracy, over every other history.

* * * *

And now a word or two about Sleepy Hollow, which many have rashly deemed a fanciful creation, like the Lubberland of mariners. It was probably the mystic and dreamy sound of the name which first tempted the historian of the Manhattoes into its spell-bound mazes. As he entered, all nature seemed for the moment to awake from its slumbers, and break forth in gratulations. The quail whistled a welcome from the corn-field; the loquacious cat-bird flew from bush to bush with restless wing, proclaiming his approach, or perked inquisitively into his face, as if to get a knowledge of his physiognomy; the woodpecker tapped a tattoo on the hollow apple-tree, and then peered round the trunk, as if asking how he relished the salutation; while the squirrel scampered along the fence, whisking his tail over his head by way of a huzza.

Here reigned the golden mean extolled by poets, in which no gold was to be found, and very little silver. The inhabitants of the Hollow were of the primitive stock, and had intermarried, and bred in and in, from the earliest time of the province—never swarming far from the parent hive, but dividing and subdividing their paternal acres as they swarmed.

Here were small farms, each having its little portion of meadow and corn-field—its orchard of gnarled and sprawling apple-trees—its garden, in which the rose, the marigold, and hollyhock grew sociably with the cabbage, the pea, and the pumpkin. Each had its low-eaved mansion, redundant with white-headed children, with an old hat nailed against the wall for the housekeeping wren; the coop on the grassplot, where the motherly hen clucked round with her vagrant brood. Each had its stone-well, with a moss-covered bucket suspended to the long balancing-pole, according to antediluvian hydraulics; while within doors resounded the eternal hum of the spinning-wheel.

Many were the great historical facts which the worthy Diedrich collected in these lowly mansions; and patiently would he sit by the old Dutch housewives, with a child on his knee, or a purring grimalkin on his lap, listening to endless ghost-stories spun forth to the humming accompaniment of the wheel.

The delighted historian pursued his explorations far into the foldings of the hills, where the Pocantico winds its wizard stream among the mazes of its old Indian haunts—sometimes running darkly in pieces of woodland, beneath balancing sprays of beech and chestnut; sometimes sparkling between grassy borders in fresh, green intervals; here and there receiving the tributes of silver rills, which came whimpering down the hillsides from their parent springs.

In a remote part of the Hollow, where the Pocantico forced its way down rugged rocks, stood Carl's Mill, the haunted house of the neighbourhood. It was indeed a goblin-looking pile, shattered and timeworn—dismal with clanking wheels and rushing streams, and all kinds of uncouth noises. A horseshoe, nailed to the door to keep off witches, seemed to have lost its power; for as Diedrich approached, an old negro thrust his head, all dabbled with flour, out of a hole above the water-wheel, and grinned and rolled his eyes, and appeared to be the very hobgoblin of the place. Yet this proved to be the great historic genius of the Hollow, abounding in that valuable information never to be acquired from books. Diedrich Knickerbocker soon discovered his merit. They had long talks together seated on a broken millstone, heedless of the water and the clatter of the mill; and to his conference with that African sage, many attribute the surprising though true story of Ichabod Crane, and the Headless Horseman of Sleepy Hollow.'

In 1835, after a period of rest from literary toil, Irving published his *Tour on the Prairies*, which cannot be classed with fictions, though its scenes and adventures derive their interest chiefly from the writer's mode of treatment. This work was followed, in the same year, by *Abbotsford and Newstead Abbey;* and in 1836, by *Astoria, or Anecdotes of an Enterprise Beyond the Rocky Mountains.*

The historical and biographical works of Irving must be separately noticed. Of the writings consisting more or less of fiction, we have still to mention the *Tales of the Alhambra*, and a series of sketches and stories first published in the *Knickerbocker Magazine* and other periodicals, and partly reprinted under the title, *Chronicles of Wolfert's Roost*. The author's latest work is a *Life of Washington*, which will be noticed in its proper place.

During his first residence in Europe (1815–1832), Irving had travelled in Spain, and stayed some time in Madrid, where he collected the materials of his *Life of Columbus*, with its sequel, the *Voyages and Discoveries of the Companions of Columbus*, and other works, including a *Life of Mohammed*, a history of the *Conquest of Granada*, and the *Tales of the Alhambra*. He had contemplated writing a history of the *Conquest of Mexico;* but when he heard that his countryman, Prescott, had already made great preparations for a work on the same subject, he courteously declined competition. In 1841, he again visited Spain, where he was appointed minister-plenipotentiary to the court of Madrid. After a four years' residence in this capital, he returned to New York, and retired to his quiet Wolfert's Roost, where his later years have been devoted to literature and friendship. He has never been married; but 'for several years has had about him a household—the daughters of his brother, who have been to him as his own children, and who bear to him all the love that a father could engage.' The best portraits of Irving shew a countenance marked by pleasant humour and refined expression, according well with the character suggested by his writings.

A cursory review of a few of Irving's tales and sketches may be pleasing to young readers, and others may be willing to revive their recollections of old favourites. *The Sketch-book* might be passed over as well known; but it is our duty to select the *best* examples of the author's style; and these will be found in his earlier works. Irving has not been a progressive writer. It has been truly said, that 'his genius reached its maturity' when he published his sketches of scenery and manners in England; and though he has added many papers on his favourite Dutch-American traditions, he has never excelled the genial humour and polished style of his tales *Rip Van Winkle* and *Sleepy Hollow*.

No reader would thank us for an attempt to criticise minutely the various writings of Washington Irving. To find faults, we must speak of what he has *not* done; for all that he has written, excepting perhaps the *Life of Mohammed*, which has little historical value, is good of its kind. His chief characteristics are elegance of language and versatility in the appropriate treatment of a wide range of topics. Of the former, nothing new can be said. The beauty of his style has been admired wherever his works are read. 'It is sprightly, pointed, easy, correct, and expressive, without being too studiously guarded against the opposite faults. It is without affectation, parade, or labour. If we were to characterise a manner which owes much of its merit to the absence of any glaring characteristic, we should perhaps say that it is above the style of all other writers of the day, marked with an expressive elegance. Washington Irving never buries the clearness and force of the meaning under a heap of fine words; nor, on the other hand, does he think it necessary to be coarse, slovenly, or uncouth in order to be emphatic.'[1] The writer of this criticism goes on to recommend young men who would excel in writing English, to study diligently the writings of Irving. This is an error. No good style can be founded on imitation. To improve our language, we should begin by cultivating clearness of thought—first learning to think well, and then it will be easy to write well. Southey, who wrote beautiful prose, says: 'Of what is called style, not a thought enters my head at any time. Look to the matter, and the manner takes care of itself.'

The variety of his topics is another characteristic of the author. 'From Irving,' says a reviewer, 'we have the humours of contemporary politics and everyday-life in America—the traditionary peculiarities of the Dutch founders of New York—the nicest shades of the school of English manners of the last century—the chivalry of the middle ages in Spain—the glittering visions of Moorish romance—a large cycle of sentimental creations, founded on the invariable experience, the pathetic sameness of the human

[1] *North American Review*, No. 88, Art. I.

heart—and, lastly, the whole unhackneyed freshness of the West—life beyond the border—a camp outside the frontier—a hunt on buffalo-ground, beyond which neither white nor Pawnee man, nor Muse can go. This is Mr Irving's range, and in every part of it he is equally at home.'[1]

Variety of mood or sentiment is another trait, obviously distinct from a mere change of topics. Irving resembles his favourite author, Goldsmith, not only in melody and simplicity of diction, but also in a healthful diversity of moods. The incessant burlesque of some writers; the unrelenting satire of others; the trick of rapid transition 'from grave to gay;' the tiresome liveliness prepared by a recipe for bringing together incongruous ideas: these and other mannerisms are only so many forms of a monotony which is no characteristic of poetic genius. A wide interval separates Goldsmith from Shakspeare. The world of thought explored by the writer of *The Traveller* and *The Vicar of Wakefield*, seems little when compared with the wide system peopled by the creations of the greatest of poets. But in the essential qualities of poetic genius, these two writers were alike: each possessed a healthful variety of moods. As Shakspeare could turn away from and utterly forget Falstaff, when he would be sad and thoughtful with Hamlet; so Goldsmith, after laughing heartily with the pedantic rogue Jenkinson, would rise to earnestness and dignity when he described the good vicar dreaming of a reformation of all criminals. Burns—another genius of the same order—could banish all thoughts of *Tam o' Shanter*, and the *Beggars' Cantata*, when, with unfeigned piety and tenderness, he wrote of the *Cottar's Saturday Night*. Irving, in other points of view, might be contrasted rather than compared with these poets; but he must be classed with the imaginative writers who have displayed variety, not merely in their choice of topics, but in their moods of thought and sentiment.

As examples of his clearness and distinct colouring in the scenery of his tales and sketches, we may quote two descriptions—one English, the other Spanish. The latter, we may observe, belongs strictly to the central parts of Old Castile, which are miserably destitute of foliage. The truthfulness of this sketch is quite as remarkable as its sombre and picturesque effect.

RURAL SCENERY IN ENGLAND.

'Nothing can be more imposing than the magnificence of English park scenery. Vast lawns that extend like sheets of vivid green, with here and there clumps of gigantic trees, heaping up rich piles

[1] *North American Review*, No. 88, Art. I.

of foliage: the solemn pomp of groves and woodland glades, with the deer trooping in silent herds across them; the hare, bounding away to the covert; or the pheasant, suddenly bursting upon the wing: the brook, taught to wind in natural meanderings, or expand into a glassy lake: the sequestered pool, reflecting the quivering trees, with the yellow leaf sleeping on its bosom, and the trout roaming fearlessly about its limpid waters; while some rustic temple or sylvan statue, grown green and dank with age, gives an air of classic sanctity to the seclusion.

These are but a few of the features of park scenery; but what most delights me, is the creative talent with which the English decorate the unostentatious abodes of middle-life. The rudest habitation, the most unpromising and scanty portion of land, in the hands of an Englishman of taste, becomes a little paradise. With a nicely discriminating eye, he seizes at once upon its capabilities, and pictures in his mind the future landscape. The sterile spot grows into loveliness under his hand; and yet the operations of art which produce the effect are scarcely to be perceived. The cherishing and training of some trees; the cautious pruning of others; the nice distribution of flowers and plants of tender and graceful foliage; the introduction of a green slope of velvet turf; the partial opening to a peep of blue distance, or silver gleam of water: all these are managed with a delicate tact, a pervading yet quiet assiduity, like the magic touchings with which a painter finishes up a favourite picture.

The residence of people of fortune and refinement in the country, has diffused a degree of taste and elegance in rural economy that descends to the lowest class. The very labourer with his thatched cottage and narrow slip of ground, attends to their embellishment. The trim hedge—the grassplot before the door—the little flower-bed, bordered with snug box—the woodbine trained up against the wall, and hanging its blossoms about the lattice—the pot of flowers in the window—the holly, providentially planted about the house, to cheat winter of its dreariness, and to throw in a semblance of green summer to cheer the fireside—all these bespeak the influence of taste, flowing down from high sources, and pervading the lowest levels of the public mind. . . . .

The effect of this devotion of elegant minds to rural occupations, has been wonderful on the face of the country. A great part of the island is rather level, and would be monotonous, were it not for the charms of culture; but it is studded and gemmed, as it were, with castles and palaces, and embroidered with parks and gardens. It does not abound in grand and sublime prospects, but rather in little home-scenes of rural repose and sheltered quiet. Every antique farmhouse and moss-grown cottage is a picture; and as the roads are continually winding, and the view is shut in by groves and hedges, the eye is delighted by a continual succession of small landscapes of captivating loveliness.

The great charm, however, of English scenery, is the moral

feeling that seems to pervade it. It is associated in the mind with ideas of order, of quiet, of sober well-established principles, of hoary usage and reverend custom. Everything seems to be the growth of ages of regular and peaceful existence. The old church of remote architecture, with its low massive portal, its Gothic tower, its windows rich with tracery and painted glass, in scrupulous preservation; its stately monuments of warriors and worthies of the olden time, ancestors of the present lords of the soil; its tombstones, recording successive generations of sturdy yeomanry, whose progeny still plough the same fields, and kneel at the same altar—the parsonage, a quaint irregular pile, partly antiquated, but repaired and altered in the tastes of various ages and occupants—the stile and footpath leading from the church-yard, across pleasant fields, and along shady hedgerows, according to an immemorial right of way—the neighbouring village, with its venerable cottages, its public green sheltered by trees, under which the forefathers of the present race have sported—the antique family mansion, standing apart in some little rural domain, but looking down with a protecting air on the surrounding scene: all these common features of English landscape evince a calm and settled security, and hereditary transmission of homebred virtues and local attachments, that speak deeply and touchingly for the moral character of the nation.'

SCENERY IN SPAIN.

'Many are apt to picture Spain to their imaginations as a soft southern region, decked out with all the luxurious charms of voluptuous Italy. On the contrary, though there are exceptions in some of the maritime provinces, yet for the greater part it is a stern melancholy country, with rugged mountains and long sweeping plains, destitute of trees, and indescribably silent and lonesome, partaking of the savage and solitary character of Africa. What adds to this silence and loneliness, is the absence of singing-birds—a natural consequence of the want of groves and hedges. The vulture and the eagle are seen wheeling about the mountain-cliffs, and soaring over the plains, and groups of shy bustards stalk about the heaths; but the myriads of smaller birds, which animate the whole face of other countries, are met with in but few provinces in Spain, and in those chiefly among the orchards and gardens which surround the habitations of man.

In the interior provinces, the traveller occasionally traverses great tracts cultivated with grain as far as the eye can reach, waving at times with verdure, at other times naked and sunburnt; but he looks round in vain for the hand that has tilled the soil. At length he perceives some village on a steep hill, or rugged crag, with mouldering battlements and ruined watchtower—a stronghold, in old times, against civil war or Moorish inroad; for the custom among the peasantry of congregating together for mutal protection, is still kept up in most parts of Spain, in consequence of the maraudings of roving freebooters.

But though a great part of Spain is deficient in the garniture of groves and forests, and the softer charms of ornamental cultivation, yet its scenery has something of a high and lofty character to compensate the want. It partakes something of the attributes of its people; and I think that I better understand the proud, hardy, frugal and abstemious Spaniard, his manly defiance of hardships and contempt of effeminate indulgences, since I have seen the country he inhabits.

There is something, too, in the sternly simple features of the Spanish landscape, that impresses on the soul a feeling of sublimity. The immense plains of the Castiles and of La Mancha, extending as far as the eye can reach, derive an interest from their very nakedness and immensity, and have something of the solemn grandeur of the ocean. In ranging over these boundless wastes, the eye catches sight here and there of a straggling herd of cattle, attended by a lonely herdsman, motionless as a statue, with his long slender pike tapering up like a lance into the air; or beholds a long train of mules slowly moving along the waste like a train of camels in the desert; or a single herdsman, armed with blunderbuss and stiletto, and prowling over the plain. Thus the country, the habits, the very looks of the people, have something of the Arabian character. The general insecurity of the country is evinced in the universal use of weapons. The herdsman in the field, the shepherd in the plain, has his musket and his knife. The wealthy villager rarely ventures to the market-town without his trabuco, and perhaps a servant on foot with a blunderbuss on his shoulder; and the most petty journey is undertaken with the preparation of a warlike enterprise.

* * * *

It has a most picturesque effect, also, to meet a train of muleteers in some mountain-pass. First you hear the bells of the leading mules, breaking with their simple melody the stillness of the airy height; or, perhaps, the voice of the muleteer admonishing some tardy or wandering animal, or chanting, at the full stretch of his lungs, some traditionary ballad. At length you see the mules slowly winding along the cragged defile, sometimes descending precipitous cliffs, so as to present themselves in full relief against the sky; sometimes toiling up the deep arid chasms below you. As they approach, you descry their gay decorations of worsted tufts, tassels, and saddle-cloths; while, as they pass by, the ever-ready trabuco, slung behind the packs and saddles, gives a hint of the insecurity of the road.

* * * *

In the wild passes of these mountains, the sight of walled towns and villages, built like eagles' nests among the cliffs, and surrounded by Moorish battlements, or of ruined watchtowers perched on lofty peaks, carries the mind back to the chivalric days of Christian and

Moslem warfare, and to the romantic struggle for the conquest of Granada. In traversing these lofty sierras, the traveller is often obliged to alight and lead his horse up and down the steep and jagged ascents and descents, resembling the broken steps of a staircase. Sometimes the road winds along dizzy precipices, without parapet to guard him from the gulfs below, and then will plunge down steep, and dark, and dangerous declivities. Sometimes it straggles through rugged barrancos, or ravines, worn by winter-torrents, the obscure path of the contrabandista; while, ever and anon, the ominous cross, the monument of robbery and murder, erected on a mound of stones at some lonely part of the road, admonishes the traveller that he is among the haunts of banditti, perhaps at that very moment under the eye of some lurking bandolero.'

The several papers on 'Christmas in England' are as racy and pleasant as anything in *The Sketch-book*, and probably suggested to American critics the suspicion that Geoffrey Crayon had enjoyed all that warm-hearted hospitality which he so vividly describes. It might well seem unlikely that such a sketch as that of the 'Christmas Dinner' had been penned in the solitary and cheerless chamber of an author writing for bread; or that the hearty old squire Bracebridge, his jocose cousin Simon, the Oxonian, the fair Julia, and her suitor—with all the appurtenances of wassail-bowl, boar's-head, ancient sirloin, fat turkey, and pheasant-pie—were 'airy nothings,' to which imagination had given 'a local habitation and a name.'[1] Making allowance for poetical hyperbole, the air of reality is admirably well sustained in these sketches. To cull choice passages is a perplexing task; for what is there that might be omitted?

THE CHRISTMAS ANTHEM.

'During service, Master Simon stood up in the pew, and repeated the responses very audibly; evincing that kind of ceremonious devotion punctually observed by a gentleman of the old school, and a man of old family connections. I observed, too, that he turned over the leaves of a folio prayer-book with something of a flourish; possibly to shew off an enormous seal-ring which enriched one of his fingers, and which had the look of a family relic. But he was evidently most solicitous about the musical part of the service,

[1] 'At the time of the first publication of this paper, the picture of an old-fashioned Christmas in the country was pronounced by some as out of date. The author had afterwards an opportunity of witnessing almost all the customs above described, existing in unexpected vigour in the skirts of Derbyshire and Yorkshire, where he passed the Christmas holidays. The reader will find some notice of them in the author's account of his sojourn at Newstead Abbey.'

keeping his eye fixed intently on the choir, and beating time with much gesticulation and emphasis.

The orchestra was in a small gallery, and presented a most whimsical grouping of heads, piled one above the other, among which I particularly noticed that of the village-tailor, a pale fellow with a retreating forehead and chin, who played on the clarionet, and seemed to have blown his face to a point; and there was another, a short pursy man, stooping and labouring at a bass-viol, so as to shew nothing but the top of a round bald head, like the egg of an ostrich. There were two or three pretty faces among the female singers, to which the keen air of a frosty morning had given a bright rosy tint; but the gentlemen choristers had evidently been chosen, like old Cremona fiddles, more for tone than looks; and as several had to sing from the same book, there were clusterings of odd physiognomies, not unlike those groups of cherubs we sometimes see on country tombstones.

The usual services of the choir were managed tolerably well, the vocal parts generally lagging a little behind the instrumental, and some loitering fiddler now and then making up for lost time by travelling over a passage with prodigious celerity, and clearing more bars than the keenest fox-hunter to be in at the death. But the great trial was an anthem that had been prepared and arranged by Master Simon, and on which he had founded great expectation. Unluckily, there was a blunder at the very onset; the musicians became flurried; Master Simon was in a fever; everything went on lamely and irregularly, until they came to a chorus beginning "Now let us sing with one accord," which seemed to be a signal for parting company: all became discord and confusion; each shifted for himself, and got to the end as well, or rather, as soon as he could, excepting one old chorister in a pair of horn spectacles, bestriding and pinching a long sonorous nose, who happened to stand a little apart, and being wrapped up in his own melody, kept on a quavering course, wriggling his head, ogling his book, and winding all up by a nasal solo of at least three bars' duration.'

The details of an orthodox old Christmas banquet may be passed over; yet not without notice of the nice gradation of the mirth after dinner. It goes on with a natural flow to the brink of propriety; and here, just at the right moment, it is checked by the tact of the host, whose jovialty is 'tempered with a proper love of decorum.' This passage may be quoted as a good example of a *crescendo* in the descriptive style:—

THE CHRISTMAS DINNER.

'Much of the conversation during dinner turned upon family topics, to which I was a stranger. There was, however, a great deal of rallying of Master Simon about some gay widow, with whom he was accused of having a flirtation. This attack was commenced by the ladies; but it was continued throughout the dinner by the fat-headed old gentleman next the parson, with the persevering assiduity of a slow hound; being one of those long-winded jokers, who, though rather dull at starting game, are unrivalled for their talent in hunting it down. At every pause in the general conversation, he renewed his bantering in pretty much the same terms; winking hard at me with both eyes whenever he gave Master Simon what he considered a home-thrust. The latter, indeed, seemed fond of being teased on the subject, as old bachelors are apt to be; and he took occasion to inform me, in an under-tone, that the lady in question was a prodigiously fine woman, and drove her own curricle.

The dinner-time passed away in this flow of innocent hilarity; and though the old hall may have resounded in its time with many a scene of broader rout and revel, yet I doubt whether it ever witnessed more honest and genuine enjoyment. How easy it is for one benevolent being to diffuse pleasure around him; and how truly is a kind heart a fountain of gladness, making everything in its vicinity to freshen into smiles! The joyous disposition of the worthy squire was perfectly contagious: he was happy himself, and disposed to make all the world happy; and the little eccentricities of his humour did but season, in a manner, the sweetness of his philanthropy.

When the ladies had retired, the conversation, as usual, became still more animated; many good things were broached which had been thought of during dinner, but which would not exactly do for a lady's ear; and though I cannot positively affirm that there was much wit uttered, yet I have certainly heard many contests of rare wit produce much less laughter. Wit, after all, is a mighty tart, pungent ingredient, and much too acid for some stomachs; but honest good-humour is the oil and wine of a merry-meeting, and there is no jovial companionship equal to that where the jokes are rather small, and the laughter abundant.

The squire told several long stories of early college pranks and adventures, in some of which the parson had been a sharer; though, in looking at the latter, it required some effort of imagination to figure such a little dark anatomy of a man into the perpetrator of a madcap gambol. Indeed, the two college-chums presented pictures of what men may be made by their different lots in life. The squire had left the university, to live lustily on his paternal domains, in the vigorous enjoyment of prosperity and sunshine, and had flourished on to a hearty and florid old age; whilst the poor parson, on the contrary, had dried and withered away, among dusty tomes, in the silence and shadows of his study. Still there seemed to be a spark of almost extinguished fire, feebly glimmering in the bottom of his soul; and as the squire hinted at a sly story of the parson and a pretty milkmaid, whom they once met on the banks of the Isis, the old gentleman made an "alphabet of faces," which, as far as I could decipher his physiognomy, I verily believe was indicative of laughter; indeed, I have rarely met with an old gentleman that took absolute offence at the imputed gallantries of his youth.

I found the tide of wine and wassail fast gaining on the dry land of sober judgment. The company grew merrier and louder as their jokes grew duller. Master Simon was in as chirping a humour as a grasshopper filled with dew; his old songs grew of a warmer complexion, and he began to talk maudlin about the widow. He even gave a long song about the wooing of a widow, which he informed me he had gathered from an excellent black-letter work, entitled *Cupid's Solicitor for Love*, containing store of good advice for bachelors, and which he promised to lend me. The first verse was to this effect:—

> "He that will woo a widow must not dally,
> He must make hay while the sun doth shine;
> He must not stand with her—shall I, shall I?
> But boldly say: Widow, thou must be mine."

This song inspired the fat-headed old gentleman, who made several attempts to tell a rather broad story out of *Joe Miller*, that was pat to the purpose; but he always stuck in the middle, everybody recollecting the latter part excepting himself. The parson, too, began to shew the effects of good cheer, having gradually settled down into a doze, and his wig sitting most suspiciously on one side. Just at this juncture we were summoned to the drawing-room, and, I suspect, at the private instigation of mine host, whose joviality seemed always tempered with a proper love of decorum.'

We must now leave the English sketches, and give some notice of the Dutch-American legends.

For its quiet humour, graphic skill, and melody of style, the *Legend of Sleepy Hollow* is more worthy of notice than many fictions of greater pretension. It is said that on one of the wide coves on the eastern shore of the Hudson, there lies a rural port named Tarry-town; and about two miles inland from this place lies 'a little valley, or rather lap of land, among high hills, which is one of the quietest places in the whole world. . . . . From the listless repose of the place, and the peculiar character of its inhabitants, who are descendants from the original Dutch settlers, this sequestered glen has long been known by the name of Sleepy Hollow, and its rustic lads are called the Sleepy Hollow Boys throughout all the neighbouring country. A drowsy, dreamy influence seems to hang over the land, and to pervade the very atmosphere. Some say that the place was bewitched by a high German doctor, during the early days of the settlement; others, that an old Indian chief, the prophet or wizard of his tribe, held his powwows there before the country was discovered by Master Hendrick Hudson. Certain it is, the place still continues under the sway of some witching power, that holds a spell over the minds of the good people, causing them to walk in a continual reverie. They are given to all kinds of marvellous beliefs; are subject to trances and visions; and frequently see strange sights, and hear music and voices in the air.'

In another paper, intended to quell the doubts of all who would regard 'this pleasant land of drowsy-head' as a mere dream-picture, the writer completes the sketch by adding a notice of the church in the Hollow: 'The congregation, in those days, was of a truly rural character. City fashions had not as yet stolen up to Sleepy Hollow. Dutch sun-bonnets and honest homespun still prevailed. Everything was in primitive style, even to the bucket of water and tin-cup near the door in summer, to assuage the thirst caused by the heat of the weather or the drouth of the sermon. . . . . The drowsy influence of Sleepy Hollow was apt to breathe into this sacred edifice; and now and then an elder might be seen with his handkerchief over his face to keep off the flies, and apparently listening to the dominie, but really sunk into a summer slumber, lulled by the sultry notes of the locust from the neighbouring trees.'

The genius of the Hollow was a schoolmaster—an intellectual pioneer, named Ichabod Crane. 'The cognomen of Crane was not inapplicable to his person. He was tall, but exceedingly lank, with narrow shoulders, long arms and legs, hands that dangled a mile out of his sleeves, feet that might have served for shovels, and his whole frame most loosely hung together. His head was small, and flat at top, with huge ears, large green glassy eyes, and a long snipe-nose, so that it looked like a weather-cock, perched upon his spindle neck, to tell which way the wind blew. To see him striding along the profile of a hill on a windy day, with his clothes bagging and fluttering about him, one might have mistaken him for the genius of Famine descending upon the earth, or some scarecrow eloped from a cornfield. The school-house stood in a rather lonely but pleasant situation, just at the foot of a woody hill, with a brook running close by, and a formidable birch-tree growing at one end of it. From hence the low murmur of his pupils' voices, conning over their lessons, might be heard in a drowsy summer-day, like the hum of a bee-hive; interrupted now and then by the authoritative voice of the master, in the tone of menace or command; or, peradventure, by the appalling sound of the birch, as he urged some tardy loiterer along the flowery path of knowledge.'

The accomplishments of the schoolmaster were various: he was the singing-master of the neighbourhood; he assisted the farmers occasionally in the lighter labours of their farms;

and knew how, by pleasing discourse on dreamy and ghostly topics, to make himself welcome at the hearths of the good Dutch housewives, with whom he occasionally tarried. To help out his maintenance, he was, according to country custom in those parts, boarded and lodged at the houses of the farmers whose children he instructed. With these, he lived successively a week at a time, thus going the rounds of the neighbourhood, with all his worldly effects tied up in a cotton handkerchief. His musical powers were too remarkable to be left unnoticed. 'It was a matter of no little vanity to him, on Sundays, to take his station in front of the church-gallery, with a band of chosen singers, where, in his own mind, he completely carried away the palm from the parson. Certain it is, his voice resounded far above all the rest of the congregation; and there are peculiar quavers still to be heard in that church, and which may even be heard half a mile off, quite to the opposite side of the mill-pond, on a still Sunday morning, which are said to be legitimately descended from the nose of Ichabod Crane.'

One of the infirmities in the mental constitution of Ichabod Crane, caused partly by his residence in this haunted valley, was his 'appetite for the marvellous:'—

'No tale was too gross or monstrous for his capacious swallow. It was often his delight, after his school was dismissed in the afternoon, to stretch himself on the rich bed of clover, bordering the little brook that whimpered by his school-house, and there con over old Mather's direful tales, until the gathering dusk of the evening made the printed page a mere mist before his eyes. Then, as he wended his way by swamp, and stream, and awful woodland, to the farm-house where he happened to be quartered, every sound of nature, at that witching hour, fluttered his excited imagination: the moan of the whip-poor-will[1] from the hillside; the boding cry of the tree-toad, that harbinger of storm; the dreary hooting of the screech-owl, or the sudden rustling in the thicket of birds frightened from their roost. The fireflies, too, which sparkled most vividly in the darkest places, now and then startled him, as one of uncommon brightness would stream across his path; and if by chance a huge blockhead of a beetle came winging his blundering flight against him, the poor varlet was ready to give up the ghost, with the idea that he was struck with a witch's token. His only resource on such occasions, either to drown thought or drive away evil spirits, was to sing psalm-tunes; and the good people of Sleepy Hollow, as they sat by their doors of an evening, were often filled with awe at hearing his nasal melody, "in linked sweetness long drawn out," floating from the distant hill, or along the dusky road.'

[1] The whip-poor-will is a bird which is only heard at night. It receives its name from its note, which is thought to resemble those words.

Even in such an abode as the Hollow, full repose cannot be enjoyed by mortals who allow ambition to enter their minds. We forebode mischief for Ichabod when we are told that, 'among the musical disciples who assembled one evening in each week to receive his instructions in psalmody, was Katrina Van Tassel, the daughter and only child of a substantial Dutch farmer. She was a blooming lass of fresh eighteen, plump as a partridge, ripe and melting, and rosy-cheeked as one of her father's peaches, and universally famed, not merely for her beauty, but her vast expectations.' The picture of the farmer's homestead might well captivate the imagination of the dominie. 'A great elm-tree spread its broad branches over it, at the foot of which bubbled up a spring of the softest and sweetest water in a little well, formed of a barrel, and then stole sparkling away through the grass to a neighbouring brook that bubbled along among alders and dwarf willows.' But all the poetry of the rural mansion and its lively farmyard was lost in Ichabod's visions of substantial benefits :—

'The pedagogue's mouth watered as he looked upon his sumptuous promise of luxurious winter fare. In his devouring mind's-eye, he pictured to himself every roasting-pig running about with a pudding in his belly, and an apple in his mouth ; the pigeons were snugly put to bed in a comfortable pie, and tucked in with a coverlet of crust ; the geese were swimming in their own gravy ; and the ducks pairing cosily in dishes, like snug married couples, with a decent competency of onion-sauce. In the porkers, he saw carved out the future sleek side of bacon and juicy relishing ham ; not a turkey but he beheld daintily trussed-up, with its gizzard under its wing, and, peradventure, a necklace of savoury sausages ; and even bright chanticleer himself lay sprawling on his back in a side-dish, with uplifted claws, as if craving that quarter which his chivalrous spirit disdained to ask while living.

As the enraptured Ichabod fancied all this, and as he rolled his great green eyes over the fat meadow-lands, the rich fields of wheat, of rye, of buckwheat, and Indian corn, and the orchards burdened with ruddy fruit, which surrounded the warm tenement of Van Tassel, his heart yearned after the damsel who was to inherit these domains, and his imagination expanded with the idea, how they might be readily turned into cash, and the money invested in immense tracts of wild land and shingle-palaces in the wilderness. Nay, his busy fancy already realised his hopes, and presented to him the blooming Katrina, with a whole family of children, mounted on the top of a wagon loaded with household trumpery, with pots and kettles dangling beneath ; and he beheld himself bestriding a pacing mare, with a colt at her heels, setting out for Kentucky, Tennessee, or the Lord knows where.'

Before this delightful dream of Katrina, with her sundry appurtenances, could be realised, a formidable rival must be vanquished. This was 'Brom Bones, a roistering Dutch lad, broad-shouldered and double-jointed, with short, curly black hair. He was always ready for either a fight or a frolic, but had more mischief than ill-will in his composition; and with all his overbearing roughness, there was a strong dash of waggish good-humour at bottom. This rantipole hero had for some time singled out the blooming Katrina for the object of his uncouth gallantries.' By the soothing powers of his psalmody, aided by 'a quiet and gently insinuating manner,' the schoolmaster contrived to maintain awhile an apparent advantage over his rival. Their competition arrived at its crisis at a family-gathering in the home of Van Tassel, to which Ichabod Crane was of course invited. As he rode along to the house of feasting, no bad omens of coming disappointment vexed his mind. The scenery of the journey is given in a passage which shews how well Irving can blend the beautiful with the humorous:—

'It was, as I have said, a fine autumnal day; the sky was clear and serene, and nature wore that rich and golden livery which we always associate with the idea of abundance. The forests had put on their sober brown and yellow, while some trees of the tenderer kind had been nipped by the frosts into brilliant dyes of orange, purple, and scarlet. Streaming files of wild-ducks began to make their appearance high in the air; the bark of the squirrel might be heard from the groves of beech and hickory nuts, and the pensive whistle of the quail at intervals from the neighbouring stubble-field.

The small birds were taking their farewell banquets. In the fulness of their revelry, they fluttered, chirping and frolicking, from bush to bush and tree to tree, capricious from the very profusion and variety around them. There was the honest cock-robin, the favourite game of stripling sportsmen, with its loud querulous note; and the twittering black-birds flying in sable clouds; and the golden-winged woodpecker, with his crimson crest, his broad black gorget, and splendid plumage; and the cedar-bird, with its red-tipt wings and yellow-tipt tail, and its little monteiro cap of feathers; and the blue jay, that noisy coxcomb, in his gay light-blue coat and white under-clothes; screaming and chattering, nodding and bobbing and bowing, and pretending to be on good terms with every songster of the grove.

As Ichabod jogged slowly on his way, his eye, ever open to every symptom of culinary abundance, ranged with delight over the treasures of jolly autumn. On all sides he beheld vast stores of apples; some hanging in oppressive opulence on the trees; some gathered into baskets and barrels for the market; others heaped up in rich piles for the cider-press. Further on, he beheld great fields of Indian corn, with its golden ears peeping from their leafy coverts, and holding out the promise of cakes and hasty-pudding; and the yellow pumpkins lying beneath them, turning up their fair round bellies to the sun, and giving ample prospects of the most luxurious of pies; and anon he passed the fragrant buckwheat-fields, breathing the odour of the bee-hive; and as he beheld them, soft anticipations stole over his mind of dainty slapjacks, well buttered and garnished with honey or treacle by the delicate little dimpled hand of Katrina Van Tassel.

Thus feeding his mind with many sweet thoughts and "sugared suppositions," he journeyed along the sides of a range of hills which look out upon some of the goodliest scenes of the mighty Hudson.'

The interior of the state-parlour of Van Tassel realised all the dominie's anticipations; for here were spread out, in a bewildering profusion, 'apple-pies and peach-pies and pumpkin-pies; besides slices of ham and smoked beef; and, moreover, delectable dishes of preserved plums and peaches, and pears and quinces; not to mention broiled shad and roasted chickens.' The hopes of Ichabod Crane were excited to an almost extravagant degree. 'He was a kind and thankful creature, whose heart dilated in proportion as his skin was filled with good cheer; and whose spirits rose with eating as some men's do with drink. He could not help, too, rolling his large eyes round him as he ate, and chuckling with the possibility that he might one day be lord of all this scene of almost unimaginable luxury and splendour. Then he thought how soon he'd turn his back upon the old school-house, snap his fingers in the face of Hans Van Ripper, and every other niggardly patron, and kick any itinerant pedagogue out of doors that should dare to call him comrade!'

Meanwhile, filled with substantial good things, he had almost forgotten that Sleepy Hollow was a haunted glen; and that, after the feast, he must ride homeward by a route including some localities not quite 'canny.' These were recalled to his mind by the talk after supper. Several dreamy ghost-stories were solemnly told as the darkness gathered, and among others, the old and well-known story of the 'headless Hessian trooper,' whose body was buried in the church-yard of Sleepy Hollow, and whose 'ghost rides forth to the scene of battle in nightly quest of his head.' Brom Bones, the rival, took a prominent part in the talk about the headless horseman; and Ichabod, to maintain his superiority, told of fearful sights which he had seen in his nightly walks about the valley. When the revel broke up, the schoolmaster lingered behind to have a tête-à-tête with the heiress, which, for some unexplained reason, must have been unsatisfactory, as he 'sallied forth, after no very great interval, with an air quite desolate and chop-fallen.' As he pursued his way homeward, 'all the stories of ghosts and goblins that he had heard in the afternoon came crowding upon his recollection. When he approached the haunted bridge, he was fully prepared to see the phantom of which his rival had given such a graphic account, and, lo! 'in the dark shadow of the grove, on the margin of the brook, he beheld something huge, misshapen, black, and towering.' Ichabod quickened his steed, and a lively chase of ghost after schoolmaster ensued. When he reached the vanishing-place of which his rival had told, he ventured to cast a look behind. 'Just then he saw the goblin rising in his stirrups, and in the very act of hurling his head at him. Ichabod endeavoured to dodge the horrible missile, but too late! It encountered his cranium with a tremendous crash—he was tumbled headlong into the dust, and Gunpowder, the black steed, and the goblin rider, passed by like a whirlwind.

The next morning, the old horse was found without his saddle, and with the bridle under his feet, soberly cropping the grass at his master's gate. Ichabod did not make his appearance at breakfast—dinner-hour came, but no Ichabod. The boys assembled at the school-house, and strolled idly about the banks of the brook; but no schoolmaster. Hans Van Ripper now began to feel some uneasiness about the fate of poor Ichabod and his saddle. An inquiry was set on foot, and after diligent investigation, they came upon his traces. In one part of the road leading to the church, was found the saddle trampled in the dirt; the tracks of horses' hoofs deeply dented in the road, and evidently at furious speed, were traced to the bridge, beyond which, on the bank of a broad part of the brook, where the water ran deep and black, was found the hat of the unfortunate Ichabod, and close beside it a shattered pumpkin.

The brook was searched, but the body of the schoolmaster was not to be discovered. Hans Van Ripper, as executor of his estate, examined the bundle which contained all his worldly effects. They consisted of two shirts and a half, two stocks for the neck, a pair or two of worsted stockings, an old pair of corduroy small-clothes, a rusty razor, a book of psalm-tunes, full of dog's ears, and a broken pitch-pipe. . . . . Brom Bones, who shortly after his rival's disappearance conducted the blooming Katrina in triumph to the altar, was observed to look exceedingly knowing whenever the story of Ichabod was related, and always burst into a hearty laugh at the mention of the pumpkin; which led some to suspect that he knew more about the matter than he chose to tell.

The old country wives, however, who are the best judges of these matters, maintain to this day that Ichabod was spirited away by supernatural means; and it is a favourite story often told about the neighbourhood round the winter-evening fire. The bridge became more than ever an object of superstitious awe, and that may be the reason why the road has been altered of late years, so as to approach the church by the border of the millpond. The school-house being deserted, soon fell to decay, and was reported to be haunted by the ghost of the unfortunate pedagogue; and the plough-boy, loitering homeward of a still summer evening, has often fancied his voice at a distance, chanting a melancholy psalm-tune among the tranquil solitudes of Sleepy Hollow.'

JAMES FENIMORE COOPER.

'No American writer has been so extensively read as JAMES FENIMORE COOPER. His novels have been translated in nearly every European tongue. . . . We have seen some of them, well thumbed and worn, at a little village in a remote mountainous district of Sicily; and in Naples and Milan, the bookstalls bear witness that *L'Ultimo dei Mohecanni* [The Last of the Mohicans] is still a popular work. In England, these American novels have been eagerly read and transformed into popular dramas; while cheap and often stupidly mutilated editions of them have been circulated through all her colonies, garrisons, and naval stations, from New Zealand to Canada.'[1] The review from which the above paragraph is quoted, also states that, 'of all American writers, Cooper is the most original, the most thoroughly national.'

These opinions, given in a review of Cooper's collected novels, are sufficient to shew that, whatever our own opinion of his merits may be, his name deserves a prominent place in this account of American literature.

He was born at Burlington, New Jersey, in 1789. His course of studies in Yale College ended in 1805, when he entered the navy. After six years of service, he retired to private life, and resided at Cooperstown, on the border of Otsego Lake, in the midst of the scenes described in one of his fictions. Soon afterwards, he published his first novel, *Precaution*, which American reviewers absurdly described as a work displaying a considerable knowledge of 'English society.' It was followed by a better fiction, *The Spy*, which was very successful, though

1 *North American Review*, No. 154, Art. VI.

it was unfavourably reviewed in America. In 1823 appeared *The Pioneers*, which may be noticed hereafter as one of a series of tales. *The Pilot*, commonly regarded as the best of the sea-stories, followed, but gained no high reputation until the praise of English critics found echoes in America. In this novel, the fate of a vessel, the *Ariel*—which might almost be described as the heroine—is narrated with a singular force and truthfulness; and Long Tom Coffin is one of the best characters portrayed by the author. *Lionel Lincoln*, the next publication, has been regarded as a failure. It was followed (1826) by *The Last of the Mohicans*, one of the most widely circulated of modern fictions.

The Prairie, *The Red Rover*, *The Wept of Wish-ton-Wish*, and *The Water-witch*, followed too rapidly—all bearing marks of hasty execution. Meanwhile the author had visited Europe, and had published his *Notions of the Americans*, a vindication of the institutions and manners of his own country. In his next work of fiction, *The Bravo*, he left the lakes and forests of the West, and selected foreign scenes and characters. It was followed by *The Heidenmauer*, *The Headsman of Berne*, and a very dull, satirical novel, *The Monikins*.

Cooper next published his *Gleanings in Europe*, consisting of ten volumes of sketches, and criticisms of scenes, society, and manners in the Old World. In his *American Democrat* (1835), he appeared as a didactic writer, and described the virtues and failings of his countrymen. In 1839, the *History of the Navy of the United States* was published. Of several novels intended to castigate the errors of American society, it would be useless to mention even the titles, for they are commonly regarded as very dull productions. *Homeward Bound* and *The Two Admirals* belong to the series of romances of naval life. *The Deerslayer* and *The Pathfinder* may be described in our notice of the series to which they belong. It is said that the writer regarded these two as his best fictions. *Mercedes of Castile*, *Wing-and-Wing*, *Wyandotte*, and *Ashore and Afloat*, displayed the author's power of diffusing a few ideas over a vast surface of paper; though they contained many passages of lively description. Altogether, in the course of thirty years, or little more, Cooper published about the same number of novels and romances, besides many volumes of history and travels. Thus every year produced, on an average, its two or three volumes. Shortly before his decease (1851), he was engaged in preparing a work, under the title, *The Middle States of America; their Origins, Customs, Conditions, and Prospects.*

With regard to his apparent productiveness, Cooper may be classed with the modern novelists who have written as if they expected that their works would be estimated according to their bulk. The number of the distinct characters portrayed in the whole series of his novels, bears a very small proportion to the number of pages, or, we might say, volumes. This seems to be commonly admitted; yet an American writer[1] has hazarded the assertion, that 'very few authors have added more than one original and striking character to the world of imagination; *none has added more than Cooper;* and his are all as distinct and actual as the personages that stalk before us on the stage of history.' It is fair to state that this assertion appears almost as singular in America as in England. The comparison of Cooper with Scott is a mere absurdity. Another American reviewer has said, that Cooper never invented more than '*two* probable and interesting characters —Long Tom Coffin and the Leather-stocking;' and that 'the latter of these, as if to shew how much the writer was delighted with his success, was made to figure in about six different novels.'[2]

This series of tales—in which the adventures of a simple hunter are described—is commonly regarded as the best; and the tales intended to have a satirical purport may be described as the worst of Cooper's fictions. The excessive dulness of the latter is explained by the fact, that the writer made them vehicles of controversy with certain neighbours and with newspaper-editors.

In the better works of Cooper—such as have their scenes in the forest, or on the sea—the plot is often grossly improbable; the conversations and the speeches of Red Indians are unreal and tedious; and the female characters are, with few exceptions, failures or nonentities. This last feature accounts for the little favour which these tales have found among female readers. They have been read chiefly by youths who love stories of adventure, narrow escapes, skirmishes with Indians, and ambuscades. These features are so often repeated, that in *The Last of the Mohicans*, and other stories, the reader becomes almost careless about heroes and heroines, knowing that, though surrounded by levelled rifles, they will be sure to make their escape. Critics who ought to have good information on the subject, have said that the characters of Cooper's Red Indians are mostly imaginary, and that their propensity to speech-making is caricatured.

The chief merits of Cooper's tales consist in their descriptions of scenery, and adventures in the forest and on the sea. In their sketches of the lakes and forests of the West, a genuine love of nature, and a tone of feeling, such as is commonly but vaguely styled poetical, redeem passages of great prolixity. A fact may

[1] Griswold's *Prose-writers of America*, Fourth Edition.
[2] *North American Review*, No. 148, Art. V.

indicate at once the merits and the defects of such tales as the Leather-stocking series. The reader of ripe years, who, for the first time, peruses *The Pathfinder* or *The Pioneers*, may very probably be offended by long conversations and other wordy passages, or by some awkward attempts in humorous writing, and may impatiently lay down the half-read book; but the man who, in his boyhood or youth, followed the career of Hawk-eye, retains memories so strong of lonely lakes and forests, beleaguered travellers, Indian scalping-parties, and thrilling adventures—like that of the battle at Glenn's Falls—that he is tempted to renew his acquaintance with Cooper's tales. Apart from distinct description, there is in these fictions the pervading influence of solitary forest-life. We might even say that, as Wordsworth's poems rather breathe the spirit than describe the exact features of our English Lake district, so Cooper's best tales have the spirit of the sombre, or tranquil, or majestic scenes in which their adventures take place. So far as they have any moral tone, it is pure and elevated; and the portraiture of that simple and manly pioneer the Pathfinder, reflects great credit on the author. As this is certainly the most successful of Cooper's creations, some account of the series of tales to which it belongs may be given here.

The first of the series is *The Deerslayer*. Its scenery is on and around Lake Otsego, in the district of New York; which, at the time of the story, was mostly 'a virgin wilderness'—'one vast expanse of woods, relieved by a comparatively narrow fringe of cultivation along the sea, dotted by the glittering surfaces of lakes, and intersected by the waving lines of rivers.' The scene of adventures is thus more fully described:—'On all sides, wherever the eye turned, nothing met it but the mirror-like surface of the lake, the placid view of heaven, and the dense setting of woods. So rich and fleecy were the outlines of the forest, that scarce an opening could be seen; the whole visible earth, from the rounded mountain-top to the water's edge, presenting one unvaried line of unbroken verdure. As if vegetation were not satisfied with a triumph so complete, the trees overhung the lake itself, shooting out towards the light; and there were miles along its eastern shore, where a boat might have pulled beneath the branches of dark Rembrandt-looking hemlocks, "quivering aspens," and melancholy pines. In a word, the hand of man had never yet defaced or deformed any part of this native scene, which lay bathed in the sunlight, a glorious picture of affluent forest-grandeur, softened by the balminess of June, and relieved by the beautiful variety afforded by the presence of so broad an expanse of water.'

Here the lonely young hunter—now styled the Deerslayer—dwells in solitude and freedom; living, like his neighbours the Indians, by the chase, but distinguishing himself by higher and better thoughts and feelings. His great characteristic was guileless truth, sincerity of feeling and expression; and his face had 'an air of integrity so simple, as to awaken the suspicion of a want of the usual means [ability?] to distinguish between truth and artifice; but few came into serious contact with the man without losing this distrust.' The story of *The Deerslayer* consists chiefly of a feud with the Indians on the banks of Lake Otsego. The two female characters, Judith and Hetty Hutter, give some variety to the tale, and the former is allowed to be Cooper's nearest approach to a faithful portraiture of woman. Judith is remarkably handsome and intelligent, but her reputation, previous to her residence in the ark on the lonely lake, had not been unsullied by suspicions. She understands and appreciates the honest, faithful, and manly heart of the Deerslayer; and, rather than return to dwell among civilised people, would share with him the dangers and the joys of his life in the forest. But the simple hunter admires only, and cannot love; nor can he understand, until it is too plainly spoken, the preference bestowed on him. After Judith has made a bold effort to save his life, while he is a prisoner among the Indians, the tale is concluded by a conversation which is very singular, and must expose the writer to the censure of all fair readers who well understand their own privileges and restrictions.

In the next tale, the hero—now known as the Pathfinder—takes a part in the adventures of the old French war. The descriptions of Lake Ontario, with its surrounding district, are distinct and interesting, but partly borrowed, it is said, from Mrs Grant's *Memoirs of an American Lady*. The opening of the story includes one of the writer's best descriptions of an Indian ambuscade; and in several other passages, situations of breathless suspense are vividly represented.

The Last of the Mohicans is the third, and the most popular, in the series of the Leather-stocking tales. Its plot is very improbable, but serves to introduce many details of perilous adventure. Two sisters, under the guidance of the hero—here known as Hawk-eye—travel through a forest infested by Indian scalping-parties. Major Heyward, the lover of Alice, with two Indians—Chingachgook and Uncas—and a ridiculous character styled David Gamut, 'a singing-master,' complete the party of travellers. The object of the journey is to reach a fort near the Hudson, commanded by a veteran officer, the father of Cora and Alice. Though there is a good and safe road connecting the two British forts, Major Heyward—for some reason not clearly explained—prefers to lead his betrothed Alice, and her sister Cora, by a very dangerous route through the forest. At the commencement of the journey, an Indian scout discovers the party, and guesses their intentions. 'The cavalcade had not long passed, before the branches of the bushes that formed the thicket were cautiously moved asunder, and a human visage, as fiercely wild as savage art and unbridled passions could make it, peered out on the retiring footsteps of the travellers. A gleam of exultation shot across the darkly painted lineaments of the inhabitant of the forest, as he traced the route of his intended victims, who rode unconsciously onward, the light and graceful forms of the females waving among the trees in the curvatures of their path, followed at each bend by the manly figure of Heyward, until finally the shapeless person of the singing-master was concealed behind the numberless trunks of trees that rose in dark lines in the intermediate space.'

From this moment the tale is occupied with the details of ambushments and conflicts of cunning and stratagem between the Mingo Indians on one side, and the travelling-party on the other. The first object of the scout Hawk-eye is to throw the cunning Mingoes 'on a wrong scent.' For this purpose, he enjoins on his companions that they must preserve a strict silence, let what will happen—and guides them to a place of shelter on an island at the foot of Glenn's Falls, a romantic cataract. This position gives great advantages in a contest against superior numbers, but the odds against the travelling-party are formidable. A strange cry alarms them, soon after they have concealed themselves in the cavern at the Falls, and it becomes evident that the Mingoes have tracked the white people to their hiding-place. The subsequent adventures cannot be understood without a description of the locality :—

'The river was confined between high and cragged rocks, one of which impended above the spot where the canoe rested. As these, again, were surmounted by tall trees, which appeared to totter on the brows of the precipice, it gave the stream the appearance of running through a deep and narrow dell. All beneath the fantastic limbs and ragged tree-tops, which were here and there dimly painted against the starry zenith, lay alike in shadowed obscurity. Behind them, the curvature of the banks soon bounded the view, by the same dark and wooded outline ; but in front, and apparently at no great distance, the water seemed piled against the heavens, whence it tumbled into caverns, out of which issued those sullen sounds that had loaded the evening atmosphere. It seemed, in truth, to be a spot devoted to seclusion, and the sisters imbibed a soothing impression of increased security, as they gazed upon its romantic, though not unappalling beauties. A general movement among their conductors, however, soon recalled them from a contemplation of the wild charms that night had assisted to lend the place, to a painful sense of their real peril.

* * * *

"We are then on an island?" [said Heyward.]

"Ay!" [the scout replied]—"there are the Falls on two sides of us, and the river above and below. If you had daylight, it would be worth the trouble to step up on the height of this rock, and look at the perversity of the water. It falls by no rule at all: sometimes it leaps, sometimes it tumbles; there it skips, here it shoots; in one place 'tis white as snow, and in another 'tis green as grass; hereabouts it pitches into deep hollows, that rumble and quake the 'arth, and thereaway it ripples and sings like a brook, fashioning whirlpools and gullies in the old stone, as if 'twas no harder than trodden clay. The whole design of the river seems disconcerted."'

When the party had found shelter in the cavern at the Falls, David Gamut, teacher of psalmody, began to 'offer up evening praise' after a day of jeopardy, and sang, amid the thunders of the cataract, a slow and solemn psalm-tune. The sisters, Cora and Alice, blended their voices in the pious strain, which was interrupted by a cry that 'seemed neither human nor earthly.' This was followed, after an interval, by a tumult of yells, filling the woods, the caverns of the Falls, the rocks, the bed of the river, and the upper air; 'as if demons had possessed themselves of the air, and were venting their savage humours in barbarous sounds.' As David, the singing-master, incautiously exposed himself, in looking out for the source of these noises, the reports of rifles were heard. Meanwhile, a party of Indians had made the hazardous experiment of swimming down the rapids, and several had succeeded in reaching the head of the island. 'Four human heads could be seen peering above a few logs of drift-wood that had lodged on these naked rocks, and which had probably suggested the idea of the practicability of the hazardous undertaking. At the next moment, a fifth form was seen floating over the green edge of the fall, a little from the true line of the island. The savage struggled powerfully to gain the point of safety, and, favoured by the glancing water, he was already stretching forth an arm to meet the grasp of his companions, when he shot away again with the whirling current, appeared to rise in the air, with uplifted arms and starting eyeballs, and then fell with a sullen plunge into the deep and yawning abyss over which he hovered. A single wild, despairing shriek rose from the cavern above the dull roar of the cataract, and all was hushed again as the grave.'

Four of the adventurous savages had made a landing, and now sprang from the cover of drift-wood, and attacked the travellers. A desperate hand-to-hand contest followed on the brink of the Falls. The rifle of Hawk-eye brought the foremost Indian to the ground; Uncas, the young Mohican, encountered the second; and the fate of the other two is thus narrated:—

'With ready skill, Hawk-eye and his antagonist each grasped that uplifted arm of the other which held the dangerous knife. For near a minute they stood looking one another in the eye, and gradually exerting the power of their muscles for the mastery. At length the toughened sinews of the white man prevailed over the less-practised limbs of the native. The arm of the latter slowly gave way before the increasing force of the scout, who, suddenly wresting his armed hand from the grasp of his foe, drove the sharp weapon through his naked bosom to the heart. In the meantime, Heyward had been pressed in a more deadly struggle. His slight sword was snapped in the first encounter. As he was destitute of any other means of defence, his safety now depended entirely on bodily strength and resolution. Though deficient in neither of these qualities, he had met an enemy every way his equal. Happily, he soon succeeded in disarming his adversary, whose knife fell on the rock at their feet, and from this moment it became a fierce struggle who should cast the other over the dizzy height into a neighbouring cavern of the Falls. Every successive struggle brought them nearer to the verge, where Duncan perceived the final and conquering effort must be made. Each of the combatants threw all his energies into that effort, and the result was that both tottered on the brink of the precipice. Heyward felt the grasp of the other at his throat, and saw the grim smile the savage gave, under the revengeful hope that he hurried his enemy to a fate similar to his own, as he felt his body slowly yielding to a resistless power, and the young man experienced the passing agony of such a moment in all its horrors. At that instant of extreme danger, a dark hand and glancing knife appeared before him: the Indian released his hold as the blood flowed freely from around the severed tendons of his wrist; and while Duncan was drawn backward by the saving arm of Uncas, his charmed eyes were still rivetted on the fierce and disappointed countenance of his foe, who fell sullenly and disappointed down the irrecoverable precipice.'

The failure of ammunition at last compels the scout and his companions to abandon the hope of defending their position, and there is every prospect that the party must fall into the hands of the Indians; yet at this crisis the writer again indulges his peculiar notions of humour. David Gamut, the professor of psalmody, now pulls out his pitch-pipe, gives the key-note, and proposes that his friends should refresh their courage by joining in singing a delectable psalm-tune, commonly known as the *Isle of Wight.* This performance is hardly concluded, when it is found that the Hurons have made themselves masters of the island, and soon afterwards, the sisters Cora and Alice, with Major Heyward and the tuneful Gamut, are made prisoners. A rescue is effected by Hawk-eye, assisted by the friendly Mohicans—Chingachgook, surnamed 'the Great Serpent,' and his son Uncas—but not without a terrible struggle, which concludes with a fierce duel between the Indians Magua, or 'the Cunning Fox,' and the Great Serpent. The description of this combat is a fair example of the zest with which Cooper often narrated such adventures, and includes some features which have made his works repulsive to readers of refined taste.

After all the tragedy, the writer affords some relief to the reader's feelings, and brings upon the stage his solitary humorous character—David Gamut—who now draws out of his pockets the psalm-book and the pitch-pipe, and, having adjusted upon his nose a pair of iron-rimmed spectacles, lifts up his voice and says: 'I invite you, friends, to join in praise for this signal deliverance from the hands of barbarians and infidels, to the comfortable and solemn tones of the tune called *Northampton*.' Accordingly, he sings the said *Northampton* to a psalm of long or common metre, as a song of victory over the Hurons. Such was Cooper's taste in the supposed comic style!

In *The Pioneers*—which American critics have described as the best of this series of tales—the hero is found in new circumstances, and surrounded by scenes and characters belonging to the times which in America may be styled old, as they are recollected only by the oldest settlers. The primitive hunter—formerly

> 'As free as Nature first made man
> When wild in woods the noble savage ran'—

now finds himself closed in by the restrictions of an advancing civilisation. The unbounded forest, without a proprietor, has been invaded; other laws than those of the sure rifle are acknowledged; and though the old hunter conceives that his rights in the forest are as well founded as any that can be secured on parchment, he finds that his antiquated notions must lead him further westward. The once lonely district of Otsego Lake, where first we found him—as the Deerslayer—is now a settlement, and is broken into several estates; game is becoming scarce; the Indians are departing, or vanishing away under the influence of contact with the white men; and Leather-stocking has been so long a man accustomed to unrestricted freedom, that he cannot breathe freely near houses, gardens, and enclosures.

Several scenes in this story were derived from the writer's recollections of his boyhood, and are well described.

The Prairie—the last of this series of fictions—is, on the whole, an inferior and improbable story. The hero, whose life has been described as a gradual retreat westward from the progress of society, ever spreading more and more from the east, is discovered, at last, as an aged trapper in the Far West, and here, among a tribe of Indians, his adventures come to a close. The story is connected with that of *The Last of the Mohicans*, as here, in the western prairie, the old trapper—formerly known as the scout Hawk-eye—recognises in the young officer, Middleton, the grandson of Major Heyward and Alice Munro, whom, half a century before, he had protected in the contest on the island at Glenn's Falls. Several passages of description relieve the general dulness of this story. The humorous character, Dr Obed Battius, the naturalist, is a worse specimen than the singing-master, David Gamut, in *The Mohicans*. As a favourable example of the writer's descriptive power, we may quote from *The Prairie* the following scene:—

THE PRAIRIE ON FIRE.

'The sleep of the fugitives lasted for several hours. The trapper was the first to shake off its influence, as he had been the last to court its refreshment. Rising, just as the gray light of day began to brighten that portion of the studded vault which rested on the eastern margin of the plain, he summoned his companions from their warm lairs, and pointed out the necessity of their being once more on the alert. . . . .

"See, Middleton!" exclaimed Inez in a sudden burst of youthful pleasure that caused her for a moment to forget her situation. "How lovely is that sky; surely it contains a promise of happier times!"

"It is glorious!" returned her husband. "Glorious and heavenly is that streak of vivid red, and here is a still brighter crimson—rarely have I seen a richer rising of the sun."

"Rising of the sun!" slowly repeated the old man, lifting his tall person from its seat with a deliberate and abstracted air, while he kept his eye rivetted on the changing and certainly beautiful tints that were garnishing the vault of heaven. "Rising of the sun! I like not such risings of the sun. Ah's me! the imps have circumvented us with a vengeance. The prairie is on fire!"

"God in heaven protect us!" cried Middleton, catching Inez to his bosom under the instant impression of the imminence of their danger. "There is no time to lose, old man; each instant is a day; let us fly."

"Whither?" demanded the trapper, motioning him with calmness and dignity, to arrest his steps. "In this wilderness of grass and reeds, you are like a vessel in the broad lakes without a compass. A single step on the wrong course might prove the destruction of us all. It is seldom danger is so pressing that there is not time enough for reason to do its work, young officer; therefore, let us await its biddings."

"For my own part," said Paul Hover, looking about him with no unequivocal expression of concern, "I acknowledge, that should this dry bed of weeds get fairly in a flame, a bee would have to make a flight higher than common to prevent his wings from scorching. Therefore, old trapper, I agree with the captain, and say mount and run."

"Ye are wrong—ye are wrong—man is not a beast to follow the gift of instinct, and to snuff up his knowledge by a taint in the air, or a rumbling in the sound; but he must see and reason, and then conclude. So follow me a little to the left, where there is a rise in the ground, whence we may make our reconnoitrings."

The old man waved his hand with authority, and led the way without further parlance to the spot he had indicated, followed by the whole of his alarmed companions. An eye less practised than that of the trapper might have failed in discovering the gentle elevation to which he alluded, and which looked on the surface of the meadow like a growth a little taller than common. When they reached the place, however, the stinted grass itself announced the absence of that moisture which had fed the rank weeds of most of the plain, and furnished a clue to the evidence by which he had judged of the formation of the ground hidden beneath. Here a few minutes were lost in breaking down the tops of the surrounding herbage, which, notwithstanding the advantage of their position, rose even above the heads of Middleton and Paul, and in obtaining a look-out that might command a view of the surrounding sea of fire. . . .

The examination which his companions so instantly and so intently made, rather served to assure them of their desperate situation than to appease their fears. Huge columns of smoke were rolling up from the plain, and thickening in gloomy masses around the horizon. The red glow which gleamed upon their enormous folds, now lighting their volumes with the glare of the conflagration, now flashed to another point, as the flame beneath glided ahead, leaving all behind enveloped in awful darkness, and proclaiming louder than words the character of the imminent and rapidly approaching danger.

"This is terrible!" exclaimed Middleton, folding the trembling Inez to his heart. "At such a time as this, and in such a manner!"

"The gates of heaven are open to all who truly believe," murmured the pious devotee in his bosom.

"This resignation is maddening! But we are men, and will make a struggle for our lives! How now, my brave and spirited friend, shall we yet mount and push across the flames, or shall we stand here and see those we most love perish in this frightful manner without an effort?"

"I am for a swarming-time, and a flight before the hive is too hot to hold us," said the bee-hunter, to whom it will be at once seen that the half-distracted Middleton addressed himself. "Come, old trapper, you must acknowledge this is but a slow way of getting out of danger. If we tarry here much longer, it will be in the fashion that the bees lie around the straw after the hive has been smoked for its honey. You may hear the fire begin to roar already; and I know by experience, that when the flame once gets fairly into the prairie-grass, it is no sloth that can outrun it."

"Think you," returned the old man, pointing scornfully at the mazes of the dry and matted grass which environed them, "that mortal feet can outstrip the speed of fire on such a path?"

"What say you, friend doctor," cried the bewildered Paul, turning to the naturalist with that sort of helplessness with which the strong are often apt to seek aid of the weak when human power is baffled by the hand of a mightier being—"what say you; have you no advice to give away in a case of life and death?"

The naturalist stood, tablets in hand, looking at the awful spectacle with as much composure as though the conflagration had been lighted in order to solve the difficulties of some scientific problem. Aroused by the question of his companion, he turned to his equally calm though differently occupied associate, the trapper, demanding, with the most provoking insensibility to the urgent nature of their situation—"Venerable hunter, you have often witnessed similar prismatic experiments"——

He was rudely interrupted by Paul, who struck the tablets from his hands with a violence that betrayed the utter intellectual confusion which had overset the equanimity of his mind. Before time was allowed for remonstrance, the old man, who had continued during the whole scene like one much at a loss how to proceed, though also like one who was rather perplexed than alarmed, suddenly assumed a decided air, as if he no longer doubted on the course it was most advisable to pursue.

"It is time to be doing," he said, interrupting the controversy that was about to ensue between the naturalist and the bee-hunter; "it is time to leave off books and moanings, and to be doing."

"You have come to your recollections too late, miserable old man," cried Middleton; "the flames are within a quarter of a mile of us, and the wind is bringing them down in this quarter with dreadful rapidity."

"Anan! the flames! I care but little for the flames. If I only knew how to circumvent the cunning of the Tetons, as I know how to cheat the fire of its prey, there would be nothing needed but thanks to the Lord for our deliverance. Do you call this a fire? If you had seen what I have witnessed in the eastern hills, when mighty mountains were like the furnace of a smith, you would have known what it was to fear the flames, and to be thankful that you were spared! Come, lads, come: 'tis time to be doing now, and to cease talking; for yonder curling flame is truly coming on like a trotting moose. Put hands upon this short and withered grass where we stand, and lay bare the 'arth."

"Would you think to deprive the fire of its victims in this childish manner?" exclaimed Middleton.

A faint but solemn smile passed over the features of the old man as he answered: "Your gran'ther would have said, that when the enemy was nigh, a soldier could do no better than to obey."

The captain felt the reproof, and instantly began to imitate the industry of Paul, who was tearing the decayed herbage from the ground in a sort of desperate compliance with the trapper's direction. Even Ellen lent her hands to the labour, nor was it long before Inez was seen similarly employed, though none amongst them knew why or wherefore. When life is thought to be the reward of labour, men are wont to be industrious. A very few moments sufficed to lay bare a spot of some twenty feet in diameter. Into one edge of this little area the trapper brought the females, directing Middleton and Paul to cover their light and inflammable dresses with the blankets of the party. So soon as this precaution was observed, the old man approached the opposite margin of the grass, which still environed them in a tall and dangerous circle, and selecting a handful of the driest of the herbage, he placed it over the pan of his rifle. The light combustible kindled at the flash. Then he placed the little flame into a bed of the standing fog, and withdrawing from the spot to the centre of the ring, he patiently awaited the result.

The subtile element seized with avidity upon its new fuel, and in a moment forked flames were gliding among the grass, as the tongues of ruminating animals are seen rolling among their food apparently in quest of its sweetest portions.

"Now," said the old man, holding up a finger, and laughing in his peculiarly silent manner, "you shall see fire fight fire! Ah's me! many is the time I have burnt a smooth path from wanton laziness to pick my way across a tangled bottom."

"But is this not fatal?" cried the amazed Middleton; "are you not bringing the enemy nigher to us instead of avoiding it?"

"Do you scorch so easily?—your gran'ther had a tougher skin. But we shall live to see; we shall all live to see."

The experience of the trapper was in the right. As the fire gained strength and heat, it began to spread on three sides, dying of itself on the fourth for want of aliment. As it increased, and the sullen roaring announced its power, it cleared everything before it, leaving the black and smoking soil far more naked than if the scythe had swept the place. The situation of the fugitives would have still been hazardous had not the area enlarged as the flame encircled them. But by advancing to the spot where the trapper had kindled the grass, they avoided the heat, and in a very few moments the flames began to recede in every quarter, leaving them enveloped in a cloud of smoke, but perfectly safe from the torrent of fire that was still furiously rolling onward.

The spectators regarded the simple expedient of the trapper with that species of wonder with which the courtiers of Ferdinand are said to have viewed the manner in which Columbus made his egg to stand on its end, though with feelings that were filled with gratitude instead of envy.

"Most wonderful!" said Middleton, when he saw the complete success of the means by which they had been rescued from a danger that he had conceived to be unavoidable. "The thought was a gift from Heaven, and the hand that executed it should be immortal!"

"Old trapper," cried Paul, thrusting his fingers through his shaggy locks, "I have lined many a loaded bee into his hole, and know something of the nature of the woods, but this is robbing a hornet of his sting without touching the insect!"

"It will do—it will do," returned the old man, who, after the first moment of his success, seemed to think no more of the exploit. . . . . "Let the flames do their work for a short half-hour, and then we will mount. That time is needed to cool the meadow, for these unshod beasts are tender on the hoof as a barefooted girl."

The veteran, on whose experience they all so implicitly relied for protection, employed himself in reconnoitring objects in the distance, through the openings which the air occasionally made in the immense bodies of smoke, that by this time lay in enormous piles on every part of the plain.'

We have not space to review the nautical tales, of which *The Pilot* is perhaps the best specimen. In this tale, the descriptions of the *Ariel* among the shoals, and the death of Long Tom Coffin, may be classed with the writer's best passages. The interest of Cooper's fictions depends rather on scenery and situation than on development of characters or construction of plot. 'The women in his novels are utterly characterless and insipid. There is no variety, no grace, no life in them.' Of the Indian characters, it is truly said that 'Cooper has given us Cato and Coriolanus dressed in blankets and moccasons. As mere imaginative creations, these may do; but they have no more resemblance to the Red Men of our forests, than to the aboriginal Britons.'[1] The reviewer whose opinions are here quoted, says of Cooper's best descriptive passages: 'There is something wanting. They are evidently thrown off in a hurry, drawn with little care from the exuberant stores of a retentive memory, and committed to paper with little effort to make the effect on the reader correspond to the vivid impression existing in the writer's mind.' In the five stories which we have briefly reviewed, there are materials from which an artist might have produced a classical American book of permanent value; but the fatal facility of diffuse writing, which has made these tales

[1] *North American Review*, No. 93, Art. I.

profitable articles in circulating libraries, must more and more reduce their value, as readers grow wiser in their expenditure of time.

BACKWOODS' LITERATURE.

IRVING'S STORY OF RALPH RINGWOOD—HALL—BIRD—HOFFMAN—SIMMS—THORPE—HOOPER—NEVILLE—HERBERT—HAWES.

Cooper in his *Pioneers* gave the first examples of backwoods' romance, in his sketches of the manners of a rising settlement. The scenes of turkey-shooting at Christmas, fish-spearing by moonlight on Otsego Lake, the burning of the woods, and other incidents and features of a life that has passed away within the last eighty years, might have reminded American writers that, while in some respects their country was poor in the materials of national prose-fiction, it contained elements which, if treated with good taste and artistic skill, might have partly supplied the want of old traditions. The tale of the first fifty years of Ohio might have made a good romance; but it has passed away, leaving only scattered memorials of early exploits. Writers who have endeavoured to follow in the track left by *The Pioneers*, have too often trusted in the freshness and natural interest of their materials, and have forgotten that forest scenes and adventures require taste and skill to secure for them a permanent place in national literature. It must be regretted that Irving never found in the stories of the old backwoodsmen the charm that has attracted him so often to the Dutch colonists of New Amsterdam. His sketch of *Ralph Ringwood* is the best of its kind.[1] We quote the part which describes forest-life in Kentucky about the close of the last century.

WOODCRAFT IN KENTUCKY.

'In the course of my first day's trudge, I shot a wild-turkey, and slung it on my back for provisions. The forest was open, and clear from underwood. I saw deer in abundance, but always running, running! It seemed to me as if these animals never stood still.

As night drew near, I prepared for camping. My first care was to

[1] 'Ralph Ringwood, though a fictitious name, is a real personage—the late Governor Duval of Florida. I have given some anecdotes of his early and eccentric career in, as nearly as I can recollect, the very words in which he related them. They certainly afford strong temptations to the embellishments of fiction; but I thought them so strikingly characteristic of the individual, and of the scenes and society into which his peculiar humours carried him, that I preferred giving them in their original simplicity.'—IRVING.

collect dry wood, and make a roaring fire to cook and sleep by, and to frighten off wolves, and bears, and panthers. I then began to pluck my turkey for supper. I had camped out several times in the early part of my expedition, but that was in comparatively more settled and civilised regions, where there were no wild animals of consequence in the forest. This was my first camping out in the real wilderness; and I was soon made sensible of the loneliness and wildness of my situation.

In a little while, a concert of wolves commenced; there might have been a dozen or two, but it seemed to me as if there were thousands. I never heard such howling and whining. Having prepared my turkey, I divided it into two parts, thrust two sticks into one of the halves, and planted them on end before the fire—the hunter's mode of roasting. The smell of roast-meat quickened the appetites of the wolves, and their concert became truly infernal. They seemed to be all around me, but I could only now and then get a glimpse of one of them, as he came within the glare of the light.

I did not much care for the wolves, whom I knew to be a cowardly race; but I had heard terrible stories of panthers, and began to fear their stealthy prowlings in the surrounding darkness. I was thirsty, and heard a brook bubbling and tinkling along at no great distance, but absolutely dared not go there, lest some panther might lie in wait, and spring upon me. By and by a deer whistled. I had never heard one before, and thought it must be a panther. I now felt uneasy lest he might climb the trees, crawl along the branches overhead, and plump down upon me; so I kept my eyes fixed on the branches until my head ached. I more than once thought I saw fiery eyes glaring down from among the leaves. At length I thought of my supper, and turned to see if my half turkey was cooked. In crowding so near the fire, I had pressed the meat into the flames, and it was consumed. I had nothing to do but toast the other half, and take better care of it. On that half I made my supper, without salt or bread. I was still so possessed with the dread of panthers, that I could not close my eyes all night, but lay watching the trees until daybreak, when all my fears were dispelled with the darkness; and as I saw the morning sun sparkling down through the branches of the trees, I smiled to think how I suffered myself to be dismayed by sounds and shadows: but I was a young woodsman, and a stranger in Kentucky.

Having breakfasted on the remainder of my turkey, and slaked my thirst at the bubbling stream without further dread of panthers, I resumed my wayfaring with buoyant feelings. I again saw deer, but, as usual, running, running! I tried in vain to get a shot at them, and began to fear I never should. I was gazing with vexation after a herd in full scamper, when I was startled by a human voice. Turning round, I saw a man at a short distance from me in a hunting-dress.

"What are you after, my lad?" cried he.—"Those deer," replied I pettishly; "but it seems as if they never stand still." Upon that he burst out laughing. "Where are you from?" said he.—"From Richmond." "What! in old Virginny?"—"The same." "And how on earth did you get here?"—"I landed at Green River from a broad-horn." "And where are your companions?"—"I have none." "What! all alone?"—"Yes." "Where are you going?"—"Anywhere." "And what have you come here for?"—"To hunt." "Well," said he laughingly, "you'll make a real hunter, there's no mistaking that! Have you killed anything?"—"Nothing but a turkey: I can't get within shot of a deer; they are always running." "Oh, I'll tell you the secret of that. You're always pushing forward, and starting the deer at a distance, and gazing at those that are scampering; but you must step as slow, and silent, and cautious as a cat, and keep your eyes close around you, and lurk from tree to tree, if you wish to get a chance at deer. But come; go home with me. My name is Bill Smithers; I live not far off; stay with me a little while, and I'll teach you how to hunt."

I gladly accepted the invitation of honest Bill Smithers. We soon reached his habitation—a mere log-hut, with a square hole for a window, and a chimney made of sticks and clay. Here he lived with a wife and child. He had "girdled" the trees for an acre or two around, preparatory to clearing a space for corn and potatoes. In the meantime, he maintained his family entirely by his rifle, and I soon found him to be a first-rate huntsman. Under his tutelage I received my first effective lessons in woodcraft.

The more I knew of a hunter's life, the more I relished it. The country, too, which had been the promised land of my boyhood, did not, like most promised lands, disappoint me. No wilderness could be more beautiful than this part of Kentucky in those times. The forests were open and spacious, with noble trees, some of which looked as if they had stood for centuries. There were beautiful prairies, too, diversified with groves and clumps of trees, which looked like vast parks, and in which you could see the deer running at a great distance. In the proper season, these prairies would be covered in many places with wild-strawberries, where your horse's hoofs would be dyed to the fetlock. I thought there could not be another place in the world equal to Kentucky—and I think so still.

After I had passed ten or twelve days with Bill Smithers, I thought it time to shift my quarters, for his house was scarce large enough for his own family, and I had no idea of being an encumbrance to any one. I accordingly made up my bundle, shouldered my rifle, took a friendly leave of Smithers and his wife, and set out in quest of a Nimrod of the wilderness, one John Miller, who lived alone, nearly forty miles off, and who, I hoped, would be well pleased to have a hunting-companion.

I soon found out that one of the most important items in woodcraft, in a new country, was the skill to find one's way in the wilderness. There were no regular roads in the forests, but they were cut up and perplexed by paths leading in all directions. Some of these were made by the cattle of the settlers, and were called "stock-tracks;" but others had been made by the immense droves of buffaloes which roamed about the country, from the Flood until recent times. These were called "buffalo-tracks," and traversed Kentucky from end to end like highways. Traces of them may still be seen in uncultivated parts, or deeply worn in the rocks where they crossed the mountains. I was a young woodsman, and sorely puzzled to distinguish one kind of track from the other, or to make out my course through this tangled labyrinth. While thus perplexed, I heard a distant roaring and rushing sound; a gloom stole over the forest: on looking up, when I could catch a stray glimpse of the sky, I beheld the clouds rolled up like balls, the lower part as black as ink. There was now and then an explosion, like a burst of cannonry afar off, and the crash of a falling tree. I had heard of hurricanes in the woods, and surmised that one was at hand. It soon came crashing its way; the forest writhing, and twisting, and groaning before it. The hurricane did not extend far on either side, but in a manner ploughed a furrow through the woodland; snapping off or uprooting trees that had stood for centuries, and filling the air with whirling branches. I was directly in its course, and took my stand behind an immense poplar, six feet in diameter. It bore for a time the full fury of the blast, but at length began to yield. Seeing it falling, I scrambled nimbly round the trunk like a squirrel. Down it went, bearing down another tree with it. I crept under the trunk as a shelter, and was protected from other trees which fell around me, but was sore all over, from the twigs and branches driven against me by the blast.

This was the only incident of consequence that occurred on my way to John Miller's, where I arrived on the following day, and was received by the veteran with the rough kindness of a backwoodsman. He was a gray-haired man, hardy and weather-beaten, with a blue wart, like a great bead, over one eye, whence he was nicknamed by the hunters Blue-bead Miller. He had been in these parts from the earliest settlements, and had signalised himself in the hard conflicts with the Indians, which gained Kentucky the appellation of The Bloody Ground. In one of these fights, he had an arm broken; in another, he had narrowly escaped, when hotly pursued, by jumping from a precipice thirty feet high into a river.

Miller willingly received me into his house as an inmate, and seemed pleased with the idea of making a hunter of me. His dwelling was a small log-house, with a loft or garret of boards, so that there was ample room for both of us. Under his instruction, I soon made a tolerable proficiency in hunting. My first exploit of any consequence was killing a bear. I was hunting in company with two brothers, when we came upon the track of Bruin, in a wood where there was an undergrowth of canes and grape-pines.

He was scrambling up a tree, when I shot him through the breast: he fell to the ground, and lay motionless. The brothers sent in their dog, which seized the bear by the throat. Bruin raised one arm, and gave the dog a hug that crushed his ribs. One yell, and all was over. I don't know which was first dead, the dog or the bear. The two brothers sat down and cried like children over their unfortunate dog. Yet they were mere rough huntsmen, almost as wild and untamable as Indians; but they were fine fellows.

By degrees I became known, and somewhat of a favourite among the hunters of the neighbourhood; that is to say, men who lived within a circle of thirty or forty miles, and came occasionally to see John Miller, who was a patriarch among them. They lived widely apart, in log-huts and wigwams, almost with the simplicity of Indians, and well-nigh as destitute of the comforts and inventions of civilised life. They seldom saw each other; weeks, and even months would elapse without their visiting. When they did meet, it was very much after the manner of Indians; loitering about all day, without having much to say, but becoming communicative as evening advanced, and sitting up half the night before the fire, telling hunting-stories and terrible tales of the fights of the Bloody Ground.

Sometimes several would join in a distant hunting-expedition, or rather campaign. Expeditions of this kind lasted from November until April, during which we laid up our stock of summer provisions. We shifted our hunting-camps from place to place, according as we found the game. They were generally pitched near a run of water, and close by a canebrake, to screen us from the wind. One side of our lodge was open towards the fire. Our horses were hoppled, and turned loose in the canebrakes, with bells round their necks. One of the party stayed at home to watch the camp, prepare the meals, and keep off the wolves; the others hunted. When a hunter killed a deer at a distance from the camp, he would open it and take out the entrails; then climbing a sapling, he would bend it down, tie the deer to the top, and let it spring up again so as to suspend the carcass out of reach of the wolves. At night, he would return to the camp, and give an account of his luck. The next morning early he would get a horse out of the canebrake, and bring home his game. That day he would stay at home to cut up the carcass, while the others hunted.

Our days were thus spent in silent and lonely occupations. It was only at night that we would gather together before the fire, and be sociable. I was a novice, and used to listen with open eyes and ears to the strange and wild stories told by the old hunters, and believed everything I heard. Some of their stories bordered upon the supernatural. They believed that their rifles might be spell-bound, so as not to be able to kill a buffalo, even at arm's length. This superstition they had derived from the Indians, who often think the white hunters have laid a spell upon their rifles. Miller partook of this superstition, and used to tell of his rifle's having a spell upon it; but it often seemed to me to be a shuffling way of accounting for a bad shot. If a hunter grossly missed his aim, he would ask: "Who shot last with this rifle?"—and hint that he must have charmed it. The sure mode to disenchant the gun was to shoot a silver bullet out of it.

By the opening of spring, we would generally have quantities of bear's meat and venison salted, dried, and smoked, and numerous packs of skins. We would then make the best of our way home from our distant hunting-grounds; transporting our spoils, sometimes in canoes along the rivers, sometimes on horseback over land, and our return would often be celebrated by feasting and dancing, in true backwoods' style.

* * * *

I had now lived some time with old Miller, and had become a tolerably expert hunter. Game, however, began to grow scarce. The buffalo had gathered together, as if by universal understanding, and had crossed the Mississippi never to return. Strangers kept pouring into the country, clearing away the forests, and building in all directions. The hunters began to grow restive. Jemmy Kiel, the same of whom I have already spoken for his skill in racoon-catching, came to me one day; "I can't stand this any longer," said he; "we're getting too thick here. Simon Schultz crowds me so, that I have no comfort of my life."

"Why, how you talk!" said I: "Simon Schultz lives twelve miles off."

"No matter; his cattle run with mine, and I've no idea of living where another man's cattle can run with mine. That's too close neighbourhood: I want elbow-room. This country, too, is growing too poor to live in—there's no game: so two or three of us have made up our minds to follow the buffalo to the Missouri, and we should like to have you of the party." Other hunters of my acquaintance talked in the same manner. This set me thinking; but the more I thought, the more I was perplexed. I had no one to advise with. Old Miller and his associates knew of but one mode of life, and I had no experience in any other; but I had a wider scope of thought. When out hunting alone, I used to forget the sport, and sit for hours together on the trunk of a tree, with rifle in hand, buried in thought, and debating with myself—"Shall I go with Jemmy Kiel and his company, or shall I remain here? If I remain here, there will soon be nothing left to hunt. But am I to be a hunter all my life? Have not I something more in me, than to be carrying a rifle on my shoulder day after day, and dodging about after bears, and deer, and other brute beasts?" My vanity told me I had; and I called to mind my boyish boast to my sister, that I would never return home until I returned a member of Congress for Kentucky.'

JAMES HALL (born 1793), author of *The Wilderness and the War-path*, and one of the chief contributors to the illustrated

History of the Indian Tribes, is a judge in Illinois. His *Letters from the West*, *Notes on the Western States*, and other writings, contain many interesting sketches of scenery, manners, and customs on the frontiers; and his style is refined and pleasant, except, perhaps, when he has to describe faithfully the extravagant language in which the Kentuck settler loves to indulge. In the tale of *Pete Featherton*, he ventures to introduce supernatural agency into the backwoods, where a bold hunter follows the trail of a 'stranger' whose footprints are very odd. The only explanation given is in the fact, that Pete Featherton had tarried too long at a store where strong waters were sold. It would require the tact shewn in Irving's *Sleepy Hollow* to domesticate ghosts in Illinois and Kentucky. The difficulty is admitted by Judge Hall in the introduction to the story:

'We who live on the frontier have little acquaintance with imaginary beings. These gentry never emigrate; they seem to have strong local attachments, which not even the charms of a new country can overcome. A few witches, indeed, were imported into New England by the Puritans; but were so badly used, that the whole race seems to have been disgusted with new settlements. With them the spirit of adventure expired, and the weird-women of the present day wisely cling to the soil of the old countries. That we have but few ghosts, will not be deemed a matter of surprise by those who have observed how miserably destitute we are of accommodations for such inhabitants. We have no baronial castles, nor ruined mansions; no turrets crowned with ivy, nor ancient abbeys crumbling into decay; and it would be a paltry spirit who would be content to wander in the forest by silent rivers and solitary swamps.'

Among the several descriptions of the western prairies, or vast grassy plains, we can hardly find one more distinct and faithful than Judge Hall's; but we prefer laying before our readers the following portrait of a genu*ine* backwoodsman:—

A BACKWOODSMAN OF KENTUCKY.

'The inmates of a small cabin on the margin of the Ohio were commencing with the sun the business of the day. A stout, rawboned forester plied his keen axe, and lugging log after log, erected a pile on the ample hearth, sufficiently large to have rendered the last honours to the stateliest ox. A female was paying her morning-visit to the cow-yard, where a numerous herd of cattle claimed her attention. The plentiful breakfast followed—corn-bread, milk, and venison crowned the oaken-board; while a tin coffee-pot of ample dimensions supplied the beverage which is seldom wanting at the morning-repast of the substantial American farmer.

The breakfast over, Mr Featherton reached down a long rifle from the rafters, and commenced certain preparations fraught with danger to the brute inhabitants of the forest. The lock was carefully examined, the screws tightened, the pan wiped, the flint renewed, and the springs oiled; and the keen eye of the backwoodsman glittered with an ominous lustre as its glance rested on the destructive engine. His blue-eyed partner, leaning fondly on her husband's shoulder, essayed those coaxing and captivating blandishments which every young wife so well understands, to detain her husband from the contemplated sport. Every pretext was urged with affectionate pertinacity which female ingenuity could supply—the wind whistled bleakly over the hills, the snow lay deep in the valleys, the deer would surely not venture abroad in such bitter cold weather, the adventurous hunter might get his toes frost-bitten, and her own hours would be sadly lonesome in his absence. He smiled in silence at the arguments of his bride, for such she was, and continued his preparations with the cool but good-natured determination of one who is not to be turned from his purpose.

He was indeed a person with whom such arguments, except the last, would not be very likely to prevail. Mr Peter Featherton, or, as he was familiarly called by all who knew him, Pete Featherton, was a bold rattling Kentuckian of twenty-five, who possessed the characteristic peculiarities of his countrymen—good and evil—in a striking degree. His red hair and sanguine complexion announced an ardent temperament; his tall form and bony limbs indicated an active frame inured to hardships; his piercing eye and high cheek-bones evinced the keenness and resolution of his mind. He was adventurous, frank, and social—boastful, credulous, illiterate, and at times wonderfully addicted to the marvellous. His imagination was a warm and fruitful soil, in which "tall oaks from little acorns grew," and his vocabulary was overstocked with superlatives. He loved his wife—no mistake about that—but next to her his affections entwined themselves about his gun, and expanded over his horse; he was true to his friends, never missed an election-day, turned his back upon a frolic, nor affected to dislike a social glass.

He believed that the best qualities of all countries were combined in Kentucky; and had the most whimsical manner of expressing his national attachments. He was firmly convinced that the battle of the Thames was the most sanguinary conflict of the age—"a raal reg'lar skrimmage"—and extolled Colonel Dick Johnson as a "severe old colt." He would admit freely that Napoleon was a great genius—Metternich, Castlereagh, "and them fellows" knew "a thing or two," but then they "were no part of a priming to Henry Clay."

When entirely "at himself"—to use his own language—that is to say, when duly sober, Pete was friendly and rational, courteous and considerate, and a better-tempered fellow never shouldered a rifle. But he was a social man, who was liable to be "overtaken;" and let him get a glass too much, and there was no end to his extravagance. Then it was that his genius bloomed, and brought forth strange boasts and strong oaths, his loyalty to old Kentuck waxed warm, and his faith in his horse, his gun, and his own manhood grew into idolatry. Always bold and self-satisfied, and habitually energetic in the expression of his predilections, he now became invested with the agreeable properties of the snapping-turtle, the alligator, and the steam-boat, and gifted with the most affable and affectionate spirit of autobiography. It was now that he would dwell upon his own bodily powers and prowess with the enthusiasm of a devotee, and as the climax of this rhetorical display, would slap his hands together, spring perpendicularly into the air, and after uttering a yell worthy of the stoutest Winnebago, swear that he was "the best man in the country," and "could whip his weight in wild cats," "no two ways about it"—he was "not afraid of no man, no way you could fix it;" and finally, after many other extravagances, he would urge, with no gentle asseveration, his ability to "ride through a crab-apple orchard on a streak of lightning."

In addition to all this, which one would think was enough for any reasonable man, Pete would sometimes brag that he had the best gun, the prettiest wife, the best-looking sister, and the fastest nag in all Kentuck; and that no man dare say to the contrary. It is but justice to remark, that there was more truth in this last boast than is usually found on such occasions, and that Pete had good reason to be proud of his horse, his gun, and his lady-love.'

ROBERT MONTGOMERY BIRD, born at Newcastle, in Delaware, about the year 1803, is the author of several historical romances, and other fictions, including tales of border life and adventure. His first work, *Calavar, or the Knight of the Conquest, a Romance of Mexico*, appeared in 1834, and was commended for its picturesque character and fidelity in descriptions of the costumes, manners, and military usages of the Aztecs. The same traits appeared in a sequel, entitled *The Infidel, or the Fall of Mexico*, which was published in 1835. In the same year appeared *The Hawks of Hawk Hollow*, a tale of Pennsylvania. 'It contains,' says Mr Griswold, 'some vigorous writing, and original and powerful sketches of character, but more of the tumult and brutality of border-life than is worth preserving in literature.'

After writing, in the course of a few years, several other fictions —*Sheppard Lee* (1836), *Nick of the Woods* (1837), *Peter Pilgrim* (1838), and *The Adventures of Robert Day* (1839)—Dr Bird 'suddenly and entirely abandoned the field of letters. His latest work appeared about the time of the commencement of the system of cheap publishing [that is, of British works], since which there have been comparatively few original books issued in America.'[1]

[1] Griswold.

Dr Bird's fictions are varied in their style, and contain many passages of graphic power. We notice the tale of *Nick of the Woods*, not as the best of the series, but because it affords another specimen of backwoods' literature. It is intended to give some account of that fiercely vindictive feeling which existed between the early settlers and the Indians of Kentucky in the days of Boone, Kenton, M'Colloch, and Wetzel. The writer says of the so-called Indian characters portrayed by Chateaubriand and Cooper, who have made of the Red Men 'a chivalry of the forest,' that 'such conceptions as Atala and Uncas are beautiful unrealities and fictions merely, as imaginary and contrary to nature as the shepherd swains of the old pastoral school of rhyme and romance; at all events, one does not find beings of this class, or anything in the slightest degree resembling them, among the tribes now known to travellers and legislators.' He adds: 'The Indian is doubtless a gentleman, but he is a gentleman who wears a very dirty shirt, and lives a very miserable life, having nothing to employ him or keep him alive except the pleasures of the chase and of the scalp-hunt, which we dignify with the name of war.' It is singular that writers living where means of gaining true information respecting the aborigines of North America were easily available, should have chosen to substitute dreams for realities. The falsification of facts is not the true way of approaching the ideal, though it is the way of too many romancists and novelists.

Being written in the taste which delights in the narration of horrors, Dr Bird's tale is very objectionable, and, accordingly, we should hardly choose to notice it; but an American critic has said, doubtless with some truth, that the story may be classed with such legends as the *Life of David Crockett*, and *The Big Bear of Arkansas*—books which have emanated from, or are adapted to, the unschooled classes of the people, and therefore reflect some national characteristics. On this ground, some notice of this tale of wild adventures may have its place here.

The chief interest of the story depends on the capture of a young officer, Roland, and his fair kinswoman Edith, who for some time are retained as prisoners among the Indians, and are at last released by the extraordinary daring of the hero, Nick of the Woods. One of the several strange characters introduced is Ralph Stackpole, an extravagant boaster, often guilty of making inroads on his neighbours' property, and consequently in danger of falling a victim to Lynch-law; yet he is spared from time to time on account of his valour in conflicts with the Indians. A singular example of trial by jury in Kentucky is explained by that vehement hatred of the savages which in early times prevailed there. Ralph Stackpole was arraigned—not for the first time—on a charge of horse-stealing, and matters went hard against him, his many offences in that line having steeled the hearts of all against him, and the proofs of his guilt in this particular instance being both strong and manifold. 'Many an angry and unpitying eye was bent upon the unfortunate fellow, when his counsel rose to attempt a defence, which he did in the following terms:—"Gentlemen of the jury," said the man of law, "here is a man, Captain Ralph Stackpole, indicted before you on the charge of stealing a horse; and the affa'r is pretty considerably proved on him." Here there was a murmur heard throughout the court, evincing much approbation of the counsel's frankness. "Gentlemen of the jury," continued the orator, elevating his voice, "what I have to say in reply is, first, that that man thar, Captain Ralph Stackpole, did, in the year seventeen seventy-nine, when this good state of Kentucky, and particularly those parts adjacent to Bear's Grass, and the mouth thereof, where now stands the town of Louisville, were overrun with yelping Injun savages—did, I say, gentlemen, meet two Injun savages in the woods on Bear's Grass, and take their scalps, single-handed—a feat, gentlemen of the jury, that an't to be performed every day, even in Kentucky! . . . . Secondly, gentlemen of the jury," exclaimed the attorney-at-law, with a still louder voice, "what I have to say, *secondly*, gentlemen of the jury, is, that this same identical prisoner at the bar, Captain Ralph Stackpole, did, on another occasion, in the year seventeen eighty-two, meet another Injun savage in the woods—a savage armed with rifle, knife, and tomahawk—and met him with—you suppose, gentlemen, with gun, axe, and scalper, in like manner?—No, gentlemen of the jury! with his *fists*, and" (with a voice of thunder) "licked him to death in the natural way!—Gentlemen of the jury, pass upon the prisoner—guilty or not guilty?" The attorney resumed his seat: his arguments were irresistible. The jurors started up in their box, and roared out, to a man, "*Not guilty!*"'

Another remarkable character is described as 'a Quaker,' who is often derided by the 'fighting-men' of Kentucky, because he is a man of peace, and refuses to join in the exterminating warfare carried on against the Indians. At the time when the tale opens, a panic was excited among the savages by the frequent occurrence of the slaying of Indians by some unknown hand; and a tale prevailed that an unearthly being, styled Nick of the Woods among the settlers, and known as Jibbenainosay among the aborigines, walked in the forest, destroying the Red Men, and leaving upon every victim a mark of two knife-cuts in the shape of a cross. The mystery is at last explained. Captain Roland, with his kinswoman Edith, on their solitary journey through the forest, are surrounded by the savages, and rescued from the danger by the guidance of Nathan the Quaker. For some time Nathan, though proving himself well acquainted with the stratagems of Indian warfare, preserves the garb and mien of 'a man of peace,' and assists only by good counsel and guidance; but at last, in a desperate struggle for the lives of the travelling-party, he is compelled to throw off the disguise. Edith is carried away as a prisoner by the savages, and when Roland despairingly bewails her fate, Nathan reproves him, and makes a confession of the dreadful circumstances which had changed his own character from that of a man of peace to that of Nick of the Woods, the slayer of the Red Men.

The remainder of the tale consists mostly of a series of sanguinary contests with Indians, and ends in the release of the prisoners Roland and Edith. The apparent gross improbability of making Nathan the Quaker identical with the murderous Nick of the Woods, is excused by the author, on the ground that terrible calamity had made the former man of peace insane in his thirst for revenge.[1] Too many passages in this story belong to the literature of horrors; and the several descriptions of deeds of violence and bloodshed supply, we think, an unwholesome excitement to the imaginations of young readers who may be attracted by the title.

For obvious reasons, our selections from the backwoods' literature must be rather scanty. The breadth of humour allowed in old Kentucky might not be relished by our readers. One specimen by Dr Bird may perhaps be tolerated, especially as it explains the zoological name of a race formerly existing on the Lower Mississippi. Of the several technical terms used in the sketch, we can give no better explanation than that afforded by the context. They must be regarded as so many expressions of exuberant energies of the pugnacious order. In literal terms, the animal described is one of the early freebooters of Kentucky. His incursions on the property of neighbours have made him liable to the infliction of Lynch-law, and some allusion to this fact has excited his anger.

SKETCH OF AN ALLIGATOR.

'"And whar are you going?" demanded Bruce.

"To St Asaph's"—which was a station some twenty or thirty miles off—replied Captain Stackpole.

[1] There can be no good excuse for this misrepresentation. It contradicts the important and memorable fact, that while exterminating wars with the Indians were supposed to be necessary for the settling of New England and other colonies, Pennsylvania was settled without bloodshed, and no Quaker was ever molested by the Indians.

"Too far for the Regulators[1] to follow, Ralph," said Colonel Bruce; at which the young men present laughed louder than ever, and eyed the visitor in a way that seemed both to disconcert and offend him.

"Cunnel," said he, "you're a man in authority, and my superior officer; wharfo' thar can be no scalping between us. But my name's Tom Dowdle the ragman!" he screamed, suddenly skipping into the thickest of the throng, and sounding a note of defiance—"my name's Tom Dowdle the ragman, and I'm for any man that insults me! log-leg or leather-breeches, green shirt or blanket-coat, land-trotter or river-roller—I'm the man for a massacree!" Then giving himself a twirl upon his foot that would have done credit to a dancing-master, he proceeded to other antic demonstrations of hostility, which, when performed in after-years on the banks of the Lower Mississippi, by himself and his worthy imitators, were, we suspect, the cause of their receiving the name of the mighty Alligator. It is said by naturalists of this monstrous reptile, that he delights, when the returning warmth of spring has brought his fellows from their holes, and placed them basking along the banks of a swampy lagoon, to dart into the centre of the expanse, and challenge the whole field to combat. He roars, he blows the water from his nostrils, he lashes it with his tail, he whirls round and round, churning the water into foam; until, having worked himself into a proper fury, he darts back again to the shore, to seek an antagonist. Had the gallant captain of horse-thieves boasted the blood, as he afterwards did the name, of an "alligator half-breed," he could have scarce conducted himself in a way more worthy of his parentage. He leaped into the centre of the throng, where, having found elbow-room for his purpose, he performed the gyration mentioned before, following it up by other feats expressive of his hostile humour. He flapped his wings and crowed, until every chanticleer in the settlement replied to the note of battle; he snorted and neighed like a horse; he bellowed like a bull; he barked like a dog; he yelled like an Indian; he whined like a panther; he howled like a wolf; until one would have thought he was a living menagerie, comprising within his single body the spirit of every animal noted for its love of conflict. Then, not content with such a display of readiness to fight the field, he darted from the centre of the area allowed him for his exercise, and invited the lookers-on individually to battle. "Whar's your buffalo-bull," he cried, "to cross horns with the roarer of Salt River? Whar's your full-blood colt that can shake a saddle off? H'yar's an old nag can kick off the top of a buck-eye![2] Whar's your cat of the Knobs? your wolf of the Rolling Prairies? H'yar's the old brown bar can claw the bark off a gum-tree! H'yar's a man for you, Tom Bruce! Same to you, Sim Roberts! to you, Jimmy Big-nose! to you, and to you, and to you! Arn't I a ring-tailed

[1] The amateur executioners of Lynch-law.
[2] A tall tree: the American horse-chestnut.

squealer? Can go down Salt on my back, and swim up the Ohio! Whar's the man to fight Roaring Ralph Stackpole?"

CHARLES FENNO HOFFMAN (born 1806), the writer of several lyrical poems which have been highly praised by American critics, is a well-known contributor to magazines, and has edited *The Knickerbocker*, *The American Monthly*, and *The New York Mirror*. In 1837, after a tour in the western territories, he published in London a volume of sketches and legends, entitled *Wild Scenes in the Forest and the Prairie;* which was followed in 1840 by the tale of *Greyslaer*, founded on a remarkable criminal trial, which has also been made the basis of Mr Simms's novel entitled *Beauchampe*. The incidents of the novel are so extraordinary, that critics have condemned them as unsuitable in a fiction intended to seem probable; while others have referred to the proverbial saying, that 'truth is stranger than fiction,' and have shewn that the facts of the trial have been mitigated in the tale of *Greyslaer*. The description of horrible circumstances and adventures is, to our taste, a repulsive feature in Hoffman's writings: for example, in *Ben Blower's Story*, and *The Flying Head*. One specimen may be enough to justify our objection. Hoffman tells the story of 'a steam-boat race' on one of the great rivers; and the destruction of human lives is described in the following style:—

'"You have seen the *Flame*, then, afore, Strannger? Six year ago, when new upon the river, she was a raal out and outer, I tell ye. I was at that time a hand aboard of her. Yes, I belonged to her at the time of her great race with the 'Go-liar.' You've heern, mayhap, of the blow-up by which we lost it? They made a great fuss about it; but it was nothing but a mere fiz of hot water, after all. Only the springing of a few rivets, which loosened a biler-plate or two, and let out a thin spirting upon some niggers that hadn't sense enough to get out of the way. Well, the 'Go-liar' took off our passengers, and we ran into Smasher's Landing to repair damages, and bury the poor fools that were killed."'

After this, the narrator describes his own adventure of falling asleep in the engine-boiler, where he is parboiled, but escapes in time to relish a mint-julep:—

'"I heard the cry of horror . . . . . the shout to drown the fire—the first stroke of the cold water-pump. They say, too, that I was conscious when they took me out—but I—I remember nothing more till they brought a julep to my bedside arterwards. AND *that julep!*"——

"Cooling! was it?"

"STRANNGER!!!"

Ben turned away his head, and wept—he could no more.'

Can anything be said in defence of this species of fiction?

William Gilmore Simms (born 1807) is a planter, residing at Midway, in South Carolina, and one of the most voluminous of American writers of fiction. Having lost his inherited property by an attempt to maintain an unpopular newspaper, *The Charlestown City Gazette*, he determined to retrieve his fortune by literary industry; and in the course of about twenty years wrote more than fifty volumes of novels, shorter tales, poems, and miscellanies—including *Martin Faber*, a very gloomy story (1833), *Guy Rivers* (1834), *Beauchampe, or the Kentucky Tragedy* (1842); and *The Wigwam and the Cabin*—a collection of stories, which is esteemed as one of his best works. An American writer—Griswold—whose opinions seem free from prejudice, gives the following account of the numerous works of fiction by Mr Simms:—'His novels are interesting, but the interest arises more from situation than from character. Our attention is engrossed by actions, but we feel little sympathy with the actors. He gives us too much of ruffianism. . . . . He delights in action, whether of men or of the elements, and is most successful in strife, storm, and tumult. It is worth mentioning, that the German author Sealsfield has borrowed very largely from his works, and that whole pages which he has translated, almost literally, from *Guy Rivers*, have been praised abroad as superior to anything done by Americans in describing their own country.' The remarks suggested by Sealsfield's books may be applied to several similar works having an indefinite character between fiction and true narratives of travel. American readers will understand that we allude to tales of wondrous and romantic adventures in the far west, written by authors who were never exposed to the dangers from grizzly bears and other monsters, so vividly described. These tales, manufactured in London or New York, or even in Berlin, belong, in fact, to the class exemplified in Barnum's mermaid, and woolly horse of the Rocky Mountains.

Several works of the kind here referred to have been reprinted in England, and widely circulated as books of travel. In some instances, grave reviewers have based certain opinions upon statements made by writers of absurd fictions, under the disguise of travels. These tourists have enjoyed a wonderful facility in acquiring the Indian dialects. One narrates his conversations with the Sioux, the Winnebagoes, and other tribes; and tells us how he escaped from a herd of wolves, which tore away 'forty-five out of the fifty grouse of the prairies that hung at his saddle-bow;' how he rode 120 miles in one day, carrying for a part of the way a load of '200 pounds of prairie-hens;' how he caught, and, after a struggle, landed 'a maskinonge [a fish] weighing 57 pounds;' and, finally, how he made a voyage up the Mississippi, from Rock

Island in Iowa to the source, and down to Lake Superior, visiting in a leisurely way several other places—all in the space of one month—a feat which makes the real adventures of such travellers as Emory, Colonel Fremont, and Schoolcraft, seem ludicrously tame.

We have good authority for saying, that many of the tales of adventures, encounters with Indians, and grizzly bears, and similar spices used to season narrations of tours in the far west, have about the same degree of historical value that may be found in *The Big Bear of Arkansas*, or Thorpe's account of farming in this colony. 'I once planted,' says the hero, 'a few potatoes and beets. About that time I went off to old Kentuck on business, and stumbled on a fellow who had stopped at my place, with an idea of buying me out. "How did you like things?" said I. "Pretty well," said he: "but that bottom-land is full of cedar-stumps and Indian mounds."' The farmer explained that the cedar-stumps were beets, and the Indian mounds were 'tater-hills,' and added: 'The crop was overgrown and useless: the *sile* [soil] is too rich, and planting in Arkansaw is *dangerous*.' So is the fabrication of travels in the far west; for, unfortunately, prosaic men, like Schoolcraft, Nicollet, and Allen, have visited these regions, and described their true features.[1]

These remarks are enough to suggest that many accounts of travels and adventures in the West, 'having all the breathless interest of romance,' should be regarded with suspicion. We have properly classified them with the novels and romances written by Mr Simms.

T. B. THORPE, author of *Mysteries of the Backwoods*, *The Big Bear of Arkansas*, and other humorous sketches of life and manners on the frontier, was born in Westfield, Massachusetts, in 1815. During his youth, he made some progress in the art of painting; but circumstances induced him to lay aside the pencil, and try his skill in writing of the scenery and people of Louisiana, where he fixed his residence in 1836. Some years later, he commenced a newspaper styled *The Conservator*. His tale of *The Big Bear* is included, with other stories, in a volume edited by William T. Porter—conductor of the New York *Spirit of the Times*—and published in 1835. In 1846, another volume of humorous tales and sketches appeared, under the same editorship, and included Thorpe's *Mysteries of the Backwoods*, with the story of *Captain Simon Suggs*, the *Taking the Census*, and other Alabama sketches by Johnson Hooper; *A Quarter Race in Kentucky*, and other tales, mostly selected from the *Spirit of the Times*.

In connection with these specimens of backwoods' literature,

[1] See *North American Review*, No. 145, Art. 7.

we may notice the racy story of *Mike Fink, the Last of the Boatmen*, by MORGAN NEVILLE; the tales of the chase of HENRY W. HERBERT, better known by his pseudonym Frank Forrester; and the *Sporting Scenes* of WILLIAM P. HAWES.

Thorpe has written, with genial humour, of several grotesque features of frontier-life, but has failed to preserve the tone of good taste which would have made his sketches more attractive. His tale of *The Big Bear* has been so often mentioned, as a specimen of indigenous literature, that we must give some short account of it. It must be premised that the humour of the story is of the most simple kind, as it consists chiefly of a free use of one figure of speech—hyperbole. The use of this mode of speech must be characteristic of the backwoodsman, if we may trust the reports of Thorpe and other writers.

We enter the cabin of a steamer on the Mississippi. Soon after the boat has left the wharf, an original specimen of an Arkansas settler and bear-hunter comes in. He is a man in rude health, having a face full of good-humour, and eyes of singular brightness. Making himself at home, he takes a chair, puts up his feet on the stove, salutes the 'strangers' in a hearty familiar style, and, without waiting for a question, informs them that, for the first time in his life, he has been to New Orleans, where the 'perlite chaps' have been inquiring respecting the game in his part of the country. 'Game, indeed!' he says—'that's what city folks call it. Maybe such trash live in my diggins, but I arn't noticed them yet: a bird anyway is too trifling. I never did shoot at but one, and I'd never forgiven myself for that, had it weighed less than forty pounds. I wouldn't draw a rifle on anything less than that; and when I meet with another wild-turkey of the same weight, I will drap him.'

'A wild-turkey weighing forty pounds!' exclaimed twenty voices in the cabin at once. . . . . 'Where did all that happen?' asked a cynical-looking Hoosier. . . . . This expression of a doubt excites the hyperbolical man of Arkansas; he scorns to talk of such poor things as wild-turkeys, and begins his story of the Big Bear of Arkansas.

'"Happen! happened in Arkansaw. Where else could it have happened but in the creation state, the finishing-up country—a state where the *sile* runs down to the centre of the 'arth, and government gives you a title to every inch of it? Then its airs—just breathe them, and they will make you snort like a horse. It's a state without a fault, it is." . . . .

"What season of the year do your hunts take place?" inquired a gentlemanly foreigner, who, from some peculiarities of his baggage, I suspected to be an Englishman, on some hunting-expedition, probably at the foot of the Rocky Mountains.

"The season for bar-hunting, stranger," said the man of Arkansaw, "is generally all the year round, and the hunts take place about as regular. I read in history that varmints have their fat season and their lean season. That is not the case in Arkansaw—feeding as they do upon the *spontenacious* productions of the *sile*, they have one continued fat season the year round: though in winter, things in this way is rather more greasy than in summer, I must admit. For that reason, bar with us run in warm weather, but in winter they only waddle. . . . . Run a bar in this fat condition, and the way it improves the critter for eating is amazing; it sort of mixes the ile up with the meat until you can't tell t'other from which. I've done this often." . . . .

A timid little man inquired if the bear in Arkansaw ever attacked the settlers in numbers.

"No," said our hero, warming with the subject; "no, stranger, for you see it ain't the natur of bar to go in droves; but the way they squander about in pairs and single ones is edifying. And then the way I hunt them—the old black rascals know the crack of my gun as well as they know a pig's squealing. They grow thin in our parts—it frightens them so, and they do take the noise dreadfully, poor things. That gun of mine is a perfect *epidemic among bar*: if not watched closely, it will go off as quick on a warm scent as my dog Bowie-knife will: and then that dog—whew! why, the fellow thinks that the world is full of bar, he finds them so easy. It's lucky he don't talk as well as think; for with his natural modesty, if he should suddenly learn how much he is acknowledged to be ahead of all other dogs in the universe, he would be astonished to death in two minutes. . . . . I never could tell whether he was made expressly to hunt bar, or whether bar was made expressly for him to hunt."'

In the same extravagant style, the narrator goes on in his talk of bears, and makes a digression on the danger of planting in a soil so enormously productive as that of Arkansas. At last, he tells the story of the death of the Big Bear, and so concludes a wild strain of hyperbole. For the amusement of readers who like tales of this kind, we may mention here *The Sketches and Eccentricities of Colonel David Crockett*, containing many examples of skill in the use of the long-bow.

It would be hardly fair to conclude our notices of backwoods' literature without a better specimen of Thorpe's sketches. The following portrait of a bee-hunter describes, says the author, 'a fraternity of men of genius,' who have passed away, 'unwept and unsung,' in the backwoods:—

TOM OWEN THE BEE-HUNTER.

'It was on a beautiful southern October morning, at the hospitable mansion of a friend, where I was staying to drown dull care, that I first had the pleasure of seeing Tom Owen. He was straggling, on this occasion, up the rising-ground that led to the hospitable mansion of mine host, and the difference between him and ordinary men was visible at a glance. Perhaps it shewed itself as much in the perfect contempt of fashion he displayed in the adornment of his outward man, as it did in the more elevated qualities of his mind that were visible in his face. His head was adorned with an outlandish pattern of a hat; and his nether limbs were ensconced in a pair of inexpressibles, beautifully fringed by the brier-bushes through which they were often drawn. Coats and vests he considered as superfluities. Hanging upon his back were a couple of pails; and he had an axe in his right hand. Such were the varieties that characterised the corpus of Tom Owen. As is usual with great men, he had his partisans, and with a courtier-like humility, they depended upon the expression of his face for all their hopes of success. The common salutations of meeting were sufficient to draw me within the circle of his influence, and I at once became one of his most ready followers. "See yonder!" said Tom, stretching his long arm into the air—"see yonder—there's a bee." We all *looked* in the direction he indicated, but that was the extent of our observation. "It was a fine bee," continued Tom, "black body, yellow legs, and into that tree"—pointing to a towering oak, blue in the distance. "In a clear day, I can see a bee over a mile easy!" When did Coleridge "talk" like that? And yet Tom Owen uttered such a saying with perfect ease.

After a variety of meanderings through the thick woods, and clambering over fences, we came to our place of destination as pointed out by Tom. . . . . The felling of a great tree is a sight that calls up a variety of emotions; and Tom's game was lodged in one of the finest in the forest. But "the axe was laid at the root of the tree," which, in his mind, was made expressly for bees to build their nests in, that he might cut it down and obtain possession of the honey. The sharp sound of the axe as it played in the hands of Tom, was replied to by a stout negro from the opposite side; and by the rapidity of their strokes, they fast gained upon the heart of the lordly sacrifice. There was a little poetry in the thought, that long before this mighty empire of states was formed, Tom Owen's bee-hive had stretched its brawny arms to the winter's blast, and grown green in the summer's sun. Yet such was the case; and how long I might have moralised I know not, had not the enraged buzzing about my ears convinced me that the occupants of the tree were not going to give up their home and treasure without shewing considerable practical fight. No sooner had the little insects satisfied themselves that they were about to be attacked, than they began one after another to descend from their airy abode, and fiercely pitch into our faces; anon, a small company, headed by an old veteran, would charge with its entire force upon all parts of our body at once. It need not be said that the better part of valour was displayed by a precipitate retreat from such attacks.

* * * *

Cut-thwack! sounded through the confused hum at the foot of the tree, marvellously reminding me of the interruptions that occasionally broke in upon the otherwise monotonous hours of my school-days. A sharp cracking finally told me the chopping was done; and looking aloft, I saw the mighty tree balancing in the air. Slowly and majestically, it bowed for the first time towards its mother-earth, gaining velocity as it descended, shivering the trees that interrupted its course, and falling with thundering sound, splintering its gigantic limbs, and burying them deeply in the ground.

The sun, for the first time in at least two centuries, broke uninterruptedly through the chasm made in the forest, and shone with splendour upon the magnificent Tom, standing a conqueror among his spoils.'

BRYANT—VERPLANCK—LEGGETT—SANDS—NEAL—KENNEDY—WARE—JUDD—LONGFELLOW—POE—FAY—MITCHELL—MELVILLE—MAYO—WISE—SANDERSON—JOSEPH NEAL—MATTHEWS.

WILLIAM CULLEN BRYANT, whose poems have been reviewed, has distinguished himself as a prose-writer chiefly by his numerous articles in the *Evening Post* newspaper, which he has edited during more than twenty years. He has written several short works of fiction, including contributions to *The Talisman*, published in 1827–1829, and some portions of the work entitled *Tales of Glauber Spa* (1832). In these two miscellanies, Bryant was assisted by his friends VERPLANCK, LEGGETT, and SANDS. His own tales were marked rather by correct style and good taste than by any extraordinary display of invention. Among the contributions of his friends, the tale of *Major Egerton*, by Verplanck, is one of the best. It is lively and pleasant in its style of narrative and description, though highly improbable and fantastic in its incidents. Verplanck's most important contribution to literature is an edition of Shakspeare, published in 1844–46.

JOHN NEAL, already noticed as a writer of verse, wrote a great number of novels, tales, sketches, reviews, and magazine papers. His first novel, oddly entitled *Keep Cool*, is described by himself as 'a foolish fiery thing,' and was followed by *Logan*, which a critic characterises as 'a sort of rhapsody in two thick volumes.' *Seventy-six*, a better fiction, was written during 'odd hours, in less than a month;' and within two or three months after, the author produced another novel in two volumes, *Randolph*, which attracted notice by its sketches of living public characters.

During a visit to England, Neal wrote several articles in *Blackwood's Magazine*, and resided for some time with Jeremy Bentham, whose *Principles of Legislation* he translated from the French of Dumont. After his return to his native country, Neal wrote *Rachel Dyer*, a story of the days of Cotton Mather (1828); *Authorship*, a tale (1830); *The Down-easters* (1831), and *Ruth Elder;* besides numerous papers in his weekly miscellany, *The Yankee.* The whole of his writings in prose and verse are strongly marked by the faults of extreme haste and carelessness. In attempting fine writing, he seldom avoids the step from the sublime to the ridiculous.

JOHN PENDLETON KENNEDY (born 1795), author of *Swallow Barn, or a Sojourn in the Old Dominion* (1832), and other fictions giving sketches of life and manners in Virginia, Carolina, and Maryland, is a politician, whose leisure has been partly devoted to light literature. His tales, marked by considerable skill in portraiture of characters, and containing many pleasant descriptive passages, have been very successful. The first has been characterised as resembling in plan Irving's *Bracebridge Hall.* The scene is laid in Lower Virginia (the 'Old Dominion'), and the object is to describe the state of society in the ancient commonwealth. The leading character, a wealthy country gentleman, is described with genial humour, and the series of adventures is so arranged as to illustrate the various aspects of life in Virginia.

A second novel by Mr Kennedy was entitled *Horse-shoe Robinson* (1835), and was even more popular than the first. It narrates the adventures of a yeoman who took a prominent part in the civil war. A more carefully written, yet less successful fiction, *Rob of the Bowl*, appeared in 1838. Its scene was in Maryland, at the time when the quarrels of Protestants and Catholics disturbed the colony.

In his first work, Kennedy wrote in the manner of Washington Irving. There may be no proofs of direct imitation in *Swallow Barn*, but the tone, as well as the plan of the book, reminds us of the Crayon sketches. The portrait drawn in the passage appended as a specimen, bears too close a resemblance to the studies of other country gentlemen in *Bracebridge Hall* and *The Sketch-book.* In his later works, Kennedy assumed a more original style.

A COUNTRY GENTLEMAN.

'Frank Meriwether is now in the meridian of life—somewhere close upon forty-five. Good cheer and a good temper both tell well upon him. The first has given him a comfortable full figure; and the latter certain easy contemplative habits, that incline him to be lazy and philosophical. He has the substantial planter look that belongs to a gentleman who lives on his estate, and is not much vexed with the crosses of life.

I think he prides himself on his personal appearance, for he has a handsome face, with a dark blue eye, and a high forehead that is scantily embellished with some silver-tipped locks that, I observe, he cherishes for their rarity: besides, he is growing manifestly attentive to his dress, and carries himself erect, with some secret consciousness that his person is not bad. It is pleasant to see him when he has ordered his horse for a ride into the neighbourhood, or across to the court-house. On such occasions, he is apt to make his appearance in a coat of blue broadcloth, astonishingly new and glossy, and with a redundant supply of plaited ruffle strutting through the folds of a Marseilles waistcoat: a worshipful finish is given to this costume by a large straw-hat, lined with green silk. There is a magisterial fulness in his garments that betokens condition in the world, and a heavy bunch of seals, suspended by a chain of gold, jingles as he moves, pronouncing him a man of superfluities.

It is considered rather extraordinary that he has never set up for Congress; but the truth is, he is an unambitious man, and has a great dislike to currying favour—as he calls it. And, besides, he is thoroughly convinced that there will always be men enough in Virginia willing to serve the people, and therefore does not see why he should trouble his head about it. Some years ago, however, there was really an impression that he meant to come out. By some sudden whim, he took it into his head to visit Washington during the session of Congress, and returned, after a fortnight, very seriously distempered with politics. He told curious anecdotes of certain secret intrigues which had been discovered in the affairs of the capital, gave a pretty clear insight into the views of some deep-laid combinations, and became all at once painfully florid in his discourse, and dogmatical to a degree that made his wife stare. Fortunately, this orgasm soon subsided, and Frank relapsed into an indolent gentleman of the opposition; but it had the effect to give a much more decided cast to his studies, for he forthwith discarded *The Whig* and took to *The Inquirer*, like a man who was not to be disturbed by doubts; and as it was morally impossible to believe what was written on both sides, to prevent his mind from being abused, he, from this time forward, gave an implicit assent to all the facts that set against Mr Adams. The consequence of this straightforward and confiding deportment was an unsolicited and complimentary notice of him by the executive of the state. He was put into the commission of the peace; and having thus become a public man against his will, his opinions were observed to undergo some essential changes. He now thinks that a good citizen ought neither to solicit nor decline office; that the magistracy of Virginia is the sturdiest pillar that supports the fabric of the constitution;

and that the people, "though in their opinions they may be mistaken, in their sentiments they are never wrong"—with some other such dogmas, that, a few years ago, he did not hold in very good repute. In this temper, he has of late embarked upon the millpond of county affairs, and notwithstanding his amiable and respectful republicanism, I am told he keeps the peace as if he commanded a garrison, and administers justice like a cadi.

He has some claim to supremacy in this last department; for during three years of his life he smoked cigars in a lawyer's office at Richmond; sometimes looked into *Blackstone* and the *Revised Code;* was a member of a debating-society that ate oysters once a week during the winter; and wore six cravats and a pair of yellow-topped boots as a blood of the metropolis. Having in this way qualified himself for the pursuits of agriculture, he came to his estate a very model of landed gentlemen. Since that time, his avocations have had a certain literary tincture; for having settled himself down as a married man, and got rid of his superfluous foppery, he rambled with wonderful assiduity through a wilderness of romances, poems, and dissertations, which are now collected in his library, and, with their battered blue covers, present a lively type of an army of continentals at the close of the war, or an hospital of veteran invalids. These have all at last given way to the newspapers—a miscellaneous study very enticing to gentlemen in the country—that have rendered Meriwether a most discomfiting antagonist in the way of dates and names.

He has great suavity of manners, and a genuine benevolence of disposition that makes him fond of having his friends about him; and it is particularly gratifying to him to pick up any genteel stranger within the purlieus of Swallow Barn, and put him to the proof of a week's hospitality, if it be only for the pleasure of exercising his rhetoric upon him. He is a kind master, and considerate towards his dependents, for which reason, although he owns many slaves, they hold him in profound reverence, and are very happy under his dominion. All these circumstances make Swallow Barn a very agreeable place, and it is accordingly frequented by an extensive range of his acquaintances.

There is one quality in Frank that stands above the rest: he is a thoroughbred Virginian, and consequently does not travel much from home, except to make an excursion to Richmond, which he considers emphatically as the centre of civilisation. Now and then, he has gone beyond the mountain, but the upper country is not much to his taste, and, in his estimation, only to be resorted to when the fever makes it imprudent to remain upon the tide. He thinks lightly of the mercantile interest, and, in fact, undervalues the manners of the cities generally; he believes that their inhabitants are all hollow-hearted and insincere, and altogether wanting in that substantial intelligence and honesty that he affirms to be characteristic of the country. He is a great admirer of the genius of Virginia, and is frequent in his commendation of a toast in which the state is compared to the mother of the Gracchi: indeed, it is a familiar thing with him to speak of the aristocracy of talent as only inferior to that of the landed interest—the idea of a freeholder inferring to his mind a certain constitutional pre-eminence in all the virtues of citizenship, as a matter of course.

The solitary elevation of a country gentleman, well to do in the world, begets some magnificent notions. He becomes as infallible as the pope; gradually acquires a habit of making long speeches; is apt to be impatient of contradiction, and is always very touchy on the point of honour. There is nothing more conclusive than a rich man's logic anywhere; but in the country, amongst his dependents, it flows with the smooth and unresisted course of a gentle stream irrigating a verdant meadow, and depositing its mud in fertilising luxuriance. Meriwether's sayings about Swallow Barn import absolute verity; but I have discovered that they are not so current out of his jurisdiction. Indeed, every now and then, we have some obstinate discussions when any of the neighbouring potentates, who stand in the same sphere with Frank, come to the house; for these worthies have opinions of their own, and nothing can be more dogged than the conflict between them. They sometimes fire away at each other with a most amiable and inconvincible hardihood for a whole evening, bandying interjections, and making bows, and saying shrewd things with all the courtesy imaginable: but for unextinguishable pertinacity in argument, and utter impregnability of belief, there is no disputant like your country gentleman who reads the newspapers. When one of these discussions fairly gets under-way, it never comes to an anchor again of its own accord—it is either blown out so far to sea as to be given up for lost, or puts into port in distress for want of documents, or is upset by a call for the boot-jack and slippers—which is something like the previous question in Congress.

If my worthy cousin be somewhat over-argumentative as a politician, he restores the equilibrium of his character by a considerate coolness in religious matters. He piques himself upon being a high-churchman, but he is only a rare frequenter of places of worship, and very seldom permits himself to get into a dispute upon points of faith. If Mr Chub, the Presbyterian tutor in the family, ever succeeds in drawing him into this field, as he occasionally has the address to do, Meriwether is sure to fly the course: he gets puzzled with Scripture names, and makes some odd mistakes between Peter and Paul, and then generally turns the parson over to his wife, who, he says, has an astonishing memory.'

WILLIAM WARE, born 1797, a Unitarian clergyman, and a descendant from one of the earliest settlers of Massachusetts, is the author of two well-known romances founded on ancient history—*The Fall of Palmyra* (1836), and *Probus, or Rome in the Third Century* (1838). The first of these works is given in the form of letters, addressed by Lucius Manlius Piso to his friend Marcus Curtius. The supposed writer is represented as visiting Palmyra about the close of the third century, beholding the city in its days of grandeur, and witnessing its overthrow by Aurelian. The second romance is written in the form of letters from Piso at Rome, to Fausta, daughter of one of the ministers of Queen Zenobia, and gives an account of Piso's conversion to Christianity. A third work of a similar character is entitled *Julian*, and narrates the adventures of a Roman citizen of Hebrew descent, who visits Judæa in the early part of the first century.

The writings of Mr Ware have been generally commended for their graceful style, pleasing descriptions, and pious and benevolent sentiments. Soon after their appearance in America, they were reprinted in England with new titles. We may notice here, as the only other American work resembling the fictions of Ware, the tale of *Philothea* by Mrs Child. In its scenery, it belongs to Athens in the days of Pericles and Phidias, but the philosophical talk belongs rather to Boston, United States, in the days of Ralph Waldo Emerson.

THE JOURNEY TO PALMYRA.

'I will not detain you long with our voyage, but will only mark out its course. Leaving the African shore, we struck across to Sicily, and coasting along its eastern border, beheld with pleasure the towering form of Ætna, sending up into the heavens a dull and sluggish cloud of vapours. We then ran between the Peloponnesus and Crete, and so held our course till the Island of Cyprus rose like her own fair goddess from the ocean, and filled our eyes with a beautiful vision of hill and valley, wooded promontory, and glittering towns and villas. A fair wind soon withdrew us from these charming prospects, and after driving us swiftly and roughly over the remainder of our way, rewarded us with a brighter and more welcome vision still—the coast of Syria, and our destined port Berytus.

As far as the eye could reach, both towards the north and the south, we beheld a luxuriant region, crowded with villages, and giving every indication of comfort and wealth. The city itself, which we rapidly approached, was of inferior size, but presented an agreeable prospect of warehouses, public and private edifices, overtopped here and there by the lofty palm, and other trees of a new and peculiar foliage. Four days were consumed here in the purchase of slaves, camels, and horses, and in other preparations for the journey across the desert. Two routes presented themselves—one more, the other less direct; the last, though more circuitous, appeared to me the more desirable, as it would take me within sight of the modern glories and ancient remains of Heliopolis. This, therefore, was determined upon; and on the morning of the fifth day we set forward upon our long march. Four slaves, two camels, and three horses, with an Arab conductor, constituted our little caravan; but for greater safety, we attached ourselves to a much larger one than our own, in which we were swallowed up and lost—consisting of travellers and traders from all parts of the world, and who were also on their way to Palmyra, as a point whence to separate to various parts of the vast east. It would delight me to lay before you, with the distinctness and minuteness of a picture, the whole of this novel and, to me, interesting route; but I must content myself with a slight sketch, and reserve fuller communications to the time when, once more seated with you upon the Cœlian, we enjoy the freedom of social converse.

Our way through the valleys of Libanus was like one long wandering among the pleasure-grounds of opulent citizens. The land was everywhere richly cultivated, and a happier peasantry, as far as the eye of the traveller could judge, nowhere exists. The most luxuriant valleys of our own Italy are not more crowded with the evidences of plenty and contentment. Upon drawing near to the ancient Baalbec, I found, on inquiry of our guide, that we were not to pass through it, as I had hoped, nor even very near it—not nearer than between two and three miles; so that in this I had been clearly deceived by those of whom I had made the most exact inquiries at Berytus. The event proved, however, that it was not for nothing; for soon after we had started on our journey, on the morning of the second day, turning suddenly around the projecting rock of a mountain-ridge, we all at once beheld, as if a veil had been lifted up, Heliopolis and its suburbs spread out before us in all their various beauty. The city lay about three miles distant. I could only, therefore, identify its principal structure, the Temple of the Sun, as built by the first Antonine. This towered above the walls and over all the other buildings, and gave vast ideas of the greatness of the place, leading the mind to crowd it with other edifices that should bear some proportion to this noble monument of imperial magnificence. As suddenly as the view of this imposing scene had been revealed, so suddenly was it again eclipsed by another short turn in the road, which took us once more into the mountain valleys. But the overhanging and impenetrable foliage of a Syrian forest shielding me from the fierce rays of a burning sun, soon reconciled me to my loss—more especially as I knew that in a short time we were to enter upon the sandy desert which stretches from the Anti-Libanus almost to the very walls of Palmyra.

Upon this boundless desert we now soon entered. The scene which it presented was more dismal than I can describe. A red moving sand—or hard and baked by the heat of a sun such as Rome never knows—low gray rocks just rising here and there above the level of the plain, with now and then the dead and glittering trunk of a vast cedar whose roots seemed as if they had outlasted centuries—the bones of camels and elephants, scattered on either hand, dazzling the sight by reason of their excessive whiteness—at a distance, occasionally an Arab of the desert, for a moment surveying our long line, and then darting off to his fastnesses—these were the objects which, with scarce any variation, met our eyes during the four wearisome days that we dragged ourselves over this wild and inhospitable region. A little after the noon of the fourth day, as we started on our way, having refreshed ourselves and our exhausted animals at a spring which here poured out its warm but still grateful waters to the traveller, my ears received the agreeable news that towards the east there could now be discerned the dark line which indicated our approach to the verdant tract that encompasses the great city. Our own excited spirits were quickly imparted to our beasts; and a more rapid movement soon revealed into distinctness the high land and waving groves of palm-trees which mark the site of Palmyra.

It was several miles before we reached the city, that we suddenly found ourselves—landing, as it were, from a sea upon an island or continent—in a rich and thickly peopled country. The roads indicated an approach to a great capital in the increasing numbers of those who thronged them, meeting and passing us, overtaking us, or crossing our path. Elephants, camels, and the dromedary, which I had before seen only in the amphitheatres, I here beheld as the native inhabitants of the soil. Frequent villas of the rich and luxurious Palmyrenes, to which they retreat from the greater heats of the city, now threw a lovely charm over the scene. Nothing can exceed the splendour of the sumptuous palaces. Italy itself has nothing which surpasses them. The new and brilliant costumes of the persons whom we met, together with the rich housings of the animals they rode, served greatly to add to all this beauty. I was still entranced, as it were, by the objects around me, and buried in reflection, when I was aroused by the shout of those who led the caravan, and who had attained the summit of a little rising-ground, saying: "Palmyra! Palmyra!" I urged forward my steed, and in a moment the most wonderful prospect I ever beheld—no, I cannot except even Rome—burst upon my sight. Flanked by hills of considerable elevation on the east, the city filled the whole plain below as far as the eye could reach, both towards the north and towards the south. This immense plain was all one vast and boundless city. It seemed to me to be larger than Rome; yet I knew very well that it could not be—that it was not. And it was some time before I understood the true character of the scene before me, so as to separate the city from the country, and the country from the city, which here wonderfully interpenetrate each other, and so confound and deceive the observer. For the city proper is so studded with groups of lofty palm-trees, shooting up among its temples and palaces; and, on the other hand, the plain in its immediate vicinity is so thickly adorned with magnificent structures of the purest marble, that it is not easy, nay, it is impossible, at the distance at which I contemplated the whole, to distinguish the line which divided the one from the other. It was all city and all country—all country and all city. Those which lay before me, I was ready to believe were the Elysian Fields. I imagined that I saw under my feet the dwellings of purified men and of gods; certainly, they were too glorious for the mere earth-born. There was a central point, however, which chiefly fixed my attention, where the vast Temple of the Sun stretched upward its thousand columns of polished marble to the heavens, in its matchless beauty casting into the shade every other work of art of which the world can boast. I have stood before the Parthenon, and have almost worshipped that divine achievement of the immortal Phidias; but it is a toy by the side of this bright crown of the eastern capital. I have been at Milan, at Ephesus, at Alexandria, at Antioch; but in neither of these renowned cities have I beheld anything that I can allow to approach in united extent, grandeur, and most consummate beauty, this almost more than work of man. On each side of this, the central point, there rose upward slender pyramids, pointed obelisks, domes of the most graceful proportions, columns, arches, and lofty towers, for number and for form beyond my power to describe. These buildings, as well as the walls of the city, being all either of white marble or of some stone as white, and being everywhere in their whole extent interspersed, as I have already said, with multitudes of overshadowing palm-trees, perfectly filled and satisfied my sense of beauty, and made me feel for the moment as if in such a scene I should love to dwell, and there end my days. Nor was I alone in these transports of delight. All my fellow-travellers seemed equally affected; and from the native Palmyrenes, of whom there were many among us, the most impassioned and boastful exclamations broke forth. "What is Rome to this?" they cried. "Fortune is not constant. Why may not Palmyra be what Rome has been—mistress of the world? Who more fit to rule than the great Zenobia? A few years may see great changes. Who can tell what shall come to pass?" These, and many such sayings, were uttered by those around me, accompanied by many significant gestures and glances of the eye. I thought of them afterwards. We now descended the hill, and the long line of our caravan moved on towards the city.'

Among the numerous fictions written as vehicles of moral and religious sentiments, the tales of *Margaret* and *Richard Edney*, by the Rev. SYLVESTER JUDD, a clergyman of Augusta, Maine, may be noticed. In their object, these stories are good; but the author seems to write with a deliberate eccentricity of style. Many scenes of daily life in New England are vividly described, while in other parts of the story the mixture of sacred with ludicrous matters is very offensive. In a poem entitled *Philo, an Evangeliad*, the author of *Margaret* surpasses the oddity of his prose-style, and introduces, in the discussion of the most solemn themes, such words as muzzy, soggy, munch, mucker, princock, dowse, and queachy. On the whole, it may be said of Mr Judd's writings, that they are unique in American literature. '*Philo*,' says a reviewer, 'is strictly an original work,' and we might extend the same praise to the two novels already named. The phrase 'solitary and alone,' ascribed to egotistic orators who boast of their own exploits, might be an excusable pleonasm if used by Mr Judd in describing his own choice of diction. We will venture to say, that nothing like it can be found in the whole range of literature. We must give one short specimen of the mode of inserting odd words in passages of a serious character. Speaking of the Sabbath in New England, the author says: 'All days are holy; this is the *cream* of the week. . . . Its light, its air, its warmth, its sound, its sun, the shimmer of the dawn on the brass cock of the steeple, the look of the meeting-house itself, —all things were not as on other days. And now, when those old Sabbaths are almost gone, some latent, indefinable impression of what they were comes over us, and *wrenches* us into awe, stillness, and regret.'

The prose-writings of LONGFELLOW, whose poems have been noticed in our review, can hardly be classed with fictions. The first entitled *Outre-mer, or a Pilgrimage beyond the Sea*, consists of sketches of travel in France, Spain, and Italy, interspersed with meditative passages. *Hyperion*, published in 1839, is partly written on the same plan, but includes a slight texture of narrative, having a moral purport. Its scenes are laid in Germany and Switzerland; and the tone of thought and sentiment assures us that the work was written under the influence of the study of German literature, especially its poetry and philosophy. *Kavanagh, a Tale*, has some degree of narrative interest, but the story is broken by several digressions on literary topics. The appended quotation gives the writer's views of national literature. The stranger, Mr Hathaway, must be supposed to represent the young authors who have a wish to cultivate an intensely American style of writing.

NATIONAL LITERATURE.

FROM KAVANAGH.

'He announced himself as Mr Hathaway. Passing through the village, he could not deny himself the pleasure of calling on Mr Churchill, whom he knew by his writings in the periodicals, though not personally. He wished, moreover, to secure the co-operation of one already so favourably known to the literary world, in a new magazine he was about to establish, in order to raise the character of American literature, which, in his opinion, the existing reviews and magazines had entirely failed to accomplish. A daily increasing want of something better was felt by the public; and the time had come for the establishment of such a periodical as he proposed. After explaining in rather a florid and exuberant manner his plan and prospects, he entered more at large into the subject of American literature, which it was his design to foster and patronise.

"I think, Mr Churchill," said he, "that we want a national literature commensurate with our mountains and rivers; commensurate with Niagara and the Alleghanies, and the great lakes!"

"Oh!"

"We want a national epic that shall correspond to the size of the country; that shall be to all other epics what Banvard's Panorama of the Mississippi is to all other paintings—the largest in the world!"

"Ah!"

"We want a national drama in which scope enough shall be given to our gigantic ideas, and to the unparalleled activity and progress of our people!"

"Of course."

"In a word, we want a national literature altogether shaggy and unshorn, that shall shake the earth like a herd of buffaloes thundering over the prairies!"

"Precisely," interrupted Mr Churchill; "but excuse me!—are you not confounding things that have no analogy? Great has a very different meaning when applied to a river, and when applied to a literature. Large and shallow may perhaps be applied to both. Literature is rather an image of the spiritual world than of the physical, is it not?—of the internal, rather than the external. Mountains, lakes, and rivers are, after all, only its scenery and decorations—not its substance and essence. A man will not necessarily be a great poet because he lives near a great mountain. Nor, being a poet, will he necessarily write better poems than another, because he lives nearer Niagara."

"But, Mr Churchill, you do not certainly mean to deny the influence of scenery on the mind?"

"No, only to deny that it can create genius. At best, it can only develop it. Switzerland has produced no extraordinary poet; nor, as far as I know, have the Andes, or the Himalaya Mountains, or the Mountains of the Moon in Africa."

"But, at all events," urged Mr Hathaway, "let us have our literature national. If it is not national, it is nothing."

"On the contrary, it may be a great deal. Nationality is a good thing to a certain extent, but universality is better. All that is best in the great poets of all countries, is not what is national in them, but what is universal. Their roots are in their native soil; but their branches wave in the unpatriotic air, that speaks the same language unto all men, and their leaves shine with the illimitable light that pervades all lands. Let us throw all the windows open;

let us admit the light and air on all sides; that we may look towards the four corners of the heavens, and not always in the same direction."

"But you admit nationality to be a good thing?"

"Yes, if not carried too far; still, I confess, it rather limits one's views of truth. I prefer what is natural. Mere nationality is often ridiculous. Every one smiles when he hears the Icelandic proverb: 'Iceland is the best land the sun shines upon.' Let us be natural, and we shall be national enough. Besides, our literature can be strictly national only so far as our character and modes of thought differ from those of nations. Now, as we are very like the English—are, in fact, English under a different sky—I do not see how our literature can be very different from theirs. Westward, from hand to hand, we pass the lighted torch, but it was lighted at the old domestic fireside of England."

"Then you think our literature is never to be anything but an imitation of the English?"

"Not at all. It is not an imitation, but, as some one has said, a continuation."

"It seems to me that you take a very narrow view of the subject."

"On the contrary, a very broad one. No literature is complete until the language in which it is written is dead. We may well be proud of our task and of our position. Let us see if we can build in any way worthy of our forefathers."

"But I insist upon originality."

"Yes; but without spasms and convulsions. Authors must not, like Chinese soldiers, expect to win victories by turning somersets in the air."

"Well, really, the prospect from your point of view is not very brilliant. Pray, what do you think of our national literature?"

"Simply, that a national literature is not the growth of a day. Centuries must contribute their dew and sunshine to it. Our own is growing slowly, but surely, striking its roots downward, and its branches upward, as is natural; and I do not wish, for the sake of what some people call originality, to invert it, and try to make it grow with its roots in the air. And as for having it so savage and wild as you want it, I have only to say, that all literature, as well as all art, is the result of culture and intellectual refinement."'

The prose-writings of EDGAR A. POE include a series of short stories. Of these, several consist chiefly of details of circumstantial evidence in criminal trials; others have, as we think, a very morbid character in their topics and mode of treatment. The command of language, power of description, and analytical skill displayed in Poe's tales, are wasted when expended on revolting subjects. The ingenuity of his plots, and the graphic power shewn in many passages, have been very highly commended; but we have found nothing to modify our opinion of the morbid tone of mind so prevalent in his fictions.

THEODORE S. FAY, who in 1837 was appointed secretary of legation for the United States at the court of Berlin, is the author of several novels, besides shorter tales and magazine-papers. His most successful work, *The Countess Ida*, published in 1840, is intended as a protest against the custom of duelling. The hero, Claude Wyndham, resides at Berlin, where he endures for some time the insults offered by a certain Lord Elkington, who at last, when other means of bringing about a duel have failed, strikes Wyndham at a court-ball. Denham, the hero's friend, takes up the quarrel, meets the duellist, and is fatally wounded; while Wyndham, in solitude, is endeavouring to master his passions and maintain his principle. He is exposed to the bitter reproaches of the widow of Denham, and is branded as a coward, and deserted by his best friends. In the end, he vindicates the courage which has sustained him in the midst of his trials. The tale has the faults commonly found in works of fiction constructed with a view to some moral purport. The same purpose is seen in another work by Mr Fay—*Hoboken, a Romance of New York*, published in 1843. The other fictions by this author include *Norman Leslie* (1835) and *Robert Rueful* (1844).

Under the assumed name of Ik. Marvel, one of the younger American authors, DONALD G. MITCHELL, has acquired a reputation by various tales and sketches, published under the titles of *Reveries of a Bachelor*, *Dream-life*, and *Lorgnette, or Studies of the Town*. These are partly sentimental, and have too much sameness in their tone of melancholy. It has been remarked, that the study of Irving's sketches has left traces of imitation too evident in the writings of Mitchell. His style has, in many passages, a certain charm of dreamy quietude and pleasurable pensiveness; but when we have read a few pages, we have a desire to vary the tune, or, indeed, to change the key-note. The author of *Dream-life* might be compared with a musician who knows little of the resources of modulation, and attempts to write a symphony on a few simple chords in one scale. It seems strange to find in American books by young authors a want of the freshness and variety of life. Pathos has its place in fiction, but should leave room for other moods of mind. For more detailed characteristics of this writer, we may refer to a review,[1] from which a passage may be quoted here: 'Mr Mitchell does not bear reading from cover to cover. The want of sustained

[1] In *Putnam's Monthly*, No. 1.

interest in his books, and the very fragmentary manner in which he arranges them, are indeed unfavourable to a continuous perusal. . . . . There is a sameness about their very perfections that wearies us as we go on. They are the champaign lands of sentiment; beautiful levels, over which an hour's gallop or a day's meditation is charming; but to stay there for any length of time, induces terrible lassitude and mental depression.'

The reader who is wearied by sentimental fiction, may find relief in turning to the tales of adventure by Dr MAYO, Lieutenant WISE, and HERMANN MELVILLE. To write a grave critique on these books, would be ridiculous; and to make any protest against the extravagances of the writer last named, would be useless; for it would never be read by those who find delight in the pages of *Mardi*, *Kaloolah*, and similar tales. It must not be supposed that we deny the peculiar merits of these romances: we intend only to shew the impossibility of giving any critical account of them. They must be received as reports of the fluent, careless, and often brilliant talk of imaginative travellers, or dreamers of travel, who have written without any care for rules of art, or fear of critics. The passion for reading of the class to which we refer, is a curious feature in recent years. It prevails in England and Germany as in America. As practical life becomes tame and monotonous, the youthful imagination goes back to barbarism and the wildness of nature, to find excitement. Tales of adventure by land and sea, in the forests, or on the prairies of the far west, or highly coloured pictures of sensuous and luxurious life in the islands of the South Seas—these supply the intellectual refreshment of numerous young readers, and lure away their minds from the study of realities. The wildness of Melville's stories—*Typee*, *Omoo*, *Mardi*, and others—seems to be infectious; for in a review of *Mardi*, we find *a critic* writing in the following style:—'Reading this wild book, we can imagine *ourselves* mounted upon some Tartar steed, golden caparisons clank around our person, ostrich plumes of driven whiteness hang over our brow, and cloud our vision with dancing snow. . . . . Away, away, along the sandy plain!' &c. This is perhaps our most concise mode of indicating the rhapsodical style of the book itself. *Typee*, the first of Melville's books, tells the story of two sailors who escaped from their ship, and landed on an island of the Pacific, where they were received by the Typee natives, with whom they lived luxuriously, feasting on sucking-pigs and bread-fruit, and enjoying all the licence of a primitive state of society. *Mardi* intermingles with its voluptuous scenery a dreamy philosophy of which we can give no clear account.

Kaloolah, by Dr Mayo, is a comparatively sober tale of adventures, beginning among the Red Indians, and ending with an account of the hero's marriage with the princess of Kiloam, a highly civilised country in the interior of Africa. *Los Gringos*, by Lieutenant Wise, is a lively series of adventures, including the author's perils while engaged in carrying dispatches during the Mexican war.

Mr Kimball's *St Leger; Harry Franco*, by Mr Briggs; and *The Confessions of a Poet*, by Laughton Osborn, may be mentioned here as fictions which have gained some reputation. It has been frequently asserted, that America is deficient in humorous, imaginative literature. Among the writers in this department, we find the names of Irving, Paulding, Verplanck, Sanderson, Neal, Matthews, and others who have written light satirical sketches of character and manners. Among recent publications, several books of a light humorous description have been produced in the southern and western states.

JOHN SANDERSON (1785–1844) commenced writing for the periodical press in the beginning of the present century. In 1820, he wrote the first and second of the eight volumes of the *Lives of the Signers of the Declaration of Independence.* After a tour in Europe, he published his series of letters, entitled *The American in Paris* (1839), which was reprinted in London; and commenced a similar work, *The American in London*, of which some parts appeared in the *Knickerbocker Magazine.* Sanderson is described by his friends as a quiet and amiable man, whose satirical powers were always restrained by his good-nature. On one occasion, when he had satirised with an unusual freedom an absent person, he went out after midnight, and in a storm, to express his regret for having indulged in such a licence. It may be supposed that a man of this temper could not be a very pungent satirist.

Our want of knowledge of the originals may perhaps explain the fact, that we cannot appreciate the humour of the burlesque sketches of low characters found in the writings of NEAL and Matthews. The *Charcoal Sketches* of the former have had a wide circulation in America, and have been partly reprinted in London. But in these times, when a mere apparent cheapness is regarded, by many booksellers, as almost the sole quality wanted in a popular book, a wide circulation proves nothing in favour of the real worth of the American works so profusely reprinted. 'Mr Neal's style,' says Griswold, 'is neat and graceful, and frequently sparkling and witty. He writes as if he had little or no sympathy with his creations, and as if he were a calm spectator of acts and actors, whimsical or comical—an observer rather by accident than from desire. It is not always so, however, since in some of his sketches he exhibits not only a happy faculty for the burlesque, and singular skill in depicting character, but a geniality and heartiness of appreciation which carry the reader's feelings along with his fancy.'

The Career of Puffer Hopkins, by CORNELIUS MATTHEWS, professes to be 'characteristic and national in its features,' and is intended to represent the progress of 'a vulgar politician.' Its sketches of the lower classes in New York indicate that the author has studied and imitated the manner of Dickens. One specimen may be quoted. It describes the labours of a political canvasser, named Hobbleshank, who is employed to collect votes among the sailors residing in Water Street :—

THE CANVASSER.

'There was one that toiled in Puffer's behalf more like a spirit than a man—a little shrunken figure, that was everywhere for days before the canvass—a universal presence, breathing in every ear the name of Puffer. There was not a taproom that he did not haunt; no obscure alley into which he did not penetrate, and make its reeking atmosphere vocal with his praises. Wherever a group of talkers or citizens were gathered, the little old man glided in and dropped a word that might bear fruit at the ballot-box. At nightfall he would mix with crowds of shipwrights, 'prentices, and labourers, and kindle their rugged hearts with the thought of the young candidate.

He stopped not with grown men and voters, but seizing moments when he could, he whispered the name in children's ears, that, being borne to parents by gentle lips, it might be mixed with kindly recollections, and so be made triumphant.

It was given out that the Blinkerites had established or discovered in some under-ground tenements that never saw light of day, a great warren of voters. When the toilsome old man learned of this burrow that was to be sprung against his favourite, he looked about for an equal mine, whence voters might be dug in scores, at a moment's notice, should occasion demand. With this in view, one afternoon he entered Water Street, at Peck Slip, like a skilful miner, as though a great shaft had been sunk just there.

* * * *

He passed from house to house, making friends in each. Sometimes he made his way into the bar-room, where, seated against the wall, on benches all around the sanded floor, with dusty bamboo rods, alligator skins, outlandish eggs, and sea-weeds plucked among the Caribbees or the Pacific islands, or some far-off shore, he would linger by the hour, listening with all the wondering patience of a child, to their ocean-talk. And when they were through, he would draw a homely similitude between their story—the perils their ship had crossed—with the good ship of state; and then tell them of a young friend of his, who was on trial before the ship's crew for a master's place. Before he left, in nine cases out of ten they gave their hands for Puffer, sometimes even rising and confirming it with a cheer that shook the house, and brought their messmates thronging in from the neighbourhood, when the story would be recited to them by a dozen voices, and new recruits to Puffer's side enrolled.

* * * *

The little old man—true to the interest he had first shewn—bent himself with such hearty good-will to his task, that when, after many days' labour, he left Water Street at its other extremity, there was not a ripe old Salt that was not gathered, nor a tall young sailor that was not harvested for the cause. And so he pursued the task he had set to himself without faltering, without a moment's pause. For days before the contest came on, he was out at sunrise, moving about wherever a vote could be found; nursing and maturing it for the polling-day, as a gardener would a tender plant; watching and tending many out-of-the-way places, and by a skilful discourse, a chance word, an apt story, ripening it against the time when it was to be gathered.'

NATHANIEL PARKER WILLIS.

A biographical notice of N. P. WILLIS has already been given, with some account of his poems. His prose-writings include *Pencillings by the Way*, *Inklings of Adventure*, *Dashes at Life with a Free Pencil*, *Loiterings of Travel*, *Letters from under a Bridge*, and various sketches of scenery, travels, and manners, first published in the *Home Journal*, and reprinted under the title *Hurrygraphs*. It must be noticed, that the same writings by Willis have appeared under several titles. Thus the *Pencillings* have partly been reprinted under the title, *Famous Persons and Famous Places*. *Life Here and There* consists of a collection of 'sketches of society and adventure, at far apart times and places.' *People I have Met*, is a remarkable specimen of a book with a false title; for while it professes to give 'pictures of society and people of mark, drawn under a thin veil of fiction,' its sketches are imaginary and extravagant. We have still to mention *Fun Jottings*, and *A Summer Cruise in the Mediterranean*.

It is obvious that it must be difficult to classify strictly these several miscellanies. We notice them in the department of fiction, as they include many tales, though the descriptive and gossipping papers are more characteristic and entertaining than the stories. In all his writings, Willis sustains the lively, conversational style he represents as 'the present fashion' in literature. In recommending his own fluency, he refers to the examples of other successful writers, and informs us that 'Thackeray's novels are stenographed from his everyday rattle with his intimates. . . . . In writing a book now-a-days, the less you "smell of the shop," the better it sells.' The maxim of Horace, too trite to be quoted, suggests itself here. We do not see clearly why, in this world of variety, a writer or a speaker should confine himself to one tone or manner, however lively it may be. Even Bottom could leave 'Ercles' vein,' and take up a 'more condoling' strain. The incessant liveliness of Willis may suit a short story or a single chapter of gossip; but in the course of a whole volume, it becomes wearisome. It has another defect, as it injures the writer's descriptive powers. He never forgets himself in the object described, but is himself constantly present to the reader. Two of his best descriptive passages are the sketches of Trenton Falls and the promontory of Nahant; but in these, as in others, the prominent object is the writer himself, as modified by the influence of these localities. At Niagara, his vivacity is so remarkable, that the proper title of the description would be—'A lively Sketcher, as seen at the Falls.'

The *Pencillings by the Way* include some of the best specimens of the writer's descriptive talent. The prose is fluent, and free from the extremes of the 'hurrygraph' style seen in later sketches. With regard to personalities, enough has been said on both sides; and we will remark only that Willis, in writing sketches of the talk and manners of eminent living men, adopted a style of gossip which, in recent times, has become too common. We have now on our table a sketch of the living editor of a well-known newspaper. It seems to have been written as a climax, and for the purpose of exposing to ridicule all similar attempts. With a well-sustained air of seriousness, the writer informs the public that Mr G. looks rather old when seen by a spectator walking behind him; that he wears occasionally a white coat, whereby hangs a tale (relative to its purchase); that one of his legs is slightly shorter than the other; that, standing without his shoes, he measures so many feet and inches in height; and that he weighs so many stones, allowing for each fourteen pounds.[1] This

[1] *Life of Horace Greeley, Editor of the New York Tribune.* By J. Parton.

caricature will, we hope, have some good effect on the literature of personalities.

There is some ingenuity in the apology offered by Willis for his own portraitures of living authors and public characters. He observes that the 'Atlantic' between England and America is equal to a century in removing contemporaries to a suitable distance. Of course, this argument applies only to American readers, and is made futile by reprints in England. Another mode of defence is very objectionable:

'For the living portraitures of the book, I have a word to say. That sketches of the whim of the hour, its manners, fashions, and those ephemeral trifles which, slight as they are, constitute in a great measure its "form and pressure"—that these, and familiar traits of persons distinguished in our time, are popular and amusing, I have the most weighty reasons certainly to know. *They sell.*'

Scenes in 'high life' occupy too much space in these and other sketches. A foreign writer, having the graphic talent of Willis, might have found in England a far greater variety of aspects of life and society; and, without offence, might have written freely and instructively on many characteristics which can hardly be viewed impartially by Englishmen. But his attention was too much occupied by the gilded cupola, and sparingly bestowed on the main structure of our society. Many of the lighter traits noticed in the sketcher's diary might be suitable for a newspaper, but appear ridiculous when reprinted and circulated in numerous editions.

In his contrasts of manners at home and abroad, the sketcher is sometimes too severe with regard to his own countrymen, or at least he seems to imply more than is true. His rather solemn and overdrawn sketch of the 'repose of high life,' would suggest that loud talking and 'overpowering' demeanour are common in the best circles of American society; but this, we believe, is not true. Most probably there is a degree of caricature on both sides of the picture; for, we trust, it would not be easy to find 'the high-bred Englishman' who is 'just as calm' and 'technical' 'in describing the death of his friend' 'as in discussing the weather.' A want of guarded expressions in writing judgments on whole classes of society, is seen in another passage. No doubt, there is some truth in it: every impartial traveller in America has noticed the hopefulness and consequent activity of numerous sober, industrious, and intelligent workmen who there see an open path to success and comfort; and he must have contrasted these traits with the sad apathy of all higher feelings too common among the lowest class in England. But the following sketch is exaggerated, or not properly qualified. We quote it, however, because it is *quite as fair* as some English sketches of American classes :—

'During the four or five hours that I was playing the hanger-on to a vulgar and saucy custom-house officer at Liverpool, one or two contrasts crept in at my dull eyes—contrasts between what I had left, and what was before me. The most striking was the *utter want of hope* in the countenances of the working-classes—the look of dogged submission and animal endurance of their condition of life. They act like horses and cows. A showy equipage goes by, and they have not the curiosity to look up. Their gait is that of tired donkeys, saving as much trouble at leg-lifting as possible. Their mouths and eyes are wholly sensual, expressing no capability of a want above food. Their dress is without a thought of more than warmth and covering—drab covered with dirt. Their voices are a half-note above a grunt. Indeed, comparing their condition with the horse, I would prefer being an English horse to being an English working-man. And you will easily see the very strong contrast there is between this picture and that of the ambitious and lively working-men of our country.'

'It is extraordinary,' says Willis, 'how *universal*' [in England and Scotland, he means to say] 'the feeling seems to be against America.' This is a fair specimen of many vague and unfounded statements which have a tendency to produce that bad feeling which they presuppose. What inquiry had the sketcher made before he hazarded this broad assertion? To say nothing of any other class of society, a universal national antipathy must be shared by the working-classes, the vast majority of the people of Great Britain; but what signs have they ever given of this supposed hatred of America? It is ludicrous to read the trivial anecdote on which so grave a statement is made to hang. The tourist, on his way to Edinburgh, was annoyed by a rude and talkative individual in the cabin of a steamer. 'Opposite me,' he says, 'sat a pale, severe-looking Scotchman, who had addressed one or two remarks to me, and, upon an uncommon burst of uproariousness' [among a party of ladies], 'he laughed with the rest, and remarked—"that the ladies were excusable, for they were doubtless Americans, and knew no better."'

'"It strikes me," said I, "that both in manners and accent they are particularly Scotch."

"Sir!" said the pale gentleman.

"Sir!" said several of my neighbours on the right and left.

"Have you ever been in Scotland?" asked the pale gentleman with rather a ferocious air.

"No, sir! Have you ever been in America?"

"No, sir! but I have read Mrs Trollope."

"And I have read *Cyril Thornton;* and the manners delineated in Mrs Trollope, I must say, are rather elegant in comparison."

I particularised the description I alluded to, which will occur immediately to those who have read the novel I have named; and then confessing I was an American, and withdrawing my illiberal remark, which I had only made to shew the gentleman the injustice and absurdity of his own, we called for another glass of whisky, and became very good friends. Heaven knows, I have no prejudice against the Scotch, or any other nation—but it is extraordinary how universal the feeling seems to be against America. A half-hour incog. in any mixed company in England, I should think would satisfy the most rose-coloured doubter on the subject.'

In the same style, Willis writes of a supposed English prejudice against books written by American authors! 'There is little need,' he says, 'of widening the ditch of prejudice over which American books must jump to be read in England.' The success of Irving might have induced the sketcher to reconsider his assertion. Later American writers have surely had no reason to complain. The fact is notorious, that American literature has been more than fairly represented in the English market. On account of the state of copyright-law, the number of cheap reprints of works issued from the presses of New York, Philadelphia, and Boston, has been so great, that we might rather complain of a prejudice *in favour* of the works of Willis, Longfellow, Hawthorne, and other Americans. In fact, such has been the prominence of their names on our railway-book stalls and the counters of provincial cheap booksellers, that a foreigner, judging by appearances, might conclude that England, for its current literature, depended on America! It would be useless to say more of a mere absurdity, deserving notice only as a specimen of many random assertions made by travellers.

In several short papers, originally published in his own newspaper, and afterwards collected and reprinted under the odd title *Hurrygraphs*, Mr Willis undertakes the duties of *arbiter elegantiarum* in American society. Of the faithfulness of his sketches, or the justice of his strictures on fashions and manners, we do not profess to be able to give an opinion. The writer asserts that, after all the criticism called forth by his sketches of English society, not a single incorrectness has ever been proved, or even charged upon them. It is reasonable, therefore, to suppose that his accounts of life in New York must be accurate, at least with regard to certain classes.

We pass over many criticisms and eulogies on musical artists and lecturers, and can find little to say in commendation of the tales *Ernest Clay*, *Edith Linsey*, *Lady Rachel*, and others included in the writer's miscellanies. His best qualities are seen in his descriptive passages; and it appears probable that, if he had concentrated on a well-selected task the attention which has been engaged upon a wide range of miscellaneous topics, he might have fulfilled the promise made in one of his prefaces. As an example of his quiet and more accurate style of description, we select the following passage from *Pencillings by the Way:*—

THE CLIMATES OF ENGLAND AND AMERICA COMPARED.

'It is almost a matter of course to decry the climate of England. The English writers themselves talk of *suicidal months;* and it is the only country where part of the livery of a mounted groom is his master's great-coat, strapped about his waist. It is certainly a damp climate, and the sun shines less in England than in most other countries. But to persons of full habit, this moisture in the air is extremely agreeable; and the high condition of all animals in England, from man downward, proves its healthfulness. A stranger who has been accustomed to a brighter sky, will at first find a gloom in the gray light so characteristic of an English atmosphere; but this soon wears off, and he finds a compensation, as far as the eye is concerned, in the exquisite softness of the verdure, and the deep and enduring brightness of the foliage. The effect of this moisture on the skin is singularly grateful. The pores become accustomed to a healthy action, which is unknown in other countries; and the bloom by which an English complexion is known all over the world, is the index of an activity in this important part of the system, which, when first experienced, is almost like a new sensation. The transition to a dry climate such as ours, deteriorates the condition and quality of the skin, and produces a feeling, if I may so express it, like that of being *glazed.* It is a common remark in England, that an officer's wife and daughters follow his regiment to Canada at the expense of their complexions; and it is a well-known fact, that the bloom of female beauty is, in our country, painfully evanescent.

The climate of America is in many points very different from that of France and Great Britain. In the middle and northern states, it is a dry, invigorating, and bracing climate, in which a strong man may do more work than in almost any other, and which makes continual exercise, or occupation of some sort, absolutely necessary. With the exception of the "Indian summer," and here and there a day scattered through the spring and the hot months, there is no weather tempered so finely, that one would think of passing the day in merely enjoying it, and life is passed by those who have the misfortune to be idle, in continual and active dread of the elements. The cold is so acrid, and the heat so sultry, and the changes from one to the other are so violent, that no enjoyment can be depended upon out of doors, and no system of clothing or protection is good for a day together. He who has full occupation for head and hand

—as by far the greatest majority of our countrymen have—may live as long in America as in any portion of the globe—*vide* the bills of mortality. He whose spirits lean upon the temperature of the wind, or whose nerves require a genial and constant atmosphere, may find more favourable climes; and the habits and delicate constitutions of scholars, and people of sedentary pursuits generally, in the United States, prove the truth of the observation.

The habit of regular exercise in the open air, which is found to be so salutary in England, is scarcely possible in America. It is said, and said truly, of the first, that there is no day in the year when a lady may not ride comfortably on horseback; but with us the extremes of heat and cold, and the tempestuous character of our snows and rains, totally forbid to a delicate person anything like regularity in exercise. The consequence is, that the habit rarely exists; and the high and glowing health so common in England, and consequent, no doubt, upon the equable character of the climate in some measure, is with us sufficiently rare to excite remark. "Very English-looking!" is a common phrase, and means very healthy-looking. Still, our people *last;* and though I should define the English climate as the one in which the human frame is in the highest condition, I should say of America, that it is the one in which you could get the most work out of it.'

As specimens of livelier and more fanciful sketches, we might select, if our space would permit, the papers on several interesting localities in America. A sketch of the promontory of Nahant is one of the best; but here, on the shore of the Atlantic, the writer places himself in the foreground, and makes the description serve as an introduction to the tale of a quarrel about a 'hair-brush.' A passage from the account of a visit to Niagara may be quoted, as it is characteristic of the writer, and will at least explain, if it does not justify, our censures:—

NIAGARA.

'As I came nearer the Fall, a feeling of disappointment came over me. I had imagined Niagara a vast body of water descending as if from the clouds. The approach to most falls is *from below*, and we get an idea of them as of rivers pitching down to the plain from the brow of a hill or mountain. Niagara River, on the contrary, comes out from Lake Erie through a flat plain. The top of the cascade is ten feet, perhaps, below the level of the country around—consequently invisible from any considerable distance. You walk to the bank of a broad and rapid river, and look over the edge of a rock, where the outlet flood of an inland sea seems to have broken through the crust of the earth, and, by its mere weight, plunged with an awful leap into an immeasurable and resounding abyss. It seems to strike and thunder upon the very centre of the world, and the ground beneath your feet quivers with the shock till you feel unsafe upon it.

Other disappointment than this I cannot conceive at Niagara. It is a spectacle so awful, so beyond the scope and power of every other phenomenon in the world, that I think people who are disappointed there, mistake the incapacity of their own conception for the want of grandeur in the scene.

The "hell of waters" below needs but a little red ochre to out-Phlegethon Phlegethon. I can imagine the surprise of the gentle element, after sleeping away a se'nnight of moonlight in the peaceful bosom of Lake Erie, at finding itself of a sudden in such a coil! A Mediterranean sea-gull, which had tossed out the whole of a January in the infernal "yeast" of the Archipelago—(was I not all but wrecked every day between Troy and Malta in a score of successive hurricanes?)—I say, the most weather-beaten of sea-birds would look twice before he ventured upon the roaring caldron below Niagara. It is astonishing to see how far the descending mass is driven under the surface of the stream. As far down towards Lake Ontario as the eye can reach, the immense volumes of water rise like huge monsters to the light, boiling and flashing out in rings of foam, with an appearance of rage and anger that I have seen in no other cataract in the world.

"A *nice* fall, as an Englishman would say, my dear Job."

"Awful!"

Halleck, the American poet—a better one never "strung pearls"—has written some admirable verses on Niagara, describing its effect on the different individuals of a mixed party, among whom was a tailor. The sea of incident that has broken over me in the years of travel, has washed out of my memory all but the two lines descriptive of its impression upon Snip:—

> "The tailor made one single note—
> 'Gods! what a place to sponge a coat!'"

"Shall we go to breakfast, Job?"

"How slowly and solemnly they drop into the abysm!"

It was not an original remark of Mr Smith's. Nothing is so surprising to the observer, as the extraordinary deliberateness with which the waters of Niagara take their tremendous plunge. All hurry, and foam, and fret, till they reach the smooth limit of the curve, and then the laws of gravitation seem suspended; and, like Cæsar, they pause, and determine, since it is inevitable, to take the death-leap with becoming dignity.

"Shall we go to breakfast, Job?" I was obliged to raise my voice, to be heard, to a pitch rather exhausting to an empty stomach.

His eyes remained fixed upon the shifting rainbows bending and vanishing in the spray. There was no moving him, and I gave in for another five minutes.

"Do you think it probable, Job, that the waters of Niagara strike on the axis of the world?"

No answer.

"Job!"

"What?"

"Do you think his majesty's half of the cataract is finer than ours?"

"Much."

"For *water*, merely, perhaps. But look at the delicious verdure on the American shore, the glorious trees, the massed foliage, the luxuriant growth even to the very rim of the ravine! By Jove! it seems to me things grow better in a republic. Did you ever see a more barren and scraggy shore than the one you stand upon?"

"How exquisitely," said Job soliloquising, "that small green island divides the Fall! What a rock it must be founded on, not to have been washed away in the ages that these waters have split against it!"

"I'll lay you a bet it is washed away before the year two thousand —payable in any currency with which we may then be conversant."

"Don't trifle."

"With time, or geology, do you mean? Isn't it perfectly clear, from the looks of that ravine, that Niagara has *backed up* all the way from Lake Ontario? These rocks are not adamant, and the very precipice you stand on has cracked, and looks ready for the plunge. It must gradually wear back to Lake Erie, and then there will be a sweep I should like to live long enough to see. The instantaneous junction of two seas, with a difference of two hundred feet in their levels, will be a spectacle—eh, Job?"

"Tremendous!"

"Do you intend to wait and see it, or will you come to breakfast?"

He was immovable. I left him on the rock, went up to the hotel, and ordered mutton-chops and coffee; and when they were on the table, gave two of the waiters a dollar each to bring him up *nolens volens*. He arrived in a great rage, but with a good appetite; and we finished our breakfast just in time to meet Miss —— as she stepped, like Aurora, from her chamber.'

NATHANIEL HAWTHORNE.

The author of *The House of the Seven Gables*, and other tales and romances, is a native of the dull old town of Salem, in Massachusetts, so famous for its witchery in the days of Cotton Mather. Hawthorne, in one of his prefaces, seems to ascribe to the traditions of his birthplace a certain influence on his own imagination. Of the incidents of his life, we have little to record. He graduated in 1825 at Bowdoin College, in Maine, and soon afterwards began to write tales and sketches, which appeared in periodicals, but failed to attract general notice. Several of these early writings are included in the two volumes of *Twice-told*

Tales, published in 1837 and 1842. The author was at one time a member of the company who endeavoured to establish a co-operative fraternity at Brook Farm, in Roxbury. At another time, we find him musing in the solitude of the Old Manse, by the river at Concord, of which he has given a very pleasant description in the introduction to his work, *Mosses from an Old Manse* (1846). From his quiet hermitage at Concord, Hawthorne returned to Salem, where he was appointed surveyor of customs. After three years of enjoyment, or suffering, in this place, the Whigs expelled him from office, and he reappeared as a writer of fiction. Since the publication of his *Blithedale Romance*, he has received another appointment under government, and now resides in England.

It is not easy to characterise briefly such writings as the *Twice-told Tales*, *Mosses*, and *The House of the Seven Gables*. To say that they consist of tales, sketches, and allegories, tells nothing of Hawthorne's peculiarities. 'There is not unfrequently an incompleteness in his choicest productions. . . . . His plots are seldom well devised or skilfully developed. . . . . Indeed, he is often most successful where he does not even attempt narration, but selects some single scene, object, or incident, as the nucleus for a cluster of fancies and musings—melancholy, grave, humorous, or gay.' These fragments of criticism are true, but fail to make a complete portrait. To apply to Hawthorne the praise bestowed on another writer: 'He seems to enter into the very tone of feeling, the spirit of a landscape, or the atmosphere of a household, and reproduce them, not only to our perceptions, but almost to our sensations.' It is easy to notice separate characteristics; but we are not sure of success in attempting to explain clearly the general purport of Hawthorne, or the peculiar vein of thought which gives individuality to his stories. We have heard of a reflective man who, on all ordinary occasions, conversed 'like a man of this world,' but on certain topics intruded a quasi-German and not very transparent phraseology. It was hinted that his style might be improved with regard to clearness. 'Sir,' he replied, 'for many years my favourite study has been—psychology.' This is the best key we can find to the riddles in Hawthorne's tales. He employs fiction, not to illustrate practical life, not to add to the creations of the imaginative world, but to elucidate psychological problems. In our reading of several characters drawn in *The House of the Seven Gables* and *The Blithedale Romance*, we regard them not as men and women, but as walking and talking psychological problems, wandering in search of a solution. These remarks are not applicable to the strictly allegorical writings of Hawthorne; for example, his *Celestial Railroad*. In other tales, more or less allegorical, he partly adopts the manner of Tieck and Fouqué. The best critique on his earlier writings is found in one of his own magazine-papers, but is too long to be quoted here.

The external features of a work of fiction may be fantastic and visionary, while the *heart* of the story, if so we may speak of its inner meaning, may be sound and true. This rule is exemplified in the best specimens of dreamy tales by German authors—for instance, the goblin-story of *Red-mantle*, by Fouqué—and may be fairly applied to several of the tales or sketches of Hawthorne. Considered merely as tales, they are often poor, and the poverty of characters and plot-interest suggests that the writer would have succeeded better in allegory. This opinion is supported by the skill displayed in the satirical allegory of *The Celestial Railroad*, which is nothing less than a sequel to *The Pilgrim's Progress* of Bunyan. The nature of the subject precludes quotation of the most pointed passages in the satire, but a few incidents of a humorous description may be noticed.

It must be premised, that the railroad is intended as a vast modern improvement on the old difficult and dangerous route so well described by Bunyan. 'The old enemies of the foot-travellers have been "bought over" by offices on the new road,' and several ancient incumbrances have been set aside. For example, ' the enormous burdens, instead of being carried on our shoulders, as had been the custom of old, were snugly deposited in the baggage-car, and, as I was assured, would be delivered to their respective owners at the journey's end.' Mr Great-Heart's services were set aside. He had grown 'preposterously stiff and narrow in his old age,' having so often guided pilgrims over the road on foot, that he considered it a sin to travel in any other fashion. A bridge has been made over the Slough of Despond, but in a rather hasty mode of construction, so that it vibrates uncomfortably as the car passes over. However, the travellers, without accident, arrive at the station-house, where a supposititious 'Evangelist' presides at the ticket-office. The satire in the sketch of the Dark Valley is rather too serious to be noticed here, excepting a single portrait of one of the most difficult subjects that ever tried the skill of an artist. Even Theodore Parker and his friends must smile at such a sketch as the following:—

'At the end of the valley, as John Bunyan mentions, is a cavern, where, in his days, dwelt two cruel giants, Pope and Pagan, who had strewn the ground about their residence with the bones of slaughtered pilgrims. These vile old troglodytes are no longer there; but in their deserted cave another terrible giant has thrust himself, and makes it his business to seize upon honest travellers, and fat them for his table with plentiful meals of smoke, mist, moonshine, raw potatoes, and saw-dust. He is a German by birth, and is called Giant Transcendentalist; but as to his form, his features, his substance, and his nature generally, it is the chief peculiarity of this huge miscreant, that neither he for himself, nor anybody for him, has ever been able to describe them. As we rushed by the cavern's mouth, we caught a hasty glimpse of him, looking somewhat like an ill-proportioned figure, but considerably more like a heap of fog and duskiness. He shouted after us, but in so strange a phraseology, that we knew not what he meant, nor whether to be encouraged or affrighted.'

Escaping from this 'heap of fog and duskiness,' we arrive safely in Vanity Fair, where we purpose making a long stay, as we learn that there is no longer that 'want of harmony between the towns-people and pilgrims' of which Bunyan complained. We cannot touch the theological improvements in the ancient 'city of Vanity,' but must notice lighter matters, such as the substitutes for study, learning, and so-called heavy literature. This is all superseded by the labours of 'innumerable lecturers, who diffuse such a various profundity in all subjects of human or celestial science, that any man may acquire an omnigenous erudition without the trouble of even learning to read. . . . . Thought and study are done to every person's hand, without his putting himself to the slightest inconvenience in the matter.' But the grand attractions of the old city are found in its splendid bazaars :

'It was well worth one's while, even if he had no idea of buying or selling, to loiter through the bazaars, and observe the various sorts of traffic that were going forward.

Some of the purchasers, I thought, made very foolish bargains. For instance, a young man having inherited a splendid fortune, laid out a considerable portion of it in the purchase of diseases, and finally spent all the rest for a heavy lot of repentance and a suit of rags. A very pretty girl bartered a heart as clear as crystal, and which seemed her most valuable possession, for another jewel of the same kind, but so worn and defaced as to be utterly worthless. In one shop, there were a great many crowns of laurel and myrtle, which soldiers, authors, statesmen, and various other people, pressed eagerly to buy ; some purchased these paltry wreaths with their lives ; others by a toilsome servitude of years ; and many sacrificed whatever was most valuable, yet finally slunk away without the crown. There was a sort of stock or scrip, called Conscience, which seemed to be in great demand, and would purchase almost anything. Indeed, few rich commodities were to be obtained without paying a heavy sum in this particular stock, and a man's business was seldom very lucrative, unless he knew precisely when and how to throw his hoard of Conscience into the market. Yet as this stock was the only thing of permanent value, whoever parted with it was sure to find himself a loser in the long-run. Several of the speculations were of a questionable character. Occasionally, a member of Congress recruited his pocket by the sale of his constituents; and I was assured that public officers have often sold their country at very moderate prices. Thousands sold their happiness for a whim. Gilded chains were in great demand, and purchased with almost any sacrifice. In truth, those who desired, according to the old adage, to sell anything valuable for a song, might find customers all over the Fair; and there were innumerable messes of pottage, piping hot, for such as chose to buy them with their birthrights. A few articles, however, could not be found genuine at Vanity Fair. If a customer wished to renew his stock of youth, the dealers offered him a set of false teeth and an auburn wig; if he demanded peace of mind, they recommended opium or a brandy-bottle.'

Hawthorne has written nothing more pleasant and characteristic, than the sketch of his own experience in the custom-house at Salem. The dilapidated old wharf, and the custom-house, with its drooping banner of the Republic, and an 'enormous specimen of the American eagle' over the entrance of the great brick building, are graphically treated; but the writer's skill is more apparent in the portraits of the officials and other persons who haunt the place: 'the sea-flushed shipmaster, just in port, with his vessel's papers under his arm in a tarnished tin-box;' the owner cheerful or sombre, according to the success of his adventure, and 'the germ of the wrinkle-browed, grizzly-bearded, care-worn merchant, the smart young clerk, who gets the taste of traffic as a wolf-cub does of blood, and already sends adventures in his master's ships when he had better be sailing boats upon a mill-pond.' On ascending the steps, we find in the entry 'a row of venerable figures sitting in old-fashioned chairs, which were tipped on their hind-legs back against the wall. Oftentimes they were asleep, but occasionally might be heard talking together in voices between speech and a snore, and with that lack of energy that distinguishes the occupants of alms-houses and all other human beings who depend for subsistence on charity, on monopolised labour, or on anything else but their own independent exertions. These old gentlemen, seated, like Matthew, at the receipt of custom, but not very liable to be summoned thence, like him, for apostolic errands, were custom-house officers. . . . . They were ancient sea-captains for the most part, who, after being tossed on every sea, and standing up sturdily against life's tempestuous blast, had finally drifted into this quiet nook.'

'Two or three of their number, as I was assured being gouty and rheumatic, or perhaps bedridden, never dreamed of making their appearance at the custom-house during a large part of the year; but, after a torpid winter, would creep out into the warm sunshine of May or June, go lazily about what they termed duty, and at their own leisure and convenience betake themselves to bed again. I must plead guilty to the charge of abbreviating the official breath of more than one of these venerable servants of the Republic. They were allowed, on my representation, to rest from their arduous labours; and soon afterwards—as if their sole principle of life had been zeal for their country's service, as I verily believe it was—withdrew to a better world. It is a pious consolation to me, that, through my interference, a sufficient space was allowed them for repentance of the evil and corrupt practices into which, as a matter of course, every custom-house officer must be supposed to fall. Neither the front nor the back entrance of the custom-house opens on the road to Paradise.

* * * *

It pained, and at the same time amused me, to behold the terrors that attended my advent—to see a furrowed cheek, weather-beaten by half a century of storm, turn ashy pale at the glance of so harmless an individual as myself—to detect, as one or another addressed me, the tremor of a voice which in long-past days had been wont to bellow through a speaking-trumpet, hoarsely enough to frighten Boreas himself to silence. They knew, these excellent old persons, that, by all established rule—and, as regarded some of them, weighed by their own lack of efficiency for business—they ought to have given place to younger men more orthodox in politics, and altogether fitter than themselves to serve our common Uncle. I knew it too, but could never quite find in my heart to act upon the knowledge. Much and deservedly to my own discredit, therefore, and considerably to the detriment of my official conscience, they continued, during my incumbency, to creep about the wharfs, and loiter up and down the custom-house steps. They spent a good deal of time, also, asleep in their accustomed corners, with their chairs tilted back against the wall—awaking, however, once or twice in a forenoon, to bore one another with the several thousandth repetition of old sea-stories and mouldy jokes, that had grown to be pass-words and countersigns among them.

* * * *

It was pleasant, in the summer forenoons, when the fervent heat, that almost liquefied the rest of the human family, merely communicated a genial warmth to their half-torpid systems—it was pleasant to hear them chatting in the back-entry, a row of them all tipped against the wall, as usual; while the frozen witticisms of past generations were thawed out, and came bubbling with laughter from their lips. Externally, the jollity of aged men has much in common with the mirth of children; the intellect, any more than a deep sense of humour, has little to do with the matter; it is, with both, a gleam that plays upon the surface, and imparts a sunny and cheery aspect alike to the green branch and gray mouldering trunk. In one case, however, it is real sunshine; in the other, it more resembles the phosphorescent glow of decaying wood.'

As a specimen of quiet humour, this sketch of the old men in Salem custom-house may be compared with the best passages of the same kind in the writings of Washington Irving. A more satirical humour, yet without bitterness, appears in the portrait of the inspector—a man of fourscore years, 'one of the most wonderful specimens of winter-green,' with his florid cheek and compact figure, brisk and vigorous step, and smartly arrayed in a bright-buttoned blue coat. 'The careless security of his life in the custom-house, on a regular income, and with but slight and infrequent apprehensions of removal, had no doubt contributed to make time pass lightly over him. The original and more potent causes, however, lay in the rare perfection of his animal nature, the moderate proportion of intellect, and the very trifling admixture of moral and spiritual ingredients; these latter qualities, indeed, being in barely enough measure to keep the old gentleman from walking on all-fours.'

'One point, in which he had vastly the advantage over his four-footed brethren, was his ability to recollect the good dinners which it had made no small portion of the happiness of his life to eat. His gourmandism was a highly agreeable trait; and to hear him talk of roast-meat was as appetising as a pickle or an oyster. As he possessed no higher attribute, and neither sacrificed nor vitiated any spiritual endowment by devoting all his energies and ingenuities to subserve the delight and profit of his maw, it always pleased and satisfied me to hear him expatiate on fish, poultry, and butcher's meat, and the most eligible methods of preparing them for the table. His reminiscences of good cheer, however ancient the date of the actual banquet, seemed to bring the savour of pig or turkey under one's very nostrils. There were flavours on his palate that had lingered there not less than sixty or seventy years, and were still apparently as fresh as that of the mutton-chop which he had just devoured for his breakfast. I have heard him smack his lips over dinners, every guest at which, except himself, had long been food for worms.'

These sketches are enough to prove that Hawthorne has a peculiar graphic power, and writes with genial humour. The quiet and easy, yet original style, marked by natural yet unhackneyed combinations, assures us that the writer thinks and speaks for himself, and in his own way—a great merit, and quite distinct from mere eccentricity. That such a style should have been so often employed to treat unpleasant, and even revolting subjects, must be regretted. In other cases, where the author has selected homely and familiar themes, his skilful touches remind us of

Ostade's pictures, in which beautiful effects of light are reflected from brass kettles, earthen pots, and other culinary utensils.

The personal narrative which serves as a preface to *The Scarlet Letter*, is, to our taste, more agreeable than the romance, which, while it has all the charms of Hawthorne's style, is in substance a very unpleasant story. In this, as in other works, the writer's powers of mind seem superior to his themes; and the reader may suppose that, in Hawthorne, a truly poetical genius has been depressed, and otherwise injured, by poring over the rather gloomy annals of New England in the olden time. The characters in the story may be regarded as so many curious specimens in morbid psychology, rather than as real men and women. The general effect is gloomy; but an exception must be made in favour of the visionary little girl Pearl, whose presence in many scenes is like a ray of light in a dark wood. The passions chiefly portrayed are remorse in one character—Dimmesdale; and long-cherished implacable revenge in another—Chillingworth. There is something dreamy—or perhaps we might say mystical—in many passages; but the mysticism is not in the language, which a reviewer has happily likened to 'a sheet of transparent water, reflecting from its surface blue skies, nodding woods, and the smallest spray or flower that peeps over its grassy margin; while in its clear yet mysterious depths we espy rarer and stranger things, which we must dive for, if we would examine.'[1] Here and there deep thoughts are uttered, as when we read of one 'who wanted—what some people want throughout life—a grief that should deeply touch her, and thus humanise and make her capable of sympathy.'

The tale is rich in passages of picturesque beauty, and the writer has a singular power of breathing, if we may so speak, a sentiment through every picture. Thus we read of a forest-walk:—

'The road, after the two wayfarers had crossed from the peninsula to the mainland, was no other than a footpath. It straggled onward into the mystery of the primeval forest. This hemmed it in so narrowly, and stood so black and dense on either side, and disclosed such imperfect glimpses of the sky above, that to Hester's mind it imaged not amiss the moral wilderness in which she had so long been wandering. The day was chill and sombre. Overhead was a gray expanse of cloud, slightly stirred, however, by a breeze; so that a gleam of flickering sunshine might now and then be seen at its solitary play along the path. This flitting cheerfulness was always at the further extremity of some long vista through the forest. The sportive sunlight—feebly sportive, at best, in the

[1] *North American Review*, No. 143, p. 146.

predominant pensiveness of the day and scene—withdrew itself as they came nigh, and left the spots where it had danced the drearier because they had hoped to find them bright.'

Little Pearl, the child whose infancy is overshadowed by the sorrow and shame of her parents, attends her mother in this walk through the forest; and by an exquisite art the scenery is made to symbolise the life of the child :—

'Thus conversing, they entered sufficiently deep into the wood to secure themselves from the observation of any casual passenger along the forest-track. Here they sat down on a luxuriant heap of moss, which, at some epoch of the preceding century, had been a gigantic pine, with its roots and trunk in the darksome shade, and its head aloft in the upper atmosphere. It was a little dell where they had seated themselves, with a leaf-strewn bank rising gently on either side, and a brook flowing through the midst, over a bed of fallen and drowned leaves. The trees impending over it had flung down great branches, from time to time, which choked up the current, and compelled it to form eddies and black depths at some points; while, in its swifter and livelier passages, there appeared a channel-way of pebbles, and brown sparkling sand. Letting the eyes follow along the course of the stream, they could catch the reflected light from its water, at some short distance within the forest, but soon lost all traces of it amid the bewilderment of tree-trunks and underbrush, and here and there a huge rock, covered over with gray lichens. All these giant trees and boulders of granite seemed intent on making a mystery of the course of this small brook; fearing, perhaps, that, with its never-ceasing loquacity, it should whisper tales out of the heart of the old forest whence it flowed, or mirror its revelations on the smooth surface of a pool. Continually, indeed, as it stole onward, the streamlet kept up a babble—kind, quiet, soothing, but melancholy—like the voice of a young child that was spending its infancy without playfulness, and knew not how to be merry among sad acquaintance and events of sombre hue.

"O brook! O foolish and tiresome little brook!" cried Pearl, after listening awhile to its talk. "Why art thou so sad? Pluck up a spirit, and do not be all the time sighing and murmuring!"

But the brook, in the course of its little lifetime among the forest trees, had gone through so solemn an experience, that it could not help talking about it, and seemed to have nothing else to say. Pearl resembled the brook, inasmuch as the current of her life gushed from a well-spring as mysterious, and had flowed through scenes shadowed as heavily with gloom. But, unlike the little stream, she danced and sparkled, and prattled airily along her course. . . . .

The child went singing away, following up the current of the brook, and striving to mingle a more lightsome cadence with its melancholy voice. But the little stream would not be comforted, and still kept telling its unintelligible secret of some very mournful mystery that had happened—or making a prophetic lamentation about something that was yet to happen—within the verge of the dismal forest. So Pearl, who had enough of shadow in her own little life, chose to break off all acquaintance with this repining brook. She set herself, therefore, to gathering violets and wood-anemones, and some scarlet columbines that she found growing in the crevices of a high rock.'

It should be observed, that the passages here quoted are by no means fair specimens of the whole story, for its most powerful scenes are those of a gloomy character. The internal sufferings of the fallen minister Dimmesdale, are described with an ability as remarkable as the author's choice of a subject; but the malignant and revengeful Chillingworth is so darkly coloured, that the man vanishes, and we see only a dismal goblin.

The House of the Seven Gables is the most complete and characteristic of the writer's works. We have not space to give the incidents of its story, but may point to the photograph portraiture of the old house, with its heir-loom of misery, presented to the imagination with such oppressive fulness of details, that at last we sympathise with one of the inmates who longs to pull down the whole structure. The sufferings of pride and poverty in the person of the old maid, during her commencement of petty shop-keeping, are described with admirable fidelity.

The Blithedale Romance will disappoint readers who expect to find in it any fair account of the socialist experiment at Brook Farm; for the colony serves merely as scenery, the characters are fictitious, and the result is produced by accidents, proving nothing, either good or bad, respecting the theory or working of co-operative societies. Hollingsworth, the leading character, may be described as a professor of abstract benevolence, who does not condescend to ordinary human kindness. Several scenes and detached passages are marked by the writer's usual graphic power; but the story is forced to lead to a certain moral: the catastrophe is unreal, and in the concluding misery of the hero we have no sympathy; we do not see a human being suffering—all we observe is a rather curious psychological problem involved in certain difficulties.

PROSE-FICTION AND MISCELLANEOUS WRITINGS.

CATHERINE M. SEDGWICK—MRS CHILD—SARAH J. HALE—CAROLINE M. KIRKLAND—ELIZA LESLIE—MRS STOWE—MISS PLANCHE—'FANNY FERN'—MISS COOPER—MARGARET FULLER.

It may be well to repeat, in this place, our remark that the relative merits of writers cannot in every instance be fairly represented by the proportions of our notices. While we endeavour, on the whole, to give prominence to the more national and characteristic portions of American belles-lettres, we must decline the task of arranging strictly every work in the order of merit: it would be especially difficult in the department of fiction, where so many questions of taste may occur.

CATHERINE M. SEDGWICK, born in the village of Stockbridge, first appeared as an authoress in 1822, when her *New England Tale* was published. Two years later, the tale of *Redwood* attracted notice, and was followed in 1827 by *Hope Leslie;* in 1830, by *Clarence;* in 1832, by *Le Bossu;* and in 1835, by *The Linwoods*, and a collection of tales gathered from the magazines. In the following year, Miss Sedgwick commenced a series of moral tales under the titles—*The Poor Rich Man and the Rich Poor Man; Live and Let Live* (1837); and *Means and Ends*. Besides these, the amiable authoress has written several stories for children, magazine-articles, a *Life of the Poetess Lucretia M. Davidson*, and notices of a tour in Europe.

In descriptions of the joys and sorrows of domestic life, and in development of the affections belonging to home, Miss Sedgwick has been very successful. Her tales, without injury to their readable quality, have been made vehicles of sound practical wisdom and healthy sentiment; while the characters introduced have, in several instances, a marked individuality. The manners of New England are faithfully portrayed, and the relations described as existing between the several classes of society may suggest some useful lessons to English readers. Miss Sedgwick is an American writer, not only in her choice of subjects, but also in her tone of thought and feeling, her warm sympathy with the labouring-classes, her contempt of the tinsel, and her respect for the realities of life. It is well that American literature, in the department of fiction, should begin with such tales as *Home*, or *Live and Let Live;* and the legislation, or rather want of legislation, which would discourage this home-bred literature, and would afford unfair facilities for the spread of morbid French stories and fashionable English novels, is a melancholy proof that astute politicians may understand little of the best wealth of nations. It is not easy to select from Miss Sedgwick's tales short specimens of independent interest. We might notice the admirable letter of Mrs Fletcher in *Hope Leslie*, but it requires to be prefaced by a sketch of character. The following passage may be chosen, because it describes faithfully one of the characteristics of old times in America :—

THE SABBATH IN NEW ENGLAND.

FROM HOPE LESLIE.

'The observance of the Sabbath began with the Puritans, as it still does with a great portion of their descendants, on Saturday night. At the going down of the sun on Saturday, all temporal affairs were suspended ; and so zealously did our fathers maintain the letter, as well as the spirit of the law, that, according to a vulgar tradition in Connecticut, no beer was brewed in the latter part of the week, lest it should presume to *work* on Sunday.

It must be confessed that the tendency of the age is to laxity ; and so rapidly is the wholesome strictness of primitive times abating, that should some antiquary, fifty years hence, in exploring his garret rubbish, chance to cast his eye on our humble pages, he may be surprised to learn that, even now, the Sabbath is observed, in the interior of New England, with an almost Judaical severity.

On Saturday afternoon, an uncommon bustle is apparent. The great class of procrastinators are hurrying to and fro to complete the lagging business of the week. The good mothers, like Burns's matron, are plying their needles, making "auld claes look amaist as weel's the new ;" while the domestics, or *helps* (we prefer the national descriptive term), are wielding with might and main their brooms and *mops* to make all *tidy* for the Sabbath.

As the day declines, the hum of labour dies away, and after the sun is set, perfect stillness reigns in every well-ordered household, and not a footfall is heard in the village street. It cannot be denied, that even the most scriptural, missing the excitement of their ordinary occupations, anticipate their usual bedtime. The obvious inference from this fact is skilfully avoided by certain ingenious reasoners, who allege that the constitution was originally so organised as to require an extra quantity of sleep on every seventh night. We recommend it to the curious to inquire how this peculiarity was adjusted when the first day of the week was changed from Saturday to Sunday.

The Sabbath-morning is as peaceful as the first hallowed day. Not a human sound is heard without the dwellings, and but for the lowing of the herds, the crowing of the cocks, and the gossipping of the birds, animal life would seem to be extinct, till, at the bidding of the church-going bell, the old and young issue from their habitations, and, with solemn demeanour, bend their measured steps to the meeting-house—the families of the minister, the squire, the doctor, the merchant, the modest gentry of the village, and the mechanic and labourer, all arrayed in their best, all meeting on even ground, and all with that consciousness of independence and equality, which breaks down the pride of the rich, and rescues the poor from servility, envy, and discontent. If a morning salutation is reciprocated, it is in a suppressed voice; and if, perchance, nature, in some reckless urchin, burst forth in laughter—"My dear, you forget it's Sunday," is the ever-ready reproof.

Though every face wears a solemn aspect, yet we once chanced to see even a deacon's muscles relaxed by the wit of a neighbour, and heard him allege, in a half-deprecating, half-laughing voice, "The squire is so droll, that a body must laugh, though it be Sabbath-day."

The farmer's ample wagon, and the little one-horse vehicle, bring in all who reside at an inconvenient walking-distance—that is to say, in our riding community, half a mile from the church. It is a pleasing sight, to those who love to note the happy peculiarities of their own land, to see the farmers' daughters, blooming, intelligent, well-bred, pouring out of these homely coaches, with their nice white gowns, prunel shoes, Leghorn hats, fans and parasols, and the spruce young men, with their plaited ruffles, blue coats, and yellow buttons. The whole community meet as one religious family, to offer their devotions at the common altar. If there is an outlaw from the society—a luckless wight, whose vagrant taste has never been subdued—he may be seen stealing along the margin of some little brook, far away from the condemning observation and troublesome admonitions of his fellows.

Towards the close of the day, or, to borrow a phrase descriptive of his feelings who first used it, "when the Sabbath begins to *abate*," the children cluster about the windows. Their eyes wander from their Catechism to the western sky, and, though it seems to them as if the sun would never disappear, his broad disc does slowly sink behind the mountain; and while his last ray still lingers on the eastern summits, merry voices break forth, and the ground resounds with bounding footsteps. The village belle arrays herself for her twilight walk; the boys gather on "the green;" the lads and girls throng to the "singing-school;" while some coy maiden lingers at home, awaiting her expected suitor; and all enter upon the pleasures of the evening with as keen a relish as if the day had been a preparatory penance.'

Mrs David Lee Child, the author of several moral stories and other works which have been reprinted in England, commenced writing as a novelist in *Hobomok*, a tale of New England in the times of the Pilgrims. This was followed by *The Rebels* (1825); *Philothea*, a romance of Athens in the days of Pericles (1835); *Fact and Fiction;* and various other tales, besides numerous contributions to periodicals, chiefly marked by benevolent and sometimes rather mystical tendencies. In other works, Mrs Child has appeared as a practical utilitarian, and has discoursed of the secrets of good housekeeping. In her most ambitious book, *Philothea*, an attempted modern-antique, she introduces Plato as one of the chief characters, and makes the philosopher talk in a style more characteristic of Boston than of ancient Athens. The authoress is more successful in her minor works—such as the *Neighbour-in-law*, or the *Beloved Tune*—in which the hopeful benevolence of her own character finds expression. Of the mystical and speculative portions of her miscellanies, we can give no clear account. The *Letters from New York* may be described as the most characteristic of Mrs Child's writings.

Northwood, by SARAH J. HALE, is described as a tale containing faithful portraitures of society in New England. Among many other fictions which might be noticed, if our space would permit, we may allude to the writings of Mrs O. Smith, Mrs Farrar, Mrs Stephens, Miss Macintosh, Mrs Gilman, and Mrs Judson, who has written under the pseudonym of Fanny Forrester. *Dollars and Cents*, a tale by Amy Lothrop, *The Wide, Wide World*, and *Queechy*, by Miss Warner, must be mentioned as tales that have had a wide circulation, and have been commended for their moral and religious tendency. *The Lamplighter* belongs to the same class of fictions.

CAROLINE M. KIRKLAND, the authoress of several lively tales and sketches of society in the western settlements, is a native of New York. Of her biography, we know little more than that she married the amiable and accomplished William Kirkland, with whom she lived some years at Geneva, on the Seneca Lake, and afterwards in Michigan and in New York, until 1846, when her husband was accidentally drowned in the Hudson river.

In 1839, Mrs Kirkland published, under a pseudonym, her first book of western sketches, entitled a *New Home*, which was followed in 1842 by a work of similar character, *Forest Life;* and in 1845, her *Western Clearings* appeared. These tales and sketches give, in fresh and lively colours, portraits and groups evidently taken from life on the western frontiers of civilisation. The traits of character are often boldly drawn; but caricature is avoided, and the truthfulness of Mrs Kirkland's portraits is admitted by all who are competent to judge. The unrestrained manners; the assertion of equality, almost bordering upon Communism; the plain-speaking selfishness, not so intense as that species found in cities, but perfectly undisguised: these, and other features of society in the West, are portrayed by the authoress in a racy style, and with as much delicacy and refinement as her subjects would allow. Good sense, genial humour, and poetical feeling in descriptions of nature, are the chief characteristics of these truly American sketches.

Mrs Kirkland has also published *Holidays Abroad*, giving the impressions of her travels in England and on the continent in 1837, or about that time. As an example of the errors into which even a shrewd and sensible tourist may fall, in making statements without due inquiry, we may notice, in this book, the grave assertion, that the court of Great Britain is almost entirely closed against men of eminence in literature and science, and that learning, or the power of writing a good book, implies 'loss of caste' in the highest circles of British society. Another American writer states, very confidently, that when the death of Dr Southey left the office of poet-laureate vacant, the name of the proposed successor—Wordsworth—was unknown at the court of England!

To return to the West—where we find Mrs Kirkland at home—it would be unfair to select from her books the grotesque sketches of rude life, and leave them without their context. The coarseness must be taken with its redeeming accompaniments of honesty, hospitality, and enterprise. It is almost startling to read of the extent to which the habit of 'loaning' (borrowing) is carried. 'This excellent reason, "cause you've got plenty,"' says Mrs Kirkland, 'is conclusive as to sharing with your neighbours. Whoever comes into Michigan with nothing, will be sure to better his condition; but wo to him that brings with him anything like an appearance of abundance, whether of money or mere household conveniences! To have them, and not be willing to share them in some sort with the whole community, is an unpardonable crime. You must lend your best horse *qui que ce soit* to go ten miles over hill and marsh, in the darkest night, for a doctor; or your team to travel twenty after a "gal:" your wheel-barrows, your shovels, your utensils of all sorts, belong, not to yourself, but to the public, who do not think it necessary even to *ask* a loan, but take it for granted. The two saddles and bridles of Montacute spend most of their time travelling from house to house a-man-back; and I have actually known a stray martingale to be traced to four dwellings two miles apart, having been lent from one to another, without a word to the original proprietor, who sat waiting, not very patiently, to commence a journey.'

This is nothing to the climax of a woman who wished 'to borrow her neighbour's *baby!*'—but we must remember that the habit carried to this absurd extreme, arose from the necessities of forest-life.

SCENE AT A POPULAR ELECTION.

'"Gentlemen!" said the orator, taking off his hat, and waving it in a courteous and inviting manner, while he wiped his brow with a faded cotton handkerchief—"Gentlemen! may I beg your attention for a few moments. You are aware that I do not often draw very largely on your patience, and also that I am not a man who is fond of talking about himself. It is indeed a most unpleasant thing to me, to be in a manner forced to advocate my own cause; and nothing short of the desire I feel to have an opportunity of advancing the interest of my friends and neighbours in the legislature, would induce me to submit to it."

Somebody groaned: "Oh, Tim, that's tough!"

"Yes, gentlemen! as you observe, it *is* tough; it is a thing that always hurts a man's feelings. But, as I was observing, we must go through with whatever is for the good of our country. The greatest good of the greatest number, *I* say!"

By this time the auditory had greatly increased, and comprised indeed nearly all the voters. Mr Rice went on with increasing animation.

"This is the principle to go upon, and if this was only carried out, we should all have been better off long ago. This is where the legislature wants mending. They always stop short of the right mark. They get frightened, gentlemen!—yes, frightened, scar't! They always have a lot of these small souls among them—souls cut after a scant pattern—souls that are afraid of their own shadows—that object to all measures that would really relieve the people, so they just give the people a taste to keep them quiet, and no more, for fear of what folks a thousand miles off would say! You've heard of the jackass that was scar't at a penny-trumpet—well, these jackasses are scar't at what isn't louder than a penny-trumpet, nor half so loud."

Here was a laugh, which gave the orator time to moisten his throat from a tumbler handed up by a friend.

"Now you see, gentlemen, nobody would have said a word against that exemption bill, if everybody was as much in favour of the people as I am. I don't care who knows it, gentlemen—*I* am in favour of the people. Don't the people want relief? And what greater relief can they have, than not to be obliged to pay their debts, when they have nothing to pay them with? that is, nothing that they can spare conveniently. I call that measure a half-way measure, gentlemen—it is a measure that leaves a way open to take a man's property if he happens to have a little laid by—a little of his hard earnings, gentlemen; and you all know what hard earnings are.

"What is the use of having the privilege of making laws, if we can't make them to suit ourselves? We might as well be a Territory again, instead of a sovereign State, if we are a-going to legislate to favour the people of other States, at the expense of our own people. I don't approve of the plan of creditors from other States coming here to take away our property. Folks are very fond of talking about honesty and good faith, and all that. As to faith, they may talk, but I'm more for works; and the man that works hard and can't pay his debts, is the one that ought to be helped, in my judgment.

"They'll tell you that the man that sues for a debt is owing somebody else, and wants his money to pay with. Now, *I* say, he's just the man that ought to feel for the other, and not want to crowd him hard up. Besides, if we pass exemption laws, don't we help him too? Isn't it as broad as it's long?"

A murmur of applause.

"Then as to honesty; where'll you find an honest man, if not among the people? and such measures are on purpose to relieve the people. The aristocracy don't like 'em perhaps, but who cares what *they* like? They like nothing but grinding the face of the poor."

Here a shout of applause, and a long application to the tumbler.

"Gentlemen," continued Mr Rice, "some people talk as if what debts were not paid were lost, but it is no such thing. What one man don't get, t'other keeps; so it 's all the same in the long-run. Folks ought to be accommodating, and if they are accommodating, they won't object to any measures for the relief of the people; and if they don't want to be accommodating, we'll just make 'em, that's all!

"Some say it 's bad to keep altering and altering the laws, till nobody knows what the law is. That's a pretty principle, to be sure! What do we have a legislature for, I should be glad to know, if not to make laws? Do we pay them two dollars and fifty cents a day to sit still and do nothing? Look at the last legislature. They did not hold on above two months, and passed rising of two hundred laws, and didn't work o' Sundays neither! Such men are the men you want, if they'll only carry the laws far enough to do some good.

"Now, gentlemen, I see the poll's open, and I s'pose you want to be off, so I will not detain you much longer. All I have to observe is, that although I am far from commending myself, I must give you my candid opinion, that a certain person, who has thrust himself before the public on this occasion, is unworthy of the suffrages of a free and enlightened community like this. He's a man that's always talking about doing justice to all, and keeping up the reputation of the State, and a great deal more stuff of the same sort; but it's all humbug! nothing else; and he has an axe of his own to grind, just like the rest of us. And worse than all, gentlemen, as you very well know, he's one of these tee-totallers, that are trying to coax free-born Americans to sign away their liberty, and make hypocrites of 'em. I'm a man that will never refuse to take a glass of grog with a fellow-citizen because he wears a ragged coat.

Liberty and equality, *I* say—Hurrah for liberty and equality! three cheers for liberty and equality, and down with the tee-totallers!"

The orator had been so attentive to the tumbler, that the sincerity of the latter part of his speech at least could not be doubted; and, indeed, his vehemence was such as to alarm Seymour, who felt already somewhat ashamed of the cause he was bound to advocate, and who feared that a few more tumblers would bring Tim to a point which would render his advocacy unavailing. He therefore sought an opportunity of a few moments' private talk with the candidate, and ventured to hint that, if he became so enthusiastic that he could not stand, he would have very little chance of sitting in the legislature.

Now, Mr Rice liked not such quiet youths as our friend Seymour, and especially in his present elevated frame did he look down with supreme contempt upon anything in the shape of advice on so delicate a subject; so that Seymour got an answer which by no means increased his zeal in Mr Rice's service, though he still resolved to do his best to fulfil the wishes of Mr Hay.

Rice's conduct throughout the day was in keeping with the beginning which we have described; and such was the disgust with which it inspired Seymour, that he at length concluded to quit the field, and tell Mr Hay frankly that it was impossible for him to further the interests of so unprincipled a candidate.'

ELIZA LESLIE, sister of the eminent painter C. R. Leslie, is a lively and sarcastic sketcher of manners. Her *Pencil Sketches* give some remarkable instances of the power of an easy and fluent style in carrying the reader through a story of which the incidents are very trivial. For example, in the sketch of 'That Gentleman,' the passengers on a liner bound for New York are curious to learn the name of a reserved individual, and the captain refuses to give it. At last, after many pages of suspense, when we hope for some striking explanation of the mystery, we find nothing more than the fact, that the name is Sir St John St Ledger, and that it was kept secret because its sibilation offended the ears of the captain. In caricatures of vulgarity and affectation, Miss Leslie writes with great zest and liveliness, as may be seen in the sketch of 'Mrs Washington Potts;' but ridiculous traits should be contrasted with the better features of society, in order to make satire truthful and wholesome.

The story of Mrs Marsden's ambition to become acquainted with Mrs Potts, a vulgar woman of fashion, is a fair satire on the petty worship of aristocracy which prevails here and there in the United States. As this feature in American society has been frequently ridiculed, it should not be forgotten that it is the genuine growth of the old country. Our British homage, paid, in season and out of season, to the distinctions of rank and title, is a common object of ridicule among continental people. A German prince cannot travel through our country without laughter at the solemnities of our court-circular and other 'records of movements in high life.' Mrs Kirkland observes that this species of worship appears more ridiculous in America, because it is there copied on a small scale. 'We must laugh,' says she, 'when we see the managers of a city-ball admit the daughters of *wholesale* merchants, while they exclude the families of merchants who sell at retail; and still more, when we come to the "new country," and observe that Mrs Penniman, who takes *in* sewing, utterly refuses to associate with her neighbour Mrs Clay because she goes *out* sewing by the day; and that our friend Diggins, being raised a step in the world by the last election, signs all his letters of friendship—"D. Diggins, Sheriff."'

To return to Miss Leslie's satirical story. Mrs Washington Potts is described as 'a charming woman, who makes strange mistakes in talking.' She is travelling in America with an English family—the Montagues—who assume the style of aristocracy. Their exclusiveness excites the ambition of Mrs Marsden, who employs all possible means of attracting their notice. At last she succeeds, and the distinguished travellers accept her invitation. Among other arrangements for the entertainment of the party, a certain homespun and rather uncouth relative of the Marsdens—Aunt Quimby—is set aside or confined to her own chamber. But in the midst of all the charming talk of high life, this original old lady escapes from her room, and introduces herself to the guests. Miss Leslie must narrate the sequel:—

'At this juncture—to the great consternation of Mrs Marsden and her daughter—who should make her appearance but Aunt Quimby, in the calico gown which Albina now regretted having persuaded her to keep on! The old lady was wrapped in a small shawl and two large ones, and her head was secured from cold by a black silk handkerchief tied over her cap and under her chin. She smiled and nodded all around to the company, and said: "How do you do, good people? I hope you are all enjoying yourselves. I thought I must come down and have a peep at you. For after I had seen all the ladies take off their hoods, and had my tea, I found it pretty dull work sitting up stairs with the mantua-maker, who had no more manners than to fall asleep while I was talking."

Mrs Marsden, much discomfited, led Aunt Quimby to a chair between two matrons, who were among the "unavoidably invited," and whose pretensions to refinement were not very palpable. But the old lady had no idea of remaining stationary all the evening between Mrs Johnson and Mrs Jackson. She wisely thought that "she could see more of the party" if she frequently changed her place; and being of what is called a sociable disposition, she never hesitated to talk to any one that was near her, however high or however low. . . . .

"And now," said Albina starting, "I will shew you a far worse mortification than the failure of the ice-cream. Only look—there sits Aunt Quimby between Mr Montague and Mrs Washington Potts!"

"How in the world did she get there?" exclaimed Mrs Marsden.

"I daresay she walked up, and asked them to make room for her between them. There is nothing now to be done but to pass her off as well as we can, and to make the best of her. I will manage to get as near as possible, that I may hear what she is talking about, and take an opportunity of persuading her away."

As Mrs Marsden approached within hearing distance, Mr Montague was leaning across Aunt Quimby, and giving Mrs Potts an account of something that had been said or done during a splendid entertainment at Devonshire House.—"Just at that moment," said he, "I was lounging into the room with Lady Augusta Fitzhenry on my arm (unquestionably the finest woman in England), and Mrs Montague was a few steps in advance, leaning on my friend the Marquis of Elvington."

"Pray, sir," said Mrs Quimby, "as you are from England, do you know anything of Betsy Dempsey's husband?"

"I have not the honour of being acquainted with that person," replied Mr Montague after a withering stare.

"Well, that's strange," pursued Aunt Quimby, "considering that he has been living in London at least eighteen years—or perhaps it is only seventeen. And yet I think it must be near eighteen, if not quite. Maybe seventeen and a half. Well, it's best to be on the safe side, so I'll say seventeen. Betsy Dempsey's mother was an old schoolmate of mine. Her father kept the Black Horse Tavern. She was the only acquaintance I ever had that married an Englishman. He was a grocer, and in very good business; but he never liked America, and was always finding fault with it; and so he went home, and was to send for Betsy. But he never sent for her at all; and for a very good reason, which was, that he had another wife in England, as most of them have—no disparagement to you, sir."

Mrs Marsden now came up, and informed Mrs Potts in a whisper, that the good old lady beside her was a distant relation or rather connection of *Mr* Marsden's, and that though a little primitive in appearance and manner, she had considerable property in bank-stock.'

Among the writers who have employed fiction to convey moral lessons, Mrs STOWE, the author of the celebrated tale of *Uncle Tom's Cabin*, has been eminently successful. Harriet Beecher Stowe is the daughter of Dr Lyman Beecher, an able congregational minister. Her early writings, including tales and sketches of New England life, published under the title of *The Mayflower*, gave promise of the graphic powers of narrative which appeared more fully in *Uncle Tom's Cabin.* We shall not attempt to criticise a book so well known all over the world. Its pathos, and rich variety of scenes and characters, have recommended it to unnumbered readers.

The success of the work was very remarkable. In the course of less than a year after its publication, more than 200,000 copies were sold in the United States. To supply the demand, 'the publishers kept four steam-presses running night and day, Sundays alone excepted, and at double the ordinary speed, being equal to sixteen presses worked ten hours a day at the usual speed.' The several editions printed in nine months consumed 75 tonweights of paper, and 200 hands were constantly employed in binding. In England, the sale was still more extraordinary, and the statistics of the several reprints would be curious; but we cannot give them with accuracy. It has been stated that thirty editions were issued in London in the course of six months. One was recommended by a preface written by the Earl of Carlisle. The rights of the author were forgotten in the warmth of zeal for the liberation of slaves. A small percentage of the profits derived from the several reprints, would have enabled Mrs Stowe to purchase the freedom of many negroes; but we have not heard that any share of these funds was devoted to that purpose.

The popularity of the book, arising, in the first place, from its own merit, was increased by the efforts of persons who had an interest in spreading the epidemic. Lecturers, who had failed to attract by other themes, found crowded houses ready to listen to the tale of *Uncle Tom*, illustrated in coarse paintings. Vocalists of a commonplace order were encored when they sang ballads written by poets whose existence had been revealed by *Uncle Tom.* Children cried for printed handkerchiefs, as memorials of the 'Cabin.' Mozart and Beethoven were set aside to make room for 'Uncle Tom's Polka.' The theatres assisted in maintaining the furor: even the itinerant circus was compelled to assume a moral and anti-slavery tendency; and 'Uncle Tom' might be seen careering in the arena, and appealing to the sympathies of the spectators.

In this place, the names of several female writers of descriptive sketches and other light papers may be mentioned, though they do not belong to the class of novelists. The *Trap to Catch a Sunbeam*, by Miss PLANCHE, is partly allegorical, and, like so many other tales by female writers, is made a vehicle of moral doctrine. *Fern Leaves*, by FANNY FERN—the pseudonym of a lady who is said to be the sister of N. P. Willis—is the title of a rather large collection of short and familiar sketches of manners, stories, passages of sentiment or satire, and fragments of gossip, written in an easy, careless style, not without a certain audacity of censure directed against one-half of the human family. The most remarkable trait in these papers, is their rather angry complaint of a want of 'gentlemen' in the United States. The justice or injustice of the writer's frequent censure of the characters, as well as the manners of her countrymen, is a question of facts which, happily, it is not our duty to determine. The facility with which these numerous *Fern Leaves* have been thrown off, reminds us of Jean Paul's prediction, that 'the days will come when all men [and all women], from the North Pole to the South, will write books;' and we may add, as a natural consequence, that nobody will read them.

One of the pleasantest of the books descriptive of nature in America, is the volume entitled *Rural Hours*, by Miss COOPER, who has also written a work on *The Rhyme and Reason of Country Life*. In the former volume, we find faithful sketches of the change of the seasons, and the habits of birds, insects, and plants. The descriptions have a quiet truthfulness of detail, which distinguishes them from passages written for effect. For example, many writers have attempted to paint in words the glory of American forest-scenery in autumn, but we have seen no sketch that can rival Miss Cooper's in distinctness and brilliancy. Without some preface, it might appear too highly coloured.

The Indian summer and autumn include the most beautiful days in the American year. Bryant, Lowell, and other poets have described the glory of this season. Emerson has almost forgotten himself and his abstractions, when speaking of the halcyon-days that sleep 'over the broad hills and warm wide fields.' First come the calm, clear days of the early grain-harvest, while the forests wear all their rich foliage, without a trace of decay; and one day after another passes beneath an unclouded blue sky, and closes with a brilliant sunset. Next, when the ripe maize has been gathered in, and the orchards have yielded their stores of apples, plums, peaches, and other fruits, light frosts follow, and the first sign of the dying year is seen here and there in the woods, where a maple-tree is glowing with the colours of decay. Still the greater part of the forest preserves its glossy green or russet foliage. But a few nights, nay, even one night, of sharper frost, will change the colouring of the landscape from its varied shades of green to deep red, bright yellow, gold, orange, scarlet, and other rich hues, such as Turner might have envied. In such a scene, we can hardly see a poetical truth in the words 'melancholy autumn.' As Bryant says: 'The woods have put their glory on'—

'The mountains that enfold,
In their wide sweep, the coloured landscape round,
Seem groups of giant kings, in purple and gold,
That guard the enchanted ground.'

Another stanza in the same poem might be regarded as hyperbole; but it is nothing more than the natural truth—

'Beneath yon *crimson* tree,
Lover to listening maid might breathe his flame,
Nor mark, within its roseate canopy,
Her blush of maiden shame.'

AUTUMNAL CHANGES.

'We behold the green woods becoming one mass of rich and varied colouring. It would seem as though Autumn, in honour of this high holiday, had collected together all the past glories of the year, adding them to her own; she borrows the gay colours that have been lying during the summer months among the flowers, in the fruits, upon the plumage of the bird, on the wings of the butterfly, and working them together in broad and glowing masses, she throws them over the forest to grace her triumph. Like some great festival of an Italian city, where the people bring rich tapestries and hang them in their streets; where they unlock chests of heir-looms, and bring to light brilliant draperies, which they suspend from their windows and balconies, to gleam in the sunshine.

The hanging woods of a mountainous country are especially beautiful at this season; the trees throwing out their branches, one above another, in bright variety of colouring and outline, every individual of the gay throng having a fancy of his own to humour. The oak loves a deep rich red, or a warm scarlet, though some of his family are partial to yellow. The chestnuts are all of one shadeless mass of gold-colour, from the highest to the lowest branch. The bass-wood, or linden, is orange. The aspen, with its silvery stem and branches, flutters in a lighter shade, like the wrought gold of the jeweller. The sumach, with its long pinnated leaf, is of a brilliant scarlet. The pepperidge is almost purple, and some of the ashes approach the same shade during certain seasons. Other ashes, with the birches and beech, hickory and elms, have their own tints of yellow. That beautiful and common vine, the Virginia creeper, is a vivid cherry-colour. The sweet-gum is vermilion. The Viburnum tribe and dogwoods are dyed in lake. As for the maples, they always rank first among the show; there is no other tree which contributes singly so much to the beauty of the season, for it unites more of brilliancy, with more of variety, than any of its companions; with us it is also more common than any other tree. Here you have a soft maple, vivid scarlet from the highest to the lowest leaf; there is another, a sugar maple, a pure sheet of gold; this is dark crimson like the oak, that is vermilion; another is party-coloured, pink and yellow, green and red; yonder is one of a deep purplish hue; this is still green, that is mottled in patches, another is shaded; still another blends all these colours on its own branches, in capricious confusion—the different limbs, the separate twigs, the single leaves, varying from each other in distinct colours, and shaded tints. And in every direction a repetition of this magnificent picture meets the eye: in the woods that skirt the dimpled meadows, in the thickets and copses of the fields, in the bushes which fringe the brook, in the trees which line the streets and roadsides, in those of the lawns and gardens—brilliant and vivid in the nearest groves, gradually lessening in tone upon the further woods and successive knolls, until, in the distant background, the hills are coloured by a mingled confusion of tints, which defy the eye to seize them.'

Several works by the authoress of *Woman in the Nineteenth Century*, may be noticed in connection with a brief sketch of her life and character. The *Memoirs of Margaret Fuller*, written by several of her friends, consist partly of personal notices, but include many letters and papers on art and literature. The tendencies of certain modes of intellectual culture are illustrated in this singular book.

MARGARET FULLER was born in Cambridge, Massachusetts, in 1810. At an early age, she displayed a remarkable activity of intellect. Her father overworked the child's memory to a degree which proved very injurious to her mental and physical health. The details of this cruelty, as given in her memoirs, may serve as a warning against that stimulant-system of early training, which has arisen from a want of knowledge of the relations existing between the mind and the body. When Margaret was nine years old, her father, who acted as her tutor, was accustomed to require from her the composition of a number of Latin verses every day, besides other tasks in various branches of knowledge. The doctrine that the mind of a child requires a large proportion of rest and play, was no part of his creed. 'At the very beginning,' says his daughter, 'he made one great mistake, more common, it is to be hoped, in the last generation, than the warnings of physiologists will permit it to be with the next: he thought to gain time by bringing forward the intellect as early as possible. Thus I had tasks given me, as many and various as the hours would allow, and on subjects beyond my age; with the additional disadvantage of reciting to him in the evening, after he returned from his office. As he was subject to many interruptions, I was often kept up very late; and as he was a severe teacher, both from his habits of mind and his ambition for me, my feelings were kept on the stretch till the recitations were over. Thus, frequently, I was sent to bed several hours too late, with nerves unnaturally stimulated. The consequence was, a premature development of the brain, that made me a "youthful prodigy" by day, and by night a victim of spectral illusions, nightmare, and somnambulism, which at the time prevented the harmonious development of my bodily powers, and checked my growth; while, later, they induced continual headache, weakness, and nervous affections of all kinds. As these again reacted on the brain, giving undue force to every thought and every feeling, there was finally produced a state of being both too active and too intense, which wasted my constitution, and will bring me—even although I have learned to understand and regulate my now morbid temperament—to a premature grave.' The statements of her friends confirm her own account.

This explanation of the cause of various eccentricities disarms ridicule. Unhappily, after her father's death, Margaret's education, under her own management, was continued in a mode hardly less injurious than her early training. In the course of a few years, we find her reading largely and discursively in English, French, and German literature; attempting abstruse metaphysics, and losing herself in a bewildering misuse of books. One of her friends, Mr Clark, states, that 'in about *three months* from the time (1832) that Margaret commenced German, she was reading with ease the master-pieces of its literature. Within the year, she had read Goethe's *Faust*, *Tasso*, *Iphigenia*, *Hermann and Dorothea*, *Elective Affinities*, and *Memoirs*; Tieck's *William Lovel*, *Prince Zerbino*, and other works; Körner, Novalis, and something of Richter; all of Schiller's principal dramas, and his lyric poetry'—to say nothing of English books.

In the same year, we find the authoress venturing, without a guide, into the dim recesses of German philosophy! She confesses, in a letter to a friend, that she '*could not understand Fichte*;' and adds this curious paragraph, which must excite the compassion of every reader who is acquainted with the mazes of bewilderment in the works of Fichte, Jacobi, and his friend Hamann: 'Jacobi I could understand in details, but not in *system* (*!*) It seemed to me that his mind must have been moulded by some other mind, with which I ought to have been acquainted in order to know him well—perhaps Spinoza's.[1] Since I came home, I have been consulting Buhle's and Tennemann's histories of philosophy,

[1] Jacobi had no system, but wrote *against* the views of Spinoza.

and dipping into Brown, Stewart, and that class of books.' The same letter mentions a contemplated *Life of Goethe*. After all this diversity of study in one year, the authoress writes to her friend: 'New lights are constantly dawning on me; and I think it possible I shall come out from the Carlyle view.' This last obscure expression seems to imply that Margaret had studied the writings of Thomas Carlyle. She found comfort in the fact, that even Sir James Mackintosh had been puzzled by the metaphysical problems which had baffled her own intellect! 'It is quite gratifying,' she writes, 'after my late chagrin, to find Sir James, with all his metaphysical turn and ardent desire to penetrate it, puzzling so over the German philosophy, and particularly what I was myself troubled about at Cambridge—*Jacobi's Letters to Fichte*.' After this, she commenced reading Bacon's *Novum Organum*, and was shocked by finding that her own knowledge, acquired by discursive reading, was 'vague and superficial.'

In 1839, Margaret Fuller published a translation of Eckermann's *Conversations with Goethe;* and in the following year, wrote several papers for *The Dial*, a periodical conducted by Ralph Waldo Emerson. At Concord, where she resided for some time, she enjoyed the society of Hawthorne, then living at the Old Manse, William Ellery Channing, Emerson, and other literary friends. Her conversation, as described by her best friends, was characterised by an excessive self-esteem. After a tour in 1843, she published a work entitled *Summer on the Lakes*, consisting of descriptions interspersed among various speculations.

When Emerson discontinued *The Dial*, Margaret went to New York, where she resided with Horace Greeley, editor of *The Tribune*, and wrote for his paper the reviews of current literature. In 1845, she published her most characteristic work—*Woman in the Nineteenth Century;* an earnest protest against the commonly received views of the social position of women. Her views are explained by her friend, Mr Greeley, in a letter from which we may quote a passage:—'She demanded [for her sisters] the fullest recognition of social and political equality with the rougher sex; the freest access to all stations, professions, and employments which are open to any. To this demand, I heartily acceded. It seemed to me, however, that her clear perceptions of abstract right were often overborne, in practice, by the influence of education and habit; that, while she demanded absolute equality for women, she exacted a deference and courtesy from men to women, *as* women, which was entirely inconsistent with that requirement.'

During a visit to England in 1845, Miss Fuller was introduced to several celebrated persons, of whom she gave some accounts in letters published in *The Tribune*. In 1846 and following years, she travelled and resided in Italy, where she was married to an impoverished nobleman, the Marquis d'Ossoli, who was engaged in the revolutionary movement of 1849. In the following year, she embarked with her husband and their child in a vessel bound for New York. Their voyage was disastrous: but they had almost reached the American coast, when the ship was wrecked by a violent gale off the shore of Fire Island. There was a good chance of saving the lives of all the passengers; but Margaret refused to be parted from Ossoli and their son. Her literary ambition had been almost forgotten in her love for her boy, named Angelino. While the seamen were vainly persuading her to leave the child in the care of the steward, a heavy sea washed over the forecastle, and carried all away. Margaret sank with her husband, and the lifeless body of the child was carried to the beach.

It is not our purpose to criticise the writings named in this biographical sketch. It appears clear that the eccentricity and unhappiness of Margaret Fuller, though partly constitutional, were in a great measure caused by the errors of her early training; and in this point of view, her biography affords a useful warning. With regard to the style and the general characteristics of her writings, the opinions of an American editor—Mr Griswold—may be quoted. Of the work, entitled *Woman in the Nineteenth Century*, he says: 'It is difficult to understand what is its real import, further than to the extent, that the author was ill satisfied that there should be difference in the rank or opportunity of the sexes. . . . . *Summer on the Lakes* evinces considerable descriptive power, and contains some good verses. . . . . The *Papers on Literature and Art* are all forcible, and brilliant in a degree, but frequently pointed with pique or prejudice.' . . . . The authoress 'was fond of epigram, and shewed everywhere a willingness to advance any opinion for the sake of making a point. . . . . She rarely attempted particular or analytical criticism, but commended or censured all books with about an equal degree of earnestness, being generally most severe upon those of home-production, excepting a few by personal friends.

She had remarkable quickness, but not much subtlety of apprehension; general, but not solid acquirements; and an astonishing facility in the use of her intellectual furniture, which secured her the reputation of being one of the best talkers of the age.'

HISTORY.

BANCROFT—HILDRETH—PARKMAN—TICKNOR, AND OTHER WRITERS.

'More than four hundred large historical works,' says an American writer, 'have been written in the United States.' Of these, however, a large majority may be described as consisting rather of compilations of materials than of complete and well-executed books. The names of Bancroft, Prescott, Hildreth, and Sparks, are the most prominent in the departments of history and historical biography.

The work of Bancroft on the *History of the United States* was preceded by the writings of Hutchinson, Belknap, Ramsay, Holmes, Marshall, Botta, Pitkins, and Grahame, besides several local histories already named. Judge Marshall's *History of the Colonies planted by the English on the Continent of North America*, appeared in 1824. In the same year, James Grahame, a Scotch advocate, commenced writing a *History of the United States*, which was completed and published in four octavo volumes (1836). This work was very coldly received in England, and its publication occasioned a pecuniary loss of L.1000 sterling. It is described as a valuable work based upon diligent research. Botta's *History of the War of the Revolution* is a treatise of considerable merit, but has the disadvantage of being written by a foreigner. American readers had too long borrowed their knowledge of the history of their own country, when, in 1834, Mr Bancroft published the first volume of his *History of the Colonisation of the United States*. The materials for the work were abundant, but no American before Bancroft had attempted to collect and organise them. A few brief notices of the works of several local historians may precede our remarks on Bancroft's history.

A *History of the State of Maine*, by WILLIAM D. WILLIAMSON, includes the period 1602–1820, and has been highly commended for its fidelity and completeness of narrative, its judicious arrangement, and neat and perspicuous style.

The *Historical Sketches of Michigan* comprise a series of discourses delivered before the Historical Society of that state by Lewis Cass, Henry Whiting, John Biddle, and Henry R. Schoolcraft. These papers are rather fragmentary, but include several interesting memoirs.

Another collection of materials for American history was supplied by SALMON P. CHASE in his three volumes of the

Statutes of Ohio and of the North-western Territory (1788–1833). The *Collections of the New York Historical Society* include numerous valuable materials and curious old works. Gayarré's *History of Louisiana*—written in French—embodies several important documents, but does not claim notice as a complete history. An *Introduction to the History of the Colony and Ancient Dominion of Virginia*, by CHARLES CAMPBELL, and *A History of Georgia*, by the Rev. W. B. STEVENS, must be classed with the more valuable contributions to national historical literature.

A *History of the Commonwealth of Kentucky*, by MANN BUTLER, must be commended as a work of research, though its style is inelegant. It introduces us to the early settlers, men of hardy and daring character, among whom the most celebrated was Daniel Boone.

Several other works of the same class might be mentioned; but the preceding notices may be sufficient to indicate the abundance of materials for a *History of the United States*. This wealth of details made the task of the historian very difficult. To combine the annals of the several states, and to sustain a connected narrative interest throughout the details of the colonial period; to correct the errors of early writers on the affairs of the several colonies; and to find unity of purpose and tendency in the development of the various local governments—such was the arduous undertaking of Mr Bancroft. He has written in a high tone of enthusiasm, and has given a warmth of colouring to many topics which had been coldly treated by other writers. There can be no doubt of his industry and fidelity in research; but critics have censured his immoderate use of eulogy, and have complained that his views are sometimes American rather than philosophical.

GEORGE BANCROFT, the historian of the United States, is the son of a congregational minister, and was born at Worcester, in Massachusetts, in the year 1800. His father had some reputation as a historical writer, and published in 1807 a *Life of Washington*, which passed through many editions.

In 1817, Bancroft graduated with the first honours of his class in Harvard College, and gained one of the Bowdoin prizes by an *Essay on the Use and Necessity of Revelation*. At this time, he had determined to enter the Christian ministry; and after a visit to Europe, he appeared, on some few occasions, as a successful preacher; but his love of literature soon prevailed over his first choice of a profession. During his stay in Germany, he had studied history and philosophy under the learned professor Heeren, and had enjoyed the society of the historian Schlosser.

In 1824, Bancroft published a translation of Heeren's *Reflections on the Politics of Ancient Greece*, which was followed by several translations of German works on philology; and in 1828, by Heeren's histories of the states of antiquity, and of the political system of Europe and its colonies, from the discovery of America to the time of independence. Meanwhile, the translator, not trusting in the precarious gains of literary labour, had opened a school at Northampton. In his political views, he had seen reasons for leaving the Whig party, and joining the democracy. An article from his pen, 'The Progress of Civilisation,' published in *The Boston Quarterly Review*, explained his motives in making this change.

The first volume of the *History of the Colonisation of the United States* appeared in 1834, and was received with general approbation. The services of the writer were rewarded by his appointment as collector of the customs at Boston. The second volume of the History appeared in 1837, and the third in 1840. After a considerable interval of time, partly occupied by the author's official duties, the fourth volume, giving a view of the first epoch of the American Revolution, or the overthrow of the colonial system, appeared in 1852, and has been followed by the history of the revolution. Besides this principal work, Bancroft has published an abridgment of the History, and has contributed several articles to the North American and Boston Quarterly Reviews. His services have been justly recognised in his own country, and the eminent political and social position he holds has been won by literature. America has unwisely refused to insure to the scholar a fair share of the profits of his own toil, but has not yet adopted the policy of treating learning and intellectual power as disqualifications for public service. In 1844, Bancroft was appointed secretary of the navy; and in this office, his zeal and foresight in planning reforms and instituting a Nautical School and Astronomical Observatory, made his services highly important and valuable. In 1846, he was sent as minister-plenipotentiary to Great Britain.

The *History of the United States* is based on extensive research in original documents, and corrects the errors of former works. Its failings are very intimately connected with its best qualities. It is too exclusively American in its tone. The generous enthusiasm of the writer must be commended, and is well displayed in eulogy of the heroes of early colonisation; but in the warmth of sympathy, Bancroft sometimes appears rather as the advocate than the historian. With regard to the institutions of his country, too, the strong national feeling of the writer has led him aside from the path of careful analysis.

Among the most characteristic portions of the History, we must notice the narratives of the early colonisation of New England and Pennsylvania. The several sketches of character are written in an enthusiastic and eloquent style. A summary of the early annals of Connecticut may be mentioned as one of the best examples of the author's manner. In other parts of the work, digressions on topics which do not belong strictly to American history are too freely introduced. To quote the remarks of an American Review—'Mr Bancroft likes to expatiate on a boundless theme, passing swiftly from one portion of it to another; here presenting a striking event, and there portraying a brilliant character, and colouring the whole with the glare of ambitious rhetoric and a somewhat overstrained republican philosophy.'

The style of the historian, in speaking of the heroes of liberty and civilisation, is so hearty and enthusiastic, that he seems to identify himself with the characters portrayed by his pen. The narration of the deeds of George Fox and William Penn is so warmly eulogistic, that we might imagine the author to be a descendant of the American Quakers; but his zeal has a broader character than that of the sectarian, and is as readily called forth by the exploits of the Jesuit missionary as by the courage of Roger Williams. In both instances, the same grandeur of character and nobility of purpose awaken the sympathy of Bancroft. He forgets the creed, and sees only the man. His narrative of the adventure of the Catholic missionaries in the Western territory, is one of the most attractive episodes in American history.

As the Reformation gave rise to the settlement of New England, so the counter-movement commenced by Loyola, first introduced civilisation into Canada and the West. In 1634, the two Jesuit missionaries Brebeuf and Daniel, joined a tribe of Huron Indians, and travelled more than 300 leagues through dense forests, and along the Ottawa and its confluents, enduring all the miseries of savage-life, resting at night on the bare earth, and subsisting on a scanty supply of maize. Near a bay of Lake Huron, in the Indian territory, they raised their first chapel, and began their labours among the natives. Six years later, Montreal was selected as a mission-station; and a plan was formed for establishing settlements among the northern Indians, as in Michigan, the south of Lake Huron, and other regions of the West. Serious difficulties opposed this design, for the animosities of the tribes made the proposed routes of travel impracticable. Some years elapsed before the missionary Jogues was deputed to visit the Mohawks, in order to establish friendly relations with the tribes known as the Five Nations. He obeyed the order, but, as he departed, said: '*Ibo, et non redibo*' (I shall go, but shall not return). His foreboding was true, for he was condemned by the Mohawk council, and put to death as an enchanter who had blighted their harvest.

These and other efforts excited the enmity of the surrounding tribes against the Hurons and their missionaries. Their villages were invaded; men, women, and children were put to death, or driven into the woods; and their teachers were made prisoners, and subjected to tortures. The sufferings of Brebeuf and his colleague Lallemand—too dreadful to be detailed—were borne with a firmness which excited the wonder of their Indian executioners. Other victims followed, for religious enthusiasm was kindled anew by every martyrdom. The aged René Mesnard travelled from Quebec to the south of Lake Superior, and on his way to another station—not clearly indicated—was lost in the forest, and never seen again. The Sioux Indians, whom he had visited, preserved as charms his cassock and breviary.

So far as the conversions of the Indians may be judged by their results, the labours of the French missionaries were vainly continued, year after year, in the wilderness. No permanent success was obtained. Indians learned to talk of the white man's 'manitou,' regarded the priest as a skilful 'medicine-man,' submitted themselves to the rite of baptism, and suspended their thank-offerings of rich furs and crimson belts on the crosses set up by the Jesuits; but these external innovations passed away. As the pioneers of civilisation, the illustrious missionaries Alloüez, Dablon, Joliet, and Marquette, earned for themselves immortal honour. While engaged in extending the power of France through vast regions, they had heard, from time to time, the Indian stories of 'the Great River.' It was described as abounding in monsters, which swallowed both men and canoes; and when the fearless Marquette resolved to attempt the discovery, the friendly natives who heard the proposal, warned him of the excessive heats on the banks of the river, and of warlike tribes who would never spare the strangers. The sequel must be narrated by Bancroft:—

THE FRENCH DISCOVERY OF THE MISSISSIPPI.

'Behold, then, in 1673, on the tenth day of June, the meek, single-hearted, unpretending, illustrious Marquette, with Joliet for his associate, five Frenchmen as his companions, and two Algonquins as guides, lifting their two canoes on their backs, and walking across the narrow portage that divides the Fox River from the Wisconsin. They reach the water-shed: uttering a special prayer to the immaculate Virgin, they leave the streams that, flowing onwards, could have borne their greetings to the castle of Quebec; already they stand by the Wisconsin. "The guides returned," says the gentle Marquette, "leaving us alone, in this unknown land, in the hands of Providence." France and Christianity stood in the valley of the Mississippi. Embarking on the broad Wisconsin, the discoverers, as they sailed west, went solitarily down the stream, between alternate prairies and hillsides, beholding neither man nor the wonted beasts of the forest: no sound broke the appalling silence, but the ripple of their canoe, and the lowing of the buffalo. In seven days, "they entered happily the Great River, with a joy that could not be expressed;" and the two birch-bark canoes, raising their happy sails under new skies and to unknown breezes, floated down the calm magnificence of the ocean stream, over the broad, clear sand-bars, the resort of innumerable water-fowl—gliding past islets that swelled from the bosom of the stream, with their tufts of massive thickets, and between the wide plains of Illinois and Iowa, all garlanded with majestic forests, or checkered by island-groves, and the open vastness of the prairie.

About sixty leagues below the mouth of the Wisconsin, the western bank of the Mississippi bore on its sands the trail of men; a little footpath was discerned leading into a beautiful prairie; and, leaving the canoes, Joliet and Marquette resolved alone to brave a meeting with the savages. After walking six miles, they beheld a village on the banks of a river, and two others on a slope, at a distance of a mile and a half from the first. The river was the Mou-in-gou-e-na, or Moingona, of which we have corrupted the name into Des Moines. Marquette and Joliet were the first white men who trod the soil of Iowa. Commending themselves to God, they uttered a loud cry. The Indians hear; four old men advance slowly to meet them, bearing the peace-pipe, brilliant with many-coloured plumes. "We are Illinois," said they—that is, when translated, "We are men;" and they offered the calumet. An aged chief received them at his cabin with upraised hands, exclaiming: "How beautiful is the sun, Frenchman, when thou comest to visit us! Our whole village awaits thee; thou shalt enter in peace into all our dwellings." And the pilgrims were followed by the devouring gaze of an astonished crowd.

At the great council, Marquette published to them the one true God, their Creator. He spoke also of the great captain of the French, the governor of Canada, who had chastised the Five Nations, and commanded peace; and he questioned them respecting the Mississippi, and the tribes that possessed its banks. For the messengers who announced the subjection of the Iroquois, a magnificent festival was prepared of hominy and fish, and the choicest viands from the prairies.

After six days' delay, and invitations to new visits, the chieftain of the tribe, with hundreds of warriors, attended the strangers to their canoes; and selecting a peace-pipe embellished with the head and neck of brilliant birds, and all feathered over with plumage of various hues, they hung round Marquette, the mysterious arbiter of peace and war, the sacred calumet, a safeguard among the nations.

The little group proceeded onwards. "I did not fear death," says Marquette: "I should have esteemed it the greatest happiness to have died for the glory of God." They passed the perpendicular rocks, which wore the appearance of monsters; they heard at a distance the noise of the waters of the Missouri, known to them by its Algonquin name of Pekitanoni; and when they came to the most beautiful confluence of rivers in the world—where the swifter Missouri rushes like a conqueror into the calmer Mississippi, dragging it, as it were, hastily to the sea—the good Marquette resolved in his heart, anticipating Lewis and Clarke, one day to ascend the mighty river to its source; to cross the ridge that divides the oceans, and, descending a westerly flowing stream, to publish the gospel to all the people of this New World.

In a little less than forty leagues, the canoes floated past the Ohio, which was then, and long afterwards, called the Wabash. Its banks were tenanted by numerous villages of the peaceful Shawnees, who quailed under the incursions of the Iroquois.

The thick canes begin to appear so close and strong, that the buffalo could not break through them; the insects become intolerable; as a shelter against the suns of July, the sails are folded into an awning. The prairies vanish; and forests of whitewood, admirable for their vastness and height, crowd even to the skirts of the pebbly shore. It is also observed that in the land of the Chickasas the Indians have guns.

Near the latitude of 33 degrees, on the western bank of the Mississippi, stood the village of Mitchigamea, in a region that had not been visited by Europeans since the days of De Soto.* "Now," thought Marquette, "we must indeed ask the aid of the Virgin." Armed with bows and arrows, with clubs, axes, and bucklers, amidst continual whoops, the natives, bent on war, embark in vast canoes made out of the trunks of hollow trees; but at the sight of the mysterious peace-pipe held aloft, God touched the hearts of the old men, who checked the impetuosity of the young; and throwing their bows and quivers into the canoes, as a token of peace, they prepared a hospitable welcome.

The next day, a long wooden canoe, containing ten men, escorted the discoverers, for eight or ten leagues, to the village of Akansea, the limit of their voyage. They had left the region of the Algonquins, and in the midst of the Sioux and Chickasas, could speak only by an interpreter. A half-league above Akansea, they were met by two boats, in one of which stood the commander, holding in his hand the peace-pipe, and singing as he drew near. After offering the pipe, he gave bread of maize. The wealth of his

* Ferdinand de Soto, a Spaniard, first discovered the Mississippi in 1541. As he found no 'golden land' such as his fancy had painted, his voyage was regarded as a failure, and no use was made of his discovery. He died of fever, and was buried in the Mississippi, 1542.

tribe consisted in buffalo-skins; their weapons were axes of steel—a proof of commerce with Europeans.

Thus had our travellers descended below the entrance of the Arkansas, to the genial climes that have almost no winter, but rains, beyond the bound of the Huron and Algonquin languages, to the vicinity of the Gulf of Mexico, and to tribes of Indians that had obtained European arms by traffic with Spaniards or with Virginia.

So, having spoken of God and the mysteries of the Catholic faith; having become certain that the father of rivers went not to the ocean east of Florida, nor yet to the Gulf of California, Marquette and Joliet left Akansea, and ascended the Mississippi.

At the 38th degree of latitude, they entered the river Illinois, and discovered a country without its paragon for the fertility of its beautiful prairies, covered with buffaloes and stags—for the loveliness of its rivulets, and the prodigal abundance of wild-ducks and swans, and of a species of parrots and wild-turkeys. The tribe of Illinois, that tenanted its banks, entreated Marquette to come and reside among them. One of their chiefs, with their young men, conducted the party, by way of Chicago, to Lake Michigan; and before the end of September, all were safe in Green Bay.

Joliet returned to Quebec to announce the discovery, of which the fame, through Talon, quickened the ambition of Colbert: the unaspiring Marquette remained to preach the gospel to the Miamis, who dwelt in the north of Illinois, round Chicago. Two years afterwards, sailing from Chicago to Mackinaw, he entered a little river in Michigan. Erecting an altar, he said mass, after the rites of the Catholic church; then, begging the men who conducted his canoe to leave him alone for a half-hour—

> "in the darkling wood,
> Amidst the cool and silence, he knelt down,
> And offered to the Mightiest solemn thanks
> And supplication."

At the end of the half-hour, they went to seek him, and he was no more. The good missionary, discoverer of a world, had fallen asleep on the margin of the stream that bears his name. Near its mouth, the canoemen dug his grave in the sand. Ever after, the forest-rangers, if in danger on Lake Michigan, would invoke his name. The people of the West will build his monument.'

The *History of the United States*, by RICHARD HILDRETH, has been characterised as a laborious compilation of facts, arranged mostly in chronological order, but deficient in the higher qualities of historical writing. One of the most prominent features of this work, is its low estimate of the Puritan Fathers of New England, and its very unfavourable representation of their theocratic form of government. The author brings forward many undoubted facts to support his charges of bigotry and religious persecution; but he has neglected to consider dispassionately the circumstances of the Pilgrims and their followers, and the characteristics of the time. These remarks are applicable only to certain portions of Mr Hildreth's extensive work; but a coldness of tone, strongly contrasted with the national fervour of Bancroft, may be ascribed to the whole history. 'Of centennial sermons and Fourth of July orations,' says the author, 'there are more than enough.' He suggests that historians and orators have described with theatrical pomp and exaggeration the supposed heroes of the colonial and the revolutionary period, and asserts that his own purpose is to wipe away the 'patriotic rouge,' to strip off 'the fine-spun cloaks of excuses and apology,' and to exhibit, for the first time, the heroes of American history in their true character. 'The history of the revolution,' says a reviewer, 'is clearly and succinctly told, but in as cold-blooded a manner as if the writer had been engaged with an account of a long struggle between two tribes of savages in the heart of Africa. *Nil admirari* might be inscribed on the volume as its motto. The account of the battle of Bunker Hill, which "figures in history as having tested the ability of the provincials to meet a British army in the field," closes with the characteristic remark, that "the men engaged in it were not all heroes. The conduct of several officers on that day was investigated by court-martial, and one at least was cashiered for cowardice."'

A History of the Conspiracy of Pontiac, and the War of the North American Tribes against the English Colonies, has been ably written by FRANCIS PARKMAN. It comprises a curious and interesting account of the aborigines, and narrates, in a spirited style, the incidents of savage warfare, including the obstinate and memorable siege of Detroit by the Indian forces under Pontiac. Mr Parkman's work has been based on careful researches, and is one of the most valuable contributions to the history of the aborigines of America. The well-known *Naval History of the United States*, by JAMES FENIMORE COOPER, the novelist, and a *History of the Northmen*, by HENRY WHEATON, may be mentioned in this place.

In the department of literary history, America has produced one work of first-rate character—the *History of Spanish Literature*, by GEORGE TICKNOR. The writer, one of the most accomplished of American scholars, preceded Longfellow in the chair of Modern Literature in Harvard College. During his travels in Europe, he collected the numerous materials which have been skilfully employed in the composition of his work. It is rich in its details, including reviews of the poetry, romance, and all the general literature of Spain; its critical views are genial, and at the same time judicious; and the plan combines literary history with a view of the moral and intellectual life of the Spanish nation. The merits of the work have been universally recognised by European scholars, and several translations have already appeared.

INDIAN HISTORY AND BIOGRAPHY.

One of the duties of American literature, has been to collect and preserve the records of the various tribes of Red Indians now passing away from their ancestral dwelling-places. To this task several writers, including Thatcher, Stone, Drake, Catlin, Schoolcraft, Gallatin, Bradford, M'Kenney, and Hall, have contributed their services. Their researches have greatly modified the representations given by romantic writers; but when fiction has been put aside, there still remains a history which must excite compassion for the fate of the aborigines. Of all the descriptions of these wandering tribes, the most unfair is that given by GRUND, a German, who wrote on America. He asserts, that the expelled Indians never had any right to dwell on their native soil; that they were justly treated as wild animals; and that their extinction was necessary, and by no means to be regretted.

Other writers have described, in a more humane manner, the characteristics and the destiny of the red race in America. Mr STONE, in a series of memorials of the Six Nations, has preserved many fragments of Indian history and biography. THATCHER'S *Indian Biography* gives many sketches of tribes and individuals; and a more comprehensive work, *The History of the Indian Tribes of North America*, has been published by M'KENNEY and HALL. The portraits given in this work were taken from the Indian chiefs, or delegates, who visited the seat of legislature for the purpose of making treaties or transacting other business. But among all the writers of Indian history and biography, Schoolcraft is probably the highest authority. He has lived among the Red Men; has studied their dialects, and translated their legends; and though he speaks warmly of their virtues, he is not a one-sided advocate. HENRY ROWE SCHOOLCRAFT (born 1793) has a high reputation as a man of general cultivation and scientific attainments. His first work, a scientific treatise on *Vitreology*, published in 1817, described modes of applied chemistry in the fusion of silica and kali for making glass and enamel. His *View of the Lead Mines of Missouri* (1819), was followed in the next year by the *Journal of a Tour in the Interior of Missouri and Arkansas*, and soon afterwards by a *Narrative Journal of a Tour in the Copper*

Region of Lake Superior. In 1821, the author was appointed secretary to the commission for treating with the Indian tribes at Chicago, and afterwards devoted his studies chiefly to Indian ethnology. After all the attempts of fiction-writers to portray the Red Men, readers who would find truth must study the works of Schoolcraft. His statements are founded on extensive observation during his years of service among the remnants of the Indian tribes. He married a lady who was descended, on the maternal side, from the hereditary chief of Lake Superior. In 1839, he published *Algic Researches*, consisting of two volumes of Indian legends; and after a visit to Europe and other travels, commenced in 1844 the publication, in numbers, of *Oneota*, or the 'Red Race in America.' In this and other works, Schoolcraft established his reputation as an authority on the history, traditions, customs, and dialects of the Algic tribes. In 1846, he presented to the legislature of his native state a report, consisting of *Contributions to the Statistics, Aboriginal History, and General Ethnology of Western New York.*

The writings of Schoolcraft, and other authors already named, enable us to correct the erroneous impressions made by works of fiction respecting the red race.

We have no facts to support the statements of writers who have found refinement and philosophy among the children of the forest. The wigwam was no fit abode for such Indian characters as are seen in romances. It was a smoky den, where families were huddled together in circumstances which made decency and cleanliness impossible. For food, the Indian depended partly on the chase of wild animals; but he was not wholly ignorant of agriculture. With some few exceptions, all the tribes south of the St Lawrence tilled the soil. The use of milk was unknown, which fact distinguishes the American Indians from nomadic tribes of the Old World. The plants cultivated included maize, the vine styled the squash, beans, and tobacco. Arrows tipped with hartshorn, eagles' claws, or sharp flint, were used in the chase; and fish were taken with nets and spears.

The squaw, or Indian's wife, was his slave. When he returned from the chase, he remained idle until hunger again moved him; while the wife tilled the ground, reaped the harvest, pounded the maize, and, in travelling, carried the poles of the wigwam. Scarcity of food was a frequent cause of suffering; for when provisions were plentiful, appetite knew no bounds. The condition of afflicted individuals and old and infirm people was very miserable. Decoctions of herbs and a simple form of vapour-bath were the favourite remedies for various diseases.

The wars, or rather 'scalp-hunts,' of the natives consisted

chiefly of ambuscade and surprise. Remarkable cunning and keenness of the senses were evinced in following the trail of an enemy. Commonly, a scalping-party included about six or seven Indians, sometimes only two or three; though, on great occasions, as many as forty would go out together, traverse the forest, enter the foe's domain, and lurking behind rocks or trees, wait for their victims. The taking of the scalp of an enemy was the first ambition of the young men.

The treatment of prisoners was even more revolting than the custom of taking scalps. The captive doomed to die was made to pass through lingering tortures, such as Cooper has described in his forest-romances. By his fortitude in bearing all the cruelty of his foes, the Indian gained the highest honour for himself and his tribe. Councils of war or negotiations for peace were conducted with a solemn decorum, and the patience of the Indian in listening to a speech or argument was always exemplary. He seldom interrupted the speech of his opponent.

The oratory of the Red Men has been misrepresented: the tedious long-drawn argument, or the rambling after-dinner speech, was never a characteristic of the Indian. When sober, he was seldom talkative. He spoke in metaphors, reasoned by analogy, and never employed abstract terms. Happiness was a bright sun or a clear blue sky; burying a tomahawk signified peace; a thorny plant symbolised adversity. This metaphorical style naturally gave rise to eloquent but short addresses. A Choctaw chief, who died while on a visit to Washington, finding his end approaching, sent the following message to his people:—'I shall die,' said he, 'but you will return to our brethren. As you go along the paths, you will see the flowers and hear the birds sing; but Pushmataha will see them and hear them no more. When you shall come to your home, they will ask you: "Where is Pushmataha?" and you will say to them: "He is no more." They will hear the tidings like the fall of a mighty oak in the stillness of the woods.'

The only style of writing was pictorial. Rude outlines of animals sketched on the bark of a tree, or on a smooth stone, served as symbols of tribes, or as memoranda of events. Remembrance of transactions was assisted by a sort of rosary of shells, or by a small bundle of sticks held in the hand. When Roger Williams, conversing with a chief, spoke of the good faith of the white men, the chief took a stick, and breaking it into ten pieces, related ten instances of bad faith, laying down a short stick to mark each *item*.

The same want of the power of abstraction or generalisation observed in the language, is found also in the religious notions of the Indian. Yet he was not a materialist. He could discern between cause and effect; he believed in an unseen power, the manitou, or spirit, as residing in every plant, or animal, or other natural object. As he conceived, there was a manitou, a spirit, which gave the spark from the flint, lived in every blade of grass, flowed in the streams, shone in the stars, and thundered in the water-falls; but in each example the notion of deity was concrete and particular. When missionaries suggested the unity of the Great Spirit pervading all beings, it was very readily received; but it does not appear that this generalisation had been made by the Indian previous to his intercourse with white men.

The specimens given by Schoolcraft in his *Oneota* of the myths and legends, or unwritten poetry of the Indians, have the simplicity of stories for children. We may give one example, translated from one of the dialects of the Algonquin language.[1] It bears strong internal evidence of genuineness.

SHINGEBISS:[2] AN INDIAN FABLE.

'There was once a Shingebiss living alone in a solitary lodge on the shores of the deep bay of a lake, in the coldest winter weather. The ice had formed on the water, and he had but four logs of wood to keep his fire. Each of these would, however, burn a month; and as there were but four cold winter months, they were sufficient to carry him through till spring.

Shingebiss was hardy and fearless, and cared for no one. He would go out during the coldest day, and seek for places where flags and rushes grew through the ice, and plucking them up with his bill, would dive through the openings in quest of fish. In this way he found plenty of food while others were starving; and he went home daily to his lodge, dragging strings of fish after him on the ice.

Kabebonicca[3] observed him, and felt a little piqued at his perseverance and good-luck, in defiance of the severest blasts of wind he could send from the north-west. "Why, this is a wonderful man!" said he; "he does not mind the cold, and appears as happy and contented as if it were the month of June. I will try whether he cannot be mastered." He poured forth tenfold colder blasts and drifts of snow, so that it was next to impossible to live in the open air. Still the fire of Shingebiss did not go out; he wore but a single strip of leather around his body, and he was seen in the

[1] The Algonquin language (so called by the French) was spoken, though not exclusively, in a territory that extended through 60 degrees of longitude, and more than 20 degrees of latitude.—*Bancroft*.

[2] The Indian name of a species of wild-duck.

[3] A personification of the north-west or wintry wind.

worst weather searching the shores for rushes, and carrying home fish.

"I shall go and visit him," said Kabebonicca one day, as he saw Shingebiss dragging along a quantity of fish; and accordingly that very night he went to the door of his lodge. Meantime Shingebiss had cooked his fish and finished his meal, and was lying, partly on his side, before the fire, singing his songs. After Kabebonicca had come to the door, and stood listening there, he sang as follows:—

"Spirit of the North-west,
You are but my fellow-man!"

The hunter knew that Kabebonicca was at his door, for he felt his cold and strong breath; but he kept on singing his songs, and affected utter indifference. At length Kabebonicca entered, and took his seat on the opposite side of the lodge; but Shingebiss did not regard or notice him. He got up as if nobody were present, and taking his poker, pushed the log, which made his fire burn brighter, repeating as he sat down again:

"You are but my fellow-man!"

Very soon the tears began to flow down Kabebonicca's cheeks, which increased so fast that presently he said to himself: "I cannot stand this; I must go out." He did so, and left Shingebiss to his songs; but resolved to freeze up all the flag orifices, and make the ice thick, so that he could not get any more fish. Still Shingebiss, by dint of great diligence, found means to pull up new roots and dive under for fish. At last, Kabebonicca was compelled to give up the contest. "He must be aided by some Monedo,"[1] said he: "I can neither freeze him nor starve him; he is a very singular being. I will let him alone."'

Besides their faith in the manitou, which was so easily led up to a belief in one Great Spirit, the Indians had several forms of superstition regarding charms, incantations, and dreams—such as are commonly found among tribes who live in intimate dependence on the powers of nature.

The medicine-man was a professed sorcerer, prophet, and rain-maker. His spells were supposed to have virtues in making the arrow swift and sure, drawing fish into the net, and outwitting the cunning of the moose-deer. For the cure of sickness, he would prescribe fanciful remedies in some cases, while, in others, he recommended means which might have some good effect—such as rolling in the snow, or exposure to excessive heat. His powers were ascribed to his friendship with a strong manitou, and cases of failure were easily explained—some manitou stronger than his own had attacked the patient. All the logic of

[1] A spirit or god.

certain modern medical theories may be found in the doctrine of the Indian quack.

It is hardly necessary to say, that dreams exercised a great influence on the mind of the Red Man. He would expose himself to great hardship in order to comply with the supposed commands of a manitou as given in dreams. His faith in immortality was firm, though not refined. He believed in a life beyond the grave, but it was not an ideal life, abstracted from all the common sights and sounds of mother-earth. The spirit of the Red Man goes to the happy hunting-ground in the far south-west; there he finds abundance of game, with beans and maize; there he has still his quiver, arrows, and moccasons, his pipe and tomahawk; and there he feasts joyfully with his friends.

For accounts of the condition of the Indian tribes after their intercourse with Europeans, we refer to the writings of the authors already named. Thatcher's *Indian Biography* gives many interesting sketches of character, and is written in a spirit of sympathy with the aborigines, yet without injustice to the early settlers. The Life of Black-Hawk is a curiosity, as it gives a narrative of adventures written under the dictation of the chief so named. There is no doubt of the truth of its statements, for 'an Indian's word of honour is as good as a white man's oath.' Black-Hawk boasts of having taken his first scalp when he was only fifteen years old, and justifies his subsequent warfare with white men. After signing a treaty of peace, he remarks: 'What do we know of the laws and customs of the white people? They might buy our bodies for dissection, and we would touch the goose-quill to confirm it, without knowing what we are doing.' This aptly describes the mode in which lands have been sold by the Indians. The forced sale of his own village compelled the chief to question whether the Americans could discern between right and wrong. When a very small fraction of the lands, bought for a trifle, was resold at a high price, he could not understand the transaction. Indeed, the sale of land, or claiming fields, and rivers, and woods, as private property, was a mystery to the Indian. The chief Tecumthé on one occasion concisely expressed the views of his people. 'Sell a country!' said he; 'why not sell the air, the clouds, and the great sea, as well as the earth? Did not the Great Spirit make them all for the use of his children?'

From the days of the apostle John Eliot to the present time, endeavours to convert the Indians to Christianity have commonly been failures. The schools, churches, and villages, formerly planted by missionary effort in the forest, have all vanished. The Indian Bible translated by Eliot is a dead-letter, for all the people who spoke its language have been long extinct. In almost all instances of natives educated by white men, savage life has won back the weary students. All that the Indians learned from the settlers was the use of 'fire-water' or alcohol. The chief Red-jacket gave, in its most simple form, the common Indian argument against the adoption of Christianity. 'If,' said he, 'the Great Spirit had intended that the Red Men should be Christians, he would have made his revelation to them as well as to the whites; and not having made it, it was clearly his will that they should continue in the faith of their fathers.' He also made use of another argument when he replied to the missionaries: 'Go, try your hand in the town of Buffalo for one year. If in that time you shall have done them [the white people] any good, and made them any better, then we will let you come among our people.' The fact that, during more than two centuries, these aborigines have lived, more or less, in intercourse with civilised and Christian men, and yet have refused the new ideas offered by their neighbours, is very remarkable, and suggests queries not readily answered. The tribes now remaining, says Schoolcraft, 'desire neither our knowledge nor our religion. They distrust our power, decry our refinements, and condemn our laborious industry.'

For speculations on the probable origin of the North-American tribes, we refer to the writings of GALLATIN and DRAKE (*Biography and History of the Indians of North America*), BRADFORD (*American Antiquities*), and SQUIER and DAVIS (*Ancient Monuments of America*). It is commonly said that America has no antiquity: this is true of the United States; but the New World has its archæology, more shadowy and seemingly unreal than the story of ancient Egypt.[1] Whence came the Red Men? Who were the 'mound-builders' in the valley of the Mississippi? and how were they related to the Toltec race in Central America? These questions make the exploration of Aztec and Inca monuments seem comparatively an easy matter. No answers better than mere guesses have hitherto been given. Of course, the Ten Tribes have been traced in America, as in all other lands, and so-called affinities of language have been found between the Algonquin and the Hebrew. With equal facility, analogies would be found between the Huron dialect and the Sanscrit. Many of the theories based on comparison of languages, are

[1] Of the supposed 'mound-builders of the north,' a writer in the *North American Review* says: 'We know not what fearful pestilence or what terrible enemy may have overcome them. Other perished nations have survived in the history of their conquerors. But no historian existed for this people. No wandering poet, singing for all ages, told the story of their deeds, or the tale of their wrongs. Ruler and subject, priest and warrior, are buried in one overwhelming oblivion. Forgotten by men, their record is with God alone.'

scarcely better than the characteristic notion of old Cotton Mather, who explained almost everything mysterious by a simple reference to the devil. 'We may guess,' said he, 'that probably the devil decoyed those miserable salvages hither, in hopes that the gospel . . . . would never come here to destroy or disturb his absolute empire over them. But our Eliot,' he continues, referring to the great missionary, 'was willing to rescue as many of them as he could from that old usurping *landlord* of America.'

Leaving this mythological theory, we may quote from the work of Squier a summary of its statements respecting the so-called 'ancient earthworks' in the West:—

'The mounds,' says Mr Squier, 'are of all dimensions, from those of but a few feet in height and a few yards in diameter, to those which, like the celebrated structure at the mouth of Grave Creek, in Virginia, rise to the height of 70 feet, and measure 1000 feet in circumference at the base. The great mound in the vicinity of Miamisburgh, Montgomery county, Ohio, is 68 feet in perpendicular height, and 852 in circumference at the base, containing 311,353 cubic feet. The truncated pyramid at Cahokia, Illinois, has an altitude of 90 feet, and is upwards of 2000 feet in circumference at the base. It has a level summit of several acres' area. The great mound at Selzerstown, Mississippi, is computed to cover 6 acres of ground. Mounds of these extraordinary dimensions are most common at the south, though there are some of great size at the north. The usual dimensions are, however, considerably less than in the examples here given. The greater number range from 6 to 30 feet in perpendicular height, by 40 to 100 feet diameter at the base.'

It is now generally admitted, that early explorers of the Mississippi valley would have been less successful in finding aboriginal earthworks, if they had enjoyed a greater share of geological science. It has been clearly shewn that, with regard to the more gigantic mounds and fortifications, nature was the engineer. The imagination of theorists gave a complete and artificial form to every conical elevation, and made a fortress of every hill approaching a quadrangular form.

WILLIAM H. PRESCOTT.

WILLIAM H. PRESCOTT, the historian, is the descendant of one of the most prominent families of New England, and was born in Salem in 1796. After a course of classical studies at Harvard University, he travelled in Europe, and returned in 1817 to Boston, where he applied his mind to the study of modern languages, and wrote several articles chiefly for the *North*

American Review. In 1819, he began to meditate the plan of some extensive historical work, and determined to devote ten years to preliminary studies. Subsequently, he found a field of research in the times of Ferdinand and Isabella of Spain—the age of revolutions in the political system of Europe, and marked by a brilliant assemblage of historical characters and events, including, among the former, Henry VIII. of England, Charles VIII. of France, Ximenes the statesman, Cordova the soldier, and Columbus the navigator; among the latter, the overthrow of the Moorish kingdom, the establishment of the Inquisition, and the discovery of the New World. This last feature of the age especially recommended it to the American historian.

Through the aid of Mr Alexander H. Everett, minister at the court of Spain, Mr Prescott obtained from the libraries of the Peninsula many valuable materials, including Llorente's History of the Inquisition, Condé's version of the Spanish-Arab chronicles, and the writings of Marina, Sempere, and Capmany on the ancient political institutions of Spain. These and other rare and valuable works enabled the historian to commence his work with resources far superior to any known by his predecessors in the same field—the Abbé Mignot, and the German author Rupert Becker. The historical works of Mr Prescott are remarkable as proofs of what may be done by zeal and industry in circumstances of great difficulty. In his youth, an accident had deprived the writer of the sight of one eye, and the other suffered so much from literary labours, that the task of writing the history of Ferdinand and Isabella required the use of a writing-case such as is sometimes used by persons totally blind. In consulting authorities, he was obliged to be satisfied with the services of a reader who did not understand Spanish. After some years of labour under these disadvantages, the author's eyesight improved, though it still remained so imperfect that it could only be employed with great moderation and by daylight. The wide extent of research shewn in the numerous citations and references in *Ferdinand and Isabella*, appears very remarkable when the circumstances of the writer are considered. After twelve years of meditation and labour, the book was published in 1838, and was universally received as an elaborate and important work on a period in history which had previously been very meagerly treated. It fulfilled far more than the promise of its title-page, as it gave a history not only of the reign of Ferdinand and Isabella, but also of the reigns of John II. of Aragon, John II. and Henry IV. of Castile, Philip and Joanna, and the regencies of Ferdinand and Ximenes.

In the two parts of the introduction to his work, the historian has given comprehensive views of the political, religious, and social condition of the kingdoms of Castile and Aragon about the middle of the fifteenth century. This summary is followed by notices of the reigns of the two kings, John II. of Aragon, father of Ferdinand, and John II. of Castile, father of Isabella, whose crowns were united by the marriage of their heirs. The factions and wars preceding this union are narrated with numerous details not found in any previous history of the time. A chapter is devoted to the institution of the Inquisition, and the persecution of the Jews in Spain—the darkest features of the age. This is one of the most graphic and original portions of the history. It is followed by an account of the Spanish Arabs, which serves as an introduction to the wars of Granada. The first part of the work closes with historical notices of Spanish literature.

The foreign affairs of Spain; the Italian wars, and the triumph of the great captain, Gonsalva; the death of Isabella, and the consequent disturbances; Ferdinand's second marriage, and his resignation of the regency, followed by his return to power; the extraordinary career of that able and versatile hermit, cardinal, despot, scholar, soldier, and saint, Ximenes: these are among the chief topics of the second part. It is obvious that the story of a work of such magnitude cannot be sufficiently direct and simple to allow an unbroken narrative interest. The writer has, with good judgment, deviated in many places from the chronological order of events, so as to avoid the intermixture of too many topics, and to give to each a certain degree of completeness. Perhaps, it may be objected that the treatment of some topics—for example, the Spanish literature—is too minute for the purpose of a general history of a period. The portraits of the leading characters—Isabella, Ferdinand, Columbus, Gonsalvo, Ximenes, and others—are very carefully drawn.

Five years after the publication of his first historical work, Mr Prescott produced a second—the *History of the Conquest of Mexico*. In this work, the subject is of an inferior nature; indeed, it is nothing more than the extermination of a helpless nation; the perpetrators of which cannot, by any fair historical treatment, be raised to the rank of heroes. With this defect, the *Conquest of Mexico* had the advantage of a clear, direct and marvellous narrative, and afforded abundant scope for the exercise of powers of description. The landing of the Spaniards on the shore of Mexico; their march over the coast, and through the tropic scenery of the plain, to the table-land; their skirmishes and negotiations with the several native tribes; the rapid fall of an empire; the beginning of that work of desolation which has made the history of South America more melancholy than that of any other section of the world: these striking features made Mr Prescott's second work even more successful than his first. It has been widely circulated in America and Great Britain; and, besides several reprints, translations have appeared in Paris, Berlin, Rome, Madrid, and Mexico. Though the author's share of profit has been by no means commensurate with the extensive sale of his works, it is pleasing to know that his success in his own country has added a considerable sum to his inherited property.

In the introduction to the *History of the Conquest of Mexico*, the historian gives the results of extensive researches in a general view of Aztec civilisation; and throughout the work he makes use of numerous materials unknown to the preceding writers on the same subject—Dr Robertson, and the Spaniard Antonio de Solis. The summary of Aztec culture is exceedingly interesting, and prepares the reader to study with sympathy the following narrative. We borrow from this summary a few of the more prominent facts.

In his physical structure, the Aztec was less robust than the European, and in some respects resembled the Hindoo. His hair was straight and black; the beard was usually plucked away or thinned; the complexion was a reddish brown or copper colour, the cheek-bones high, and the eyes obliquely set. The women were exempted from the hard bodily labour imposed upon them by savage tribes; and the wife was the companion, not the slave of her husband. This one trait proves that a considerable degree of civilisation had been attained. The agriculture of the Aztecs was skilful; and in other useful arts, great progress had been made. Vessels for domestic use were made of clay or lackered or painted wood; and articles of luxury included gold and silver ornaments, jewellery, and especially splendid dresses and tapestry, made of the plumage of tropical birds.

The tables of the wealthy were supplied with such delicacies as sauces, confectionary, chocolate flavoured with vanilla, and fish brought from a sea-shore 200 miles distant. The dark fact that cannibalism formed a part of their luxurious banquets, seems scarcely conceivable among a people otherwise refined and gentle in their manners.

As a specimen of Aztec literature, Mr Prescott notices the poems ascribed to one of the kings of the Tezcucans—the most civilised of all the tribes who inhabited the valley of Mexico. The strains of this royal poet have a melancholy tone, reminding the reader of a troubled life, not without crime, of remorse and forebodings mixed with the pleasures of a palace. A system of picture-writing served for the publication of laws and the record of memorable events. Time was accurately measured; and the advanced state of the Aztec astronomy is perhaps the most remarkable fact brought to light by recent researches.

The religion and the political system of the Aztecs were very closely connected. The education of the people was one of the duties of the priesthood, which was not bound by vows of celibacy. Temples were richly endowed, and the priests received first-fruits and many voluntary offerings. The surplus of the church-revenues was distributed in alms. One supreme Creator and Lord of the universe was the central object of worship; but homage was also paid, as by the Hindoos, to a multitude of subordinate deities. A ceremony, having some likeness to baptism, was used in naming children, and a cleansing power, in a moral sense, was ascribed to the water. Roman Catholic missionaries have recognised in the monuments of the Aztecs the rites of confession and absolution. The cross seems to have been an object of adoration. These and other coincidences have suggested the theory of connecting Aztec religion and civilisation with Jewish traditions; but, on the other side, the Aztec worship was as degraded and cruel as that of the lowest savages. Human sacrifices were commonly offered on the altars of the gods, and the flesh of enemies seized in battle was served up at luxurious banquets.

The Aztec government was an elective monarchy. A numerous aristocracy depended on the throne. Judges in the superior courts were appointed by the crown; while, in the lower, they were chosen by the people. For numerous details of a people whose civilisation, so far as researches have hitherto extended, seems an isolated fact in the world's history, connecting itself with nothing before or after it, we have to thank Mr Prescott; but he has wisely abstained from theorising on the origin of Mexican culture. He has left it as he found it—a problem presenting the greatest difficulties to students who hold the traditional theory of civilisation. The end of this Mexican system seems as mysterious as the beginning. Other nations have perished, but not without leaving some heritage to their successors. Where are the inheritors of Aztec culture? For what great purpose connected with the world's general history did it exist? These are questions to which human reason can find no reply. The melancholy fate of the Aztecs has no parallel in all history. Other nations have passed away, but not without having fulfilled a destiny more or less important as a part of the whole life of mankind. So natural is the belief that all culture must, in some form or other, perpetuate itself, that we cannot, without some feeling of scepticism, read

Mr Prescott's able and interesting summary of Aztec civilisation, especially his account of the character and poetical writings of the king of Tezcuco, who might be styled the Aztec Solomon. We read that the latter part of his life 'was devoted to astronomical, and, probably, astrological studies; to meditation on his immortal destiny; and to giving utterance to his feelings in songs, or rather hymns, of much solemnity and pathos.' An extract from one of these will convey some idea of his religious speculations.

HYMN ON MORTALITY.

BY THE KING OF TEZCUCO.

'All things on earth have their term, and, in the most joyous career of their vanity and splendour, their strength fails, and they sink into the dust. All the round world is but a sepulchre; and there is nothing which lives on its surface, that shall not be hidden and entombed beneath it. Rivers, torrents, and streams move onward to their destination. Not one flows back to its pleasant source. They rush onward, hastening to bury themselves in the deep bosom of the ocean. The things of yesterday are no more to-day; and the things of to-day shall cease, perhaps, on the morrow. The cemetery is full of the loathsome dust of bodies once quickened by living souls, who occupied thrones, presided over assemblies, marshalled armies, subdued provinces, arrogated to themselves worship, were puffed up with vainglorious pomp, and power, and empire.

But these glories have all passed away, like the fearful smoke that issues from the throat of Popocatepetl,[1] with no other memorial of their existence than the record on the page of the chronicler.

The great, the wise, the valiant, the beautiful—alas! where are they now? They are all mingled with the clod; and that which has befallen them shall happen to us, and to those that come after us. Yet, let us take courage, illustrious nobles and chieftains, true friends and loyal subjects—let us aspire to that heaven, where all is eternal, and corruption cannot come. The horrors of the tomb are but the cradle of the Sun, and the dark shadows of death are brilliant lights for the stars.'

The writer of this hymn died about the year 1470, or half a century before the desolation commonly called the Conquest of Mexico.

After a clear and comprehensive introduction, giving an account of the Aztec civilisation, Mr Prescott proceeds to give the narrative of the rapid conquest of Mexico; and in doing this, he supplies many details which reduce the vague, marvellous, and

[1] A volcano.

seemingly fabulous account, rendered by the preceding historian, Robertson, to a statement that may be readily understood and credited. At first sight, it seems a mere story of romance that a handful of adventurers, landing in Mexico, scantily furnished with the means of warfare, and fighting at their own cost, could, in the space of two years, overthrow an empire and destroy an ancient civilisation. Besides the facts, that these adventurers were excited by a thirst for gold to the highest degree of valour; that they were led on by a bold, enthusiastic, and yet cunning commander; and that their victims were a singularly unwarlike people, dismayed even by the sound of firearms; we require other circumstances to explain how one Spaniard literally put to flight a thousand Mexicans.

In the first place, we learn that the empire of the Aztecs was a mere aggregate of several distinct communities, without the centralisation required for a common defence. Cortés conquered one tribe after another, and made the vanquished his allies. In doing this, he was greatly assisted by the jealousies excited against the Indian monarch, Montezuma. Though his military prowess was celebrated in Mexico, it was little better than the courage of a mere child when opposed to the discipline of the invaders; for of the art of war, the irresolute and bewildered king knew nothing.

The prediction current in Mexico, that the empire must fall into the hands of invaders coming from the east, was no slight aid to the adventurers; but their greatest auxiliaries were found in the divisions of the Indian tribes and the vacillation of the monarch. Montezuma acted as a fatalist who sees his destiny, and submits. When he heard of the strange men, if men they could be called, who had landed on his coast, and, accompanied by unknown terrors of thunder and lightning, were marching on his capital, his superstitious mind remembered the prophecy of invasion from the east; and when he declined the proffered visit, it was not through indignation or simple fear, but with the deep melancholy of a man who has foreseen a gloomy fate, and knows that his hour is come.

When the invaders appeared before him, he at once resigned everything into their hands—as his subjects said, 'he became a woman.' As Mr Prescott states—Montezuma died 'quite as much under the anguish of a wounded spirit as under disease. . . . . Perceiving his end approach, some of the cavaliers present in the fortress, whom the kindness of his manners had personally attached to him, were anxious to save the soul of the dying prince from the sad doom of those who perish in the darkness of unbelief. They accordingly waited on him, with Father Olmedo at their head, and in the most earnest manner implored him to open his eyes to the error of his creed, and consent to be baptised. But Montezuma, whatever may have been suggested to the contrary, seems never to have faltered in his hereditary faith, or to have contemplated becoming an apostate—for surely he merits that name, in its most odious application, who, whether Christian or Pagan, renounces his religion without conviction of its falsehood. Indeed, it was a too implicit reliance on its oracles which had led him to give such easy confidence to the Spaniards. His intercourse with them had doubtless not sharpened his desire to embrace their communion; and the calamities of his country he might consider as sent by his gods, to punish him for his hospitality to those who had desecrated and destroyed their shrines.

When Father Olmedo, therefore, kneeling at his side, with the uplifted crucifix, affectionately besought him to embrace the sign of man's redemption, he coldly repulsed the priest, exclaiming: "I have but a few moments to live, and will not at this hour desert the faith of my fathers." One thing, however, seemed to press heavily on Montezuma's mind—this was the fate of his children, especially of three daughters, whom he had by his two wives; for there were certain rites of marriage which distinguished the lawful wife from the concubine. Calling Cortés to his bedside, he earnestly commended these children to his care, "as the most precious jewels that he could leave him." He besought the general to interest his master, the emperor, in their behalf, and to see that they should not be left destitute, but be allowed some portion of their rightful inheritance. "Your lord will do this," he concluded, "if it were only for the friendly offices I have rendered the Spaniards, and for the love I have shewn them, though it has brought me to this condition. But for this I bear them no ill-will." Such, according to Cortés himself, were the words of the dying monarch. Not long after, on the 30th of June 1520, he expired in the arms of some of his own nobles, who still remained faithful in their attendance on his person.'

The preceding notices have shewn how clearly the historian explains the circumstances which make credible so romantic a story as the conquest of Mexico by Cortés and his followers. The march of the adventurers is described in a vivid style. Considering all the circumstances conspiring to aid their enterprise, we still must admire their courage, and might follow them with sympathy if some better motive than the thirst for gold had impelled them. When they marched boldly from the coast through the gorgeous low tropical district, discovering every day new wonders in the surrounding scenes, they knew little or nothing of the power of the people whom they went to conquer. They knew not that jealousies and divisions existed among the native tribes; that the monarch was superstitious and irresolute; and that the Aztec oracles would be found in alliance with the invaders. Through a land of mystery, they marched on from the tropic climate of the lowlands to the temperate slopes or terraces; and still on, over the high table-lands and through the passes, where tempests of snow and arrowy sleet beat upon them. Here the larch, oak, and cypress appeared in place of the tropical aloes and bananas, and rich groves adorned a landscape which has been desolated by the Spaniards—a people whose taste in arboriculture equals their success in colonisation. After hard toil and suffering from cold, the invaders reached the summit of the mountain-chain of Ahualco. So far, the country had appeared less and less attractive as they had ascended the table-land.

'Their progress was now comparatively easy, and they marched forward with a buoyant step, as they felt they were treading the soil of Montezuma.

They had not advanced far, when, turning an angle of the sierra, they suddenly came on a view which more than compensated the toils of the preceding day. It was that of the valley of Mexico, or Tenochtitlan, as more commonly called by the natives; which, with its picturesque assemblage of water, woodland, and cultivated plains, its shining cities and shadowy hills, was spread out like some gay and gorgeous panorama before them. In the highly rarefied atmosphere of these upper regions, even remote objects have a brilliancy of colouring and a distinctness of outline which seem to annihilate distance. Stretching far away at their feet, were seen noble forests of oak, sycamore, and cedar, and beyond, yellow fields of maize, and the towering maguey, intermingled with orchards and blooming gardens; for flowers, in such demand for their religious festivals, were even more abundant in this populous valley than in other parts of Anahuac. In the centre of the great basin were beheld the lakes, occupying then a much larger portion of its surface than at present; their borders thickly studded with towns and hamlets; and in the midst—like some Indian empress with her coronal of pearls—the fair city of Mexico, with her white towers and pyramidal temples, reposing, as it were, on the bosom of the waters—the far-famed "Venice of the Aztecs." High over all rose the royal hill of Chapoltepec, the residence of the Mexican monarchs, crowned with the same grove of gigantic cypresses which at this day fling their broad shadows over the land. In the distance, beyond the blue waters of the lake, and nearly screened by intervening foliage, was seen a shining speck, the rival capital of Tezcuco; and still further on, the dark belt of porphyry, girdling the valley around, like a rich setting which nature had devised for the fairest of her jewels. Such was the beautiful vision which broke on the eyes of the conquerors.

And even now, when so sad a change has come over the scene; when the stately forests have been laid low, and the soil, unsheltered from the fierce radiance of a tropical sun, is in many places abandoned to sterility; when the waters have retired, leaving a broad and ghastly margin white with the incrustation of salts, while the cities and hamlets on their borders have mouldered into ruins: even now that desolation broods over the landscape, so indestructible are the lines of beauty which nature has traced on its features, that no traveller, however cold, can gaze on them with any other emotions than those of astonishment and rapture.

What, then, must have been the emotions of the Spaniards, when, after working their toilsome way into the upper air, the cloudy tabernacle parted before their eyes, and they beheld these fair scenes in all their pristine magnificence and beauty! It was like the spectacle which greeted the eyes of Moses from the summit of Pisgah, and in the warm glow of their feelings they cried out: "It is the promised land!"'

Mr Prescott lavishes the charms of his style to invest with dignity the marches and battles of the merciless freebooters who desolated Mexico. He feels the difficulty of describing massacres with the pomp of great actions of warfare, and therefore often turns aside from the direct course of events to relieve the tale of carnage by interspersed descriptions of cities, architecture, and the grandeurs of natural scenery. But he describes Cortés as a hero, and even hazards the assertion that he 'was not cruel; at least, not cruel as compared with most of those who followed his iron trade.' This appears a bold statement, when we look at the plain facts of the conqueror's career. It was rapid, and its success is easily explained by the unwarlike character of the unhappy Aztecs, who never offered any considerable resistance until the last moment of desperation, when, driven into their capital, they defended it with that courage which even the most inoffensive bird will display in defence of the nest which contains her brood. The other so-called battles were so many massacres, like that perpetrated by Pizarro and his accomplices at Caxamalca; and the description of one might serve for the whole series. We see a mass of unarmed, naked, and timid Indians, amazed by the appearance of mounted troopers, with guns discharging deadly fire with the noise of thunder. To the wretched Mexicans, these terrors seemed supernatural; and to offer battle was as hopeless as to wage warfare with the giants and demons of mythology. The conquerors, therefore, rode over their victims. A wolf in a fold of lambs could scarcely have an easier task than many of the 'victories' of Cortés and his band. The rapidity of their march is sufficient evidence of the nature of the adventure. In August 1519, they commenced the expedition against the city of

Mexico; they arrived here in November, and passed the winter. After reducing several places on the lake, gaining victories over various tribes, and waiting for reinforcements, they captured the city, and completed the conquest of an empire in August 1521. The fact that this was achieved by a small band of hardy adventurers, and in the course of two years, can be explained only by the passive character of the subjugated people, and the alliance formed by the Spaniards with the several Indian tribes, especially the republicans of Tlascala.

We cannot agree with the historian, either in his general estimate of the character of Cortés, or in his palliation of the gross superstition and cruelty of the Spaniards. It must not be forgotten that the same form of religion professed by the invaders of Mexico, had been found, in other men, compatible with feelings of humanity. False religion, or even the darkest superstition, has been in many cases rather the pretext and disguise than the real incentive to cruelty and oppression. It was not a religious zeal that led Cortés to Mexico, and Pizarro to Peru; it was the wild spirit of adventure, and that greedy love of gold which, in our own times, has made almost a pandemonium of California. With this protest, we give the more favourable character of Cortés, as described by Mr Prescott:—

'Cortés was not a vulgar conqueror. He did not conquer from the mere ambition of conquest. If he destroyed the ancient capital of the Aztecs, it was to build up a more magnificent capital on its ruins. If he desolated the land, and broke up its existing institutions, he employed the short period of his administration in digesting schemes for introducing there a more improved culture and a higher civilisation. In all his expeditions, he was careful to study the resources of the country, its social organisation, and its physical capacities. He enjoined it on his captains to attend particularly to these objects. If he was greedy of gold, like most of the Spanish cavaliers in the New World, it was not to hoard it, nor merely to lavish it in the support of a princely establishment, but to secure funds for prosecuting his glorious discoveries. Witness his costly expeditions to the Gulf of California. His enterprises were not undertaken solely for mercenary objects, as is shewn by the various expeditions he set on foot for the discovery of a communication between the Atlantic and the Pacific. . . . .

He was a knight-errant in the literal sense of the word. Of all the band of adventurous cavaliers, whom Spain, in the sixteenth century, sent forth on the career of discovery and conquest, there was none more deeply filled with the spirit of romantic enterprise than Hernando Cortés. Dangers and difficulties, instead of deterring, seemed to have a charm in his eyes. They were necessary to rouse him to a full consciousness of his powers. He grappled with them at the outset, and, if I may so express myself, seemed to prefer to take his enterprises by the most difficult side. He conceived, at the first moment of his landing in Mexico, the design of its conquest. When he saw the strength of its civilisation, he was not turned from his purpose; when he was assailed by the superior force of Narvaez, he still persisted in it; and when he was driven in ruin from the capital, he still cherished his original idea. How successfully he carried it into execution, we have seen.'

Nine years after the publication of the *History of Ferdinand and Isabella*, the author completed the story of Spanish discovery and conquest in America. The *History of the Conquest of Peru* (1847), is the result of careful research in valuable documents which the former historian, Robertson, had not employed; but in the narrative of the conquest, Prescott has added little to the statements of his conscientious predecessor. In the preliminary view of the civilisation achieved by the Incas of Peru, the writings of the Spaniards Sarmiento and Ondegardo, contemporaries of the Pizarros, have been consulted and collated with the commentaries of Garcilasso, and all that can be known of the Peruvians at the time of the conquest has been collected. Of the origin of this civilisation, or of the history of the Incas in times preceding the conquest, we can learn nothing, as no written records were found.

The materials for the historian of Peru are, therefore, very scanty. He finds only documents describing the life of two generations—the people living during the so-called conquest, and their immediate predecessors; for of the scattered remnant who lived after the conquest, the tale is as brief as it is melancholy. We find a quiet and inoffensive nation sheltered among the valleys of Peru: they are divided into two castes—the Incas or rulers, and the common people. We see that they understand several of the useful arts. Their agriculture covers the terraces of their hills with verdure; their roads and bridges are remarkable structures; and their architecture has a rude magnificence. We are curious to learn, if possible, the origin and the traditions of this isolated system of culture; but while we contemplate it, suddenly the scene changes, and the dynasty of the Incas vanishes like a dream. Its gilded temples have attracted the avarice of a band of marauders coming from the west; they invade the land, massacre the helpless people, and so completely do the work of extermination, as to leave, in the course of a few years, nothing more than those records of rapine and oppression which fill the history of Spanish colonisation.

The origin of the Inca-system of government, like that of the Aztecs, remains a mystery. An Indian tradition tells us, that in the most ancient times all the tribes of the American continent were savages, worshipping rude natural objects, delighting in warfare, and eating the flesh of captives. A celestial man and woman, children of the sun, appeared and fixed their residence in the valley of Cuzco, where they opened a school of civilisation. Manco Capac, the husband, instructed the men in agriculture; while Mama Oello, his wife, taught the women to weave and spin. In process of time, the city of Cuzco was built, and here the mild government of the Incas—or descendants from Manco Capac and Mama Oello—was first established. There may be some germ of truth in the legend which describes a government founded on superior wisdom rather than physical force. The Incas were certainly more advanced in intellect than the common people of Peru, and the difference found in the facial angles of the two races, corresponds with this fact.

Whatever may have been its origin, the Inca-system fostered a remarkable civilisation. Agriculture was in an advanced state. The sovereign or Inca was its patron, and on one day in every year went into the fields and ploughed a furrow. A magnificent system of irrigation was employed. The surplus of abundant harvests was stored in granaries, to provide for times of scarcity. Bare rocks were cut into terraces, covered with soil, and made fruitful. Manures were liberally used; and guano, a recent improvement in Europe, was commonly applied in Peru before the 'conquest,' or rather desolation, of the country by the Spanish banditti. Among the other useful arts in which the Peruvians excelled, we find—working in gold and silver, engraving on gems, smelting copper-ore, and spinning and weaving woollen and other fabrics. The use of iron was unknown. Their architecture was simple and massive; and their great roads are perhaps more remarkable than any other results of their civilisation. 'One of these roads,' Mr Prescott says, 'passed over the grand plateau;' and its length has been estimated at from 1500 to 2000 miles. 'Its breadth scarcely exceeded twenty feet. It was built of heavy flags of freestone, and, in some parts at least, covered with a bituminous cement, which time has made harder than the stone itself. In some places, where the ravines had been filled up with masonry, the mountain-torrents, wearing on it for ages, have gradually eaten a way through the base, and left the superincumbent mass—such is the cohesion of the materials—still spanning the valley like an arch! Over some of the boldest streams, it was necessary to construct suspension-bridges, as they are termed, made of the tough fibres of the maguey or of the osier of the country, which has an extraordinary degree of tenacity and strength. These osiers were woven into cables of the thickness of a man's body. The huge ropes, then stretched across the water, were conducted through rings or holes cut in immense buttresses of stone raised on the opposite banks of the river, and there secured to heavy pieces of timber. Several of these enormous cables, bound together, formed a bridge, which, covered with planks, well secured and defended by a railing of the same osier materials on the sides, afforded a safe passage for the traveller.'

The general characteristics of the Peruvians under the Inca government were those of a mild, peaceable people living under a paternal despotism. Their want of enterprise depended probably on the want of property in the soil, which was annually distributed among them, so that each received a share. This form of communism favoured the development of a quiet, unambitious, and unwarlike character, which was ill fitted to resist the Spanish invasion. The Inca, or king, was also the high-priest, or chief-minister of religion; and the highest aristocracy consisted of the members of the royal family, who led the armies and filled the chief offices of church and state. One Supreme Being was the central object of worship, as among the Aztecs in Mexico; but homage was also paid to many subordinate deities, and especially to the sun, as the great ancestor of the Inca dynasty. The moon was worshipped as the sister, and the planet Venus as the page, or morning and evening attendant of the sun. A class of nuns, styled 'Virgins of the Sun,' served in the temples, and, among other duties, tended the sacred fire which was lighted on a certain annual festival. The four chief festivals were celebrated at the solstices and equinoxes, when sacrifices were offered, which, on some rare occasions, included among their victims a child or a beautiful virgin.

Such were the traits of government, religion, and social life among the quiet people who fell victims to the ruthless cruelty of a base adventurer. Pizarro, a rapacious marauder, who, in other times, would have reached no higher elevation than the gallows, was the natural son of a Spanish officer. Left in a state of beggary by his father, the boy was for some time engaged as a swineherd. When he attained manhood, he joined a band of military adventurers, went to seek his fortune in the New World, and, by his courage, gained promotion to the rank of lieutenant. After following Balboa, and remaining for some time with the colony on the isthmus of Panama, he sought more exciting adventures in the regions on the south, and, having found suitable companions, sailed southwards from Panama, hoping to find some golden country. This first private enterprise was a failure; but the hopes of Pizarro were not easily discouraged. A second expedition was successful; and, after great sufferings, Pizarro and his associates anchored their vessel in the harbour of Tumbez, within the dominions of the Inca. Here they were hospitably treated by the natives, and feasted their eyes on the gold and silver work of a temple.

Having made this reconnaissance of his intended victims, the adventurer prudently abstained from immediate hostilities, and sailed back to Panama to raise a stronger band of invaders. As the governor of the colony refused his assistance, Pizarro returned to Spain, and there was appointed governor of Peru, but left to find his own resources for the subjugation of the country. Among the first volunteers on his side were his own brothers, Hernando, Juan, and Gonzalo, and a relative named Francisco—all worthy associates in a scheme of enormous robbery. Many difficulties were encountered and overcome by their fanatical thirst for riches; and at last, with banditti numbering 180 men, and only 27 horses for cavalry, Pizarro was prepared to invade Peru. The invasion, at all times easy, was favoured by the circumstance, that at this time a disputed succession to the throne had divided the timid and defenceless people.

Landing near the haven of Tumbez, Pizarro, with his banditti, marched into the country. Murder and rapine marked their path from village to village, and the poor natives fled like sheep before a band of wolves. Gold and silver sent home to Panama excited other adventurers to sail for Peru; and having thus gained reinforcements, Pizarro boldly marched on the capital, and determined to seize the person of the reigning Inca. He succeeded by a base act of treachery, inviting the king to visit the Spanish quarters, where he was made a prisoner. The conditions offered to the Inca were, that he should immediately be baptised as a convert to the Catholic faith, and surrender his throne to Spain. These conditions were rejected with natural indignation. Meanwhile, the invader had concealed his forces in the temples and other buildings near the great square where the interview with the Inca had taken place. He now waved in the air a white scarf, as the signal of beginning the slaughter of the terrified people. The Spaniards rushed out from their hiding-places and fired upon the Peruvians. There was no battle; no resistance was offered by the unarmed natives. Stunned by the din of musketry, the miserable king saw his people falling around him under the storm of bullets, or cut down like grass and trampled under the hoofs of the fierce cavalry. His troops, regarding battle as a hopeless fight with demons of superhuman power, fled in all directions before the assassins, and thus the so-called conquest of Peru was achieved! The king was retained as a prisoner until his subjects handed over to the Spaniards a large ransom, and then he was murdered. One brave

Peruvian chieftain, who offered resistance to Pizarro, was taken, after a skirmish, and burned alive. The remainder of the story consists chiefly of the internal discords of the marauding Spaniards.

This is the simple account of an enormous crime which Mr Prescott has described in a very calm and lenient style, such as may be suitable to the history of honourable warfare, but is, we conceive, utterly out of place in narrating the career of a sanguinary outlaw like Pizarro. The historian has apparently attempted to treat the butchery at Caxamalca as a military exploit. It is true, he has not falsified any facts: he admits that the natives made no resistance; that they had no weapons; that the ferocious Spaniards were in no more danger than a sportsman encounters in the slaughter of pheasants; that, indeed, they did not lose a single man; but he throws a false dignity over the crime and its perpetrators. Without a word of indignation, he tells us that his hero saw that 'the hour had come;' that 'his followers shouted the old war-cry of "St Jago and at them!"' that the struggle (?) 'became fiercer than ever around the royal litter;' and so forth—but the reader who looks through the rather florid dress thrown over the massacre, will find nothing more than the fact, that Spanish ruffians shot and cut down a crowd of timid and inoffensive Indians.

BIOGRAPHY.

In this department we find several valuable works, with many others characterised by a special rather than a general interest. The section of religious biography is crowded with memoirs of eminent divines, missionaries, and other leading characters in the several churches of America. It is obvious that we cannot notice fairly any considerable number of works of this class, and to copy their titles would make our pages a bibliographical catalogue. We must therefore pass over a host of volumes, to notice a work which contains the best specimens of American biography.

JARED SPARKS, the editor of this extensive work, was born about the year 1794. His earlier writings included several essays on religious questions, and contributions to *The North American Review*, which remained under his editorship during the years 1823–30. In 1828, he commenced the series of American biographies, and since that time has chiefly devoted his studies to the illustration of the history of his country. His first biographical work, *The Life of John Ledyard*, the traveller, was followed by a *Life of Governor Morris*, and *The Diplomatic Correspondence of the American Revolution*—the latter published in twelve volumes, in the years 1829–31. In 1833, he commenced the publication of *The Life and Writings of Washington*, which was completed in twelve volumes, the last appearing in 1840. This was followed by a complete edition of the works of Benjamin Franklin, with a continuation of his autobiography and explanatory notes.

The *Library of American Biography* already includes twenty-five volumes. In the first series of ten volumes, the editor wrote the lives of Ethan Allen, Benedict Arnold, and Father Marquette, the French discoverer of the Mississippi. Among the other contributors to this extensive work, the names of the brothers EVERETT, PRESCOTT, WHEATON, CHARLES F. HOFFMAN, HENRY REED, and GEORGE HILLARD, may be mentioned. The several important contributions to historical biography by Mr Sparks, display remarkable fidelity and diligence of research. His style is sober and correct, but deficient in animation and variety.

As specimens of numerous memoirs which might be noticed if our space would allow, we may mention SABINE'S *Sketches of the American Loyalists*; RAYNER'S *Life of Jefferson*; ELLIS'S *Life of Penn*; *The Letters of Mrs Adams*, wife of the second president; and TICKNOR'S *Life of Daniel Webster*. In the department of religious biography, examples of works of general interest are found in GURLEY'S *Life of Ashmun*, a tribute to the memory of a good man who devoted his labours to the African colonisation in Liberia; the *Life of Boardman*, another contribution to the history of Christian missions; GAMMEL'S *Life of Roger Williams*; and M'LURE'S *Lives of the Fathers of New England*.

The well-known biographical works of WASHINGTON IRVING have been mentioned in a general review of his writings. We may add the remarks, that his *Life of Goldsmith* can bear no comparison with the elaborate biography written by Mr Forster, and that the *Life of Mohammed* has been generally regarded as deficient in the critical investigation required in following the statements of Oriental writers. Irving's latest work, the *Life of George Washington*, is necessarily rather historical than biographical; for it may be said of the hero of the revolution, that he scarcely had at any time a private life. 'All his actions and concerns, almost from boyhood, were connected with the history of his country.' Throughout the work, Irving has been largely indebted to the researches of that laborious and conscientious contributor to national literature—Jared Sparks; but the manuscripts of the correspondence of Washington have also been consulted and carefully collated with 'Washington's writings,' as edited by Sparks.[1]

The following notices are appended as curiosities in the biographical literature of America. The first requires no preface to indicate its general and scientific interest: the second is selected not merely as unique of its kind, but also as having a rather important purport with regard to the state of culture and popular taste in England and America.

LAURA BRIDGMAN.

Condillac, and other writers who regarded the senses as the *only* sources of intelligence, might have found some difficulty in explaining the case of a child deprived of sight and hearing, and almost destitute of smell and taste, yet capable of receiving and combining many ideas.

Laura Bridgman, born in 1829, when two years old was attacked by a violent fever, and lost the senses of sight and hearing, while that of smell was almost destroyed, and taste was much impaired. Thus the imprisoned soul of the child had only one door by which communication could take place with the surrounding world. The one sense of feeling was left as the only channel through which she could receive impressions and ideas from nature and her fellow-creatures. To educate a mind thus isolated seemed hopeless. The results of the experiment are so interesting, that readers will probably wish to know something of the process, conducted under the direction of Dr Howe.[2] At four years of age, the general health of the blind, deaf, and dumb child improved, and she began to exert the sense of touch more actively; followed her mother about the house, felt her arms and hands when they were engaged in various domestic duties, and imitated their motions. Her affections expanded—something like stubbornness appeared, but this might be merely the result of her condition. Gentle patting on the head seemed to be understood as indicating approbation; on the back, disapprobation.

[1] It was intended that a more proportionate notice of Irving's *Life of Washington* should be given in this place; but though the work has long been announced as on the eve of publication, the first volume is all that has hitherto appeared.

[2] The following account is condensed from the very interesting narrative by Dr Howe. See Ninth Annual Report of the Perkins Institution and Massachusetts Asylum for the Blind.

In 1837, when Laura was eight years old, she was brought to the Boston Institution for the Blind. The strange locality seemed awhile to bewilder her mind; but in the course of a fortnight, by continually using her one perfect sense of touch, she made herself at home, or acquainted with surrounding objects. To convey to her a knowledge of signs, words in raised letters were used. For example, the name *s-p-o-o-n* was pasted on the article signified; and in the same way the words *key* and *book* were used. Shortly she learned to put the label *book* upon a book, and so to recognise the labels for the spoon, key, and other objects. Next she learned to arrange the separate and disordered letters—for example, *o o s p n*, so as to form the word *spoon*. This process required some weeks of patient toil. Dr Howe says he could almost fix the moment when, after much bewilderment, the notion entered her mind of expressing her wishes by the arbitrary signs of embossed letters. The next step was to procure a set of metal types, with a board drilled with square holes, in which she might fix the letters when spelling names of objects. She attained great dexterity in the use of this manual alphabet, and could read very quickly, on the tips of her fingers, the names of known objects arranged by her teachers.

Having mastered the manual alphabet of the deaf mutes, and learned to spell in this mode the names of many things, Laura readily acquired the use of words denoting qualities, such as *hard* or *soft*, and naturally placed these adjectives after their respective nouns. Next, she was taught the use of words denoting relations to place. A ring was placed *on* a box, then *on* a hat, then *in* the hat or box; and these distinctions were pointed out by the usual mode of spelling. After some study, the meaning of the several little words seemed suddenly to enter her mind. She spelled the word *on*, and then laid one hand on the other; then spelled *into*, and enclosed one hand within the other. Active verbs—such as to walk, to run, to sew—were readily understood; but at first, no distinction of mood or tense could be made. In asking for bread she used the form: 'Bread, give, Laura.'

When she first understood the use of writing, and knew that by tracing letters with a pencil she could convey her thoughts to absent persons, her delight was remarkable, and her progress so rapid, that, after a few months, she was able to write a note to her mother. About the same time, Laura learned to add and subtract small numbers, and to count to one hundred. She acquired, without any great labour, a considerable accuracy in the measurement of time; knew the days of the week; could calculate on what day the 15th or 16th from a certain date would fall; and could mark upon the key-board of a pianoforte the relative durations of crotchets and quavers—in other words, she could divide a second of time into two equal parts. Her acuteness of touch became more and more remarkable, and in her eleventh year, among forty or fifty friends, she was able to recognise any person whose hand she might examine. At the same time, her vocabulary had greatly increased, so that she could construct such sentences as 'I did learn to read much with types'—'Doctor did teach me in nursery.' The use of pronouns now varied her forms of speech, and she would even correct those who used the childish repetition of the noun. When Dr Howe said, 'Doctor will teach Laura,' she eagerly shook his arm, and told him to say, 'I will teach you.' The moral qualities were developed in proportion with the intellectual. She was remarkably correct in her deportment; and her love of order, neatness, and cleanliness was exemplary. Her notions of property were very definite, and while she tenaciously claimed her own, she was never known to take anything belonging to another. In two instances of strong temptation, Laura was found capable of falsehood; but, with these exceptions, her openness and conscientiousness were very pleasing. Having offended in some trifling manner, she would at once spontaneously confess her fault, sometimes with tears, and saying, 'It was wrong. Teacher cannot love wrong girl.'

She distinguished the different degrees of intellect in others, would betray a rather unamiable contempt of dull pupils, and selected the most lively and intelligent as her friends. The traits of self-assertion and jealousy were strongly marked in her character, and a sense of the humorous was shewn by such tricks as treating her doll as a sick pupil, putting it to bed with a bottle of hot water to its feet, and laughingly requesting the doctor to apply a blister to the wooden patient. When left alone, she would soliloquise by spelling on her fingers. Dr Howe observes, of her moral character: 'It is beautiful to behold her continual gladness, her keen enjoyment of existence, her expansive love and sympathy with suffering, her truthfulness and hopefulness.' Speaking of the child when eleven years old, he adds: 'No religious feeling, properly so called, has developed itself, nor is it yet time perhaps to look for it; but she has shewn a disposition to respect those who have power and knowledge, and to love those who have goodness.'

Such were the results of a benevolent effort to liberate an imprisoned mind. The report of the case must be as interesting to the metaphysician as it is pleasing to the general reader.

We do not see how Locke and Condillac could have explained the well-authenticated facts in the education of Laura Bridgman.

PHINEAS T. BARNUM.

The *Life of P. T. Barnum*, written by himself, would scarcely claim a notice here, if regarded simply as a literary effort; but it is *a representative book*. It tells a curious tale of the tastes for amusement prevailing in large masses of respectable people in Great Britain and America. Mr Barnum was one of the most successful of showmen. While others were labouring, through heavy discouragements, to educate and refine popular taste, he determined to cater for that taste *in statu quo*, and to make a large profit by so doing. Putting aside all consideration of the honesty of such a plan, it must be admitted that the means adopted were clever. Having failed in various other schemes for raising money, the writer turned his attention to the showman's profession, and resolved to speculate on the popular love of wonders. The first curiosity to which he invited the notice of a discerning public, was described as a very old negress—'Joice Heth, aged 161 years, and formerly nurse to General Washington.' Mr Barnum liked the appearance of the old woman; for 'so far as outward indications were concerned, she might almost as well have been called a thousand years old as any other age.' Having largely advertised this curiosity, as the venerable negress who, to use her own words, had 'raised' General Washington, the showman was liberally assisted by the press. Editorial notices in literary, political, and religious papers recommended the people to make haste to behold the monument of antiquity; and the people obeyed. Her love of psalmody made the old negress a favourite object of religious sympathies.

In the course of a little time, the negress died, and dissection exposed the gross imposition, but not before it had succeeded well enough for the showman. His next remarkable adventure, after some attempts in selling fictitious Cologne-water and bear's grease, was the purchase of a collection of curiosities known as 'the American Museum.' Mr Barnum made great improvements in this place of amusement, enriching it with 'industrious fleas, educated dogs, fat boys, giants, dwarfs,' manufactured mermaids, &c.; and among his first 'extra exhibitions,' he presented to the public 'a model of Niagara Falls, with real water,' of which he gives a ludicrous account.

This was followed by an exhibition of 'the Fejee Mermaid,' a romantic specimen in natural history, manufactured with some skill, but, according to the placards, taken alive by a fisherman somewhere near the Fejee Islands. It was a miserable disappointment for the spectators who had gazed on the external bait, a 'large transparency,' representing beautiful sirens, when they saw the internal reality, 'a black-looking specimen of dried monkey and fish;' but the adventure was successful. The rage for seeing this coarse fiction infected editors of papers as well as the less enlightened public, and is described as the 'mermaid fever' by Mr Barnum, who boasts that he sold 10,000 'mermaid pamphlets.'

The next adventure cast both the mermaid and the venerable negress into the shade. Mr Barnum had heard of a remarkably small child named Charles Stratton. 'He was only *five* years old, and to exhibit a dwarf of that age might provoke the question: "How do you know that he *is* a dwarf?"' Consequently, the caterer for public amusement advertised the little boy as 'General Tom Thumb, a dwarf of *eleven* years of age, just arrived from England!' In fact, he came from Bridgeport, in Connecticut. With this curiosity, Mr Barnum started to make the tour of Europe.

Having arrived in London, he determined to begin the imposition among the highest classes of society, and accordingly hired a respectable house in the West End, whence he sent 'letters of invitation to the editors and several of the nobility,' to visit the little boy. The invitation was readily accepted, and it soon became fashionable to call on the tiny general. 'Mr Everett, the American minister, called,' and 'was highly pleased.' The Baroness Rothschild sent her carriage for 'the dwarf and Mr Barnum,' who says: 'On taking our leave, an elegant and well-filled purse was quietly slipped into my hand, and I felt that the golden shower was beginning to fall! The same trick was played upon me, shortly afterwards, at the mansion of Mr Drummond,' the eminent banker. Greater distinction followed, when a placard on the door of the Egyptian Hall announced that the exhibition would be closed one evening, as 'General Tom Thumb would be at Buckingham Palace, by command of Her Majesty.' Thrice the general appeared at court: this made success sure in town, as in the provinces. Portraits of the dwarf were given in pictorial papers—Tom Thumb Polkas and Quadrilles were published; *Punch*, as Mr Barnum states, gave caricatures, which assisted in bringing in funds. 'Besides his three public performances per day, the little general attended from three to four private parties per week, for which we were paid eight to ten guineas each.' The Queen-dowager, Adelaide, presented to the diminutive boy 'a beautiful little gold-watch, placing the chain around his neck with her own hands.' His Grace the Duke of Devonshire contributed to the Tom Thumb Museum 'an elegant gold snuff-box mounted with turquoise.' 'The Duke of Wellington called frequently to see the little general.' Mr Barnum adds: 'At the various parties which we attended, we met, in the course of the season, nearly all the nobility.'

A remarkable success rewarded the enterprising showman in France, where he 'visited King Louis-Philippe and the royal family on four different occasions.' In Paris, 'the general made a great hit as an actor. He performed for two months at one of the leading theatres, in a French play,' entitled *Petit Poucet,* written expressly for him.

Having returned to America, the dwarf was allowed to visit his native place, Bridgeport, where the people were much delighted to see their old friend 'little Charlie' again. 'They little thought, when they saw him playing about the streets a few years previously, that he was destined to create such a sensation among the crowned heads of the Old World.' 'How old are you, general?' asked one of his acquaintances. 'As Mr Barnum makes it out, I am fifteen,' said the general, laughing, for he was aware that the inquirer knew his true age to be only *nine.*

The next great speculation consisted in a contract made with the *prima donna* Jenny Lind. Mr Barnum, who had never heard this lady's voice, determined to advertise her vocal powers and private virtues throughout the Union, and to pay 1000 dollars, besides all the expenses, for each concert. The popular furor for Jenny Lind was extreme: as the speculator himself declares, 'the facts, at this late day, seem, even to myself, more like a dream than a reality.' Bayard Taylor, a poet, was employed to write a prize ode on the 'nightingale's' arrival in America. Biographies of the Swedish nightingale were largely circulated. 'Foreign correspondence glorified her talents and triumphs by narratives of her benevolence, and printer's ink was employed in every possible form to put and keep Jenny Lind before the people.'[1]

The receipts for ninety-five concerts amounted to more than 712,000 dollars, of which sum the portion of 176,000 dollars and upwards was paid to Miss Lind; while the sum of more than 535,000 dollars was claimed, according to contract, by Mr Barnum. On one occasion, the sum of 625 dollars was paid for a ticket.

This was the adventurer's climax of success. Having made his fortune, he retired to his mansion, built in the style of the Brighton pavilion, and styled Iranistan. The grandeur of his principal schemes has induced us to overlook several minor speculations which more or less assisted his progress. In 1844, he had engaged the Lancashire bell-ringers for an American

[1] In justice to this lady, it should be stated that she was ignorant of many of the stratagems practised by the showman.

tour, and one of the stipulations was, that these performers 'should suffer their moustaches to grow, assume a picturesque dress, and be known as the Swiss bell-ringers!' As a compensation to England for the loss of the bell-ringers, he sent the party of Iowa Indians to London.

Various giants and dwarfs, the Scotch Boys, the Bateman Children, and an importation of ten elephants for the Great Asiatic Caravan, Museum, and Menagerie, are included in Mr Barnum's list of all the attractions he has offered to the public.

In 1848, the daring showman observed a horse of rather small size, without any mane, and with rough or curly hair on the limbs and body. In itself, this was scarcely a wonder great enough to excite the public mind; but at this time the adventures of Colonel Fremont in the Rocky Mountains were regarded with interest. Mr Barnum now set the press to work to circulate the story, that the bold colonel, with a band of warriors, had, after a chase of incredible difficulty, captured a strange nondescript animal which might be styled 'the woolly horse.' A picture represented the animal in the act of leaping over a valley five miles wide, and an advertisement described nature as exerting 'all her ingenuity in the production of this astounding animal—extremely complex —made up of the elephant, deer, horse, buffalo, camel, and sheep.' Tolerable success rewarded this imposture, though the exhibiter was arrested on a charge of obtaining money under false pretences. On another occasion, a small herd of tamed and harmless calf-buffaloes was advertised as a 'grand buffalo-hunt,' illustrating the 'wild sports of the western prairies;' but though the poor creatures were sharply goaded, they refused to move. In justification of these and other similar exhibitions, the writer pleads that he has done good service to the state by promoting popular recreations, and adds: 'As a business-man, undoubtedly, my prime object has been to put money in my purse. I succeeded beyond my most sanguine anticipations, and am satisfied; but what I have here said will prepare the reader for what I conceive to be a just and altogether reasonable claim, that I have been a public benefactor, to an extent seldom paralleled in the histories of professed and professional philanthropists.'

There is nothing in this autobiography, regarded as a literary work, which might lead us to doubt its authorship. Undoubtedly, the man who could impose General Tom Thumb on the crowned heads of Europe, must have been clever enough to write this account of his own successes. But one feature in the life suggests the notion that some literary hack may have been employed to compile the book, and, weary of the subject, may have endeavoured, here and there, to relieve it by a stroke of satire. We allude to the passages in which the assumed author advertises his own—piety. Thus he supports some of his own views by a reference to the 'venerable and illustrious name of —Channing; eminent alike for wisdom, benevolence, piety, and purity.' Soon after making the confession of an imposition respecting the age and birthplace of the dwarf-child, he moralises in the following vein:—'Though many people may not see how my profession of a showman can be made to appear consistent with my profession of another kind, I must claim having always revered the Christian religion. I have been indebted to Christianity for the most serene happiness of my life, and I would not part with its consolations for all things else in the world. In all my journeys as a showman, the Bible has been my companion, and I have repeatedly read it attentively from beginning to end. Whether I have or have not been profited by its precepts, is a question not here to be considered; but the scriptural doctrine of the government of God, and its happy issue in the life to come, has been my chief solace in affliction and sorrow, and I hope always to cherish it as my greatest treasure.' And the writer closes his work with the self-complacent and hopeful words: 'I am at home, in the bosom of my family; and home and family are the highest and most expressive symbols of the kingdom of heaven.' These incongruities are our only reasons for entertaining any doubt of the authorship of the book. It appears, at first sight, improbable that a writer would suggest the severest censure on his own impostures by a reference to that religion which demands a rigid adherence to truth.

Our only apology for noticing this work has been already given—it is a representative book. It might be passed over in silence, if it merely reflected discredit on the writer. It would be great injustice to use it for the purpose of pointing any censure of American characteristics; but it may be fairly quoted to illustrate that state of taste and education *on both sides* of the Atlantic which has insured such success to Mr Barnum. While genius and learning were toiling vainly for recognition and reward; while plans of national education and popular improvement were, to say the least, coldly regarded by the wealthy and powerful classes; all circles of society—excepting the lower, to which he hardly condescended—were open to receive the dwarf-boy with his showman! At the time when the painter Haydon, in his misery and despair, lifted the fatal pistol to his head, the aristocracy—the best people of the realm—were crowding to the levees of Tom Thumb and Barnum. In the provinces, in our county towns—each surrounded by its ignorant and helpless peasantry, calling for aid—the higher classes, the *élite* of their respective neighbourhoods, might be seen in the train of the American speculator; and high-born and beautiful ladies, lavish of their homage, pressed forward in eager competition for a kiss from the wearied dwarf! In places where an intellectual lecturer could not calculate on 'a respectable audience,' crowds listened with delight to the tiny boy's eulogium on the British court, which he had been taught, in parrot style, to describe concisely as 'first-rate!' The book that records these facts has a certain significance—it suggests thought as well as laughter. Mr Barnum is the author of a very severe satire.

VOYAGES AND TRAVELS—NATURAL HISTORY.

A few works in this department may be classed with general literature; but the most important results of travel—including those of the *United States' Exploring Expedition* (1838–1842)—belong to the special literature of the several sciences. The *Narrative* of this expedition by CHARLES WILKES, United States' Navy, is an extensive work in five large volumes, and gives accounts of visits to Chili, Peru, and several groups of islands in the South Seas. A condensed summary in one volume has been published.

It is difficult to select from the mass of books of voyages and travels, those most worthy of notice in a review of American literature. Professor SILLIMAN'S *Journal* of travels in various parts of Europe; *A Year in Europe*, by JOHN GRISCOM; CARTER'S *Letters from Europe;* and the *Leaves of a Journal in North Britain and Ireland*, by ANDREW BIGELOW—these may be mentioned as specimens of works that have more than an ephemeral interest. The *Reminiscences of Spain*, by CALEB CUSHING, may be described as a miscellany of fact and fiction, written on a plan resembling that of Irving's *Sketch-book*. *Four Years in Great Britain*, by CALVIN COLTON, gives too many details of well-known objects. *Ship and Shore*, and *A Visit to Constantinople and Athens*, by WALTER COLTON, have been commended as lively and pleasant books.

Among the contributions to literature by sea-faring men, *A Narrative of Voyages and Commercial Enterprises*, by RICHARD J. CLEVELAND, must be mentioned. DANA'S *Two Years Before the Mast* is a well-written account of a sailor's life. The writer is the son of Richard H. Dana, the essayist.

The books of travel by Lieutenant SLIDELL, J. G. SHEA,

CARPENTER, KENDALL, CARNES, and WALLIS, might be noticed, if our limits would allow fair treatment of their respective merits.

JOHN LLOYD STEPHENS (1805–1852), author of *Incidents of Travel in Egypt, Arabia, Palestine, Yucatan, and Central America*, was a man of enterprising character, whose life was mainly spent in voyages and journeys, of which his several works gave unstudied but lively and graphic notices. He was born in New Jersey, educated in the city of New York, and, after a course of legal studies, was advised to travel for the benefit of his health. In 1834–36, he visited Italy, Greece, Turkey, and Russia, returning by the way of Poland and Germany to France. Hence he sailed for Alexandria, and ascended the Nile as far as Thebes. The results of this pilgrimage were given in his *Incidents of Travel* in the several countries mentioned, which were published in 1836–37, and had an extensive circulation in Europe, as in America. About two years later, he was appointed special ambassador to Central America, and visited Chiapas and Yucatan, returning to the latter country in 1842. Of his political objects in this journey, he jocosely said, that he had travelled over all Guatemala, looking in vain for the government to which he was accredited; so, failing to find sufficient occupation in diplomacy, he turned aside to study the antiquities of Yucatan. His speculations, though based on personal observation without the advantage of antiquarian learning, correspond with the views given by Prescott in the introduction to the *History of Mexico*. The truthfulness of Stephens has, we believe, never been doubted; but it has been suggested that a greater share of learning might have given a higher value to his laborious researches. In 1849, he engaged with others in the enterprise of the Panama Railway, and visited the isthmus for the purpose of exploring the route. His zeal in this great undertaking of connecting the two oceans, induced him to make greater exertions than his physical strength could support; and soon after his return, he died at the early age of forty-seven.

Several interesting narratives of travel might be selected from the rather extensive literature of Christian missions. As specimens of this class of books, we may mention *A Tour in Armenia*, by ELI SMITH and H. G. O. DWIGHT; and *A Visit to the South Seas*, &c., by CHARLES S. STEWART, a chaplain in the navy. Memoirs of travels in Switzerland, by the Rev. G. CHEEVER, have appeared under the titles, *The Pilgrim in the Shadow of Mont Blanc*, and *The Pilgrim in the Shadow of the Jungfrau*. A religious tendency characterises these works; and it has been remarked that the writer, in his endeavour to preserve a tone of piety, has thought it necessary to refer frequently to his own creed. Mr Cheever contributed many articles to reviews and other periodicals, and wrote several theological works, including *Lectures on the Pilgrim's Progress*, and *the Life and Times of John Bunyan.*

Among recent books of travel, the writings of J. T. HEADLEY must be noticed on account of their pleasant style. His *Letters from Italy, the Alps, and the Rhine*, published in 1844, have been followed by *Sketches and Rambles*, and several other works. It should be added, that the unassuming and easy tone of the *Letters from Italy* will not be found in the author's later works—*Napoleon and his Marshals*, and the *Sacred Mountains*. BAYARD TAYLOR'S graphic sketches of travels in the East deserve more than a passing notice; but they belong to a class of recent books too numerous to be fairly described in our review.

In connection with books of travel, we may notice here the literary portion of two of the most beautiful works in natural history—*The American Ornithology* by Wilson, and *The Birds of America* by Audubon.

Scotland must claim the honour of having sent the pioneer of ornithology—ALEXANDER WILSON—into the woods of America. He arrived in 1794, and after years of poverty and striving, was enabled to prosecute, though with much difficulty, his favourite study. His enthusiasm could not be understood by those from whom he had hoped to receive encouragement. When he sallied forth, in 1808, to find subscribers to his work on the birds of America, he was able to collect, after all his pains and humiliation, only forty-one names: in several places he was received as a singular fanatic, or as a suspicious character, cloaking political designs under pretence of the study of nature; for there were many who could not conceive how any sane man would endure poverty and hardship, and forego the winning of dollars, for the love of natural history. 'The subjects of his art and inquiry were not playthings to him: they were intimate and familiar friends; their voice was not music, but language; instead of dying away upon the ear, it went down into his soul. To him the notes with which they heralded the spring were full of glory; and when, in the autumn, they heard far off the trumpet of the storm, and sang their farewell to the woods, it was solemn and affecting, as if it were breathed from a living and beating heart. To others, this interest seemed senseless and excessive; but he was one of those who never smile at the depth and earnestness of their own emotions. When he described the birds, he spoke of their habits and manners as if they were intelligent things; and thus he has given a life and charm to his descriptions, which will make his work the chief attraction of the science in our country for many years to come.'[1] Years after Wilson had passed through his heavy discouragements, the best of the American reviews was *entreating* the wealthy classes to assist Audubon, and reminding them of the fact, that among ten millions of people, the Scotch pioneer had failed to find more than two hundred subscribers to his beautiful work.

JOHN JAMES AUDUBON, author of a splendid work on *The Birds of America*, was born in Louisiana about the year 1782. His name will ever be remembered in connection with natural history; and the graceful and happy descriptions of forest-adventures, interspersed with his sketches of birds in the *Ornithological Biography*, justly claim for him a place in our series of American authors. He was an intelligent and enthusiastic student of nature, endowed with the feeling and imagination of a poet, and blending in his deportment the refinement of a gentleman with the simplicity and frankness of a backwoodsman.[2]

After studying in Paris, where he took lessons in drawing from the painter David, Audubon, when eighteen years old, returned to America, and began farming. He was for some time engaged in commercial pursuits, but his love of art and natural history led him away from the haunts of trade; and in 1811 we find him in Florida, employed as a sportsman and artist—now shooting a deer, a squirrel, or a turkey, or hooking a trout to provide for himself a meal; then writing or drawing a sketch of some beautiful bird; spending the day in arduous journeys, to add to the pages of his Ornithology, and resting at night under a shed of green boughs. After some years of lonely wanderings in the forests of the West, he returned to Philadelphia in 1824, and visited New York, where he was encouraged to proceed in preparing his splendid work on *The Birds of America*. In 1826, he visited Edinburgh, and there found several warm friends.

Subsequently, he received the highest honours from scientific men in Paris, London, and Boston, United States, and persevered in labouring for the completion of his great undertaking. In 1830, he had issued his first volume, containing one hundred plates, representing ninety-nine species of birds, every figure of the size and colour of life. In 1834, he was again in Edinburgh, finished the second volume of *The Birds of America*, and published

[1] *North American Review*, No. 75.

[2] This is the estimate of Audubon's character given by his friend Professor Wilson, but we have not quoted the exact words.

another volume of his *Ornithological Biography*. In 1839, having returned to his native country, he commenced publishing the octavo edition of his great work, of which the seventh and last volume appeared in 1844. Of the folio edition, Cuvier said: 'It is the most splendid monument which art has erected in honour of ornithology.'

This work, and the accompanying biography, gave to the world the results of almost a whole life devoted to travel and adventure, 'amid the tall grass of the far-extended prairies of the west—in the solemn forests of the north—on the heights of the midland mountains—by the shores of the boundless ocean, and on the bosoms of our vast bays, lakes, and rivers; searching for things hidden, since the creation of this wondrous world, from all but the Indian who has roamed in the gorgeous but melancholy wilderness.'

While the people's edition of *The Birds of America* was in course of publication, Audubon recommenced his travels, to prepare materials for his new work on *The Quadrupeds of America*, of which the first volume of biographies appeared in 1847.

The following extract from Audubon's numerous lively descriptions of scenery and adventure, is beautiful in itself, and serves to illustrate the rapid progress of society in America:—

DESCENT OF THE OHIO IN 1809.

'It was in the month of October. The autumnal tints already decorated the shores of that queen of rivers, the Ohio. Every tree was hung with long and flowing festoons of different species of vines, many loaded with clustered fruits of varied brilliancy, their rich bronzed carmine mingling beautifully with the yellow foliage, which now predominated over the yet green leaves, reflecting more lively tints from the clear stream than ever landscape-painter portrayed or poet imagined.

The days were yet warm. The sun had assumed the rich and glowing hue which at that season produces the singular phenomenon called there the Indian summer. The moon had rather passed the meridian of her grandeur. We glided down the river, meeting no other ripple of the water than that formed by the propulsion of our boat. Leisurely we moved along, gazing all day on the grandeur and beauty of the wild scenery around us.

Now and then a large cat-fish rose to the surface of the water in pursuit of a shoal of fry, which, starting simultaneously from the liquid element, like so many silvery arrows, produced a shower of light, while the pursuer with open jaws seized the stragglers, and with a splash of his tail disappeared from our view. Other fishes we heard uttering beneath our bark a rumbling noise, the strange sounds of which we discovered to proceed from the white perch, for, on casting our net from the bow, we caught several of that species, when the noise ceased for a time.

Nature, in her varied arrangements, seems to have felt a partiality toward this portion of our country. As the traveller ascends or descends the Ohio, he cannot help remarking that alternately, nearly the whole length of the river, the margin on one side is bounded by lofty hills and a rolling surface; while on the other, extensive plains of the richest alluvial land are seen as far as the eye can command the view. Islands of varied size and form rise here and there from the bosom of the water, and the winding course of the stream frequently brings you to places where the idea of being on a river of great length changes to that of floating on a lake of moderate extent. Some of these islands are of considerable size and value; while others, small and insignificant, seem as if intended for contrast, and as serving to enhance the general interest of the scenery. These little islands are frequently overflowed during great *freshets* or floods, and receive at their heads prodigious heaps of drifted timber. We foresaw with great concern the alteration that cultivation would soon produce along those delightful banks.

As night came, sinking in darkness the broader portions of the river, our minds became affected by strong emotions, and wandered far beyond the present moments. The tinkling of bells told us that the cattle which bore them were gently roving from valley to valley in search of food, or returning to their distant homes. The hooting of the great owl, or the muffled noise of its wings as it sailed smoothly over the stream, were matters of interest to us; so was the sound of the boatman's horn, as it came winding more and more softly from afar. When daylight returned, many songsters burst forth with echoing notes, more and more mellow to the listening ear. Here and there the lonely cabin of a squatter struck the eye, giving note of commencing civilisation. The crossing of the stream by a deer foretold how soon the hills would be covered with snow.

Many sluggish flat-boats we overtook and passed: some laden with produce from the different head-waters of the small rivers that pour their tributary streams into the Ohio; others, of less dimensions, crowded with emigrants from distant parts, in search of a new home. Purer pleasures I never felt; nor have you, reader, I ween, unless indeed you have felt the like, and in such company. . . . .

When I think of the times, and call back to my mind the grandeur and beauty of those almost uninhabited shores; when I picture to myself the dense and lofty summits of the forest, that everywhere spread along the hills, and overhung the margins of the stream, unmolested by the axe of the settler; when I know how dearly purchased the safe navigation of that river has been by the blood of many worthy Virginians; when I see that no longer any aborigines are to be found there, and that the vast herds of elks, deer, and buffaloes which once pastured on these hills and in these valleys, making for themselves great roads to the several salt-springs, have ceased to exist; when I reflect that all this grand portion of our Union, instead of being in a state of nature, is now more or less covered with villages, farms, and towns, where the din of hammers and machinery is constantly heard; that the woods are fast disappearing under the axe by day, and the fire by night; that hundreds of steam-boats are gliding to and fro, over the whole length of the majestic river, forcing commerce to take root and to prosper at every spot; when I see the surplus population of Europe coming to assist in the destruction of the forest, and transplanting civilisation into its darkest recesses; when I remember that these extraordinary changes have all taken place in the short period of twenty years, I pause, wonder, and—although I know all to be fact—can scarcely believe its reality.'

As life becomes more and more artificial in our crowded towns and ways of commerce, we may suppose that, by a natural love of contrast, such books as these by Wilson and Audubon, breathing the spirit of the western forests, will increase in their attractiveness. It is delightful to forget, for a time, all the troubles of mankind, and the never-ending questions of social life, and to go out with the enthusiast and hold converse with the merry boblink and the versatile mocking-bird. So numerous and so charming are the sketches of birds by the pen and the pencil of Audubon, that a few specimens can give no fair idea of his rich variety. He has widened our field of observation, and has given us, at our firesides, impressions of the vivid pleasures for which he travelled so many leagues through the forests and along the rivers. The belted kingfisher, sitting, as in a trance, or glancing with a passing lustre along the bank of the lonely stream; the versatile boblink; the purple martin; the blue jay; the snowbird, drifting along in the wintry storm; the crimson oriole, falling like a flake of fire in the forest; the cat-bird, injuriously named, for he can sing sweetly; the crimson linnet, with his flute-like song: all these, and a host of other feathered friends, have their colours represented and their habits faithfully described in the splendid pages of Audubon. We here select a sketch, prefixing a short account of the writer's mode of life while pursuing his researches in the forest.

THE LIFE OF A NATURALIST.

'The adventures and vicissitudes which have fallen to my lot, instead of tending to diminish the fervid enthusiasm of my nature, have imparted a toughness to my bodily constitution, naturally strong, and to my mind, naturally buoyant, an elasticity such as to assure me that though somewhat old, and considerably denuded in the frontal region, I could yet perform on foot a journey of any length, were I sure that I should thereby add materially to our knowledge of the ever-interesting creatures which have for so long a time occupied my thoughts by day, and filled my dreams with pleasant images. Nay, reader, had I a new lease of life presented to me, I should choose for it the very occupations in which I have been engaged.

And, reader, the life which I have led has been, in some respects, a singular one. Think of a person intent on such pursuits as mine have been, aroused at early dawn from his rude couch on the alder-fringed brook of some northern valley, or in the midst of some yet unexplored forest of the west, or perhaps on the soft and warm sands of the Florida shores, and listening to the pleasing melodies of songsters innumerable saluting the magnificent orb, from whose radiant influence the creatures of many worlds receive life and light. Refreshed and reinvigorated by healthful rest, he starts upon his feet, gathers up his store of curiosities, buckles on his knapsack, shoulders his trusty firelock, says a kind word to his faithful dog, and recommences his pursuit of zoological knowledge. Now the morning is spent, and a squirrel or a trout affords him a repast. Should the day be warm, he reposes for a time under the shade of some tree. The woodland choristers again burst forth into song, and he starts anew to wander wherever his fancy may direct him, or the objects of his search may lead him in pursuit. When evening approaches, and the birds are seen betaking themselves to the retreats, he looks for some place of safety, erects his shed of green boughs, kindles his fire, prepares his meal; and as the widgeon or blue-winged teal, or perhaps the breast of a turkey or a steak of venison, sends its delicious perfumes abroad, he enters into his parchment-bound journal the remarkable incidents and facts that have occurred in the course of the day. Darkness has now drawn her sable curtain over the scene; his repast is finished, and kneeling on the earth, he raises his soul to Heaven, grateful for the protection that has been granted to him, and the sense of the Divine presence in this solitary place. Then wishing a cordial good-night to all the dear friends at home, the American woodsman wraps himself up in his blanket, and closing his eyes, soon falls into that comfortable sleep which never fails him on such occasions.'

THE HUMMING-BIRD.

'Where is the person, who, on observing this glittering fragment of the rainbow, would not pause, admire, and instantly turn his mind with reverence toward the Almighty Creator, the wonders of whose hand we at every step discover, and of whose sublime conceptions we everywhere observe the manifestations in his admirable system of creation?—There breathes not such a person, so kindly have we all been blessed with that intuitive and noble feeling—admiration!

No sooner has the returning sun again introduced the vernal season, and caused millions of plants to expand their leaves and blossoms to his genial beams, than the little humming-bird is seen advancing on fairy wings, carefully visiting every opening flower-cup, and, like a curious florist, removing from each the injurious insects that otherwise would erelong cause their beauteous petals to droop and decay. Poised in the air, it is observed peeping cautiously, and with sparkling eye, into their innermost recesses; whilst the ethereal motions of its pinions, so rapid and so light, appear to fan and cool the flower, without injuring its fragile texture, and produce a delightful murmuring sound, well adapted for lulling the insects to repose. . . . .

The prairies, the fields, the orchards and gardens, nay, the deepest shades of the forests, are all visited in their turn, and everywhere the little bird meets with pleasure and with food. Its gorgeous throat in beauty and brilliancy baffles all competition. Now it glows with a fiery hue, and again it is changed to the deepest velvety black. The upper parts of its delicate body are of resplendent changing green; and it throws itself through the air with a swiftness and vivacity hardly conceivable. It moves from one flower to another like a gleam of light—upwards, downwards, to the right, and to the left. In this manner, it searches the extreme northern portions of our country, following, with great precaution, the advances of the season, and retreats with equal care at the approach of autumn.'

THEOLOGY AND MORAL PHILOSOPHY.

In the department of Theology and Biblical literature, American works of the present century are far too numerous to be adequately described in this brief review.

Among the earlier writers of the present century, prominence may be given to the names of JOSEPH S. BUCKMINSTER, JOHN M. MASON, and EDWARD PAYSON—writers of discourses which have been described as good examples of pulpit oratory.

In polemical theology, and especially in the controversy between Orthodoxy and Unitarianism, the more eminent of the orthodox writers are NOAH WORCESTER, SAMUEL WORCESTER, MOSES STUART, and LEONARD WOODS; while on the latter side, the names of WILLIAM ELLERY CHANNING, HENRY WARE, ANDREWS NORTON, and BERNARD WHITMAN may be noticed. During the last thirty years, or rather more, an important movement has taken place in theological opinions. The Unitarians, under the leadership of Dr Channing, have become a considerable party, having a large share of influence in general literature. A distinction must be made between the Unitarians of the old school—if we may so speak—and other writers, including Dr WALKER, W. B. GREENE, and THEODORE PARKER, who have assumed a wider latitude of opinion, and have attempted to make innovations in theology and moral philosophy. The views of Theodore Parker are given in his *Discourse on Matters Pertaining to Religion.* His *Critical and Miscellaneous Writings* comprise essays on German Literature, the Education of the Labouring Class, and Thoughts on Labour, and other papers deserving commendation as examples of a clear style of writing. This is the more noticeable from its being evident that the writer has studied German authors who have buried their thoughts under a mass of confused verbiage.

Apart from controversy—some of the most valuable writings of American divines are found in the department of Biblical literature. The *Notes on the Gospels*, by ALBERT BARNES, has had a wide circulation in England as in the United States. Dr ROBINSON, formerly editor of the *Bibliotheca Sacra*, commenced in 1843, is the author of an important work, entitled *Biblical Researches in Palestine*, published in 1841. It gives the results of extensive studies and travels in the East, and has been highly commended by the best Biblical scholars of our age. GEORGE BUSH, a learned divine, who holds the views of Swedenborg, is the writer of works intended partly to oppose the literal reading of certain parts of Scripture. His principal work is a treatise entitled *Anastasis*, in which he has controverted the commonly received doctrine of the resurrection.

The commentaries on several parts of the New Testament and other theological writings by MOSES STUART, have gained a very high reputation in the Biblical literature of our times. A *New Translation of the Psalms* and other lyrical parts of the Old Testament, by G. R. NOYES, D.D.; a treatise *On the Evidences of the Genuineness of the Gospels*, by ANDREWS NORTON; and the *Lectures on the Evidences of Christianity*, by Bishop M'ILVAINE of Ohio: these are mentioned as representatives of valuable works which cannot be particularly and fairly noticed here.

Several theological writers have contributed to the department of moral philosophy and metaphysics. The treatises of JONATHAN EDWARDS, and his son, the younger Edwards, have been briefly described in a former part of this work. The writings of JOHN SMALLEY (1734–1820), including a treatise on *Natural and Moral Inability*, seem to belong to the last century. Among other works of the same class, we may mention *Outlines of Moral Science*, by Dr ALEXANDER; *The Elements of Mental and Moral Science*, by GEORGE PAYNE; *The Elements of Moral Science*, by FRANCIS WAYLAND; *Mental Philosophy*, by THOMAS C. UPHAM; the writings of H. P. TAPPAN; and several works on psychology by LAURENS P. HICKOK.

Modern writers on metaphysics may be mainly divided into

two classes—the former, including those who have adhered, more or less strictly, to the general principles of Locke, is represented by FRANCIS BOWEN, editor of the *North American Review;* while the latter—including JAMES MARSH, EMERSON, WALKER, GREENE, PARKER, and other writers—is characterised partly by a rejection of Locke's theory. Emerson is regarded as the leader of the 'transcendentalists,' and has borrowed the results of the speculations of Fichte; while others have adopted, more or less, the views of German idealism or French eclecticism. JAMES MARSH expounded the philosophical doctrine of Coleridge. More recently, the Positive Philosophy of M. Comte has been introduced in the writings of ORESTES A. BROWNSON.

In the following notices, prominence is given to the works of Dr Channing and Dr Dewey, as representatives of moral philosophy. It is hardly necessary to say that their theological opinions have no influence on our estimate of their literary merit. Channing's essays may be classed under the title of moral philosophy, and Dewey's discourses may be correctly described as practical moral essays.

WILLIAM ELLERY CHANNING.

This eminent divine and moral philosopher was born at Newport in Rhode Island, 7th April 1780. 'I thank God,' he said in one of his sermons, 'that this beautiful island was the place of my birth.' Here Roger Williams, the apostle of religious liberty, had laboured and suffered for the truth, and had left a commonwealth pervaded by his own spirit. The venerable founder of Rhode Island, in his quaint and rugged prose, had uttered, in the early part of the seventeenth century, the doctrine of religious freedom which was developed by Channing.

When fourteen years old, Channing entered Harvard College, where he graduated with the highest honours in the year 1798. After leaving Cambridge, he resided as a private tutor with a family in Virginia, and, during this time, his sedentary and studious habits impaired his health, which always remained delicate. Of a subsequent course of study in his native place he writes: 'I had two noble places of study—one the edifice, now so frequented and useful as a public library; then so deserted that I spent day after day, and sometimes week after week, amidst its dusty volumes without interruption from a single visitor: the other the beach, my daily resort, dear to me in the sunshine, still more attractive in the storm. Seldom do I visit it now without thinking of the work, which there, in the sight of that beauty, in the sound of those waves, was carried on in my soul. No spot on earth has helped to form me so much as that beach. There I lifted up my voice in praise amid the tempest. There, softened by beauty, I poured out my thanksgiving and contrite confession. There, in reverential sympathy with the mighty Power around me, I became conscious of power within. There struggling thoughts and emotions broke forth, as if moved to utterance by nature's eloquence of the winds and waves. There began a happiness surpassing all worldly pleasures, all gifts of fortune—the happiness of communing with the works of God.'

In 1803 he was ordained pastor of the church in Federal Street, Boston. Though his health was feeble, his services were so acceptable that it was soon found necessary to build a larger place of worship. In the distinctive articles of his creed he was a Unitarian; but the use of this term must remind us that such names give no fair definition of character. Channing said of himself: 'I am little of a Unitarian;' and his friends have said that he was more nearly related to Fénélon than to Priestley. His sermon on 'Unitarian Christianity,' preached at Baltimore in 1819, is perhaps the best of his writings on dogmatic theology. In the following year, he published his *Moral Argument against Calvinism.* But controversial divinity was by no means his favourite study. Of his sermon, entitled *Man the Image of his Maker*, it is said, that the reading of it has been an era in the lives of many students.

In 1823, Channing published an essay on *National Literature*, which was followed by *Remarks on the Character and Writings of John Milton* (1826), and by *Remarks on the Life and Character of Napoleon Bonaparte.* In this review, he judges the military hero by an ideal standard, rather than by fair comparison with other men of the same class. Channing found a more congenial theme in the *Character and Writings of Fénélon*, of which he wrote a review for the *Christian Examiner* in 1829. Already, in 1816, he had written against war; and again, in 1835 and 1839, he appeared as the earnest advocate of peace. In all these writings, the amiable traits of his own character appeared prominently, as in the *Address on Self-culture* (1838), which served as an introduction to a course of *Lectures on the Elevation of the Labouring Portion of the Community.* Though Channing was not connected with any anti-slavery society, he wrote with clearness and earnestness against the great social evil of the United States, and his arguments against slavery exerted a beneficial influence on public opinion. In these and other lectures and essays he founded his principles of morals, politics, and theology on his idea of the true object of human life. He subordinated all other cultivation, physical, intellectual, and social, to the culture of man as a moral and religious being. Regarded from this point of view, all his writings are consistent parts of one doctrine, and his life perfectly harmonised with his principles. He was highly esteemed as a friend and a citizen. Of his daily conversation it has been said, that it was even better than his printed discourses. 'He disliked being styled reverend,' and wished that the members of his congregation would regard him as a thoughtful brother, and not as a professional man. 'He would not have been the head of a sect if he could. He loved his religious opinions, but was anxious not to love them in such a way as to get bigoted to them.'

In his domestic life and social relations, Channing was fortunate, though often depressed by the want of physical health. He passed the last few years of his life in retirement, living in Boston during winter, and at Newport, his birthplace, in summer, where he often enjoyed the society of his friends, Allston the painter and Dana the essayist, who had shared in the pleasures of his early days. His last public address was a speech delivered in August 1842, in commemoration of the British emancipation of slaves. In October of the same year, he was seized with typhus fever while travelling, and died at Bennington, in Vermont.[1] His memoirs, as a friend has said, give emphasis to almost every sentence of his writings, 'and now his simple name is a nobler thing than even the books themselves of many other writers.'

The writings of Channing consist of essays and discourses, all marked by the characteristics of an abstract thinker. Of the thousandfold varieties of human life, its stern realities, its inconsistencies, and the difficulties it ever opposes to the schemes of the philanthropist, Channing gives no faithful delineation. He writes generally in abstract terms, of will, conscience, intellect, and moral and religious culture. The same idea everywhere presents itself in his essays and discourses; the culture of the human soul is constantly asserted as the only true end of religion, philosophy, literature, society, and government. 'The human soul,' we read, 'is greater, more sacred than the state, and must never be sacrificed to it. Thrones which have stood for ages are to meet the doom pronounced upon all man's works. . . . . But man is older than nations, and he is to survive nations. . . . . He has rights by nature. In the order of things, they precede society, lie at its foundation, constitute man's capacity for it, and are the great objects of social institutions. . . . . A human being is a member of the community—not as a limb is a member of the body, or as a wheel is a part of a machine, intended only to contribute to some

[1] *Memoirs of William Ellery Channing;* edited by his nephew, William Henry Channing.

general joint result. He was created, not to be merged in the whole, as a drop in the ocean, or as a particle of sand on the sea-shore, and to aid only in composing a mass. He is an ultimate being, made for his own perfection as his highest end—made to maintain an individual existence, and to serve others only as far as consists with his own virtue and progress.' These few sentences may indicate the purport of Channing's moral and political philosophy.

The lectures on Self-culture and the Elevation of the Labouring Classes are noble in their protest against the laws of custom which separate the various classes of society. It may be said that the writer develops nothing new—that his doctrine of the right of all men to enjoy opportunities of culture is everywhere admitted in theory, though denied in practice; but truths as old as the hills must be repeated again and again, in order to moderate, if not to abolish, the tyranny of custom. Channing was no leveller—he admitted the necessity of various degrees of wealth and power among men; but at the same time he contended that, without any disturbance of social order, the walls of separation between the several classes might be removed by the gradual process of a truly liberal education. After reading his hopeful doctrines, we regret that society in its movement remains so far behind the pioneers of progress; that truths so often repeated as to become tiresome in literature, have still to find their place in real life; and that the habits and fashions of the world, for which we can assign no good reason, are still stronger than the best philosophy.

Nothing can be clearer or more rational than Channing's main doctrine in these lectures:—'Men may work in different departments of life, and yet recognise their brotherly relation, and honour one another, and hold friendly communion with one another.' Every reader admits this abstract proposition—it is, at least, as old as Christianity, and forms a part of the creed of Christendom; but when the writer proceeds to apply it, and to suggest that, without disturbing the order of society, a true education should remove all vain distinctions, and should introduce the working-man to the saloons of the wealthy, we doubt the propriety of choosing the saloon as the meeting-ground.

The style of Channing's essays and discourses has been often commended. His style is indeed clear, generally correct, and well adapted to its purpose—the assertion of isolated propositions—but it wants variety. Its pattern, however neat, is so small, and so uniformly repeated in every part, that we may select almost any passage as a fair specimen of the whole. His essays may be divided into a number of short paragraphs, each almost as clear and self-explanatory as if it had been written without any context. One short sentence follows another; while in their general structure the several paragraphs bear a close resemblance to each other. There is a certain beauty in this mode of writing, but it is the beauty of a trim garden, laid out on a small scale, and without the charming diversities of nature.

Of Channing's theological and polemical works, no detailed account can be given in this place. He began his course of public teaching at a time when religious faith was disturbed; when the Calvinistic creed, which had prevailed ever since the settlement of New England, was losing its influence in the neighbourhood of Boston. Many inquirers were led to adopt the general principles of the Unitarians; others proceeded further in innovation, and claimed a latitude of opinion more or less resembling that of the German rationalists and idealists. Channing adhered to the Unitarians, so far as he belonged to any party. In defending his views, 'he was never betrayed by the ardour of discussion into intemperance in language or extravagance in doctrine. His controversial sermons and tracts exhibit uniformly the decorous forms of expression, and the gentle and tolerant spirit which, while they are graceful in all men, are more especially becoming in a minister of religion.'[1]

The appended extracts from Channing's essays and lectures are fair specimens of his characteristics in ethical writing and literary criticism.

THE GRAND END OF SOCIETY.

'Property continually tends to become a more vivid idea than right. In the struggle for private accumulation, the worth of every human being is overlooked. The importance of every man's progress is forgotten. We must contend for this great idea. They who hold it, must spread it around them. The truth must be sounded in the ears of men, that the grand end of society is to place within reach of all its members the means of improvement, of elevation, of the true happiness of man. There is a higher duty than to build alms-houses for the poor, and that is, to save men from being degraded to the blighting influence of an alms-house. Man has a right to something more than bread to keep him from starving. He has a right to the aids, and encouragements, and culture, by which he may fulfil the destiny of a man; and until society is brought to recognise and reverence this, it will continue to groan under its present miseries.'

[1] *North American Review*, No. 89, p. 373.

THE DOMINION OF MIND.

'In proportion as society becomes enlightened, talent acquires influence. In rude ages, bodily strength is the most honourable distinction; and in subsequent times, military prowess and skill confer mastery and eminence. But as society advances, mind, thought, becomes the sovereign of the world; and accordingly, at the present moment, profound and glowing thought, though breathing only from the silent page, exerts a kind of omnipotent and omnipresent energy. It crosses oceans and spreads through nations; and at one and the same moment, the conceptions of a single mind are electrifying and kindling multitudes, through wider regions than the Roman eagle overshadowed. This agency of mind on mind, I repeat it, is the true sovereignty of the world, and kings and heroes are becoming impotent by the side of men of deep and fervent thought.'

PARTY-SPIRIT.

'Human nature seems incapable of a stronger, more unrelenting passion. It is hard enough for an individual, when contending all alone for an interest or an opinion, to keep down his pride, wilfulness, love of victory, and other personal feelings. But let him join a multitude in the same warfare, and, without singular self-control, he receives into his single breast the vehemence, obstinacy, and vindictiveness of all. The triumph of his party becomes immeasurably dearer to him than the principle, true or false, which was the original ground of division. The conflict becomes a struggle, not for principle, but for power, for victory; and the desperateness, the wickedness of such struggles, is the great burden of history. In truth, it matters little what men divide about, whether it be a foot of land, or precedence in a procession. Let them but begin to fight for it, and self-will, ill-will, the rage for victory, the dread of mortification and defeat, make the trifle as weighty as a matter of life and death. The Greek or Eastern Empire was shaken to its foundation by parties which differed only about the merits of charioteers at the amphitheatre. Party-spirit is singularly hostile to moral independence. A man, in proportion as he drinks into it, sees, hears, judges by the senses and understandings of his party. He surrenders the freedom of a man, the right of using and speaking his own mind, and echoes the applauses or maledictions with which the leaders or passionate partisans see fit that the country should ring.'

GREAT IDEAS.

'What is needed to elevate the soul is, not that a man should know all that has been thought and written in regard to the spiritual nature—not that a man should become an encyclopædia; but that the great ideas, in which all discoveries terminate, which sum up all sciences, which the philosopher extracts from infinite details, may be comprehended and felt. It is not the quantity, but the quality of knowledge, which determines the mind's dignity. A man of immense information may, through the want of large and comprehensive ideas, be far inferior in intellect to a labourer, who, with little knowledge, has yet seized on great truths. For example, I do not expect the labourer to study theology in the ancient languages, in the writings of the Fathers, in the history of sects, &c.; nor is this needful. All theology, scattered as it is through countless volumes, is summed up in the idea of God; and let this idea shine bright and clear in the labourer's soul, and he has the essence of theological libraries, and a far higher light than has visited thousands of renowned divines. A great mind is formed by a few great ideas, not by an infinity of loose details. I have known very learned men, who seemed to me very poor in intellect, because they had no grand thoughts. What avails it that a man has studied ever so minutely the histories of Greece and Rome, if the great ideas of freedom, and beauty, and valour, and spiritual energy, have not been kindled by those records into living fires in his soul? The illumination of an age does not consist in the amount of its knowledge, but in the broad and noble principles of which that knowledge is the foundation and inspirer. The truth is, that the most laborious and successful student is confined in his researches to a very few of God's works; but this limited knowledge of things may still suggest universal laws, broad principles, grand ideas, and these elevate the mind. There are certain thoughts, principles, ideas, which by their nature rule over all knowledge, which are intrinsically glorious, quickening, all-comprehending, eternal.'

BOOKS.

'In the best books, great men talk to us, give us their most precious thoughts, and pour their souls into ours. God be thanked for books! They are the voices of the distant and the dead, and make us heirs of the spiritual life of past ages. Books are the true levellers. They give to all who will faithfully use them, the society, the spiritual presence of the best and greatest of our race. No matter how poor I am—no matter though the prosperous of my own time will not enter my obscure dwelling—if the Sacred Writers will enter and take up their abode under my roof—if Milton will cross my threshold to sing to me of Paradise, and Shakspeare to open to me the worlds of imagination and the workings of the human heart, and Franklin to enrich me with his practical wisdom —I shall not pine for want of intellectual companionship, and I may become a cultivated man, though excluded from what is called the best society in the place where I live.'

LITERATURE OF THE PRESENT AGE.

'The character of the age is stamped very strongly on its literary productions. Who, that can compare the present with the past, is not struck with the bold and earnest spirit of the literature of our times. It refuses to waste itself on trifles, or to minister to mere gratification. Almost all that is written has now some bearing on great interests of human nature. Fiction is no longer a mere amusement; but transcendent genius, accommodating itself to the character of the age, has seized upon this province of literature, and turned fiction from a toy into a mighty engine; and, under the light tale, is breathing through the community either its reverence for the old or its thirst for the new—communicates the spirit and lessons of history—unfolds the operations of religious and civil institutions—and defends or assails new theories of education or morals by exhibiting them in life and action. The poetry of the age is equally characteristic. It has a deeper and more impressive tone than comes to us from what has been called the Augustan age of English literature. The regular, elaborate, harmonious strains which delighted a former generation, are now accused, I say not how justly, of playing too much on the surface of nature and of the heart. Men want and demand a more thrilling note—a poetry which pierces beneath the exterior of life to the depths of the soul, and which lays open its mysterious workings, borrowing from the whole outward creation fresh images and correspondences with which to illuminate the secrets of the world within us. So keen is this appetite, that extravagances of imagination and gross violations—both of taste and moral sentiment—are forgiven, when conjoined with what awakens strong emotion; and, unhappily, the most stirring is the most popular poetry, even though it issue from the desolate soul of a misanthrope and a libertine, and exhale poison and death.'

ORVILLE DEWEY.

The example of Channing, who had already extended the range of topics commonly treated in the pulpit, was followed by his successor Orville Dewey (born 1794), who may be described as the most practical of the Unitarian divines. He first appeared as a minister in the pulpit left vacant by Channing when he travelled in Europe. After ten years of service as pastor of a church in New Bedford, Dr Dewey was appointed minister of the church of the Messiah, in New York, where he gained a wide reputation by his sermons and other publications. His account of a tour in Europe, published under the title of *The Old World and the New* (1836), was well received, and was followed by several collections of his sermons, essays, reviews, and tracts, marked by a sober yet animated style, and a constant application to practical life.

In 1838, he published twelve discourses, collectively entitled *Moral Views of Commerce, Society, and Politics*. The subjects treated in this volume include the Moral Laws of Trade, the Uses of Labour, a Passion for a Fortune, the Moral Limits of Accumulation, and others of a similar nature, well suited to attract the attention of men in a state of society remarkable for its commercial spirit. In defence of his own unusual choice of topics, Dr Dewey, in his preface, makes a protest against the common narrow range of topics discussed in the pulpit, and adds:—'I must confess I cannot understand by what process of enlightened reasoning and conscience, the preacher can come to the conclusion, that there are wide regions of moral action and peril around him, into which he may not enter, because such unusual words as commerce, society, politics, are written over the threshold.'

RALPH WALDO EMERSON.

The essays and lectures of Emerson have perhaps had a larger circulation than any other works of the same kind. Considering the abstruse nature of many of their topics, and their singular style, sometimes oracular and rhapsodical, it is difficult to account for the wide diffusion of such writings, though they contain many excellent passages.

RALPH WALDO EMERSON has been, during the greater part of his life, a retired student, a thinker who from time to time has given to the world the results of his own meditations, and has apparently taken very little care to adapt them to the thoughts of other men. Though his writings often oppose established opinions, and suggest many topics for discussion, he is by no means a controversial author. In reply to a letter inviting discussion, he writes: 'I could not give account of myself, if challenged. I could not possibly give you one of the arguments you cruelly hint at, on which any doctrine of mine stands. For I do not know what arguments mean in reference to any expression of a thought. I delight in telling what I think; but if you ask me why I dare say so, or why it is so, I am the most helpless of mortal men.' In the same letter he styles himself, with reference to his writings, 'a chartered libertine,' and confesses an 'incapacity of methodical writing.'

We know little of the biography of this author. He was born in 1803 at Boston, United States, and studied at Harvard University, where, in his eighteenth year, he took his degree as Bachelor of Arts. For some short period, he was pastor of a Unitarian congregation in his native city; but differences of opinion between himself and his hearers led to his retirement from this office.

Since then, he has passed his time in studious solitude, at Concord in Massachusetts, has occasionally lectured, and has paid a visit to friends in England. Having a competent fortune, he has been fully at liberty to choose his own topics and indulge in his style of soliloquy, and his writings prove that his simple object has been to think for himself and give free expression to his thoughts. He has no system of philosophy, no definite method of arriving at conclusions. In his views of man and nature—briefly, sometimes mysteriously expressed—he often coincides with the results of German writers on philosophy, and especially with the doctrines of Fichte. How far this may be ascribed to reading, we cannot say, though it is stated that Mr Emerson is well acquainted with the writings of the German idealists.

A poetical spirit pervades many passages in his essays and lectures; and brief descriptive sketches, often marked by wit and humour, relieve the more abstruse parts of his writings. His doctrine, so far as it refers to points in speculative theology, cannot be discussed here; but it may be said that his moral tone is uniformly noble and manly. The variety of thoughts suggested, but not unfolded in any orderly style; the union of the several styles of philosophy, poetry, fact, and description: these and other peculiar features make it no easy task to write a fair and complete criticism on the works of Emerson.

Remote from the pressure of active life in America, and apart from the crowd of restless politicians, buyers and sellers and practical speculators, there exists a philosophical, and perhaps rather dreamy little Germany—if we may so speak of a certain class of men devoted to abstruse studies. Of this circle of thinkers, Ralph Waldo Emerson is, to use his own words, 'the representative man.' From his quiet retirement at Concord, he has sent forth his little books, consisting of essays and lectures, full of elevated thoughts, sometimes happily but often vaguely uttered, which have exercised a considerable influence upon many readers. He has written, in an abstract manner, of man, society, government, religion, and the philosophy of nature. His religious views may be concisely described as the extreme opposite of all views based upon tradition and authority. Of that tendency of the mind and longing of the heart for unity and repose, which has led many doubters to submit their faith to the absolute guidance of a church, Emerson appears to know nothing. On the contrary, he advocates a stern self-reliance, perhaps we might say a self-isolation.

A clear criticism of Emerson's philosophical doctrines is perhaps impossible, but the main feature in his style of thinking and writing may be easily defined: it consists in the constant use of abstract terms in isolated assertions. Wherever we open his essays, we are sure to find passages like the following:—'There are no fixtures in nature. The universe is fluid and volatile. Permanence is but a word of degrees. Our globe, seen by God, is a transparent law, not a mass of facts. The law dissolves the fact, and holds it fluid.' Such abstract statements—philosophy in short-hand, as they might be styled—may have their meaning in the mind of the original thinker; but to make them commonly intelligible, they require to be *written out* and explained by details. As an extreme instance of the condensed style in which Emerson gives the results of whole volumes of German philosophy, we may quote the following:—'Nature is the incarnation of a thought, and turns to a thought again, as ice becomes water and gas. The world is mind precipitated, and the volatile essence is for ever escaping again into the state of free thought. Hence the virtue and pungency of the influence on the mind of natural objects, whether inorganic or organised. Man imprisoned, man crystallised, man vegetative, speaks to man impersonated.' This appears to be intended as a summary of a German theory; but how dark must be the expressions here used to readers not initiated in the doctrines of Schelling and Hegel! These writers developed doctrines which may be condensed into the few terms used by the American writer, but they do not use such expressions without detailed explanation. Hegel, for example, in the preface to one of his works,[1] employs the metaphor of 'making fluid,' to describe the dialectic method; but in the same preface, he clearly exposes the error of employing abstract or general assertions as substitutes for logical writing.

These remarks may be sufficient to prove what we have already said—that any methodical account of Emerson's views of the philosophy of nature is impossible. They must be regarded simply as assertions of his own thoughts and impressions, of which he confesses that he is not able to 'give account.'

It may be readily supposed that the influence of his writings upon young readers is rather exciting and disturbing than instructive. Hawthorne seems to imply this in his description of some of the disciples of Emerson:

'Severe and sober as was the Old Manse' [a house in the village of Concord], 'it was necessary to go but a little way beyond its threshold before meeting with stranger moral shapes of men than might have been encountered elsewhere in a circuit of a thousand miles.

[1] *Phaenomenologie des Geistes.* Ed. von Schulze. 1832.

These hobgoblins of flesh and blood were attracted thither by the wide-spreading influence of a great original Thinker, who had his earthly abode at the opposite extremity of our village. His mind acted upon other minds, of a certain constitution, with wonderful magnetism, and drew many men upon long pilgrimages, to speak with him face to face. Young visionaries—to whom just so much of insight had been imparted as to make life all a labyrinth around them—came to seek the clue that should guide them out of their self-involved bewilderment. Gray-headed theorists—whose systems, at first air, had finally imprisoned them in an iron framework—travelled painfully to his door, not to ask deliverance, but to invite the free spirit into their own thraldom. People that had lighted on a new thought, or a thought that they fancied new, came to Emerson, as the finder of a glittering gem hastens to a lapidary to ascertain its quality and value. Uncertain, troubled, earnest wanderers, through the midnight of the moral world, beheld his intellectual fire as a beacon burning on a hill-top, and climbing the difficult ascent, looked forth into the surrounding obscurity more hopefully than hitherto. . . . .

But it was impossible to dwell in his vicinity without inhaling, more or less, the mountain atmosphere of his lofty thought, which in the brains of some people wrought a singular giddiness—new truth being as heady as new wine. Never was a poor little country village infested with such a variety of queer, strangely-dressed, oddly-behaved mortals, most of whom took upon themselves to be important agents of the world's destiny, yet were simply bores of a very intense water. Such, I imagine, is the invariable character of persons who crowd so closely about an original thinker as to draw in his unuttered breath, and thus become imbued with a false originality.'[1]

In the series of lectures on *Representative Men*, Montaigne is selected as the example of the sceptical tendency in thought; though sincerity and liberality are equally characteristic of the French essayist, as Emerson implies in the following passage:—

'Over his name he drew an emblematic pair of scales, and wrote "Que sçais-je?" under it. As I look at his effigy, opposite the title-page, I seem to hear him say: "You may play old Poz, if you will; you may rail and exaggerate—I stand here for truth, and will not, for all the states, and churches, and revenues, and personal reputations of Europe, overstate the dry fact as I see it: I will rather mumble and prose about what I certainly know—my house and barns; my father, my wife, and my tenants; my old lean bald pate; my knives and forks; what meats I eat and what drinks I prefer; and a hundred straws just as ridiculous—than I will write, with a fine crow-quill, a fine romance. I like gray days, and autumn and

[1] Hawthorne's *Mosses from an Old Manse.*

winter weather. I am gray and autumnal myself, and think an undress and old shoes that do not pinch my feet, and old friends that do not constrain me, and plain topics where I do not need to strain myself and pump my brains, the most suitable."'

In the lecture on Goethe or the Writer, the reader must be disappointed if he expects a clear and sober statement of the merits of the celebrated German. Mr Emerson ventures to say: 'The old Eternal Genius who built the world has confided himself more to this man (Goethe) than to any other;' and yet he adds in the next sentence—'I dare not say that Goethe ascended to the highest grounds from which genius has spoken.' These two statements seem hardly to admit reconciliation. That style of speaking for which Montaigne has been commended, would be very desirable in a description of the characteristics of Goethe, for many of the criticisms and commentaries on his works are remarkably vague or contradictory. Thus we find, in contrast against the enthusiastic praises bestowed by Mr Carlyle, the opinions of such German writers as Görres, Novalis, and Börne, who condemn Goethe as 'a heathen,' an 'anti-christian writer,' and 'a preacher of moral indolence;' while Menzel carries animosity against Goethe and all his admirers to an absurd extreme; and even Theodore Parker writes: 'That Goethe, as a man, was selfish to a very high degree, a debauchee, and well-bred epicurean, who had little sympathy with what was highest in man, so long as he could crown himself with rose-buds, we are willing to admit.' Of the most enigmatical of all Goethe's writings—the second part of *Faust*—Mr Emerson says: 'It is a philosophy of literature set in poetry. . . . . This reflective and critical wisdom makes the poem more truly the flower of this time. . . . . The wonder of the book is its superior intelligence.' Yet, of this same poem, an able German critic and warm admirer of Goethe,[1] says: 'Already many passages in this second part have become riddles, and for the hopeless solution we may vainly strive until we lose our temper; while others may be readily guessed; but not without the vexation of finding, under a great array of symbols, nothing more than a trivial and insignificant result: so we may conclude, that in the course of some fifty years, the whole of this second part will be almost destitute of meaning.'

The other lectures describe as representatives—Plato, the Philosopher; Swedenborg, the Mystic; Shakspeare, the Poet; and Napoleon, the Man of the World. In all, several striking passages occur in contrast with obscure statements and exaggerated

[1] Dr Vilmar—*Vorlesungen über die Geschichte der deutschen Nationalliteratur.*

or one-sided assertions. The same characteristic of isolated propositions, which makes it impossible to find any method of thinking in Mr Emerson's works, also makes his style rather monotonous. His language, truly representing his thoughts, consists chiefly of short, aphoristic sentences. A quotation from the lecture on Plato is appended:

SOCRATES.

'Socrates, a man of humble stem, but honest enough; of the commonest history; of a personal homeliness so remarkable, as to be a cause of wit in others—the rather that his broad good-nature and exquisite taste for a joke invited the sally, which was sure to be paid. The players personated him on the stage; the potters copied his ugly face on their stone jugs. He was a cool fellow, adding to his humour a perfect temper and a knowledge of his man—be he who he might—whom he talked with, which laid the companion open to certain defeat in any debate; and in debate he immoderately delighted. The young men are prodigiously fond of him, and invite him to their feasts, whither he goes for conversation. He can drink too; has the strongest head in Athens; and, after leaving the whole party under the table, goes away as if nothing had happened, to begin new dialogues with somebody that is sober. In short, he was what our country-people call *an old one*.

He affected a good many citizen-like tastes, was monstrously fond of Athens, hated trees, never willingly went beyond the walls, knew the old characters, valued the bores and Philistines, thought everything in Athens a little better than anything in any other place. He was plain as a Quaker in habit and speech, affected low phrases and illustrations from cocks and quails, soup-pans and sycamore-spoons, grooms and farriers, and unnameable offices; especially if he talked with any superfine person. He had a Franklin-like wisdom. Thus, he shewed one who was afraid to go on foot to Olympia, that it was no more than his daily walk within doors, if continuously extended, would easily reach.

Plain old uncle as he was, with his great ears—an immense talker—the rumour ran, that on one or two occasions, in the war with Bœotia, he had shewn a determination which had covered the retreat of a troop; and there was some story that, under cover of folly, he had in the city government, when one day he chanced to hold a seat there, evinced a courage in opposing singly the popular voice, which had well-nigh ruined him. He is very poor; but then he is as hardy as a soldier, and can live on a few olives; usually in the strictest sense on bread and water, except when entertained by his friends. His necessary expenses were exceedingly small, and no one could live as he did. He wore no under garment; his upper garment was the same for summer and winter; and he went bare-footed; and it is said that, to procure the pleasure which he loves, of talking at his ease all day with the most elegant and cultivated young men, he will now and then return to his shop, and carve statues, good or bad, for sale. However that be, it is certain that he had grown to delight in nothing else than this conversation; and that, under his hypocritical pretence of knowing nothing, he attacks and brings down all the fine speakers, all the fine philosophers of Athens, whether natives or strangers from Asia Minor and the Islands. Nobody can refuse to talk with him, he is so honest and really curious to know; a man who was willingly confuted, if he did not speak the truth, and who willingly confuted others asserting what was false; and not less pleased when confuted than when confuting; for he thought not any evil happened to men of such a magnitude, as false opinion respecting the just and the unjust. A pitiless disputant, who knows nothing, but the bounds of whose conquering intelligence no man had ever reached; whose temper was imperturbable; whose dreadful logic was always leisurely and sportive; so careless and ignorant as to disarm the wariest, and draw them, in the pleasantest manner, into horrible doubts and confusion. But he always knew the way out—knew it, but would not tell it. No escape; he drives them to terrible choices by his dilemmas, and tosses the Hippiases or Gorgiases, with their grand reputations, as a boy tosses his balls. The tyrannous realist! Meno has discoursed a thousand times at length, on virtue, before many companies, and very well, as it appeared to him; but at this moment he cannot even tell what it is—this cramp-fish of a Socrates has so bewitched him.

This hard-headed humorist, whose strange conceits, drollery, and *bonhomie* diverted the young patricians, whilst the humour of his sayings and quibbles gets abroad every day, turns out, in the sequel, to have a probity as invincible as his logic, and to be either insane, or at least, under cover of this play, enthusiastic in his religion. When accused before the judges of subverting the popular creed, he affirms the immortality of the soul, the future reward and punishment; and, refusing to recant, in a caprice of the popular government, was condemned to die, and sent to the prison. Socrates entered the prison, and took away all ignominy from the place, which could not be a prison whilst he was there. Crito bribed the jailer; but Socrates would not go out by treachery. "Whatever inconveniences ensue, nothing is to be preferred before justice. These things I hear like pipes and drums, whose sound makes me deaf to everything you say." The fame of this prison, the fame of the discourses there, and the drinking of the hemlock, are one of the most precious passages in the history of the world.'

ESSAYS, REVIEWS, AND ORATIONS.

In America, as in England, the quarterly reviews and other periodicals employ the services of the best writers, and critical essays and summaries given in the form of reviews have taken the place occupied by the *Tatler*, *Spectator*, and other papers of the eighteenth century. *Salmagundi*, a miscellany written by Irving, Verplanck, and Paulding (1807), may be regarded as the last imitation of the plan of essay-writing introduced by Steele and Addison. About the same time, *The Monthly Anthology* appeared under the editorship of the Rev. Mr Emerson (father of the well-known essayist), and was continued until 1811. Four years later, *The North American Review* was established by William Tudor, and after several changes of management during the years 1815–19, was transferred to the care of Edward Everett. Subsequently, it was conducted by Jared Sparks (1822–30), Alexander Everett (1830–35), Dr Palfrey (1835–), and in 1842 passed into the hands of Francis Bowen, a gentleman highly esteemed for his acquirements in general literature and philosophy. *The North American Review* has long maintained the highest position among critical journals, and has employed the services of the best scholars in the United States.

In the year 1827, *The American Quarterly Review* was commenced in Philadelphia, under the direction of Mr Robert Walsh, and was continued until 1837. In this year, *The Boston Quarterly Review* was established. During recent years, it has been under the guidance, and, indeed, has been chiefly written by Orestes A. Brownson. *The Southern Quarterly Review*, edited by W. Gilmore Simms, was established in Charleston, 1828, suspended in 1833, and recommenced in 1842.

Of the monthly literary magazines, *The Knickerbocker*, established in 1832, has been one of the most successful, and has numbered among its contributors Irving, Paulding, Bryant, and Longfellow. *Harper's Magazine*, published in New York, has enjoyed a very extensive circulation, but cannot be classed with respectable periodicals. It has adopted the plan of seizing and appropriating, for its own use, the articles of English writers; and this has frequently been done without any form of acknowledgment. A higher character is justly claimed by *Putnam's Monthly*, a literary miscellany which deserves success, for its object is the culture and encouragement of native American talent. It already includes among its contributors several of the best writers of light literature.

The writers of reviews and essays are too numerous to be

distinctly characterised. VERPLANCK, an historical essayist, who has prepared the best American edition of Shakspeare, has written many critical articles displaying great research, especially with regard to the early colonisation of New York. The *Lectures on Shakspeare*, by H. N. HUDSON, have been commended as examples of genial criticism and delicate analysis. Among the contributors to *The North American Review*, we may mention the names of the brothers EVERETT, C. C. FELTON, GEORGE S. PERKINS, PICKERING, CHARLES SUMNER, and GEORGE HILLARD; while we omit here the names of other writers whose works have already been noticed in other parts of this volume.

In selecting a few names as representatives of a class too numerous to be fully described here, it is by no means implied that the respective merits of these and other writers can be fairly estimated by our brief notices.

JOHN QUINCY ADAMS (1767–1848) devoted his life to political studies, and rose to the office of President of the United States. Amid the cares of his public life, he found occasional solace in literature, especially in the study of Shakspeare's plays. These he viewed chiefly with regard to their moral purport; and his *Essays on the Characters of Shakspeare* contain some singular assertions respecting the great poet's ethical teaching. For example, Mr Adams gravely and elaborately contended that *Othello* was written to expose the enormity of Desdemona's marriage 'with a blackamoor.'

ALEXANDER EVERETT (1790–1847) edited *The North American Review* in the years 1830–35, and during that time contributed several articles, which have been collected, with other papers, and published under the title *Critical and Miscellaneous Essays*. He also wrote extensively for the same review while it was edited by his younger brother Edward; and at various times was a contributor to *The Boston Quarterly Review*, *The Democratic Review*, and other periodicals. His other works include an essay, entitled *New Ideas on Population* (1822), intended to refute the theory of Malthus; a work on *America;* and a collection of political addresses and occasional orations.

During a considerable part of his life, Alexander Everett was engaged in politics and diplomacy. In 1809 he went to St Petersburg, on a mission to Russia, and while he resided there, studied modern languages, public law, and political economy. After a visit to London, he returned to the United States, and in 1821 published his work, entitled *Europe; or a General Survey of the Political Situation of the Principal Powers, with Conjectures on their*

Future Prospects. In his next work, the essay on population, he argued against Malthus, that the growth of an industrious population must always be accompanied by a proportionate increase of the means of subsistence.

In 1825, he was appointed minister at the court of Madrid. During his residence in this capital, he continued his literary pursuits, and wrote, besides his work on *America*, several articles for *The North American Review*. While in Spain, he collected the valuable new materials for Prescott's *History of Ferdinand and Isabella*, and also assisted Irving in historical researches relative to the *Life of Columbus*.

In the years 1830–40, Everett was engaged in political affairs, and devoted a part of his leisure to literary pursuits. In 1845, he was appointed to succeed Caleb Cushing on a mission to China. In the following year he sailed for Canton, where he died in the summer of 1847.

It is well known that in America the public speeches of Daniel Webster, Calhoun, the brothers Everett, and other politicians, are regarded as worthy of a prominent place in national literature. The orations delivered on various occasions by Daniel Webster and Edward Everett, have been collected and published as important contributions to the American library. 'Our national literature,' says a reviewer, 'is to be found in the records of our greatest minds, and is not confined to the poems, novels, and essays which may be produced by Americans.' These remarks may serve to explain the fact, that the reputation of Alexander Everett, like that of his younger brother Edward, was not wholly founded on his essays, reviews, and other political writings, but was partly aided by his public speeches, of which several are included in the list of his publications.

As a writer and an orator, Alexander was inferior to his brother EDWARD EVERETT, who has expended, in periodical literature and public speaking, the powers which might have produced works deserving a permanent reputation. He was born at Dorchester, near Boston, in 1794; graduated at Harvard University in 1811; and succeeded Buckminster as minister of a Unitarian church in Boston. At this time, when nineteen years old, he wrote a *Defence of Christianity*. After a course of travel for the benefit of his health, he entered in 1819 on the duties of his professorship of the Greek language and literature, in Harvard University, to which he had been appointed in 1815. In the following year (1820), he commenced the editorship of *The North American Review*, and during the four years of his régime, he wrote almost one half of the work. Subsequently, when his elder brother, Alexander, undertook the duties of management, Edward Everett remained one of the leading contributors. His numerous essays and reviews include some elaborate articles; while others, the productions of the few leisure hours allowed by professional duties, have the common faults of hasty writing. Everett has rarely enjoyed the advantages of the retired student. His ten years of service in the House of Representatives; the duties of the presidency of Harvard College during three years; the cares of the office of governor of Massachusetts, and of an embassy to the court of England—these, and other public services, have left so little time for unbroken studies, that the scholarship and variety of intellectual resources found in his writings and public speeches must excite admiration.

His *Orations and Speeches*, published in 1850, include a great diversity of topics, but have one common feature in their enthusiastic national tone. In commemorating the settling of New England, or the events of the revolutionary war; in eulogies of the patriots of America; and in speeches for literary institutions, charitable associations, temperance societies; and even at agricultural dinners and cattle-shows, Everett never forgets to infuse an American spirit. His language is generally chaste and elegant, and often rises to a higher style of eloquence in accordance with the development of his subject; but he has not always resisted the peculiar seductions of public speaking.

We append an extract from Everett's oration on the arrival of the Pilgrims in New England:

THE LANDING OF THE MAYFLOWER.

'Let us go up for a moment, in imagination, to yonder hill, which overlooks the village and the bay, and suppose ourselves standing there on some bleak, ungenial morning, in the middle of November of that year [1620]. The coast is fringed with ice. Dreary forests, interspersed with sandy tracts, fill the background. Nothing of humanity quickens on the spot, save a few roaming savages, who, ill provided with what even they deem the necessaries of life, are digging with their fingers a scanty repast out of the frozen sands. No friendly light-houses had as yet hung up their cressets upon your headlands; no brave pilot-boat was hovering like a sea-bird on the tops of the waves, beyond the cape, to guide the shattered bark to its harbour; no charts and soundings made the secret pathways of the deep as plain as a gravelled road through a lawn; no comfortable dwellings along the line of the shore, and where are now your well-inhabited streets, spoke a welcome to the pilgrim; no steeple poured the music of Sabbath-morn into the ear of the fugitive for conscience' sake. Primeval wildness and native desolation brood over sea and land; and from the 9th of November, when, after a most calamitous voyage, the *Mayflower* first came to anchor in Provincetown harbour, to the end of December, the entire male portion of the company was occupied, for the greater part of every day, and often by night as well as by day, in exploring the coast, and seeking a place of rest, amidst perils from the savages, from the unknown shore, and the elements, which it makes one's heart bleed to think upon.

But this dreary waste, which we thus contemplate in imagination, and which they traversed in sad reality, is a chosen land. It is a theatre upon which an all-glorious drama is to be enacted. On this frozen soil—driven from the ivy-clad churches of their mother-land, escaped at last from loathsome prisons—the meek fathers of a pure church will lay the spiritual basement of their temple. Here, on the everlasting rock of liberty, they will establish the foundation of a free state. Beneath its ungenial wintry sky, principles of social right, institutions of civil government, shall germinate, in which, what seemed the Utopian dreams of visionary sages, are to be more than realised.

But let us contemplate, for a moment, the instruments selected by Providence for this political and moral creation. However unpromising the field of action, the agents must correspond with the excellence of the work. The time is truly auspicious. England is well supplied with all the materials of a generous enterprise. She is in the full affluence of her wealth of intellect and character. The age of Elizabeth has passed, and garnered up its treasures. The age of the Commonwealth, silent and unsuspected, is ripening towards its harvest of great men. The Burleighs and Cecils have sounded the depths of statesmanship; the Drakes and Raleighs have run the whole round of chivalry and adventure; the Cokes and Bacons are spreading the light of their master-minds through the entire universe of philosophy and law. Out of a generation of which men like these are the guides and lights, it cannot be difficult to select the leaders of any lofty undertaking; and, through their influence, to secure to it the protection of royalty. But, alas for New England! No, sir, happily for New England, Providence works not with human instruments. Not many wise men after the flesh, not many mighty, not many noble, are called. The stars of human greatness that glitter in a court are not destined to rise on the lowering horizon of the despised colony. The feeble company of Pilgrims is not to be marshalled by gartered statesmen or mitred prelates. Fleets will not be despatched to convoy the little band, nor armies to protect it. Had there been honours to be won, or pleasures to be enjoyed, or plunder to be grasped, hungry courtiers, midsummer friends, godless adventurers, would have eaten out the heart of the enterprise. Silken Buckinghams and Somersets would have blasted it with their patronage. But safe amidst their unenvied perils, strong in their inoffensive weakness, rich in their untempting poverty, the patient fugitives are permitted to pursue unmolested the thorny paths of tribulation; and, landed at last on the unfriendly shore, the hosts of God, in the frozen mail of December, encamp around the dwellings of the just—

> "Stern famine guards the solitary coast,
> And winter barricades the realms of frost."

While Bacon is attuning the sweetest strains of his honeyed eloquence to soothe the dull ear of a crowned pedant, and his great rival, only less obsequious, is on his knees to deprecate the royal displeasure, the future founders of the new republic beyond the sea are training up for their illustrious mission, in obscurity, hardship, and weary exile in a foreign land.

And now—for the fulness of time is come—let us go up once more, in imagination, to yonder hill, and look out upon the November scene. That single dark speck, just discernible through the perspective-glass, on the waste of waters, is the fated vessel. The storm moans through her tattered canvas, as she creeps, almost sinking, to her anchorage in Provincetown harbour; and there she lies, with all her treasures, not of silver and gold—for of these she has none—but of courage, of patience, of zeal, of high spiritual daring. So often as I dwell in imagination on this scene; when I consider the condition of the *Mayflower*, utterly incapable as she was of living through another gale; when I survey the terrible front presented by our coast to the navigator who, unacquainted with its channels and roadsteads, should approach it in the stormy season, I dare not call it a mere piece of good-fortune, that the general north and south wall of the shore of New England should be broken by this extraordinary projection of the Cape, running out into the ocean a hundred miles, as if on purpose to receive and encircle the precious vessel. As I now see her, freighted with the destinies of a continent, barely escaped from the perils of the deep, approaching the shore precisely where the broad sweep of this most remarkable headland presents almost the only point at which for hundreds of miles she could with any ease have made a harbour, and this perhaps the very best on the sea-board, I feel my spirit raised above the sphere of mere natural agencies. I see the mountains of New England rising from their rocky thrones. They rush forward into the ocean, settling down as they advance; and there they range themselves as a mighty bulwark around the Heaven-directed vessel. Yes, the everlasting God himself stretches out the arm of his mercy and his power, in substantial manifestation, and gathers the meek company of his worshippers as in the hollow of his hand.'

In accordance with the rule laid down by an American reviewer, we must include DANIEL WEBSTER in our list of authors, though he never wrote a book. We readily grant that his speeches are far more valuable than many books which have been noticed in our review. He was born (in 1782) at Salisbury, in New Hampshire. After he had graduated in Dartmouth College, he chose the profession of law, and for some time practised as an attorney and counsellor. In early life, he devoted a considerable share of his studies to political questions, and soon after the declaration of war (1812), was elected a member of the national House of Representatives. During his retirement from Congress (1817–23), he wrote several articles for *The North American Review*, and delivered some of his most celebrated orations. The remainder of his public life was devoted to the service of his country, and its record belongs to political history. He died in October 1852.

The collected writings of Daniel Webster, including speeches in Congress and addresses on various public occasions, with forensic arguments, and several essays, appeared in 1852–53, with a memoir written by Edward Everett. His orations are characterised as 'more remarkable for fervour of sentiment and depth of feeling than for richness of imagery or imaginative power. No one has a greater contempt for the barren shows of oratorical and poetic phraseology, or for the mere illusions of fancy.' This statement accords well with Webster's own description of eloquence, given in one of his speeches, from which the following passage may be quoted:—

'When public bodies are to be addressed on momentous occasions, when great interests are at stake, and strong passions excited, nothing is valuable in speech further than as it is connected with high intellectual and moral endowments. Clearness, force, and earnestness are the qualities that produce conviction. True eloquence, indeed, does not consist in speech. It cannot be brought from far. Labour and learning may toil for it, but they will toil in vain. Words and phrases may be marshalled in every way, but they cannot compass it. It must exist in the man, in the subject, and in the occasion. Affected passion, intense expression, the pomp of declamation, all may aspire to it; they cannot reach it. It comes, if it come at all, like the outbreaking of a fountain from the earth, or the bursting forth of volcanic fires, with spontaneous, original, native force. The graces taught in the schools, the costly ornaments and studied contrivances of speech, shock and disgust men when their own lives, and the fate of their wives, their children, and their country, hang on the decision of the hour. Then words have lost their power, rhetoric is vain, and all elaborate oratory contemptible. Even genius itself then feels rebuked and subdued, as in the presence of higher qualities. Then patriotism is eloquent; then self-devotion is eloquent. The clear conception, outrunning the deductions of logic, the high purpose, the firm resolve, the dauntless spirit, speaking on the tongue, beaming from the eye, informing every feature, and urging the whole man onward, right onward to his object—this, this is eloquence; or rather it is something greater and higher than all eloquence—it is action, noble, sublime, godlike action.'

JOSEPH STORY (1779–1845), an eminent lawyer and judge in the Supreme Court of the United States, devoted his leisure hours to literature, and wrote several occasional addresses and biographical sketches, besides his essays contributed to *The North American Review*. His writings on jurisprudence—including *Commentaries on the Constitution of the United States*, *Commentaries on the Conflict of Laws*, and on *Equity Pleadings*, and numerous written judgments—are voluminous. The following extract is taken from a *Centennial Discourse* at Salem, in which the author refers to the intolerance of the Puritans in New England :—

PERSECUTION.

'I stand not up here the apologist for persecution, whether it be by Catholic or Protestant, by Puritan or Prelate, by Congregationalist or Covenanter, by church or state, the monarch or the people. Wherever and by whomsoever it is promulgated or supported, under whatever disguises, for whatever purposes, at all times, and under all circumstances, it is a gross violation of the rights of conscience, and utterly inconsistent with the spirit of Christianity. I care not, whether it goes to life, or property, or office, or reputation, or mere private comfort, it is equally an outrage upon religion and the inalienable rights of man. If there is any right sacred beyond all others, because it imports everlasting consequences, it is the right to worship God according to the dictates of our own consciences. Whoever attempts to narrow it down in any degree, to limit it by the creed of any sect, to bound the exercises of private judgment or free inquiry by the standard of his own faith, be he priest or layman, ruler or subject, dishonours, so far, the profession of Christianity, and wounds it in its vital virtues. The doctrine on which such attempts are founded, goes to the destruction of all free institutions of government. There is not a truth to be gathered from history more certain or more momentous than this—that civil liberty cannot long be separated from religious liberty without danger, and ultimately without destruction to both. Wherever religious liberty exists, it will, first or last, bring in and establish political liberty. Wherever it is suppressed, the church establishment will, first or last, become the engine of despotism, and overthrow, unless it be itself overthrown, every vestige of political right. How it is possible to imagine, that a religion breathing the spirit of mercy and benevolence, teaching the forgiveness of injuries, the exercise of charity, and the return of good for evil—how it is possible, I say, for such a religion to be so perverted as to breathe the spirit of slaughter and persecution, of discord and vengeance for differences of opinion, is a most unaccountable and extraordinary moral phenomenon. Still more extraordinary, that it should be the doctrine, not of base and wicked men merely, seeking to cover up their own misdeeds, but of good men, seeking the way of salvation with uprightness of heart and purpose. It affords a melancholy proof of the infirmity of human judgment; and teaches a lesson of humility, from which spiritual pride may learn meekness, and spiritual zeal a moderating wisdom.'

The names already given must suffice as representative of other writers of orations—CLAY, CALHOUN, LEGARÉ, BURGESS, WRIGHT, CHOATE, and PRESTON. In the same mode of treatment, we may select a few names of writers of essays and reviews, without any intention of asserting their claims to be regarded as the chief representatives of their respective departments.

The essays and reviews written by THEODORE PARKER for *The Dial* and other periodicals, would demand more than a passing notice, if their topics might be included in the range of general literature. As specimens of clear writing on difficult subjects, they deserve the highest commendation. Their theological purport has been indicated, and cannot with propriety be discussed in this place.

ORESTES A. BROWNSON, formerly editor of *The Boston Quarterly Review*, gained a reputation rather by his rapid changes of opinions than by his ability in metaphysical and theological controversy. During his editorship (1838–43), he wrote, it is said, almost the whole of the Review; and in 1844, when *The Boston Quarterly* had been merged in *The Democratic Review*, he commenced a new quarterly to expound his own doctrines. These were subject to changes so rapid, that a weekly periodical was required to keep pace with them. By turns, Brownson advocated catholicism in religion, eclecticism in philosophy, and other systems more or less borrowed from foreign writers, and ultimately found a resting-place in the Positive Philosophy of M. Comte. Respecting this last phase of faith, Mr Griswold says: 'It is more creditable to his [Brownson's] judgment than to his candour; for I do not recollect that he has once mentioned the name of an author from whom he has rather compiled than borrowed.' This is a serious charge; and we fear that several similar charges might be justly preferred against other metaphysical writers who have borrowed without sufficient acknowledgment from the French and the German.

HUGH SWINTON LEGARÉ (1797–1843) must be mentioned as the chief contributor to *The Southern Quarterly Review*, established at Charleston in 1827, and as the writer of several able articles in *The New York Review*.

HENRY THEODORE TUCKERMAN (born 1813) may be described as one of the most imaginative and sympathetic of American critics, and as a refined and elegant writer. His essays and reviews shew a liberal cultivation of mind and heart. He is one of the few men who are well qualified to write criticism on poetry, for he has the powers required to recognise, though insufficient to create, true poetry. The poet and his competent critic must resemble each other, so far that the latter must be capable of recognising all the ideas and sentiments uttered by the former. It may be asserted that, in compass, their minds are equal, and that the difference between them is caused by the superior energy of the creative mind.

In 1835, Mr Tuckerman published, under the title of *The Italian Sketch-book*, a series of papers giving the thoughts suggested by a tour in Southern Europe. Another work of similar character, though written in the form of a romance, was entitled *Isabel; or Sicily—a Pilgrimage*, and appeared in 1839. This was followed in 1841 by a volume of miscellanies under the title of *Rambles and Reveries;* and in 1846 by the more characteristic work, *Thoughts on the Poets*—a series of essays on twenty-six Italian, English, and American poets, including Petrarch and Alfieri, Goldsmith, Gray, Burns, Cowper, Crabbe, Coleridge, Wordsworth, Tennyson, and Bryant. In his *Characteristics of Literature*, Mr Tuckerman has given a series of analytical, yet very genial and sympathetic sketches of celebrated authors, taking each as the representative of a class. He observes, in a preface to the second series, that 'the choice of writers has been quite accidental and subordinate to the principal aim—that of grouping around them something like a brief history and analysis of the species of writing in which they excelled.' Thus Sir Thomas Browne serves as the representative of philosophy; Channing is the moralist; Charles Lamb, the humorist; Burke, the rhetorician; Humboldt, the naturalist; and Godwin, the reformer.

Besides the works already mentioned, Mr Tuckerman has written a series of essays, entitled *Leaves from the Diary of a Dreamer*, a didactic essay in verse, styled *The Spirit of Poetry*, and several shorter poems and magazine articles. In one of his best essays, entitled *New England Philosophy*, and first published in *The Democratic Review*, he discusses with ability and good taste the question of the relative merits of the two departments of culture—one including the imaginative faculty and the affections; the other embracing the powers strictly called intellectual. He maintains that these latter—the faculties of practical intellect—are too often cultivated with an unwise neglect of the sentiments commonly, but vaguely, styled poetical. The whole essay may be regarded as a defence of enthusiasm—taking this word in its best and most refined meaning—and the greater portion of it is beautifully written.

A DEFENCE OF ENTHUSIASM.

'Enthusiasm is the very life of gifted spirits. Ponder the lives of the glorious in art or literature through all ages. What are they but records of toils and sacrifices supported by the earnest hearts of their votaries? Dante composed his immortal poem amid exile and suffering, prompted by the noble ambition of vindicating himself to posterity; and the sweetest angel of his paradise is the object of his early love. The best countenances the old painters have bequeathed to us are those of cherished objects intimately associated with their fame. The face of Raphael's mother blends with the angelic beauty of all his Madonnas. Titian's daughter, and the wife of Correggio, again and again meet in their works. Well does Foscolo call the fine arts the children of love. The deep interest with which the Italians hail gifted men, inspires them to the mightiest efforts. National enthusiasm is the great nursery of genius. When Cellini's statue of Perseus was first exhibited on the Piazza at Florence, it was surrounded for days by an admiring throng, and hundreds of tributary sonnets were placed upon its pedestal. Petrarch was crowned with laurel at Rome for his poetical labours; and crowds of the unlettered may still be seen on the Mole at Naples listening to a reader of Tasso. Reason is not the only interpreter of life. The fountain of action is in the feelings. Religion itself is but a state of the affections. I once met a beautiful peasant-woman in the valley of the Arno, and asked the number of her children. "I have three here, and two in Paradise," she calmly replied, with a tone and manner of touching and grave simplicity. Her faith was of the heart. Constituted as human nature is, it is in the highest degree natural that rare powers should be excited by voluntary and spontaneous appreciation. Who would not feel urged to high achievement, if he knew that every beauty his canvas displayed, or every perfect note he breathed, or every true inspiration of his lyre, would find an instant response in a thousand breasts? Lord Brougham calls the word "impossible" the mother-tongue of little souls. What, I ask, can counteract self-distrust, and sustain the higher efforts of our nature, but enthusiasm? More of this element would call forth the genius and gladden the life of New England. While the mere intellectual man speculates, and the mere man of acquisition cites authority, the man of feeling acts, realises, puts forth his complete energies. His earnest and strong heart will not let his mind rest; he is urged by an inward impulse to embody his thought. He must have sympathy—he must have results. And nature yields to the magician, acknowledging him as her child. The noble statue comes forth from the marble, the speaking figure stands out from the canvas, the electric chain is struck in the bosoms of his fellows. They receive his ideas, respond to his appeal, and reciprocate his love. . . . . . Sentiment, in its broadest acceptation, is as essential to the true enjoyment and grace of life as mind. Technical information, and that quickness of apprehension which New Englanders call smartness, are not so valuable to a human being as sensibility to the beautiful, and a spontaneous appreciation of the divine influences which fill the realms of vision and of sound, and the world of action and feeling. The tastes, affections, and sentiments, are more absolutely the man than his talent or acquirements. And yet it is by and through the latter that we are apt to estimate character, of which they are at best but fragmentary evidences. It is remarkable that, in the New Testament, allusions to the intellect are so rare, while the "heart" and the "spirit we are of," are ever appealed to. Sympathy is the golden key which unlocks the treasures of wisdom ; and this depends upon vividness and warmth of feeling. It is therefore that Tranio advises : "In brief, sir, study what you most affect." A code of etiquette may refine the manners, but the "heart of courtesy," which, through the world, stamps the natural gentleman, can never be attained but through instinct ; and in the same manner, those enriching and noble sentiments which are the most beautiful and endearing of human qualities, no process of mental training will create. To what end is society, popular education, churches, and all the machinery of culture, if no living truth is elicited, which fertilises as well as enlightens? Shakspeare undoubtedly owed his marvellous insight into the human soul to his profound sympathy with man. He might have conned whole libraries on the philosophy of the passions ; he might have coldly observed facts for years, and never have conceived of jealousy like Othello's, the remorse of Macbeth, or love like that of Juliet.'

EDWIN P. WHIPPLE (born 1819), one of the writers in *The North American Review*, has resided since 1837 in Boston, where he has been mainly occupied with commercial pursuits. Besides his lectures on Life and Literature (1850), he has written many reviews and critical papers, commonly marked by a lively and perspicuous style.[1] He is recognised as one of the most popular of the younger essayists. The following passage is taken from one of the *Lectures on Subjects connected with Literature and Life* :—

WIT AND HUMOUR.

'Wit was originally a general name for all the intellectual powers, meaning the faculty which kens, perceives, knows, understands ; it was gradually narrowed in its signification, to express merely the resemblance between ideas ; and lastly, to note that resemblance

[1] Whipple's papers in *The North American Review* include the following :—The Old English Dramatists—British Critics—Byron—Wordsworth—Talfourd—James the Novelist—Sydney Smith. In *The American Review*, he has written on the topics : Beaumont and Fletcher—English Poets of the Nineteenth Century—Coleridge as a Philosophical Critic, &c.

when it occasioned ludicrous surprise. It marries ideas, lying wide apart, by a sudden jerk of the understanding. Humour originally meant moisture, a signification it metaphorically retains, for it is the very juice of the mind, oozing from the brain, and enriching and fertilising wherever it falls. Wit exists by antipathy ; humour by sympathy. Wit laughs *at* things ; humour laughs *with* them. Wit lashes external appearances, or cunningly exaggerates single foibles into character ; humour glides into the heart of its object, looks lovingly on the infirmities it detects, and represents the whole man. Wit is abrupt, darting, scornful, and tosses its analogies in your face ; humour is slow and shy, insinuating its fun into your heart. Wit is negative, analytical, destructive ; humour is creative. The couplets of Pope are witty, but Sancho Panza is a humorous creation. Wit, when earnest, has the earnestness of passion, seeking to destroy ; humour has the earnestness of affection, and would lift up what is seemingly low, into our charity and love. Wit, bright, rapid, and blasting as the lightning, flashes, strikes, and vanishes in an instant ; humour, warm and all-embracing as the sunshine, bathes its objects in a genial and abiding light. Wit implies hatred or contempt of folly and crime, produces its effects by brisk shocks of surprise, uses the whip of scorpions and the branding-iron—stabs, stings, pinches, tortures, goads, teases, corrodes, undermines ; humour implies a sure conception of the beautiful, the majestic, and the true, by whose light it surveys and shapes their opposites. It is a humane influence, softening with mirth the ragged inequalities of existence—promoting tolerant views of life—bridging over the spaces which separate the lofty from the lowly, the great from the humble. Old Dr Fuller's remark, that a negro is "the image of God cut in ebony," is humorous ; Horace Smith's inversion of it, that the taskmaster is "the image of the devil cut in ivory," is witty. Wit can coexist with fierce and malignant passions ; but humour demands good feeling and fellow-feeling—feeling not merely for what is above us, but for what is around and beneath us.'

HENRY REED, a writer in the *Library of American Biography*, and one of the contributors to the *New York Review* (1837–1842), wrote a course of *Lectures on English Literature, from Chaucer to Tennyson*, which has been recently reprinted in London. On his return from a visit to England, this amiable and promising writer perished in the wreck of the *Arctic*.

NEWSPAPERS.

Newspapers are the representatives of the millions of people in America, while books of poetry, history, and philosophy represent only certain classes of readers. A few facts taken from the census of 1850 will suffice to prove this assertion. In that year, the number of copies of newspapers and periodicals printed in the United States amounted to 422,600,000. If we subtract from the total population of the States (23,267,498) the number of the slaves (3,197,589), we find rather more than twenty newspapers and periodicals allowed for every free man, woman, or child, in the year 1850. The details of the same census include 350 daily papers, 150 appearing thrice in a week, 125 published twice in a week, 2000 weekly papers, and 175 magazines, quarterly reviews, &c.; making a total of 2800 newspapers and periodicals, of which more than two thousand have been commenced since the year 1820.

The cheapness of newspapers in America explains their wide circulation. 'A city of 2000 inhabitants, which in England would not support a journal of its own of any description, has its daily in America; and cities of 20,000 people, which in England are content with their semi-weeklies or weeklies, in the United States support four or five dailies, with as many weeklies.' 'Even villages of a few hundred inhabitants have their papers, which, if not supported in the hamlet, draw patronage from the surrounding rural population; and almost every family takes at least one journal.'[1] A recent traveller states that 'newspapers are seen everywhere, in the hands of the labouring as well as the wealthy classes. . . . . In the streets, at the doors of hotels, and in railway-cars, boys are seen selling them in considerable numbers. Nobody ever seems to grudge buying a paper. In the parlours of public-houses and hotels in England, a newspaper is handed from one person to another, because the purchase of a copy would be expensive; but we see little of this practice in America. Every morning at the Astor House, I should think some hundreds of newspapers were bought by the guests. At breakfast, almost every man had a paper. And I believe I may safely aver, that no working-man of any respectability goes without his paper daily, or at least several times in a week. Newspapers, in a word, are not a casual luxury, but a necessary of life in the States; and the general lowness of price of the article admits of its widest diffusion.

[1] Introduction to Trübner's *Bibliographical Guide to American Literature.*

Many of these papers are only a cent—equal to a half-penny—each; but two or three cents are a more common price, and some are charged five or six cents. Compared with the expensively got-up and well-written papers of London, the American newspapers, though low-priced, are scarcely entitled to be called *cheap*. Much of their space is occupied with advertisements, and in some cases the whole readable matter amounts to a few paragraphs of news and remarks connected with party politics. Indulgence in personalities is usually, and with truth, regarded as the worst of their editorial features.'[1]

As representatives of the leading journals, we may mention—*The National Intelligencer*, published in Washington city; *The Journal of Commerce*, *Evening Post*, *Courier*, *Inquirer*, *Tribune*, and *Times*, in New York; *The Pennsylvanian Inquirer*, in Philadelphia; *The Journal*, at Louisville; and *The Patriot*, at Baltimore. 'These,' it is said, 'fairly represent the ability, scope, excellence, and tone of the respectable American press, and if more quoted from in Europe, would greatly contribute to remove the erroneous impressions respecting American newspapers.'[2]

We find no statistics of the comparative numbers of the profligate papers of which Mr Dickens has given a very dark account.[3] It is probable that a fair representation might be gained by comparing with his statement the remarks of the best American reviews, and the facts stated or implied in other notices of journalism; for example, Buckingham's *Specimens of Newspaper Literature* (1850), and a life of the editor of *The Tribune*, recently published. 'The profligate papers,' says a reviewer,[4] 'numerous as they are, and widely as their circulation ranges, neither express, nor guide, nor govern what can, with any propriety, be called the public opinion of the country; they may open their foul mouths in full cry upon a man of character, year after year, and through every state in the Union, but they can harm him no more than the idle wind. They are read, despised, and the next day utterly forgotten. A temporary prejudice may be raised, and that is all. Their cowardly malice, their ignorance, vulgarity, and profligacy, overshoot the mark.' Of invasions of private life, and attacks on personal character, it is not necessary to say more. With regard to public life, it is admitted that the violence and indecorum of party politics are prominent characteristics of a large portion of the newspaper press. A few

1 *Things as They Are in America*, by William Chambers. 1854.
2 Introduction to Trübner's *Bibliographical Guide*.
3 *American Notes for General Circulation*.
4 *North American Review*, No. 118, Art. 9.

specimens may be noticed, as warning examples of the abuse of journalism.

The style indulged by many editors and correspondents of newspapers seems to have arisen from a desire to use the pen as a substitute for the tomahawk. Among the characteristics of speakers in Congress and elsewhere, none are more applauded, in certain prints, than their abilities of speech in the cutting, flaying, or withering style. Such passages as the following are frequent in the newspapers to which we refer :—

'The most withering speech was made by ——, who seems in that line to be one of the first men in the House.' . . . . 'We publish to-day the powerful remarks of Mr —— on the Seminole war. His indignation, like the fire from the cloud, blasts wherever it falls.' . . . . 'The excoriation that Mr G—— administered the other day to Mr P—— was dreadful. Several of the Whig members were desirous of trying their hands on P——, but after the speech of Mr G——, nothing remained for them to do!' . . . . 'We have a rich treat for our readers—we allude to the speech of Mr S—— in reply to Mr D——. . . . . Such withering sarcasm, such torturing ridicule, &c. . . . . The poor doctor is literally flayed alive. Had he been on the rack of a thousand inquisitions, his torture could not have been more severe.' . . . . 'The tremendous singeing which P—— gave to G——,' &c. . . . . 'Mr P—— continued . . . . to cut deep and serve up the party,' &c.[1]

In another passage, we have a finished portrait of a Mr W——, who seems to have been the *beau idéal* of a congressional gladiator:

'"It is fortunate that he is so abstemious [with regard to alcohol, we suppose], for were it otherwise, he would be exceedingly dangerous. As a debater, he is quick and full of energy—fire is not more scorching than he is. . . . . He is ferocious in his anger. . . . . His personal rage has no interpreter save in the firm-set mouth, the unflinching and withering eye, and the compact and sullen rigidity of every muscle," &c. . . . In another place, we read that "Colonel C——'s speech was . . . . enlivened by frequent sallies of real humour. . . . . He took hold of . . . . Senator A——, and held him up before the searching fire of his sarcasm and rebuke, turning him first this way and then that, basting him now here and now there, as the blisters were seen to rise upon his epidermis, very much as a log-cabin housewife manages a roasting goose."'

It is pleasant to turn from such passages to the *facetiæ* reported in some newspapers. The G—— newspaper, commenting upon a speech made in Congress by a Mr D——, says: 'It is not a speech accommodated to rhetoricians' rules; but it will be

[1] These, and the following specimens of certain prints, are taken from an article in *The North American Review*, No. 110.

found well suited to the strong-minded, true-hearted, well-affected husbandmen of the West. . . . . Strong sense, strong feeling, generous sentiments, make up their stamina; broad humour, careless gaiety, and hardy dispositions, with some little coarseness, characterise their manners. Mr D——'s speech will be found in keeping with all these characteristics.' One passage from the said speech may be quoted:

'Mr D—— said: "Sir, I delight in the very name of a log-cabin. . . . . In the times of which I am speaking, log-cabins were what the term means—a house made of round logs," &c. . . . . "So much for the description; now for the frolic. The frolic consisted in dancing, playing and singing love-and-murder songs, eating johnny-cake and pumpkin-pies, and drinking new whisky and brown sugar out of a gourd. Our dancing, in my youthful days, and in my neighbourhood, was done to the performance of an old Irishman with one leg, with the heel of which he beat time, and a fiddle with three strings, to the air of—

Judy put the kettle on,
And we'll all take tea," &c.

. . . . "Do you desire to know the feelings of the western people in relation to Harrison, Jackson, Johnson, and their relative services? I can tell you. If a western man is asked his opinion of General Harrison, his answer will be, nineteen times out of twenty, that General Harrison is a very good man, and was a tolerable general. . . . . This, sir, I repeat, will be the general answer. In some instances, a higher opinion will be expressed—in some instances, a lower one. My colleagues on this floor, Whigs and Democrats, will bear me out in what I say; but when you hear Jackson and Johnson named, they are named in praise and song, in affection and pride. Yes, sir, in praise and song. Were you ever at a 'corn-shucking' in the West? If you were, you never left it without hearing the wool-hat and linsey hunting-shirt boys sing"'[1]——

The same speaker, in the same oration—applauded for strong sense and broad humour—ventures again into versification, when he describes the modern Whig party as consisting of—

'Coxcombs and dandies, and loafers and nibblers;
Shavers and blacklegs, and pedlers and scribblers;
Bankers and brokers, and cunning buffoons;
Thieves that steal millions, and thieves that steal spoons;
Rascals in ruffles and rascals in rags;
Beggars in coaches and beggars on nags:
* * *
Such is the crew that for Harrison bellows—
Always excepting some very fine fellows.'

[1] The song is too grotesque to be quoted.

As an example of success in American journalism, we may briefly notice here the biography of Horace Greeley, editor of *The Tribune*. The style is very diffuse, and English readers may imagine that too large a share of honour is awarded to the able editor. Horace Greeley is the son of a farmer in New England, and has raised himself from the station of a journeyman to that of the chief proprietor and editor of *The New York Tribune*. It is little more than twenty years since he arrived in New York with only ten dollars in his pocket, and commenced working, as a compositor, in West's printing-office, Chatham Street. After he had saved some small capital, he embarked in the new scheme of a penny paper, which proved a failure. It was followed by *The New Yorker*, a journal noted for its accuracy in the statement of matters of fact. A quotation from the editor's remarks, in mentioning the publication of certain works on mathematics, may supply a useful hint to many flippant reviewers. He says: 'As we are *not* ourselves conversant with the higher branches of mathematics, we cannot pretend to speak authoritatively upon the merits of these publications.' This, with certain critics, would be a simple *non sequitur*. In 1841, Mr Greeley started *The New York Tribune*, which is now the first liberal paper in America. A single fact in the history of *The Tribune* is so significant with regard to certain other papers, that it may be noticed here.

Mr Dickens, as all the world knows, had been received with the highest honours in America. He had on various occasions argued publicly in favour of international copyright, contending for the just claims of both English and American authors on some share of the profit created by their own labour. His arguments were conducted with perfect fairness and respectful treatment of opponents. But for this offence, of having spoken honestly his own thoughts on a question in which he had, of course, a personal interest, he was virulently abused by certain newspapers, and was stigmatised as a base 'mercenary,' as one who had endeavoured to *rob* the Americans while they were paying homage to him. It was even asserted and credited, that he was the hired agent of English publishers, who paid his travelling expenses! Subsequently, when he gave in the *American Notes* a very dark picture of a large portion of the newspaper press in America, the invectives against him were repeated with additions and variations. It was suddenly discovered that he had no genius, but only a certain 'knack' in caricature, that he had exhausted his store of ideas, and had not a sufficiently comprehensive intellect to appreciate the grandeur of American institutions, especially as represented in certain newspapers. In the midst of all this dull malice, the editor of *The Tribune* ventured to think for himself, and declared that he regarded the *American Notes* as 'one of the very best works of its class.' The fact that such a simple statement of opinion should be remarkable *for its boldness*, speaks more loudly than any foreign comments on the characteristics of certain news-writers in America.

SPECIAL LITERATURE AND MISCELLANEOUS WRITINGS.

Under this head, we may briefly notice a few representatives of numerous works on the several sciences, with some other writings not commonly included in a review of general literature. It is obviously impossible to characterise fairly, within our limits, the works of eminent jurists, politicians, and scientific men; yet some brief notices are required to indicate at least the fact, that the American library is comparatively rich in its special departments—law, politics, medicine, and the applied sciences.[1]

In political economy, the works of Wayland, Colton, Dew, Vethake, and other authors, have been accepted as authorities; while views opposed to the doctrines of Malthus and Ricardo are found in the several works of Henry Carey on population, wealth, wages, and other social questions. The works of Gallatin, Raguet, and Tucker, on currency and banking, have a high reputation. Clay, Matthew Carey, Alexander Everett, and Greeley, may represent the writers who have advocated the protective system in commerce; while Raguet, Bryant the poet, Biddle, Legget, and Walker, may be mentioned as free-traders.

In jurisprudence, the names of Story, Kent, Bradford, Livingston, and Wheaton, have more than a national reputation. Kent's *Commentaries on American Law* are classed beside the standard work of Blackstone. We may mention, as connected with the interests of American as well as English literature, the works of Lieber and Curtis on literary copyright.

The department of medicine, anatomy, &c., contains many valuable writings, both practical and speculative; and homœopathy has been advocated by numerous writers.

In ethnology, Morton's *Crania Americana*, and Gliddon's *Types of Mankind*, may be classed with the most important contributions to science.

Among numerous works on the exact sciences, the reports and other publications of the Smithsonian Institution have a prominent place. The history of the endowment of this institution

[1] See Trübner's *Bibliographical Guide to American Literature.*

is curious. James Smithson, from whom it derives its name, was a son of the first Duke of Northumberland, and died at Genoa in 1829. By his will, he directed that, in case of the death of his nephew and heir, or his children, during minority, the property bequeathed to them should be left to the United States of America, to found at Washington an establishment for the increase and diffusion of knowledge among men. Smithson had never visited America, had no friends there, and left no papers to shew that he had ever regarded the country or its institutions with any special interest. The income of the establishment which bears his name amounts to about 40,000 dollars per annum, and is applied to the culture of science by aiding researches, and publishing reports and other works, which are freely distributed among the literary and scientific societies of the United States and foreign countries.

The scientific reports of the *United States' Exploring Expedition* (1838–1842) include volumes on botany by Asa Gray; animal and botanical geography, by Charles Pickering; geology, by Dana; philology, by Horatio Hale; and other treatises giving the results of researches in the islands of the South Pacific and Antarctic Oceans, California, the north-west coast of Oregon, and some parts of the antarctic continent.

In chemistry, the names of Hare, Webster, Silliman, and Henry; in mineralogy, Cleveland, Dana, and Beck; in geology, Hitchcock, Maclure, Jackson, Silliman, Mather, Hall, and Percival, may be mentioned to indicate that in these sciences many valuable works have been contributed by American writers. *The Flora of North America*, by John Torrey and Asa Gray, is the latest and most complete work of its kind.

Philology and education are very fertile departments in American literature. The *Dictionary of the English Language*, by Dr Webster; the editions of the classics by Professor Anthon; Lewis, Felton, and Woolsey; the several works on the aboriginal dialects of America, and the numerous writings on philology by American missionaries in various parts of the world: these are briefly mentioned merely to indicate the existence of a large class of books in two departments of Special Literature.

The general prevalence of education throughout the States, and the circumstances arising from a want of international copyright, will explain the comparatively high number of educational books and juvenile works of instruction and entertainment produced in America. As the representative of this latter department, we must mention S. G. Goodrich, the true, original Peter Parley, whose little books have been exceedingly popular in England as in America, while his *nom de plume* has been unfairly prefixed to the works of other authors. The writings of Mrs Emma Willard on American history and geography, and many pleasant books by Jacob Abbott, Mrs Clarke, Miss M'Intosh, and other caterers for young readers, might be noticed as specimens of numerous works in which instruction and entertainment are happily united. It is well known that in the department of class-books for common schools and colleges, America is almost independent of the old country, and has supplied many acceptable works for the English market.

We have hitherto failed to find any suitable place for a number of curious books on the mysteries of Mormonism and (so-called) Spiritualism. These productions stand alone as phenomena of the 'latter days,' and have a significance with regard to the state of moral and scientific culture. Of the several records of 'rappings,' and other 'manifestations' of supposed spiritual agencies, we can give no critical account, but must simply refer inquirers to such authorities as 'the Poughkeepsie Seer' Davis, Dods, Mattison, Newman, and Oldfield. The literature produced through the mediums can hardly be criticised without a seeming irreverence; for all the specimens we have seen are as weak and commonplace as the efforts of ordinary mortals, while in many cases the 'spirits' have expressed their thoughts in ungrammatical forms.

In a literary point of view, nothing better can be said of the famous *Book of Mormon:* its incredible stupidity is the chief of its internal characteristics, but its history is one of the modern curiosities of literature. When narrated without qualifying details, the story of the rise of the sect of Mormons seems too wild and absurd to find a place even in the most fantastic work of fiction. We read that an illiterate young man of low reputation determined to set up a new sect. While he was studying by what means he might assert his own claims as an inspired teacher, he found somewhere a stupid, long story written by a needy man, and rejected by a bookseller. This tale of *Mormon* was adopted by the new 'prophet' as quite good enough for his purpose—the delusion of thousands of people in Christian and civilised countries. He printed the dull fiction, and circulated it as a revelation from Heaven! It found readers and believers in England, as in America, and the new prophet succeeded so well that, in the course of a few years, his followers formed a large community, and colonised a district of the far west, where, it is said, they have already become so powerful, that they might perhaps be able to resist any force which could be sent against them by the government of the United States. To increase the marvel of the story, it is stated, on the best authority, that emigrations *from Great Britain* have mainly supplied the population of Utah, the Mormon territory, and that this is likely, in the course of a few years, to be large enough to claim recognition as one of the United States.

The legend of the *Book of Mormon* shortly is, that it contained a revelation to the North American Indians, descendants from the Jews, but had lain buried for a certain period in a hillside, whence it was drawn forth by an inspired personage named Joseph Smith. The more practical account of it, however, is this. A poor man, named Solomon Spaulding, who had once been a preacher, and had failed in business, amused his leisure by writing, in a very feeble and incorrect style, a religious romance, which he entitled *The Manuscript Found.* It was founded on the absurd theory, that the Red Indians of America are the descendants of the Jews, or 'the lost Ten Tribes,' and gave an account of their journey from Jerusalem to America. Mormon was one of the principal characters of the story. The style of the book was extremely dry, and in numerous passages, ungrammatical. In 1812, the work was offered to a printer named Patterson, residing at Pittsburg, in Pennsylvania, who retained it for some time; and after the author's death (in 1816), restored the manuscript to Spaulding's widow. In some way, not certainly explained, the manuscript fell into the hands of one Sidney Rigdon, a compositor employed by Patterson. This Rigdon afterwards became the associate of Joseph Smith. When *The Book of Mormon* was published as a new revelation, John Spaulding, the brother of Solomon, declared upon oath that it was, to the best of his recollection and belief, nearly identical with the romance written by his brother. This statement was supported by the depositions of the author's relatives, and by his partner in business, Henry Lake.[1]

The book itself, whatever may have been its origin, is a very dull production. It contains no new doctrines. The peculiar tenets, rites, and ceremonies of the Mormons have been founded on later 'revelations.' The religious passages interwoven with the story of the Ten Tribes, are borrowed from the Old and New Testaments. The grammar is very bad, as a few specimens will shew:—'Ye are like unto *they.*' . . . 'I should have *wore* these bands.' . . . 'Ye *saith* unto him.' . . . 'He has *fell.*' Such phrases are interspersed throughout the work. It was followed

[1] *Exposé of Mormonism*, by John Bennett. Boston: 1842.

by the book of *Doctrine and Covenants*, also purporting to be a divine revelation, and containing definite doctrines and rules of church-discipline. This book, written partly by Joseph Smith, with the assistance of Rigdon, was, in fact, the new covenant of the Latter-day Saints; but its statements have not been regarded as final. From time to time, new revelations have been made, to suit various circumstances connected with the interests of the sect.

The progress of the society, founded on the doctrines of Joseph Smith and his associates, cannot be rationally explained by a mere reference to the books of the sect. The real causes of success are found partly in the circumstances of society and the state of popular education in England and Wales, but chiefly in the enterprise, industry, and able organisation of the new community. However absurd the pretensions of their leaders may appear, it is unquestionable that, in practical affairs, the Mormons have displayed remarkable energy and perseverance. Their pilgrimage from Nauvoo to the Great Salt Lake, was a fine example of union, cheerful endurance of hardship, and hopefulness sustained during a perilous journey of 1000 miles. One of the prominent features of their organisation of church and state is the great number of its functionaries. It has been calculated that every fifth man holds some office, so that work is found for every grade of talent. Though the highest officers claim exalted powers and privileges, there is some approach to the contemplated equality of communism in the free access allowed to the numerous subordinate posts of honour.[1]

We must here bring to a close this brief review of the more remarkable books published in the United States. Our topic might have been treated in a more ambitious style. Instead of a series of descriptive notices of various works, with biographical sketches of authors, we might have attempted an analysis of literature, regarded from the highest point of view, as a record of the intellectual life and moral progress of a people. But this would be an exceedingly difficult task with regard to the people of the United States, and one inconsistent with the popular character of the present work. It would be necessary, in the first place, to set aside all writings of the imitative class; all books described as 'echoes rather than as original voices—as

[1] For details of the system and doctrines of Mormonism we may refer to the following works:—*The Seer*, edited by Orson Pratt; *History of the Mormons*, by Lieutenant Gunnison; *The Mormons*, by Thomas Kane; *History, Government, &c., of the Latter-day Saints*, by B. G. Ferris; *Mormonism and the Mormons*, by D. T. Kidder; *Expedition to the Valley of the Great Salt Lake of Utah*, by Captain Stansbury.

copies from memory rather than as expressions of life, thought, and experience. Numerous productions in verse would have to be neglected, as having no distinctive features. In prose-fiction, the writings of Washington Irving and several other authors would supply few traits of real life and character in the United States. Cooper's fictions, indeed, and a few sketches already noticed under the title of 'Backwoods' Literature,' would afford interesting views of manners in rising settlements; and such stories of domestic life as have been written by Miss Sedgwick, Mrs Kirkland, and other ladies, would certainly be worthy of consideration. But, on the whole, it may be asserted, that to find American traits of character, we must read newspapers and public speeches rather than poems, novels, and essays.

Enough has been said, however, to indicate the difficulty of treating American Literature as a development of national character. It is, indeed, a continuation of our own. Well-educated men in the United States still remain Englishmen in their choice of books. They speak 'the tongue that Milton spoke.' Shakspeare, Milton, Pope, Addison, Goldsmith, Burns, and Scott, with all our other household names, are classical in the United States as in Great Britain.

To conclude—the American branch of English Literature has already produced fruit worthy of the parent stem. Its future development, we may hope, will be favourable to the friendly intercourse of two nations separated by an ocean and by differences of political institutions, but united by the sure bond of one language—both enjoying, as their inheritance, the richest literature of modern times.

INDEX.